SHADES OF BROWN

THE OFFICIAL BIOGRAPHY OF JANE ELLIOTT AND THE BLUE EYES/BROWN EYES EXERCISE

TODD M. MEALY

OXFORD SOUTHERN

an imprint of Sunbury Press, Inc.
Mechanicsburg, PA USA

OXFORD SOUTHERN

an imprint of Sunbury Press, Inc.
Mechanicsburg, PA USA

For information about special discounts for bulk purchases, please contact Sunbury Press Orders Dept. at (855) 338-8359 or orders@sunburypress.com.

To request one of our authors for speaking engagements or book signings, please contact Sunbury Press Publicity Dept. at publicity@sunburypress.com.

FIRST OXFORD SOUTHERN EDITION: June 2023

Set in Adobe Garamond | Interior design by Crystal Devine | Cover by Darleen Sedjro | Edited by Sarah Illick.

Publisher's Cataloging-in-Publication Data
Names: Mealy, Todd M., author.
Title: Shades of brown : the official biography of Jane Elliott and the blue eyes, brown eyes exercise / Todd M. Mealy.
Description: First trade paperback edition. | Mechanicsburg, PA : Oxford Southern, 2023.
Summary: *Shades of Brown: The Official Biography of Jane Elliott and the Blue Eyes, Brown Eyes Exercise* offers an unvarnished view of the origins, use, and implications of Jane Elliott and her controversial eye color exercise on discrimination.
Identifiers: ISBN : 979-8-88819-112-5 (paperback) | ISBN : 979-8-88819-113-2 (ePub).
Subjects: BIOGRAPHY & AUTOBIOGRAPHY / Educators | BIOGRAPHY & AUTOBIOGRAPHY / Women | BIOGRAPHY & AUTOBIOGRAPHY / Cultural, Ethnic & Regional / African American & Black.

Product of the United States of America
0 1 1 2 3 5 8 13 21 34 55

For the love of books!

For Sarah Elliott and her siblings, Mary, Mark, and the late Brian.

I felt desperately that there had to be a way to do more as a teacher than simply tell children that racial prejudice is irrational, that racial discrimination is wrong.

We've all been told those things. We know them, at least in the sense that we mouth them at appropriate times. Yet we continue to discriminate, or to tolerate it in others, or to do nothing to stop it.

What I had racked my brain to think of the night before was a way to letting my children find out for themselves, personally, deeply, what discrimination was really like, how it felt, what it could do to you.

—JANE ELLIOTT

CONTENTS

AUTHOR'S NOTE

Writing about Jane Elliott presents the unavoidable problem of representing the book's subject. Her government name at birth was Mabel Jane Jennison. Omitting Mabel since she was a toddler, she preferred people to call her "Jane" because her older brother, Charlie, was fascinated with Jane of the *Dick and Jane: Fun with Our Family* books. To reconstruct Jane's life in a two-parent household with six siblings, this book will use *Jane* rather than *Jennison* to describe the protagonist's actions during her formidable years. Upon marriage to Darald Elliott, Jane changed her surname to Elliott. The book subsequently balances the courtship, marriage, and growing brood, which brings into question what names to use for each family member. For clarity, I will use *Elliott* to refer to Jane Elliott, except on a few occasions where it is difficult to distinguish her from other family members. Her husband, Darald, and children, Sarah, Brian, Mary, and Mark, will be called by their first names.

A point of clarification must also be made about the name of Jane Elliott's eye color exercise. It has been called many things over the last fifty-five years: an experiment (which Elliott despises), a project, an experience, an exercise, a simulation, a lesson on bias, and the blue-eyed test are several of the phrases used by journalists and educators when describing Elliott's anti-discrimination inoculation workshop. Elliott seemingly had trouble trademarking the exercise. The initial title was "Discrimination Day." While I include many informal titles, I will use Discrimination Day lesson when speaking of the lesson formally between 1968 and 1987. During that time, Elliott facilitated eye color simulations in her Riceville elementary and middle school classrooms while instructing professional development training for educators and corporate employees in Iowa, Pennsylvania, and, among other places, Colorado. Readers will notice a change in how I frame the exercise after 1988, when Elliott became a nationally and internationally sought-after speaker on American race relations in the era noted for abundant media consumption, especially on the Internet. To that end, I will call the lesson on discrimination the Blue Eyes/Brown Eyes Exercise when retracing Elliott's footsteps from the Reagan administration to the present.

INTRODUCTION

THE ANATOMY OF JANE ELLIOTT

"If I had it my way, Jane Elliott's ingenious exercise would be repeated in every third-grade class," noted Texas newspaper editor David Crowder in an *El Paso Times* column dated July 26, 1992. Crowder, who served in the Vietnam War and saw discrimination up close while in uniform, observed that Jane Elliott's Blue Eyes/Brown Eyes Exercise on discrimination "has become a classic model" to illustrate "our prejudicial tendencies."[1] The lifelong Texan recognized the likelihood of changing the minds and behavior of adults is unlikely. Crowder felt Elliott's discrimination simulation revealed that "we all will grasp at any excuse—eye color, skin color, gender, or religion—to believe that we are better than someone else." For the children, however, Crowder claimed there is a fighting chance to lead the world into a more tolerant multicultural society. This powerful endorsement of Jane Elliott's work on prejudice reduction raises a fundamental question: why is the Blue Eyes/Brown Eyes Exercise, a system in which people are mistreated based on eye color, an ethical approach to undoing discriminatory behavior?

Jane Elliott is a lifelong Iowan: diminutive, abrasive, highly nonconformist, and the child of a family of farmers named one of the McGraw-Hill Foundation's thirty most consequential educators. She burst onto the educational scene in 1968 with a "learning exercise," as she called it, in the Community Elementary School in rural Riceville. Elliott's lesson on bias gave children an unprecedented experience confronting discrimination.[2] Dubbed the Discrimination Day lesson initially before rebranding as the "Blue Eyes/Brown Eyes Experience" after 1987, this unusual learning activity gained quick approbation among hundreds of educators, social psychologists, and civic leaders nationwide.

1

Telling the story of Elliott's efforts to undo racist behavior through the Blue Eyes/Brown Eyes Exercise is no easy task. Crowder's view was only one of many opinions about her anti-racism paradigm. More than fifty years have passed since the first eye color exercise. In each decade, nuance and context are necessary to understand Elliott's enduring work. While it is proper to call her an architect of classroom simulations, the elementary-level eye color lesson on discrimination is one of many role-playing learning experiences inspired by the civil rights era.

Shortly after the 1970 world premiere of the award-winning documentary about the Blue Eyes/Brown Eyes Exercise, *The Eye of the Storm*, Elliott survived an ethics investigation into plagiarism accusations when two teachers accused her of appropriating a segregation simulation conducted at an elementary school in Colorado Springs. Called "Project Misery," the Colorado Springs discrimination role-play was the brainchild of Wilda Wood, a tenured teacher interested in human relations. Project Misery manufactured a caste within the Pine Valley School, placing Wood's students at the bottom of the hierarchy, absent of privileges in the cafeteria, hallways, buses, and extracurricular programming. Her students were not segregated based on the color of their skin, eyes, or hair; Project Misery determined the segregated group by who was enrolled in Wood's class. After watching Riceville Elementary's third-grade students undergo the eye color exercise in ABC's *The Eye of the Storm*, Wood and a Pine Valley colleague wrote to the National Education Association accusing Elliott of passing Project Misery off as her own under an alternative name. Elliott welcomed the investigation. Upon exoneration, she pioneered diversity training, a 1980s phenomenon that occurred in the wake of a generation after the end of Jim Crow, school busing debates, discussions over truth and reconciliation emanating in nations abroad, and the integration of the corporate workforce.

While debates over the simulation's ethics have endured, the context has always substantiated its merits and preserved Elliott's voice despite her many vocal critics. Few people in twentieth-century American history are more controversial than Jane Elliott. Still, no journalist or scholar chronicling this woman's life has ever composed a comprehensive biography of her journey from a northern Iowa farm to a leading role in several documentary films, keynote speaker on hundreds of university campuses, and policy driver for many international board rooms. This book takes a deep and honest look at the woman who civil rights activist Charlie Cobb described as "determined to inoculate her students, both young and old, against the virus of bigotry."[3]

* * *

The Blue Eyes/Brown Eyes Exercise started when Elliott devised a two-day lesson plan called Discrimination Day. It began on Friday, April 5, 1968—the day after Rev. Dr. Martin Luther King, Jr.'s assassination—and concluded Monday, April 8, 1968. During the lesson, Elliott's classroom became, in her words, "a microcosm of society." To manufacture the social hierarchy, she divided her all-white, all-Christian, third-grade students into two categories based on the physical characteristic of eye color. This division generated superior and inferior expectations for each group. From her position of power, she emboldened students with the right color of eyes to tease and discriminate against their peers of the opposite eye color. She manipulated the inferior students to live down to her expectations. Once the second-class students either became unruly or underperformed, she claimed their inferiority was due to their eye color.

On the first day, she told her students that people with blue eyes were superior to those with brown eyes. She recited the hierarchical standards: "Blue-eyed people are smarter than brown-eyed people. They are cleaner than brown-eyed people, and they are more civilized than brown-eyed people."[4]

Elliott moved the desks occupied by brown-eyed students to the back of the classroom. Their recess was cut short, and she placed restrictions on how often the brown eyes could drink from the water dispenser. They were prevented from receiving a second serving at lunch. Elliott also placed green armbands on the brown-eyed children to help distinguish brown eyes from blue eyes when at a distance. That day, she made snide comments to the brown eyes and ad hominem attacks. Her behavior encouraged students with the right colored eyes to treat their brown-eyed peers just as terribly. A fight erupted between a brown-eyed student and a blue-eyed student during recess. As for learning, blue-eyed children performed that first day admirably. The brown eyes, on the other hand, needed remedial help.

The next day in class, following the weekend, Elliott reversed roles. "I lied to you when I said brown-eyed people were superior," she told the class, turning those with brown eyes into the privileged group by proclaiming them superior. With the snap of a finger, the blue eyes lost the benefit of being atop Elliott's manufactured hierarchy. She switched the placement of the desks; blue-eyed students had to wear the armbands and were transferred to the rear of the classroom—treated as pariahs by their teacher and blue-eyed peers.

"I felt desperately that there had to be a way to do more as a teacher than simply tell children that racial prejudice is irrational, that racial discrimination

is wrong," Elliott explained to the press about the controversial exercise following the murder of King. "We've all been told these things. We know them, at
least in the sense that we mouth them at appropriate times. Yet we continue
to discriminate, or to tolerate it in others, or to do nothing to stop it. What
I had racked my brain to think of the night before [Discrimination Day] was
a way of letting my children find out for themselves, personally, deeply, what
discrimination was really like, how it felt, what it could do to you. Now the
time had come to try it."[5]

Elliott's simulation on discrimination evolved considerably since the inaugural Discrimination Day lesson in 1968. Rather than executing the exercise
over two days, Elliott reduced it to one session for either ninety minutes or
three hours. She also decided to facilitate the workshop mainly with adults.
More importantly, after considering how audiences have grown more diverse
over five decades, only "Blueys," as Elliott calls them, or white participants,
would experience discriminatory treatment. The strategy eschewed levying additional trauma onto people of color.

In addition to name-calling and other forms of public shaming, she forced
Blueys to wait in a holding room for an undisclosed amount of time while
explaining the exercise's why and how to the brown-eyed group. The purpose
of the waiting room was to sucker Blueys into a child-ego state before finally
welcoming them into the workshop. Elliott had them sit in a segregated section designated "non-Brown," a space in the center of the room enveloped
by "Brownies" sitting comfortably in chairs. A few seats were available in the
"non-Brown" section, but those chairs were primarily reserved for the disabled,
making sitting on the floor impossible or unwise. Most Blueys found themselves sitting uncomfortably on the cold surface, and the staging generated a
subordinate sensation as the brown-eyed cohort looked down upon the blue-
eyed group. Instead of armbands, ugly mint green collars were used to mark
the oppressed. Signage hung from the walls, restroom doors, and session room
doors. Some of the placards declared:

"Would you want your daughter to marry one?"

"Eenie, meenie, minie, moe. Catch a Blue-Eye by the toe."

"If they don't like it here, why don't they go back to where they came from."

"God made the blue eye. He made him by night. He made him in such a
way he forgot to make him right."

"Let in one blue eye, and there goes the neighborhood."

"I'm not prejudiced. I have Brown-Eyed friends."

"Brown Eyes Only" (water fountain and bathroom signs).

Why eyes? Hair color can be changed. Height was an option, but not when teaching eight and nine-year-old children; the teacher is the only tall one in the classroom. Weight can change. Clothes can be changed. Sexism is too rampant, so it wouldn't be wise to separate students by sex. "I would do what Hitler did," Elliott said. "I would treat students positively or negatively based on the color of their eyes."[6]

Jane conducted the Blue Eyes/Brown Eyes Exercise with her elementary and middle school students sixteen times from 1968 to 1984. Since 1985, she has facilitated eye color simulations almost exclusively with professionals and—when asked—college students. The public, however, thought of Elliott as the woman who stood over eight and nine-year-old youngsters like an iron-fisted fascist to make a point about how damaging discriminatory behavior was to marginalized populations. No matter the audience, young or old, the exercise always aimed to mitigate discriminatory behavior by forcing people to interrogate conscious and unconscious prejudices about racism, sexism, homophobia, religion, and the physical and mental abilities of others. To put it bluntly, her teaching method of pitting people with one set of eyes against those of another often makes participants upset, angry, and emotional. After a debrief, Elliott believed that the short time people endure her vitriol during the workshop is the kind of experiential learning that leaves all involved with a better appreciation for diversity and overall respect for human dignity despite cultural differences.

* * *

Jane Elliott was the post-civil rights era's first renowned diversity pedagogue, a lightning rod in the field of education, and a nonconformist who paradoxically became more than respected. She was an inspiration. Seldom had a teacher lamented the shortcomings of traditional pedagogy: authoritarian discipline and rote memorization that indoctrinates students with the teacher's values in Elliott's view. The conventional pedagogical approach leaves little room for public school students to expand what they already know; it stymies curiosity and provides little incentive for learners to follow their interests. On the contrary, Jane Elliott executed a teaching method for students to learn by applying the curriculum. She encouraged learners to become critical thinkers.

Short, pale-skinned, blue-eyed, and with an ideology aligned with John Dewey, Elliott made the experiential learning mantra "learn by doing" her keynote praxis. She dedicated herself to the notion that not all learning occurs in the classroom, sitting at a desk and regurgitating what the teacher says. Elliott believed that individuals learn by having a teacher release them into the world.

With the mind of a contrarian and a steeled demeanor, she shook up the school system in Riceville with her pedagogy of active learning. A former Iowa State Teachers College student in 1952 and 1953, Elliott was all-in on Deweyan methods that trained children to think critically through exploratory, hands-on activities that generated emotional reactions to the world. Since she worked alone as an experiential learning practitioner, the world soon discovered that Elliott was ahead of her time. Her teaching practice linked student achievement to a framework encompassing four foundational principles.

1. Unpredictability: The teacher should create a classroom environment that thrives off the students' appetite to learn. To maintain engagement, the teacher must shock the system and keep students guessing what and how they are learning.

2. Act of Doing: To accomplish this, Elliott turned her classroom into a place that prioritized students' intellectual growth with hands-on activities; the construction of a public park, the planting of trees around the school, and field trips to dairy farms. Elliott's students also operated a clothing store outside her classroom, reenacted the Boston Tea Party, and curated museum exhibits by constructing and preserving teepees and paper-mâché animals.

3. Reflection: Elliott provided regular feedback on formative tasks, thus giving students enough insight to reflect, study more, and improve their work before issuing the final product for a summative grade. In her classroom, thinking and doing never stopped. Since students spent most of their time actively learning, Elliott believed the content would be enduring because the children became emotionally invested in the lesson.

4. Democratized Discussion: Before, during, and at the end of each task, Elliott engaged her students in the "Magic Circle." The circle created an atmosphere where each student's voice was affirmed and appreciated; children could speak their minds, ask questions, and seek validation without judgment. It was also a place where Elliott could gauge student needs to customize learning for each individual. While her classroom remained racially and religiously homogeneous, she commonly taught Riceville's students with reading difficulties; many had dyslexia. The Magic Circle's frank conversations enabled her to make individualized accommodations for her young learners.

The circle also existed to mitigate disciplinary problems, much like restorative and social-emotional practices help learners in current history. The best teachers create environments that prioritize students. In several chapters of this book, the details of Elliott's active learning pedagogy provides everything readers need to know to understand the origins and purpose of the Blue Eyes/Brown Eyes Exercise. Elliott's two-day lesson on discrimination was not an arbitrary undertaking or an exploitative attempt to use her students to achieve fame. An incongruous instructor, the eye color exercise was a natural aspect of her teaching style. At Riceville, she created a mold, and then she broke it.

Elliott was thirty-four when she created the Blue Eyes/Brown Eyes Exercise. In a letter to a friend on the evening of Martin Luther King Jr.'s death, April 4, 1968, she pondered the state of education after having toiled in it for a decade.

"Now, if we 'educated' adults can't understand what has happened [to King], how can I expect my nine-year-old children to? How can I explain to these white children in this white community the hazards of being black, or brown, or yellow, in this 'sweet land of liberty'?" In an age when curricular decisions were still controlled by white educators, she questioned what the world would look like if people of color had opportunities to shape the school system: "do you remember how frustrated I used to be when I'd come back to T.C. [Teacher's College] after spending a weekend at home arguing about race with my dad? Do you remember how we decided that if blue eyes ever went out of style, we'd all be in big trouble? Well, what do you suppose would happen if I introduced a color bar into my classroom tomorrow morning?" But will it help "my people" learn "a little bit about how it feels to be black?"[7]

On the eve of the eye color exercise, Elliott asked these questions with fear of what would happen. What, after all, would "the experts say" about this hands-on experience? This gap between a lesson *taught* and *performed* was accentuated in Jane Elliott's classroom and debated at universities and corporate offices for decades. To that end, she never stopped proclaiming: "I think educators should spend more time teaching people to relate to one another and less time teaching them to relate facts!"[8]

* * *

How the public reacted to Elliott's work, indeed the positions people take when debating the ethics and legacy of the eye color exercise, demonstrate how we prefer educators to teach our children. The host of Roland Martin Unfiltered and former CNN political analyst, Roland Martin, called her antiracist approach one of the most "persuasive examples" of educating white Americans about the reality of racism. Martin said the exercise "punches people in the face" and forces them to "confront the reality that they don't see." He saw the irony in the evolution of her social awareness due to that upbringing. Having emerged from a childhood of nearly complete isolation from any form of racial, ethnic, linguistic, and religious diversity, Elliott designed the Blue Eyes/Brown Eyes Exercise for people who are (color) blind, Martin attested. Through the training, she "is putting a big mirror in their face and forcing them to see something that they have not wanted to see."[9]

Elliott existed as the face of a small yet consequential movement of white activists daring enough to shock the nervous system of white America. With blunt and confounding messaging, she aimed to expose the fallacy of theories like the "great replacement," which posits that legislation and cultural shifts advocated by those left of center are working to replace straight, English-speaking, white Christian Americans. Her commitment to unmasking myths and lies makes the Blue Eyes/Brown Eyes Exercise appealing to Black liberals, white liberals, and Progressives. Martin called Elliott a "one-woman truth and reconciliation commission." He saw her as a "frank and earnest" individual working to atone for slavery, Jim Crow apartheid, and discriminatory de facto behaviors following the modern civil rights movement. The exercise "rips down layers and layers of white supremacy," Martin said.[10]

On the contrary, her loudest critics are Conservatives. Typically, a conservative rebuttal to race-conscious reasoning—in schools and out—the retort "we are the human race" signals racial colorblindness. It has made for open season on quotes like Thomas Jefferson's "All men are created equal" and King's "I look to a day when people will not be judged by the color of their skin but by the content of their character." Such phrases argue against liberal antiracist dogma, asserting that people like Elliott—who talk about anti-Black racism—are the real racists. However, when Jane Elliott decried, "There is only one race," and that everyone on earth is part of the human race "unless you're from outer space," it puzzled progressive allies and infuriated conservative critics.

Pundits who did not see her advocacy beyond the Blue Eyes/Brown Eyes Exercise have dismissed her as naïve or wrong-headed. In 1970, California Superintendent of Public Instruction Max Rafferty called the then-thirty-six-year-old's famous eye color exercise in discrimination "cyanide in the soup" and "educational malfeasance." He said her motive for creating the exercise was an "abysmal oversimplification" of why James Earl Ray assassinated Dr. King.[11] Some contemporary academics, including University of Iowa professor Stephen Bloom, calls the exercise "unethical" and "psychologically and emotionally damaging."[12] The subtitle of Bloom's 2021 book on the eye color exercise is *A Cautionary Tale of Race and Brutality*. Bloom's brutality underpinned his evaluation of Elliott's teaching methods, which claimed that the discrimination simulation was actually "a risky experiment that raised all kinds of ethical issues." He claimed that the diminutive teacher from Riceville was "a race-baiting grifter."[13] Bloom was not alone; as a whole, Jane Elliott's critics found her immensely detestable. They described her as a "traitor to the race," "deranged," "a bully," and "the scourge of modern civilization."[14]

Having lived for nine decades and witnessed every major issue of the twentieth and twenty-first centuries, Elliott cares little about her characterization. Her attitude—forthright, unfiltered, unapologetic, and somewhat cold—suggested (in her words), "I've lived long enough to know what I am talking about."[15]

Time will tell.

* * *

While Elliott has celebrated more than fifty birthdays since that first eye color exercise, her ideas are frozen in time, a consistently singular treatise that continues to inspire classroom instructors with timeless admonition. Documentaries and training videos of her Blue Eyes/Brown Eyes Exercise now exist for free online for educators' use. The most accessed resource is the 1985 *Frontline* PBS documentary, "A Class Divided," which, to an extent, is a reshowing of ABC's 1970 *The Eye of the Storm*, both directed by filmmaker William Peters. The two award-winning films show Elliott leading her third cohort of third-grade students through the Discrimination Day lesson. The films are gold for educators at every level and in varying disciplines. American history teachers use them while teaching the civil rights movement. World history instructors utilize Elliott's exercise when introducing students to Adolf Hitler. Preservice education teachers often use one of the documentaries to engage students in discussions about bias, prejudice, and social cognition in early childhood development. Addictive psychiatrists like Timmin Cermack reference Elliott's exercise in his studies on projective identification. Social psychologists, like award-winning scholar Claude Steele, use Elliott's work to inform audiences about stereotype threat.

Other films chart this fiery woman's contested eye color exercise. The first is a largely unattainable Canadian public programming feature recorded in the autumn of 1968 titled "The Way It Is." In 1987, Elliott allowed a public television station in Dade County, Florida, to film one of her workshops for its local audience. The station titled Jane's exercise "The Eye of the Beholder." Three years later, another local television crew, this time in Minneapolis, filmed *Eye to Eye* for viewers in Minnesota and northern Iowa. Elliott's international breakout as a star of documentary films occurred in 1996 with *Blue Eyed*. Produced by Denkmal Films, a German film company, *Blue Eyed* reconstructs Elliott's riven relationship with people from Riceville since the very first Blue Eyes/Brown Eyes Exercise twenty-eight years earlier. The documentary won several national and international film awards and made Jane Elliott a luminary throughout Europe, South Africa, and Australia. That year, the Magenta Foundation—an anti-discrimination organization combating hate speech on the Internet headquartered in Holland—asked Elliott to train its employees as facilitators of the eye color exercise. At age sixty-three, she was on the way to having a movie made about her and the exercise starring Susan Sarandon and produced by a film company owned by Julia Roberts. That project collapsed by the end of the decade. However, in 2001, Elliott and her entertainment lawyer, Susan Golenbock, produced *Angry Eye* with students from Bard College. It was their first of several training videos, which include *Stolen Eye*, filmed in Australia; *Indecently Exposed*, filmed in Canada; and *How Racist Are You?* produced in England.

Groups ranging from branches of the United States military to law enforcement and preservice teachers to C-suite and D-level employees use her films. Whether it be films about the Blue Eyes/Brown Eyes Exercise, professional learning sessions led by Elliott herself, or eye color simulations led by one of her certified trainers, the lessons are plentiful: the power paradox, privilege, ignorance, stereotyping, self-fulfilling prophecy, mental health, transactional analysis, crowd manipulation, conformity, synchrony, and discrimination. Those who undergo the exercise and many who study Elliott's work intently come to the same conclusions: socially invented racial categories are ridiculous.

The blue-eyed, brown-eyed perspective-taking experience will always intrigue us for Elliott's uncompromising and blunt treatment of its blue-eyed victims in contrast to the standard talking-at or group discussion style of diversity-based education. The renowned social psychologist Kenneth Clark said Elliott's exercise "Demonstrates that it is possible to educate and produce a class of human beings united by understanding, acceptance, and empathy."[16]

That has been Elliott's mission all along. While public intellectuals criticized Elliott's view as lacking depth concerning institutional power, class, and capitalism, the five feet, two inches-tall farmer's daughter from Riceville has never wavered from her argument that individuals make all the difference in closing racial gaps. "Teaching about discrimination doesn't seem to work," she said just a few years after creating the exercise, "but experiencing discrimination does."[17]

Whether one sees Elliott's tactic as a necessity for authentic learning about multicultural awareness and empathy or as an authoritarian performance that traumatizes a targeted group of participants is addressed in the following pages. However, we must consider Elliott's takeaway points to appreciate how she reached that baseline.

(1) *There is no such thing as race.*

"Every person who considers himself or herself a member of the white race, please stand," commanded Elliott while speaking alongside political activist Angela Davis at the University of Houston in 2018. "Now, will every person who considers himself or herself a member of the black race please stand?" She instructed further: "Now, the brown race. Now, the yellow race. Now, the red race."

At this point, everyone in the auditorium—approximately 1000 students, faculty, and community members—stood at attention. "Now, will everyone in this room who considers himself or herself part of the human race please sit down?" She ordered, and people sat and applauded loudly. Just feet away, Angela Davis looked on with an assenting smile. "You are all members of the same race, the human race, which started with black women," Elliott affirmed, invoking one of her favorite books, *The Myth of Race* by Robert Sussman. "White folks, you won't like it, but all you are is faded black."

The phrase "faded black" has become "shades of brown." Those who mark "white/European" on a census form, she said, are frankly "shades of brown." It is a maverick approach; she engaged in conversations about genetics. Elliott argued that testing data from DNA companies show that genes make all the difference in explaining the recklessness caused by grouping color groups into racial categories. In that, she confronted the ideological left, especially people of color inclined to hold their racialized identity dear. Elliott waged a two-front war, nonetheless. On her ideological right, many who identify as white or European, she claimed DNA testing proves all people carry African ancestry. Her point was that there is no such thing as racial purity or racial hygiene—belief systems espoused by eugenicists in the early twentieth century and implemented in such statutes as hypodescent or one-drop of blood legislation in the southern United States during and following post-Civil War reconstruction.

We are, in fact, varying shades of brown; anything contrary keeps the public divided.

Elliott represents a way of thinking and acting shaped by a far-reaching, diverse, and inclusive education, complete with windows into the worlds of others and mirrors to see herself in the American story. It is a cross-curricular education representative of the history, literature, politics, economics, geography, sociology, psychology, and anthropology of all people connected to Earth. Her teaching drives people to look for intelligent answers to combat new and old faces of racism.

Neither scientist nor anthropologist, Elliott habitually cites the scholarship of experts like Sussman and Allan Chase, who explored how race first emerged as a social construct during the Spanish Inquisition and was later exploited by nineteenth-century Darwinists to establish a hierarchy of privilege by way of the eugenics movement.[18] Racialized color descriptors (white, Black, brown, red, and yellow) have been used to classify people of varying cultures found inhabiting land within geographic borders. This practice, which led to scientific or biological racism, frames an argument that intelligence, behavior, and competencies derive from cranial shape, the size of the nose and lips, arm length, skin pigmentation, and other physical features. The science justified slavery, Jim Crow segregation, low wages, long working hours for immigrant laborers, exclusionary racial quotas, and legislation allowing for selective breeding and human sterilization.

Biological races never existed, say Elliott and her entrusted interdisciplinary experts on human population variation, immigration law, and biology. By Elliott's reasoning, all people with light to dark shades of brown skin are 30th/50th cousins. "Turn to the side," she ordered the crowd. "Shake the hand of the person in front of you, and say, 'Hi cousin!'"

It is simple logic; if one is born on Earth, that individual is part of a singular race. Differing physical features engendered due to migratory and generational evolution are physical differences caused by environmental factors. Those variances hardly qualify one as "less than" and should not lead to exclusion from the human race.

Words matter.

The words "white," "Black," and "race" make up the language of racism and perpetuate it. The need to get beyond classifying one another as racial groups are paramount to move this country beyond racism and reach a stage at which racial prejudice and discrimination are no longer social problems.[19]

Race is dead.

Long live color.

(2) *Stop teaching lies.*

Often defensive when accused of placing too much emphasis on the role of educators in undoing racism, Elliott rationalizes her stance on how much time is wasted during the school day. She argues that educators could otherwise rectify cross-curricular lies and misinformation. "We have students for eight hours a day from the time they are five to the time they are eighteen," she says. "That's thirteen years we have to turn this country into a non-racist country." Her point is that if she could turn her students and thousands of adult professionals into antiracists within a couple of hours using the eye color exercise, a school full of culturally competent teachers could drive this nation closer to post-racialism by the time a generation of students exit their senior year of high school. Elliott wishes to turn K-12 educational decisions into color-conscious calculations. This, in turn, exposes curricular myths and blatant lies preserving and propagating ideas of white supremacy. History, sociology, politics, and geography are framed in such a way that sweeps away the contributions of African, Asian, Middle Eastern, Hispanic, and Indigenous people.

Elliott offers an example of the popular narrative about Christopher Columbus as a principal component in preserving curricular lies. "Columbus didn't discover America," she says. The idea that Columbus was the first to arrive in the New World dismisses the existence of indigenous people in North and South America. It also disregards Columbus's words that African people beat him to the New World. In the journal of his second voyage, Columbus recounted a story of when indigenous people in Espanola, present-day Haiti, told him that "black-skinned people had come from the south-east in boats, trading in gold-tipped spears."[20] There is also the matter of 11.15 feet tall, 40-ton, helmeted Olmec head statues with large eyes, broad noses, and full lips, found in Central and South America and dated from 900 B.C.—a full 2,392 years before Columbus's arrival.[21]

Other constituent parts of Elliott's war on whitewashed history involve explaining to people that humans originated in Africa and about the settlement of North and South America only after two subsequent phases of migration across Asia. According to her truth, we should not dilute the story of America just so its evil deeds vanish from the public conscience. Curricular lies teach us that the United States has always been fundamentally altruistic and divinely sanctioned, a moral exemplar for the world. Her truth says how our society has treated marginalized people is problematic and that we must think critically about America's past and present to create a more perfect union for the future. Curricular lies ignore atrocities like the Mountain Meadows Massacre, the cultural genocide committed at Indian boarding schools nationwide, and the economic exploitation and resulting political unrest caused by the United Fruit Companies up and down the Americas. Her truth exposes the genocide of indigenous people, racial apartheid, lynch law, reproductive control, Mexican American repatriation, and Japanese American internment.

Curricular lies proclaim, "All men are created equal." At the same time, Elliott's truth points out the irony that when those words were written, the people barred from voting were white men without property, women of color, First Nations, and almost every Black male—regardless of free status or wealth. Curricular lies call the United States "the land of the free and the home of the brave." Her truth counters that people ascribed as white are free, while those racialized as Black are the brave. Curricular lies insist we blindly say the Pledge of Allegiance at the start of the school day. Elliott's truth revealed those moments and motivations in history when lawmakers altered the pledge. She asserts that students should have the choice to say the oath.

To Elliott, the Mercator Map is one of the most dangerous lies propping up white supremacy. This global projection distorts the shape and size of continents, with landmasses in the Global North twice those in the Global South. Additionally, the equator is two-thirds of the way down the Mercator Map instead of between the North and South Poles. This map cuts deep into the American psyche. "If that isn't conscious racism, it certainly encourages people to think in racist ways. Here are where all the light-colored people are and see how big their countries are," Elliott says.[22] She adds, "And here are all the dark-colored people and see how small their countries are." Through its visual misrepresentation, Mercator's projections signal who and what is superior and who and what is inferior. The truth, in Elliott's estimation, would be the Peters World Projection Map, which presents each continent in proportional accuracy.

During her 1992 appearance on *The Oprah Winfrey Show*, Elliott told hundreds of people in the audience and millions more television viewers that racism is learned mainly in the school setting: "Racism is not part of the human condition," she ascertained. "Racism is a learned response. You have to be taught to be racist. You are not born racist." After twenty-five years of doing the Blue Eyes/Brown Eyes Exercise with adolescents, teenagers, and adults, America saw the firebrand educator in her element. If properly listened to, Americans would have seen her argument on *Oprah*—not as one that positioned teachers as intentionally instructing students to think and behave in racist ways. Instead, she argued that a person's view on race is shaped by social exposure, what a teacher chooses to teach, not teach, and how information is presented. It is a pedagogy of value, a problematic form of exclusionary cultural instruction that impacts learners subconsciously.

Looking away from Oprah Winfrey and toward the audience, Elliott added, "Now you need to realize the contributions that have been made to society, to civilization by brown-eyed people, by people of color. I'm talking about people of color here, folks, and most of us are not aware of those things because we live in a racist society and because we are educated in a racist school system that only teaches us about white contributions [. . .] If we would start telling the truth in schools, we would not have racism in this country."[23]

Thus, in Elliott's words, curricular lies perpetuated in schools across the United States should be viewed as "indoctrination." She says that schoolteachers are not paid to indoctrinate; they are paid to educate. "The Latin root of the word educator," she often explains, means "to lead." She continues, "The prefix 'e' means 'out.' At the word's center is the combination of the letters 'a-t-e,' which means 'the act of.' The suffix 'o-r' means 'one who does.' An educator, therefore, engages in the act of leading people out of ignorance. A teacher cannot lead students out of ignorance if he or she is teaching lies."[24]

(3) *Language must change.*

Sizing up a woman standing at the microphone—an elementary school teacher—for the first time after forty-five minutes of speaking to an admirably curious audience, Jane Elliott was impressed by the question. "If there is only one race, what do we do with affinity spaces and social movements using varying racial identifiers such as Stop Asian Hate and Black Lives Matter?"

Those are movements with irreplaceable names in the present. However, Elliott's mission was to change them in the future by getting people of student age to reject widely recognized and commonly accepted racial categories and racialized labels passed down by great-grandparents, grandparents, and parents.

That is no easy task.

"We need to see a future in which we are not called polar opposites—black and white," she says. Where Elliott is concerned, a future where all people are the same race can be achieved. She spent half a century thinking about social labeling. As she commonly puts it to her audiences, teachers can give students a Pantone color guide "so they can see the color of their skin against those colors until they find one that matches their skin color." From there, students should look up the synonyms of brown, pick out the word that describes their skin color, and then look up the definition of that color in the dictionary. This process, which requires traditional yet rudimentary research skills, explains that no matter how dark or light one's skin color is, they are a shade of brown. "You can deny it until hell freezes over," she scoffs. Color is real. Culture is real. Ethnicity is real, but race is fake. "That'll still be the truth."

We need to stop using "white" and "Black" when discussing racial categories. "White and black are polar opposites. Skunks, zebras, and rabbits come in those colors. People do not. If we are unable to move beyond the vocabulary used when originally placing various ethnic groups into racial categories, which are fifteenth and sixteenth-century terms, then we should still use the means of transportation of the fifteenth and sixteenth centuries. Nobody wants to do that. So, why are we still using those terms?"[25]

There are no biracial or mixed-raced persons by her line of reasoning. She commands the audience, "Now, will every person in this room who considers himself or herself a biracial person please stand? Don't you stand!" she scolds after several crowd members rise from their seats. "Are you listening to me? There is only one race! Do you see the color of my hair? It's white. Now, look at the color of my face. It's not white. We need to get over the delusion that there are white people and black people. We do not come in those colors."[26]

This exchange leads us to yet a third way in which Elliott's work provides a framework for discerning the world. She created a color-conscious language and believed we should use it in an official context; the vernacular is not expansive. Four useful words or descriptors could move the United States closer to post-racialism.

A. Melanemic: People with low amounts of melanin in their hair, eyes, and skin commonly identify as white.

B. Melanacious: People with relative amounts of melanin causing light shades of brown, otherwise known as people of color.

C. Melanotic: People with high amounts of melanin in their hair, eyes, and skin, causing a very dark, almost black hue.

D. Mosaic: People with mixed color groupings, formerly known as biracial or mixed-raced individuals. Someone with one melanotic biological parent and one melanacious biological parent.

For Elliott, these words will kick-start the drive to unite the Left and Right; antiracists and non-racists; the heterodox and party-liners; the melanemic and melanacious. "Words are the most powerful weapon," she says. White evokes purity and that which is unvarnished; Black is the color that elicits savagery and ignorance. "As long as we use those terms, we are going to be at each other's throats."[27]

* * *

This is the story of an unlikely schoolteacher whose beginnings gave no hint as to the lightning rod she would become. Written in three parts, these pages explain the inception, use, and impact of the Blue Eyes/Brown Eyes Exercise and how that exercise is indelibly linked to the three takeaway points described above. In *Shades of Brown*, I will address many provocative questions. In part one, "Inception," this book asks: What does the eye color exercise say about the difference between education and indoctrination? To answer that question, I had to ask: Do problems of racial intolerance and societal disparities exist in communities previously made up of one cultural group like Riceville in the 1960s? In other words, can Jane Elliott's story answer what happens when attitudes, beliefs, and values collide in communities, schools, and organizations?

I tried to write about Elliott by the standard of her upbringing in a small, monolithic town where minstrelsy had been a common form of entertainment and where there was virtually no interaction with people of racialized color groups or non-Christians. While I dedicate most of the book to Elliott's life conducting the exercise on discrimination, I lean heavily on her insulated upbringing in Riceville and near-decade sojourn in Waterloo (1955-1963) for deeper understanding. We can only understand the exercise's origin by examining her bedrock roots in northern Iowa. Jane was a product of her childhood circumstances that encompassed an environment propagating racist ideas and discriminatory behavior. Not until her thirties did she understand that her culturally insulated environment up to that point did much harm to her development as a parent, educator, and member of humanity. At that harrowing moment on April 4, 1968, she created a curriculum to educate people about the truth of one race, empathy, and cultural tolerance to avert ugly episodes that often crop up following cultural collisions.

In part two, titled "Use," I question what the exercise says to the world about where racism starts and how it can be undone. In other words, what does racism do? How is racism perpetuated? Who is responsible for propagating racism? To respond to these prompts, the chapters in this part of the book reconstruct Elliott's experiences facilitating eye color workshops with adults across the United States between 1968 and 1985. During this time, three documentary films captured Jane's exercise, including *The Way It Is*, *The Eye of the Storm*, "A Class Divided," and *Eye of the Beholder*. The decades covered in part two of this book are important to understand how the exercise evolved to include adult learners and learners of color during the Watergate scandal and a fluctuating workforce.

In part three, "Results," I explore Elliott's anti-discrimination training nationally and internationally. I first explore Jane Elliott's role as an expert voice on race relations following the Los Angeles uprising and other consequential moments of the 1990s. This section, however, is a detailed reconstruction of the history of copycat teachers who attempted variations of her training exercise. It does so by interrogating community reactions to classroom simulations. I also spoke with students who experienced the exercise to obtain qualitative data addressing the impact of the exercise on a personal level. Global politics in the late-1990s concerning a turn toward truth and reconciliation in South Africa and Australia cast a spotlight on Elliott's eye color exercise. This woman, who grew up surrounded by corn fields, forged bonds with Australian Aboriginal peoples and civic leaders, military generals, and public intellectuals in Saudi Arabia, the Netherlands, Germany, Great Britain, and Canada. With help from the Internet age, the outside world saw Elliott as one of the world's foremost race relations experts. As her work pressed on into the twenty-first century, the Blue Eyes/Brown Eyes Exercise still penetrated deliberations in educational circles and the media—all the while enduring bans by school boards and attacks from members of a boisterous anti-progressive movement. As of recent, efforts to cancel Jane Elliott in 2023 have been underscored by educational gag orders on critical race theory and other "divisive concepts" statutes. These experiences allow us to better reflect on whether her tactics were ethical and effective.

This book exists as the official biography of a little woman from a farm in the small town of Riceville, Iowa. It is the story about the context, utilization, and impact of a monumental pedagogical paradigm, the Blue Eyes, Brown, Eyes Exercise.

PART ONE

INCEPTION

CHAPTER 1

A TWINKLE IN ONE'S EYE

On Thanksgiving Day, 1933, nine-month-pregnant Margaret Jennison, known affectionately by her neighbors as "Gie" (pronounced [g]-ee), prepared a holiday meal for her family, which included her husband, Lloyd, and their three toddler children. Although both sides of the family lived nearby, there would be no large gathering for this major American holiday. The twenty-one-year-old mother of three loved her life in the often misty and occasionally snowy valley of Riceville in northern Iowa, even though her parents and in-laws were at odds. When Lloyd returned from his farm duties, she planned to enjoy a typical day. Having already given birth to a boy and two girls, Gie hoped for a second son. No, she expected a boy and made it clear that she would have difficulty accepting the child were another girl. She maintained a serious expression when asked about her children. She said that if it had two X chromosomes, this fourth child would become an object of resentment.

Rather than condemning Gie as an irresponsible and cruel mother, Lloyd accepted his wife for who she was but decided he would love their child in his way. In their marriage's early years, forces seemed to get in the way of forging a blissful life together. At first, the couple tied the knot in a shotgun wedding. He was eighteen, and she was fifteen at the time of their nuptials, forced upon them days after discovering Gie had become pregnant. They were loathed by each other's in-laws, not just because the pregnancy was an accident but also due to a religious feud. Gie's Irish-Catholic upbringing clashed with Lloyd's background as a Baptist, with parents involved in the Baptist Aid Society of Riceville and grandparents that established the family as leading members of Riceville's Baptist church.[1] Then, the great economic depression sent the two into despair, forcing the couple to find a way to manage a brood of children and a massive farm during a time when bankruptcy plagued the country. In a sense, the relationship between Gie and Lloyd was star-crossed from the beginning.

Lloyd Charles Jennison was born on May 29, 1909, in Riceville, Mitchell County, Iowa—a place the *Riceville Recorder* described as "The biggest little town in northeast Iowa." Lloyd was the youngest of five children, the son of Samuel Greene Jennison and Ann Elizabeth "Lyde" Corbett.[2] He received his name from his maternal grandfather, Lloyd Corbett, who hailed from Corydon in south Iowa. His middle name came from his trailblazing paternal grandfather and Lloyd was the third generation Jennison to live in the surrounding area of Riceville. The first to arrive was his pioneering grandfather, Charles Horace Jennison (1834-1917), and grandmother, Sarah Alice Bennett. Charles, the son of a veteran of the Revolutionary War, and Sarah grew up in Swanton, Vermont. Educated in the Vermont public school system, Charles traveled west sometime after his twentieth birthday, settling in Iowa before the great land sale of 1857. He purchased a quarter section of acreage near McIntire, Iowa. In 1860, Charles returned to Swanton to wed Sarah on March 18. In 1862, the couple, now with infant child Samuel Greene (Lloyd's father), born February 2, relocated to their new homestead in McIntire. They would later purchase additional land in Round Grove, a 160-acre plot of land in the northwest corner of Jamestown Township, almost four miles north of Riceville, where he would eventually establish a farm that has since remained in the family for multiple generations.[3] To Charles, northern Iowa was "the dearest place on earth," with its sunshine and shadows.[4]

The area was so dear to the Jennisons that Charles' son, Samuel, when old enough, established his permanent residence at Round Grove to maintain that farm. Samuel would have a two-story home built in colonial style on the site. It would include a central wood and coal heater in the living room and a wood-burning stove for cooking in the kitchen, a well system, a hand pump just feet from the side door, and a milk house. Meanwhile, Charles oversaw the transfer of land to his other children spread throughout northern Iowa.[5] Agrarian to their core, Samuel and Lyde engaged in the form of mixed farming, which was generally more successful than specialization. Engulfed by cornfields, the Jennisons bred and raised cattle, chicken, sheep, and pigs. They harvested beans, oats, hay, peaches, apples, and corn. Stretched beyond the property were just a few families, yet the farmland was vast, and its rolling hills helped the fields of corn disappear in the southern horizon. Life at Round Grove took a firm grip on the spirit of each Jennison child fortunate enough to live at the estate.

Since the people living in Round Grove were small in number, the close-knit community hailed the Jennisons as their stewards, and Samuel served as its "country master." As would be imagined for a Jennison brood, Samuel exceeded Round Grove's expectations by serving multiple terms on the Riceville School Board and as a town constable during the 19-aughts.[6] Upon his father's death, Charles, in 1917, Samuel, with help from his brother Clark, assumed control over the Jennison farm empire in northern Iowa, which now included property in Round Grove, Riceville, McIntire, Cresco, Clarion, and Corwith.

Samuel's love for education bound him to Riceville's pursuit of progressive leadership in the local school district and political affairs. His activism included advocacy for child welfare and girlhood protections by increasing the age of consent from 12 to 14, then to 15—toeing the Progressive Party line by asking it to be 18.[7] Samuel's leadership in the affairs of Riceville as a member of the Round Grove community also bolstered political engagement from his wife, Lyde.

During the 1910s and 1920s, Lyde paid membership dues and was an active crusader in the Riceville Women's Christian Temperance Union (WCTU). This was a non-sectarian, apolitical special interest group initially organized in 1873 to combat liquor trafficking and support the prohibition movement in the late nineteenth and early twentieth centuries. As a guiding light of the union, Lyde advocated for initiatives related to school reform, such as a Sabbath observance and Biblical instruction in public schools, a compulsory school-attendance law, and a temperance curriculum inserted into science courses.

Upon joining Riceville's WCTU chapter around 1916, the year the Hawkeye State adopted a statutory prohibition on alcohol production, Lyde regularly played an affable host to local union meetings at the Jennison farm in Round Grove. "I will bring down the chicken, taters, and pie," she would say to attract attendees.[8] Public records indicate that Lyde assumed secretarial duties of the local chapter around March 20, 1921, a day designated "National Prohibition Rally Day." Under the auspices of the National WCTU and executed by subsidiaries such as Riceville's, the rally celebrated the enactment of the prohibition amendment to the federal constitution. It generated public interest in planning for the forthcoming fiftieth anniversary of the organization's founding. When allowed to speak at public rallies, Lyde usually delivered a rousing devotional titled "The Cup of Cold Water."[9]

Samuel and Lyde birthed Lloyd, the last of six children (one died at birth), when they were forty-seven and thirty-nine, respectively. It was a peak period of temperance activism in the Jennison household. Although he never spoke of his parents' involvement in the prohibition movement, Lloyd later passed down an ethos of intelligence, character, industry, and civic engagement to his children.

It was not that Lloyd needed to behave exactly like his father and mother to find his place in the world. He had plenty of support, both financially and in the endearing form, to take risks, realized from the success of the farming empire that began under his grandfather, Charles. When he entered high school—a path seized by few children of farmers in northern Iowa—Lloyd chose to face the slings and arrows of Iowa's interscholastic athletic competition. At Riceville High School, Lloyd shined as a three-sport athlete. His role as the star halfback on the football team while playing basketball and baseball provided a sense of independence from his parents' shadow.

Back then, Lloyd was diminutive in stature like most of his teammates. Despite standing 5'6" and weighing 129 lbs, he guided the football team to a respectable record as its star halfback during his senior year. He appeared regularly in weekend box scores as Riceville's brightest player. In the final game of his career against Nora Springs, Lloyd played splendidly, successfully executing a series of off-tackle runs, misdirection plays, and forward passes to put his team into position for the go-ahead score. Before the game's conclusion, he intercepted a Nora Springs pass to seal the victory, 7-6.[10]

While studying at Riceville High, Lloyd met Gie. Three years Lloyd's junior, Gie's real name was Margaret Rose Benson, a Catholic "to the bone and so proud of it," according to daughter Jane Elliott.[11] Born May 12, 1912, to John "Jack" Benson and Mary Ann Seavy, her family traced its roots back to Ireland, and in the state of Iowa, its members had always married within the Catholic Church. Gie's parents, who presented themselves as well-to-do "lace-curtain" Irish, were on the poorer side. In pejorative fashion, the Baptists in town (which made up the majority) called religious others like the Bensons "shanty" Irish, who were responsible for bringing insobriety, promiscuity, and overall depravity to the community. They were an affront to values espoused by temperance warriors like the Jennisons.

Nevertheless, the Bensons were unwavering followers of Rev. James J. O'Brien, pastor of the Church of Immaculate Conception in Riceville. Father O'Brien was an admired figure within the Catholic Church, the first resident pastor of Immaculate Conception, built in 1879. He and his brother, a leader in the Catholic Church with the right to ordain members, were instrumental in erecting Immaculate Conception churches across the frontier and overseeing dedications from Iowa to Washington in the late 1800s and early 1900s.[12]

O'Brien was the tower of strength that cemented the Catholic community against sectarian differences.

From an early age, Gie charmed the people of her hometown. As a second grader at the Riceville community's elementary school in 1918, school district officials asked her to pass out diplomas to Riceville seniors during the commencement ceremony.[13] By seventh grade, Gie entertained the public as a "Little Misses" piano trio member.[14] Her ability to perform was a quality that stayed throughout her lifetime. Gie directed community theater in the 1940s and served as the president of the Riceville Music Association for many years. There she worked alongside her friend Ruth Noble, mother of the internationally acclaimed conductor Weston Noble, a storied music teacher at Luther College in Decorah, Iowa.[15] Later, in 1967, Gie and Lloyd became owners of the Jennison Inn, a commonly-used venue for community events and where Gie enjoyed playing host to Ricevillians and tourists. So in-demand was the Jennison Inn that Gie gladly hosted patrons with an "iron will" and "a grand sense of humor," according to her obituary.[16]

The romantic relationship between Lloyd and Gie was both fleeting and clandestine. Indeed, family lore suggests there was no courtship. But instead, the high school's popular senior athlete wooed the freshman into sleeping with him. Then, she became pregnant by mistake (though Jane Elliott believed it was intentional).

The pregnancy brought about a collision for the Jennisons and Bensons in the summer of 1927. Just weeks after Lloyd and Gie celebrated their eighteenth and fifteenth birthdays on May 9 and May 12, respectively, the couple suspected that Gie was expecting. They were sure not long after Charles Lindbergh's flight across the Atlantic Ocean; Gie had missed a second period by then. While there are no records that the teenagers ever discussed terminating the pregnancy to prevent their parents from finding out, they both knew telling their folks that a baby was on the way would be one of the worst experiences of their young lives.

That is how Lloyd's first days out of high school began and how Gie's came to an abrupt conclusion. Lloyd's parents immediately despised Gie because she was both Catholic and much younger in the context of teenage dating. The Bensons felt the same about Lloyd, who was "barely tolerated" because he was Baptist recalled Jane years later.

The Jennisons moved quickly to have the two wed. They insisted that Gie move into a room at their Round Grove home so they could tend to their grandchild while Gie and Lloyd masqueraded as a happily married couple.

Nonetheless, Gie would be forced to sleep in her bedroom with the child, isolated from Lloyd.

Meanwhile, Gie's parents, John and Anna, declared they would never visit their new grandchild on the property of "those Baptists." The Bensons didn't disown their daughter or future grandchild. Lloyd was invited to spend time at the Benson home, which he did. However, he would never win approval from Gie's father. John was an individual who resented Protestant teetotalers like the Jennisons, who blamed America's ills on Irish Catholic immigrants. John told Lloyd at the start of their marriage, "I'll never set foot in your place until you join the [Catholic] church until you get married in the church." John kept that vow until the day he died.[17]

There is an irony behind the families' Protestant-Catholic relations. The truth was that while there were no practicing Catholics in the Jennison family, they had Catholics in their midst. Indeed, Lloyd's mother, Lyde, was a Corbett—a distant relative of the former heavyweight boxing champion, James "Gentleman Jim" Corbett, son of an Irish immigrant.[18] Lyde was a lapsed Catholic. This was one aspect of life the Jennison dynasty kept secret. It is one of the most intriguing parts of Jane Elliott's family tree, an important element that did not emerge publicly until Jane reached mid-life—when her father disclosed the information amidst revelations of her Blue Eyes/Brown Eyes Exercise. Coming of age as the wife of a farming entrepreneur in the early twentieth century, Lyde decided then to hide the Catholic side of her family for fear that deeply ingrained prejudice in northern Iowa would hurt her husband's empire. Therefore, Lloyd and his siblings remained silent on the topic for generations.

On August 25, 1927, Lloyd and Gie traveled to Cresco, Iowa, to get married by a Baptist pastor, Rev. C. S. Carroll. The only witnesses at the ceremony were one of Lloyd's older sisters, Blanche Jennison, and Gie's eldest sister, Anna Mae Benson Lammers, a newlywed who was six months pregnant—a pregnancy that, like Gie's, began before marriage.[19]

Following their nuptials, Samuel and Lyde prepared Lloyd and Gie to assume all ranching responsibilities over the Round Grove estate. According to Jane, Lyde despised Gie for trapping her son into marriage. Because of their terminal bond, Lyde wanted to get away from her daughter-in-law as soon as possible. The elder Jennisons made plans to move where they had property in town and could manage the empire as agricultural landlords.[20] It would take a few years until Samuel and Lyde would leave Round Grove. During that time, Lloyd absorbed every detail of harvesting crops, farming livestock, and conducting business with various vendors. Meanwhile, Gie learned about housekeeping duties.

Gie's contractions started during the afternoon hours of February 26, 1928. Lloyd called for Dr. Thomas G. Walker, Sr., Riceville's beloved physician and the town's original pioneering doctor. Arriving at the Jennison farm by automobile, Dr. Tom delivered a boy, Charles Vincent, named after Lloyd's grandfather, at 8:28 in the evening.[21] After the delivery, the new mother took baby Charles to her parents' home in town to be closer to Dr. Walker, whose small hospital was also in Riceville.[22] The young parents would not settle with their newborn child at the Round Grove farm until late March.

Two years later, shortly after Lloyd's twenty-first birthday and Gie's eighteenth, Samuel and Lyde turned the responsibilities of the Round Grove estate over to their son while still retaining ownership. The couple could finally share a bedroom. Gie bore seven children between Charles Vincent's birth and the last of the brood in 1943. After Charles was Mary Margaret, born May 1, 1931; Marilyn Jean, September 1932; Mable Jane, November 30, 1933; James Samuel, December 26, 1934; Anne Irene, September 28, 1941; and Steven Lloyd, February 6, 1943.

Lloyd, 33, and Gie, 30, were relatively young when their last child arrived. "There probably would have been forty of us," Jane Elliott exaggerated years later, "except the doctor said to my mother, 'If you don't stop having babies, you're going to destroy your body.'"[23]

* * *

By the summer of 1933, the worst year of the Great Depression, and not long after the inauguration of Franklin D. Roosevelt, keeping a hold on farm property became a matter of concern for farmers in Iowa. Four years earlier, the Department of Agriculture's figures showed about 6.3 million farms in the United States. When the depression peaked that summer, 2.5 million farms still carried mortgages, and that number was shrinking. The average farm measured 160 acres—the same size as Round Grove. The mortgage per acre was at $7 in 1933. With the increasing price of farm produce, the gap between ownership and tenantry widened significantly not long after Lloyd and Gie officially became farmers. However, Lloyd's father still owned the farm.[24] To the detriment of the family, the depression took away much of the Jennison farm property in northern Iowa. Lloyd's older brother, Clark, who lived in Clarion, Iowa, kept cattle, chicken, and cockerel on his property. In September, Clark's farm reached a crisis point when a herd bull gored him unconscious inside an open stall. Clark's life was spared when his wife distracted the bull with an empty pail thrown at the animal's head. She dragged Clark to safety while the enraged bull tore into the pail.[25] Fortunately, the Clarion property endured the attack on Clark's life and the depression. But the Round Grove estate near Riceville was the Jennison dynasty's most profitable farm.[26]

The Roosevelt Administration's Farm Credit Act and other government regulatory crop production interventions designed to maintain low prices on agricultural products made it possible for farmers to accept short-term loans to help with crop production. The depression-era relief, recovery, and reform programs provided a blanket of security for the Jennisons. Iowans took solace in hearing that President Roosevelt named one of their own, Henry A. Wallace, to serve as U.S. Secretary of Agriculture.[27] A few years earlier, Wallace, a corn scientist and editor of *Wallace's Farmer,* advocated for experimentation with ethyl alcohol manufactured from corn for motor fuel. Wallace maintained that if incorporated, the economic benefits for Iowa corn farmers would be exponentially greater.

Additionally, he claimed that 500 million bushels of corn would be used yearly if 10 percent of gasoline contained alcohol.[28] In Iowa, where corn is king, the power alcohol movement could have established new markets for corn at a time considered the worst stretch of the depression.[29] His "new deal" for agriculture also included plans to set up domestic allotments to control crop and tax reduction, which the Jennisons considered a "square deal" to rehabilitate production in marginal farmland.[30]

This period in Jennison's family history was uncertain. Time was spent in the confines of rural northern Iowa while trying to keep Round Grove afloat. Joy stemmed largely from the birth of their children. The unhappiness, however, materialized from persistent financial stress. The great economic depression left the Jennison family with the bare essentials. "We lived off of what my father could make selling crops from our farm," said Jane. He would sell pigs and cattle; wool sheared from his sheep was an important commodity that generated enough income to purchase equipment to keep the farm viable. The family lived off the land.[31] Lloyd also earned wages at the Oliver Tractor Plant in Charles City, Iowa. The plant was almost thirty miles from home, and he worked from three o'clock in the afternoon to eleven o'clock in the evening. Whatever playfulness and bliss that young lovers typically experience was abruptly terminated as one set of parents refused to visit, objecting to helping care for the upkeep of the farm and providing little assistance to look after the children. The other had bequeathed them nearly all responsibility to maintain the family estate during an unprecedented time. By Thanksgiving of that dreadful year, they looked forward to peaceful moments together, tender moments with the children, and thoughts about a future full of love.

For Gie, that love would be difficult to give to her new baby if it was a girl. Short of funds, mad with worry, and desiring a second son to help around the farm, the expectant mother counted on the Virgin Mary to bless her family with a boy.

On Thanksgiving Day, November 30, 1933, Gie went into labor while preparing the holiday meal. Expecting Dr. Tom to deliver the baby, it was instead his twenty-four-year-old son, Thomas "Tink" Walker, the third in the line of Doctors Walker. Called "Young Dr. Thomas" by the townspeople but not yet known to the Jennisons as a licensed physician, Tink received his medical degree from the University of Minnesota earlier that spring. He then gained experience delivering babies as an intern in Portland, Oregon, and returned to Riceville to work in his father's office.[32] The young doctor knocked at the door to attend the birth. Shocked by Tink's presence, Lloyd (just a few months older) cried out, "There's no way you're delivering this baby!" His apprehension about Young Dr. Thomas stretched beyond age. The two were neighbors growing up. As braggadocios and self-absorbed teenagers, Tink often shared with Lloyd his views about the opposite sex. As Lloyd remembered, those exchanges were reckless and unmannerly conversations preoccupied with Tink's blustering about his sexual conquests. "You're not touching my wife, Tink!" he repeated.[33]

"Look," Tink said, "my dad is busy." Dr. Tom was already preoccupied delivering twins for another couple in Riceville. "We can do this, Lloyd."

Lloyd acquiesced, and Mabel Jane Jennison entered the world later that day.

There is no record of Gie's immediate reaction to Tink announcing the baby was a girl. Her actions, however, may signal how she felt. Mabel Jane is the only child of Lloyd and Gie who did not have an announcement placed in the local newspaper. Additionally, there would be no official public record of Mabel Jane's birth for almost half a century because the young doctor failed to register baby Mabel Jane's delivery. While some in the family say Tink forgot the birth certificate in his coat pocket, some suspect Gie refused to allow Lloyd to complete the paperwork. Birth certificates and newspaper announcements exist for each of her six siblings. Mabel Jane was in her mid-forties when she finally received a birth certificate. She needed a passport to travel to London for the Blue Eyes/Brown Eyes Exercise.[34]

Mabel Jane is named after one of her father's sisters, Mabel Jennison Feyermeyer—a short-lived educator-turned life insurance secretary in Des

Moines.[35] Although she shared her aunt's name, whom Jane grew to love and deeply admire, Gie repulsed Aunt Mabel to no end. "There is no way I'm calling my daughter, Mabel," Gie told family members.[36] Aunt Mable had been the most vocal Jennison sibling to contest the union between her brother and Gie. Back in 1927, Mable said out loud what no one else would: Lloyd was not the baby's father. However, no one in either family investigated the indictment, including Lloyd. Gie always resented her sister-in-law for making the allegation. So, by November 1933, Lloyd and Gie were more than six years into their marriage, and they had just welcomed the latest child into the dynasty. While indulging Lloyd in naming their new daughter Mabel, Gie forbade anyone from speaking the name. Thus, the child was known all her life by her middle name: Jane.

* * *

"The way my mother treated me made me feel Othered, constantly," Jane said a few weeks before her eighty-eighth birthday in 2021. "I've been the Other for 87 years in my own family. I've always felt, does anyone in my family want me?"[37]

For all their drama, an observer watching the Jennisons become an institution in Riceville during the first third of the twentieth century would have predicted that someone in the family might climb to the highest political office in the state or obtain status as a national celebrity. Neither Samuel, Lyde, Lloyd, nor Gie would obtain such fame. They came close to it as the family sustained Round Grove as a revenue-generating investment beyond the Great Depression. Later in life, Lloyd and Gie added to the family's local prestige as proprietors of the only inn in Riceville. As it happened, their newborn daughter, born a Thanksgiving gift to the world and an alienated Jennison, would lift the family to national distinction—whether they liked it or not.

CHAPTER 2

DRY EYES

While much of her childhood was spent frolicking around the 160-acre farm, Jane bought into the lifestyle at Round Grove. She spent her adolescent years helping her family cope during the economic depression when all hands were needed on deck. Jane was asked to fetch water from the manual hand pump, churn butter, and collect eggs from the chicken coop. She helped her father pick corn by hand. She shocked and bundled oats by following behind a horse pulling a grain binder. The task was done shoeless, which was standard for depression-era farming by Jennison children at Round Grove. The practice made the oat stubble particularly hard on the feet. Since owning a tractor wasn't an option, the Jennisons farmed with horses. Looking back, Jane thought she labored on the farm during those early years because there was no other lifestyle for children like her, which she accepted without reservation. "It was really good for us because we grew up really strong and had terrific muscles and good bust lines," she said. "We were our own little fitness club. You worked so hard, but it was just not seen as hard work. It was just what you did."[1]

At age six, Jane discovered life outside Round Grove. The awakening began when her father acquired the family's first radio. One day, Lloyd visited with a banker in Riceville, intending to discuss the estate's business needs. During the conversation, the banker told Lloyd he would loan him $8 for a radio. "You need something out there on the farm with all those kids," the banker said, according to Jane's recollection. The radio program heard most at Round Grove during those early days was *Ma Perkins*. With the help of Oxydol scrubbing soap, housewives around the country clambered to the fifteen-minute on-air drama starring Virginia Payne as Ma Perkins, affectionately known as

"America's Mother of the Air." Initially launched in 1933 and officially called *Oxydol's Own Ma Perkins* because of funding provided by its deep-cleaning laundry detergent sponsor, Oxydol, the show featured the drama of a fictional close-knit rural community of Rushville Center. In each episode, Ma Perkins faced contemporary issues, including the economic depression, World War II, gender norms, and shifting values in a pluralistic society. Jane remembered, "Because we had nothing, we would listen to and watch and listen to my mother listening to *Oxydol's Own Ma Perkins*—the soap operas before they were called soap operas." The show aired at 2:15 in the afternoon on the commercial AM radio station WHO 1040, a network affiliate of the NBC Red Network, which broadcasted comedies, dramas, Bible readings, sports, and soap operas like *Ma Perkins*.[2] "We got a really strange education about what the rest of the world was like by listening to the radio," Jane said.[3]

Despite the challenges endured as the middle child in the Jennison family, Jane cherished moments that her family spent together listening to the radio in the living room with a kerosene lamp burning. In addition to *Ma Perkins*, the family enjoyed *Tarzan, George Burns and Gracie Allen*, and *Jack Armstrong, the All-American Boy*. Since radio listening was a skill that enhanced one's imagination, Jane and her siblings often debated their respective interpretations of each show. "We would have to picture in our minds what was happening," she explained. "We all had different pictures in our mind, of course, so we would discuss what we believed was happening in the show. Once we got television, we didn't have to make pictures in our mind anymore. It took away half the good of what we were doing with the radio because we were no longer required to listen so closely that we could create our own picture of those people in our mind."[4]

On occasions that the family turned on a musical broadcast, the children put on a show inside the Round Grove home, loud enough to be heard at the neighboring Rasmussen farm. "My mother would sit down at the piano, and she would chord while we sang," Jane recalled. "We were a loud family, and the music would travel out the window."[5]

* * *

Jane's formal education began in September 1939 at Jamestown School No. 2. Her school was one of eight local one-room schoolhouses encompassing all age levels of elementary school, kindergarten through eighth grade, located in rural Jamestown Township. Located an eighth of a mile from Jane's house but on one acre of the Jennison property, the school was often called the Round Grove School to avoid confusion with other one-room prairie schoolhouses in the township.[6] Like graded elementary schools in the Riceville borough, the school served as a feeder for Riceville High School. For instructional purposes, large desks were placed in the back of the classroom for the older students, while the desks got smaller and the younger students were in the front. In the corner of the class was a sandpit. The schoolhouse lacked electricity and an indoor toilet. Instead, the building was fitted with an antiquated potbelly wood-burning stove that was irritating for the teacher who arrived early to clean the ash and "get the room warmed up at least a little" before the students arrived, Jane recalled. Outside was a playground fitted with two swings and a chin-up bar.[7] The teacher cleaned two outdoor toilets, one for boys and another for girls. The signature feature of the Round Grove school was its bell tower.

Jane entered Jamestown School No. 2 as a darling five-year-old. Her favorable reputation was due largely to the performance of her older siblings, Charles, Mary, and Jean, who proved to be devoted and assiduous academic hotshots. The school's lone teacher—always a female, usually in her late teenage years or early twenties with virtually no formal teaching experience—was up against those dogged Jennison children, which Jane admitted were "really aggressive, abrasive, and obnoxious." About fifteen other children of varying ages and grade levels, made up of siblings from just three families, joined the Jennisons. Together, they made the job very difficult for the teacher.

Since managing a one-room school was demanding, teacher attrition at Jamestown was problematic. In most cases, Round Grove teachers stayed no longer than a year at a time, two, if lucky. The school day ran from eight in the morning until four in the afternoon. During those hours, the school's lone teacher taught curricula for nine grades and monitored the behavior of varying maturity levels and hormones. "It wasn't a treat for our teachers," Jane acknowledged. For the students, however, it was an enjoyable break from the hardships of rural life. The schoolhouse was warm, the water was accessible, and the government provided lunches for the students. It was an escape from working in the oat and cornfields. Jane's home didn't have electricity until 1943; going to school was a "real treat," she said.[8]

Jane experienced eight different teachers in nine years at the school. Although she believed that it was because of her and the other Jennison children that the school had trouble retaining its teachers, it was due to the stresses of the job. Jane poignantly described the reality of teaching at a one-room schoolhouse: "It was very difficult to be a teacher in that situation because we [Jennisons] stuck together." Five-year-olds to fourteen-year-olds stuck in the same room, eight hours a day for nine months was a bit much for teachers possessing nothing more than a four-year high school diploma or, in few cases, a first-grade teaching certification." She said, "Here you had all these kids going through all of these growth stages in the same room at the same time. It was grueling."[9]

Her kindergarten teacher, Dorothy Nelson—a twenty-two-year-old with two years of experience in the classroom and a former Riceville High School honors student—left at the end of the 1939-40 school year.[10] Nelson's replacement was Geraldine "Jay" Shipton, who taught Jane to read and write in first grade. After one year, Shipton left for a less onerous job at a larger-unit school in the McIntire Community School District, where she only had to worry about managing a single grade of students. Jane had two teachers in second grade, Helen Zilk, who passed away after a series of strokes over the Christmas and New Year holidays, and Margaret Enfield, a recent Riceville High School graduate.[11] Gertrude Austin served as the school's teacher during Jane's third-grade year (1942-43) but left in the summer of 1943 to enlist in the Women's Army Training Corps. Only once, in fourth and fifth grades, Jane had the same teacher for two consecutive years. That teacher was Grace Naab Bessman, a forty-something transplant to Riceville that Jane described as demanding. "She was mean, and she was hard, but you learned," Jane said.

Bessman was also known for her unique fashion. In middle age, she wore depression-era corsets, a garment styled in the period to focus more on "figure control, not figure alteration," as one designer put it.[12] Jane noticed what she was doing to her senescent figure by regularly wearing corsets. "From her bust down to her waist to below her hips, she was encased in this corset," Jane remembered. She also described Bessman as encompassing a love for books. Bessman introduced her to Laura Ingalls Wilder's *Little House* book series. "She read every one of those books to us, 'cause right after lunch, she would read to us K-8, and we would listen."[13]

Born in 1897, Bessman graduated from Iowa State Teachers College and became a longtime teacher in the Riceville area, with tenures in the community school district and the surrounding rural schools. During the 1940s, Bessman was a leading organizer of the Royal Home Workers Club, a social organization comprised of Riceville women. They talked seriously about politics, farming practices, schools, entertainment, and popular books. While Riceville women—many of whom participated in voluntary organizations like the WCTU—commonly debated the period's biggest issues, only some before the women's club were eager to exercise the vote. Even fewer dared to run for political office. Bessman, in 1941, tried but failed to leverage her support from the women's club into a seat on the school board of the Riceville Community School District.[14]

Bessman left Jamestown School in the spring of 1945 but returned in 1949 when Jane was a sophomore in high school.[15] Little is known about Bessman's replacement, Darlene Quinn, Jamestown's teacher, during the 1945-46 school year when Jane was in sixth grade. The instructor in 1946-47 was Ruby Servoss, a former mathematics teacher from Riceville High School and then the Girl Scout brownies leader. While loved by Jane, Servoss resigned before the end of Jane's seventh-grade year after finding one of her uncles slumped over in a chair, having suffered a heart attack.[16] Jane's instructor as an eighth grader was Ella Smith. In February 1948, Smith helped Jane win the Jamestown Township spelling bee. Victory in the township bee meant Jane could compete in the March Mitchell and Howard counties' bee. She did, and she lost.[17]

Jamestown's classes were so small that motivation to reach full academic potential emerged from the pressure of being accepted by children in higher grades. For instance, Jane was one of two students in her class when she entered kindergarten in 1939. By the following year, her only classmate had been held back, making her the only student in her class through sixth grade when a new family with a child her age moved into the Round Grove community. Often bored with her grade-level curriculum, Jane paid attention to lessons taught to her older siblings. "By the time I got to the sixth grade, I knew everything in the eighth-grade program because I had heard it for six years," she recalled. A fluctuating teaching staff aside, there is no doubt that Jane benefited from the type of education provided to her at the small rural school. "We were immersed in education all day long, and I benefited by watching what older students were learning."[18]

Jamestown School No. 2 always existed as the magnum opus of Round Grove. The schoolhouse bound together the community's families in an impossible way at the graded Riceville community schools. In truth, the fact that the school still operated in the 1940s was rare for what was currently happening to one-room rural schools across the Hawkeye State. In the 1890s, the National Education Association commenced a consolidation campaign to close independently run one-room rural schools throughout the Midwest and Pacific Northwest, claiming they were "Individualistic, inefficient and chaotic." It took some time before the movement impacted rural schools in Iowa. In 1906, the state passed its first consolidation law, which merged rural schools in McIntire with the Riceville Community School District. After World War I, the Iowa assembly passed a minimum attendance law forcing one-room schools to close if they had less than five students attending on average and less than ten students enrolled for an entire year. The legislation pressured rural schools into consolidating with larger, more urban school districts. In the year of Jane's birth, there were at least 412 consolidated schools across eighty-one counties in Iowa.[19] Rural schools throughout Jamestown Township delayed such action because enrollment tarried between fifteen and twenty-five regular students.

Jane's small schoolhouse held on as long as possible amid several legislative threats that stretched half a century. The beginning of the end of the Jamestown School started over the winter of 1944. Just after midnight, Friday, February 19, the schoolhouse burned in a devastating fire. The cause of the fire is still unknown. The historic building burnt nearly to cinders, destroying everything inside. The school's records, textbooks, desks, chalkboards, and other instructional equipment were lost. Two days before the fire, Jane had injured herself severely by stepping on a nail while playing near the family's milk house. The nail impaled her foot completely by entering its sole and exiting through the arch. While wailing in pain, her father pressed both feet down on the board and slid her foot off the nail. With her foot heavily bandaged and needing to soak in hot water most of the day, Jane struggled to fall asleep due to constant pain from the infection around the wound. This included the night of the fire. Awake past midnight, Jane was among the first in the neighborhood to notice an odd luminescence coming from the direction of the schoolhouse. "We thought it was the northern light but then realized it was the school burning," she recalled. Bedridden due to the injury, Jane stayed behind as her parents and siblings made the trek toward the light to verify that the school was on fire.

For the remainder of Jane's fourth-grade school year and all of fifth grade, the Jamestown Township board chose to enroll her and nineteen classmates into Jamestown School No. 5, also known as The Fox School, after the owner of the property, Ernest Fox.[20] The new schoolhouse for Jamestown School No. 2 at Round Grove would not open until September 1945, the start of Jane's sixth-grade school year. When ready for use, the architect fitted the new building with a line of windows extending across the western side, allowing increased natural light for instruction inside the main room. Added to the school was a basement playroom with a furnace. The architect also constructed indoor bathroom facilities and a large cloakroom. Having replaced one of the oldest buildings in Jamestown, the new schoolhouse had become the "most modern in this vicinity," reported the *Riceville Recorder*, "a fine building for their children's use."[21]

The community felt otherwise. The contractor built the new school out of concrete blocks with less than the required footing size. It often swayed. After one year, the basement was useless because two inches of standing water overwhelmed the facility. Moreover, a flat roof covered the building, causing additional drainage problems when pools of water would sit in the middle, causing leaks. Standing water became a source of mold after heavy rainfall and snow.

*　*　*

Returning to Jane's early childhood education, the world rapidly changed during Jane's first month of kindergarten in 1939. War broke out in Europe when Germany invaded Poland on the first day of September. A few days after, when the Reichsführer Heinrich Himmler ignored pleas for arbitration, the British and French declared war on the Nazi aggressors. While life in Iowa continued as usual at the outset, endless reporting of crucial moments of the conflict in Europe by the *Riceville Recorder* alarmed Lloyd and Gie. When the Soviet Union joined Germany in its assault on Poland a few weeks later, vivid memories of America's gradual entry into the Great War over twenty years earlier concerned the nation. Charles Lindbergh, an aviation hero and celebrity with a special gift for relating to the average American, tried to quell those concerns with a primetime radio address. "As long as we maintain an army, a navy, and an air force worthy of the name, as long as America does not decay within, we need fear no invasion," said Lindbergh, who had become the leading voice in the pro-isolationist movement.

A Gallup poll taken the week of September 25 found that 84 percent of the public wanted to keep U.S. ships out of war zones. However, members of Congress petitioned President Roosevelt to implement a "cash-and-carry" program that would amend the post-World War I arms neutrality embargo. The program would allow the government to trade weapons to the Allies if ratified, provided they paid cash and used their ships for transport.[22] Lloyd had been too young to serve on the Western Front in 1917, but another total war was not out of the realm of possibility. A few months into 1940, Lloyd completed his draft registration paperwork once the Roosevelt Administration convinced U.S. Congress to pass the Selective Training and Service Act, the country's first peacetime draft. Gie's brothers-in-law, David Larson, and Prosper Lamonte Jeffries, were already in the service and stationed at the Navy base in San Diego and the Great Lakes Naval Station.

The global conflict seemed ubiquitous during Jane's elementary years. Moments like the birth of her sister, Anna "Annie" Irene, on September 28, 1941, provided some escape from an otherwise distressing start to the 1940s. According to Jane, Dr. "Tink" Walker said Anne was "the most perfect child he ever delivered." Indeed, she could sing the refrain of "Ac-Cent-Tchu-Ate the Positive" by her third birthday. For a toddler, "She was brilliant," said Jane.[23]

But even those happy moments were fleeting.

In October, Jane's grandfather, Samuel, suffered a stroke and was confined to his bed in Riceville. Following the stroke, Jane's parents initially took Samuel into their home. Lloyd saw that his father received medication and the proper nursing care. Jane recalled this created friction between Lloyd and Gie, whose newborn baby girl demanded much attention. But the farm took Lloyd's focus away, as did their older kids, and now the health of Grandad Sam.

"He's got a wife. She can give him his medicine," Gie said to Lloyd.

"Ma won't give him his medicine," Lloyd replied. "I got to go give him his medicine."

Sadly, Jane recalled, "Grandpa Sam's health became an inconvenience for Mom." With reluctance, Lloyd agreed to return his father to his home in Riceville after Thanksgiving. This act ultimately entrusted his mother, Lyde, with some responsibilities for tending to his needs.

For over a month, Lloyd's daily routine included the eight-mile round trip in and out of town to ensure Lyde gave Grandad Sam his medicine. Except for the evening of December 10, a time of uncertainty caused by the congressional declaration of war against Japan two days prior, when Gie talked Lloyd into staying home. Without a telephone, Lloyd could not communicate his absence to his mother. Just as he predicted, Lyde did not give Samuel his medicine. The following day, he was dead.

"I should have gone," Lloyd repeated to himself. "I knew she wouldn't give him his medicine."[24]

While Lloyd accepted responsibility for his father's passing, Jane blamed her mother and grandmother. "It was a noble thing what my father was doing to go into town to give him his medicine," Jane posited. "We should have kept [Grandad Sam] in our house, which is what he wanted to do, but that was an inconvenience for our mother."[25]

Samuel's passing further compounded the financial troubles of the Jennison family. Now Lloyd and Gie assumed ownership rights over Round Grove, including a $3,200 mortgage and an $8,000 debt.[26] Economic stress worsened days later when a cholera outbreak on the farm took the lives of fifty-two hogs between December 11 and December 16. At the end of the depression, each family member contributed to maintaining the Round Grove farm. Hard times meant that the Jennison children were no exception. Lloyd knew that each hour the children devoted to school was an hour removed from work on the farm which could otherwise generate greater revenue. However, farming was not the life he wanted for them. To ensure his children did not end up in an agricultural hustle as he had endured, Lloyd wanted his children to focus on their education. Lloyd was determined his children received a formal education the entire year, unlike many farming families who sent their kids to school on and off when convenient.

To help make ends meet, three Jennison girls, Mary, Jean, and Jane, entered singing competitions at churches and community halls in and around Riceville. Managed by their pianist mother, the girls called themselves "The Three Jills." Mary had an unmeasured pitch, Jean had a beautiful voice, and Jane, who started singing along with her sisters at age three, could remember the words to every song.[27] The few dollars they won filled the gas tank and occasionally paid for supper. Many years after the depression, the girls welcomed to the group their younger brother, James Samuel, who went by "Jim" as an adolescent, and as an adult, preferred "Sam." The siblings became a family travel troupe called "Three Jills and a Jim" and later "The Four Jennisons." The quartet earned money performing opening acts for major orchestras and as the main entertainment at Armistice Day events, cattle banquets, and Odd Fellow and Rebekah Lodge gatherings in Minnesota and Iowa. While most of their performances were for remuneration, they performed weekly in the Riceville Methodist Church choir.[28]

A few days before Grandad Sam's death, the United States entered World War II following the surprise bombing by the Japanese Empire on the Pearl Harbor naval base. After one in the afternoon on December 7, 1941, Jane was at a Riceville service station sitting in the backseat of her father's Model A Ford when she heard about the attack.

"The sons of bitch'n Japanese just bombed Pearl Harbor," Lloyd had exclaimed upon hearing the news over the radio.[29]

Still bereft over losing his father, Lloyd felt a deep sense of sacrifice. He flirted with enlisting in the U.S. Army. His sense of duty intensified when the War Department called for men ages seventeen to fifty to join the Naval Reserves. The hometown weekly ran the names of all the men in the area who met the call to serve.[30] The pressure was almost too much to bear. Young, strong, agile, and smart, Lloyd saw his friends, coworkers, and many relatives enlist. He and Gie had terrible arguments over the war, remembered Jane. "I had never even thought about something happening so ugly that we could not just lose our farm, but we could lose our relatives and our father if he insisted on going into the military," she recalled. "It was just a strange existence that we lived at that time."

At the local Riceville drug store, the American Legion hung an Honor Roll Board, a memorial consisting of a six by sixteen feet panel fitted with a blue background with five-inch white stars possessing the names of every man and woman from Howard and Mitchell counties in the service. Featured on the board were gold stars indicating local heroes reportedly killed or missing in action.[31] As the number of gold stars increased on the honor roll, a group of mothers started a Gold Star Club in town to support one another. "It broke your heart," said Jane, who often stood on the side of the train tracks to wave at soldiers transferring through town.

Further, the wartime environment engendered deep guilt in her father, Lloyd. "Goddammit, Margaret," he exclaimed one day. "I have to join, or they are going to call me a draft dodger."

"No, Lloyd, someone has to raise these kids," Gie screamed and pointed out that they just had baby Anne, plus the demands of keeping the 160-acre farm afloat. This meant that Lloyd was the family's primary caregiver.

Fortunately for Gie, she found a way to ensure that her husband neither enlisted nor got drafted. In the summer of 1942, she informed Lloyd that they were again pregnant with a child that would become their last son, Steven Lloyd, born in February 1943. Now, there was no way that Lloyd would put on a uniform. "He couldn't possibly go to the military with a seventh child on the way," said Jane. "But we were lucky he didn't get drafted."[32]

Two of Jane's uncles were already in the throes of combat that spring. One of them, David Larson, husband to Gie's sister, Vera, was an aspiring music teacher and member of the Norway Tour Band. Larson was stationed at the 32nd Street Naval Station in San Diego on the day the Pearl Harbor attack occurred. After the attack, he was commissioned to the USS *Hornet*, the navy's famed aircraft carrier. The USS Hornet was later recognized for its role in the April 1942 Doolittle Raid and the victory at Midway two months later.[33] Uncle Larson had been present on the ship for both combat missions. He was aboard the warship during the Battle of Santa Cruz on October 27, 1942. For nearly 10 hours, Japanese torpedo planes, dive bombers, and spontaneous suicide pilots unleashed fury on the ship. Severely damaged with fires raging, the *Hornet* lost electrical power and virtually all navigation equipment. Larson and the surviving crew were forced to abandon the liner. He spent four hours floating in a life preserver with Japanese and American bodies drifting about.[34] Gunfire and artillery explosions during the battle permanently ruined Larson's hearing. When he returned home after Santa Cruz, it was impossible to continue his music career.

Jane's second uncle to see combat was Prosper LaMonte Jeffries, a graduate of Osage High School and future husband to Gie's younger sister, Mary Irene. Attaining the rank of staff sergeant, Jeffries spent four years in the army and participated in several invasions in the South Pacific.[35] Five feet, five inches, 165 pounds, Jeffries survived battles of the New Guinea campaign. His assignment was to hide in the shrubs of the jungle. There he would lie in wait for a column of Japanese troops to walk by, then ambush the last of the Japanese soldiers, strangle him with a rope, softly drop the body, and wait in the dense vegetation to do it again.[36]

The war thundered through northern Iowa in other ways. In the borough of Riceville, edgy factory hands found enough work to lift the town out of its depression-era slumber. Families registered for ration stamps, which aided the government in conserving sugar, milk, butter, gasoline, and other high-demand necessities.[37] Ruth Wells was the wife of a World War I veteran living on a farm adjacent to Round Grove. In 1942, she taught nine-year-old Jane how to exploit government-regulated systems.

"We (Jennisons) had a lot of ration stamps because there were a lot of us kids, and each one of us had a book of stamps," explained Jane. "We had milking cows, so we had milk, butter, and eggs. We didn't need ration stamps for those. So, the woman across the road [Ruth Wells] would trade us sugar for our stamps for other necessities that we already had on our farm. Ruth invited me up to her house one day and invited me upstairs. And there, in the hall against the door, was a 50-pound and a 100-pound stack of sugar. She was hoarding sugar and getting it by trading ration stamps."[38]

Living through a total war placed great stress upon every family member to contribute to American victories in Europe and the Pacific. Children in the surrounding rural areas were suddenly scouring farmland for milkweed. As it turned out, the life-saving crop contained the floss material the government needed to manufacture life preservers, aviator suits, and other lightweight floatable materials. Before 1944, the fluff material needed to fill the interior of life jackets came from kapok, which contained tiny yellowish hollow hairs covered with wax. Some kapok floss arrived from South Africa, India, the South Sea Islands, and South America. However, most of the crops arrived from Java, an island of Indonesia now occupied by the Japanese. When American manufacturers could no longer access the kapok trees in the Pacific, the navy and air corps deemed the homegrown milkweed plant a suitable replacement. Its thread-like substance was strong enough to fill life preservers, but only when properly dried and packed.[39] Accordingly, the Defense Plant Corporation opened a plant in Petoskey, Michigan, where workers separated the floss from the milkweed pod, then quilted it into life vests, rafts, and pilot jackets. Leftover milkweed pod shells were burned for fuel to heat the Petoskey plant.

In May 1944, the army and navy assigned the Department of Agriculture to oversee the milkweed drive by enlisting school children and children in youth organizations, namely the boy and girl scouts, to collect, dry, bag, and ship the pods to government authorities. Accordingly, upon the start of Jane's fifth-grade school year later that fall, under the supervision of Mrs. Bessman and directorship of the Superintendent of Howard County Schools, Jamestown School students spent several autumn days collecting milkweed pods from township farmers. The government paid the school-age milkweed army fifteen cents per bag of pods. Another five cents were allocated if the pods were dried. To get the whole twenty cents, Jane and her peers used school hours to collect and dry the pods by hanging the bags on a fence outside their schoolhouse, where the sun and wind did the job of drying the crop. Every two to six weeks after the commencement of the drive, a government agent visited the school to retrieve the bags. Children in Howard County collected almost a million milkweed pods, which amounted to about 1,255 bags.[40]

Just months after the milkweed drive, the United States closed in on victories over the Germans and the Japanese. In Europe, General George S. Patton's Third Army steamrolled through Nazi-occupied France and, by the winter months of 1945, made huge sacrifices to force a German retreat upon the conclusion of the Battle of the Bulge. In the Pacific, American troops commenced the invasion of an eight-square-mile island known as Iwo Jima. The Battle of Iwo Jima lasted thirty-six days, yielding the U.S. Army two airfields for emergency landing missions and bombing runs to the Japanese mainland.

Upon conclusion of fighting in the Ardennes region of Belgium and Luxembourg and at Iwo Jima on January 25 and March 26, 1945, respectively, the German and Japanese surrenders were just months away. At this point in her life, Jane found herself without much room to breathe freely as an adolescent. The concerns were plenty: sustaining the farm, her father's fate, and the safety of her uncles. Her role as a ration agent forced her to grow up faster than children in previous generations. While the war's end was in sight that spring, tragedy would strike inside her home with the unexpected and seemingly preventable death of one of her siblings.

On the morning of March 15, 1945, Jane's sister, Anne, now age three, acquired a fever and sore throat. Later that evening, she had difficulty swallowing. The next day, she started convulsing. Gie called a doctor to the house. Now retired as the eldest, Dr. Thomas G. Walker. The town physician before the war, Dr. Walker's son, Tink Walker, was away serving as the senior medical officer at the naval air station in Hutchinson, Kansas, after working as the flight surgeon on a small aircraft carrier in the Atlantic. That left itinerant doctor, J.A. Uran, to treat the sickly Anne. Uran administered a suppository and suggested having her soak in cool water to drive down her temperature.[41] Lloyd and Gie put

Anne in a copper boiler and watched her well-being. The treatment made Anne worse, and she convulsed throughout the night. On the morning of March 17, Gie lay on the living room sofa beside her innocent and talented daughter and watched Anne take her final breath. "She's gone, Lloyd," Gie said, and Lloyd threw back his head and let out a gut-wrenching howl.

Upon noticing what happened, Jane ran outside and knelt on the wooden step before the door. The family collie dog, Patsy, stayed beside Jane and comforted her while she prayed. Anguished by how inconsolable her father was at that moment and believing her mom would prefer to have Anne alive, Jane cried out, "God, take me instead."

Those words gob-smacked Jane, who recanted her plea to the Lord. In silence, she beseeched, "That's all right, God. You know better. You take her if you want to." She stood and wandered aimlessly through the yard. Years later, Jane admitted, "That's when I learned about being a hypocrite."[42]

Anne's death certificate says the cause of death was convulsions due to septic tonsillitis. She was "the joy of their lives," reported the *Riceville Recorder* of the three-year-old's passing. "Her sudden death has left an empty spot [. . .] that can never be filled. Surely God must have needed her very much to have taken her from the many loved ones," wrote the family in her obituary.[43]

Each member of the family mourned in their own way. For Jane's eldest brother, Charles, upon his eighteenth birthday and after receiving a diploma from high school, Uncle Sam came calling. Charles had all the traits the Jennisons valued. Standing five feet, seven inches tall, with lean shoulders and ripped biceps sculpted by hours spent on the farm, he exuded leadership skills, and all the physical traits officers looked for in good soldiers. But there was no question that Anne's death was deflating. He played football and performed in school theater during his senior year at Riceville High, but school was perfunctory. He slowed in recovering from his sister's death. A world tour courtesy of the U.S. Navy, including a deployment to Pearl Harbor, was a much-needed two-year escape from Round Grove.[44]

Jane was eleven years old when Anne passed that spring of 1945. She had been close to her younger sister. As pre-teenage girls often do, the two played games of Mommy and Daughter, happy time doll house, and tea party. They explored the Round Ground acreage's rolling hills, meadows, and creeks. Jane took to heart the fact that a treatable illness took her sister. As a result, she would spend her life attacking with special vengeance people and programs that could deliver promised care to those in need. Guilt-stricken, she eventually figured to become a nurse. Those plans would change many years later.

CHAPTER 3

CAST EYES DOWN

While divides existed between Jane and Gie, outsiders saw the Jennisons as a tight-knit, like-minded family. Lloyd made sure that it stayed that way. He taught his children that if the Jennisons found themselves in trouble, it would be dealt with internally, and the misbehavior better not harm anyone outside the clan. Having a brood of six children living isolated mainly on a farm meant he could make the family into its social clique. Since the eldest, Charles, was away in the navy, and the youngest, Steve, was just a toddler, the children in between could utilize their musical talent once showcased during the latter years of the Depression to let the community know that the Jennisons were both omnipresent and doing fine. From 1947 to 1952, Mary, Jean, Jane, and Jim, with a four-year difference from oldest to youngest, earned allowances as the regional singing troupe "Three Jills and a Jim." With Gie acting as manager, the family-friendly acapella ensemble accepted gigs at banquets and community events in northern Iowa and Minnesota. Since the *Riceville Recorder* insisted on calling them "Three Jills and a Jack," its play on the Jack and Jill nursery rhyme, the quartet rebranded itself "The Four Jennisons" after a performance in front of 152 educators at the Howard County Rural Teachers Association banquet held December 6, 1947.

The Four Jennisons provided a simple form of entertainment. Most of the time, the group sang patriotic numbers or biblical hymns. However, since the girls and Jim listened to the radio incessantly, the troupe knew all the popular songs. "We sang whatever came to our heads," Jane explained. "We were loud and on key. And we could sing every song of that era, except if it was operatic. We could sing cowboy songs. We could sing country. We could ham it up. We could sing through our noses to please the audiences."[1] Though Gie acted as the group's manager, Jane said in a colloquial manner, "She couldn't manage us."

At a time when language was still uninhibited, The Four Jennisons sang numbers that later generations would consider racist, sexist, and ageist. A few of the songs the group sang without their mother's permission were The Andrew Sisters' "I Didn't Know the Gun Was Loaded" and Tunesmith Jack Yellin and Sammy Fain's "We Gotta Put Shoes on Willie" and "Never Make Eyes (At the Gals With the Guys Who Are Bigger Than You)." In the middle of the twentieth century, the frequency of blackface minstrelsy at Riceville community events offered a glimpse into how causal racist behavior was accepted. This was particularly prevalent in parts of the United States where there were no people of color, making the thought of racism and the treatment of African Americans an uncommon practice. In March 1948, Jane's eighth-grade school year, The Four Jennisons co-headlined an event for the Saratoga AMVETS with an actress dressed up as Aunt Jemima. The benefit was advertised as a pancake dinner, and it took place at Saratoga Hall, situated east of Riceville. The event brought together local World War II veterans and their families with community members. The Jennison quartet sang George M. Cohan's "Over There" and other military ditties while Aunt Jemima sang African American folk music and told jokes, mixed, flipped, and served pancakes and sausages to an amused audience for fifty cents a ticket. [2] At the time, Jane felt no discomfort associating with an entertainer in blackface.

As each Jennison child navigated through high school, the group continued to perform together on weekends, over summer vacations, and during holidays until Jane married in 1955 and started having children. Whatever reasons convinced the siblings to continue singing together, this family business gave the Jennisons an uncommon social prominence. Jane acknowledged that The Four Jennisons projected an image of affection and affability to the public and that their love stretched beyond the boundaries of Round Grove. In hindsight, the binding would fracture relatively easily once Jane introduced the Discrimination Day lesson to her students in 1968. After Lloyd passed away in 1990, Jane's place in the family was forever lost. However, during that time, performing together generated a smokescreen covering friction between Jane and the rest of her family when behind closed doors. "Singing is when we could be friendly and [be] together," Jane maintained years later, regretting that a wedge divided her from everyone else.

The Four Jennisons also allowed Jane to practice, however sparingly, performances in front of fair-sized audiences. The experience helped her overcome stage fright: cultivating soft skills needed later to engage with her students and large crowds.

* * *

If her mother had her way, Jane, the fourth child stuck in the middle, would have disappeared years earlier when Aunt Mabel, incapable of bearing children, and Uncle Herb Fesenmeyer sought adoption. Jane was nearly age three when Mabel and Herb asked Lloyd and Gie for one of their children. Gie said, "You can take Jane," but Mabel said she wanted Jean. "No," commanded Gie. "It is Jane or none of my children."[3]

Jane and Jean were nearly identical, two inches over five feet, with short hair, gathered and waved, sometimes worn tightly curled and pushed from the side to frame their faces. Both had sapphire-blue eyes, wore black cat eyeglasses, and had skin like a rose petal. Jane was a better stage actress. Jean never acted. Jane was also a better athlete, though not nearly as athletic as her father had been twenty years earlier or what her younger brother, Jim, would become. While already established as a musical talent, Jean had more promise as a singer. Likewise, Jean's academic performance was much better than Jane's. Most of all, separating the two was Jane's penchant for challenging the status quo. Accordingly, Gie preferred celebrating Jean's successes while deflating Jane's accomplishments with dampened comments such as, "Well, Jean did it better," "You should be more like Jean," "You are an embarrassment," and "Don't be such a disappointment."[4] For her part, Jane did the best she could as a middle child enamored by one parent while despised by the other.

Since those early days, Jane and her mother were like cats itching for a fight. Gie had never disguised that she considered Jane inferior to the other Jennison children. Jean, in particular, was the anvil Gie used to hammer Jane's spirit into submission. While inseparable during their formative years, upon reaching high school Gie worked on lengthening the divide between the girls. A pithy one year separated the sisters both in age and grade—Jean, class of 1951, and Jane, class of 1952. Each was keenly aware of the other's standing and sway. However, Jane conceded that her older sister would ease through high school with one of the highest IQs ever recorded at Riceville and among the school's most decorated academic careers. "Jean was absolutely brilliant," Jane recognized. She must have felt a sense of inferiority around Jean. "I didn't compete with Jean scholastically—wouldn't dream of it." Jean was a Howard and Mitchell counties spelling bee champion, a favorite of all her teachers, and had her footprints over nearly every extracurricular at the school. Jean had an opinion on everything, including giving her peers dating advice.[5]

"At what age do you think boys and girls should start dating?" Her peers would ask.

"It is all right to date upon entering the freshman grade, but nothing steady," Jean replied.

"Do you believe in going steady while in high school?"

"No, you miss out on a lot of group fun, and you don't do your schoolwork to the best of your ability."[6]

For any existing social and academic squabble, some of which were sisterly disputes while others spurred on by their mother, Jane and Jean shared only a few moments of kinship. Jane said privately, "We were not close in philosophy, not in temperament [. . .] The only time I was close with my sisters was when we were singing." Jean would rather spend time with Mary, class of 1948, who had been an exemplary student at Riceville High. An educator and budding journalist, Mary made a name for herself in Riceville as a singer, actress, and associate editor of the school newspaper. Her columns occasionally appeared in the local *Riceville Recorder*. By 1951, Jean and Jane's senior and junior years, Mary was already three years into a teaching career, having received four years of training at Riceville High, making her eligible to teach in Iowa immediately following commencement. At age seventeen, she received her first job at the rural one-room Jamestown School No. 3. At twenty years old, Mary worked as a second and third-grade teacher at Riceville Elementary School.[7]

Meanwhile, Riceville Community School District Superintendent, Walter L. Edwards, convinced Jean and Jane to enroll together in the high school's new advanced algebra and trigonometry courses. Taught by a former instructor of military personnel during World War II, Martha Orr, the sisters were cherry-picked into the classes because they were sure to pass. Edwards would use their success to convince the school board that advanced courses, whether in the math and sciences or the humanities, were important for the school district despite the reality that many of its students would become farmers after graduation. Though Jane did pass the two courses, she said it was mainly because she "kept my mouth shut" at a time when her teacher could have gotten into trouble, an unspoken quid pro quo. Orr spent years working with military veterans. As she got to know the soldiers, Orr acquired the habit of smoking. One day she knocked her purse off her desk. Jane and Jean were in the front row and saw a pack of cigarettes that had fallen out of the purse. "We looked at each other, leaned forward to pick up the purse and its contents," recalled Jane. "The look on Mrs. Orr's face was one of total relief since smoking was one of the things that 'nice women didn't do, [*sic*] at that time."[8]

Typically razor-focused on making a fool out of her teachers, Jane's attention sometimes took a slight detour in those two math classes. Joining her in class was brainy Alfred Larsen,[9] senior class president, captain of the 1950 football team, and winner of ten varsity letters collectively in football, basketball, and baseball. Jane found Larsen both approachable and dashing. Listening to Larsen during class discussions produced an enchanting aura. Jane conspicuously avoided attaching herself to any classmate to maintain a degree of respectability over her peers. Her attraction to Larsen was something she kept to herself.

At supper one evening, Jane and her father were talking about Larsen. Lloyd turned to her and said, "Don't you date that Larsen boy," then made use of a several racial slurs.[10] Jane learned from this shocking interaction that membership in the world of the Jennisons carried lifelong responsibilities that eventually repelled her. Because she loved her father deeply, she hardly confronted him when he said the N-word or drew on anti-Black stereotypes. The few times she did, he retorted: "If you don't like the way I think, you can always leave; the road's not crowded." Jane usually retreated to her friends and complained, "If hazel eyes ever go out of style, my dad's in big trouble."[11] She figured he was a product of his environment. "He was the most moral man I've ever met in my life," Jane told an interviewer for the Iowa Women's Archive in 2009. However, she added, "He was a racist. 'Cause he didn't know any better. Everybody else was; why shouldn't he be?"[12] With all that said, Larsen, the young man she was told to steer clear of, wound up pursuing multiple degrees in physical education, athletic coaching, and science at Iowa State College. He married his high school sweetheart.

Also in the two classes was junior Edward "Burl" Armstrong. Like Larsen, Burl served as Riceville's football team captain in 1951. He came from a large farming family that needed every durable Armstrong kid to help pay the bills. One with below-average test scores due to chronic absenteeism, Burl worked as a trucker that hauled livestock to vendors in and out of Iowa because his family needed a second income. He possessed the intelligence and skill to drive a truckload of cattle long distances into the stockyards, so he prioritized the job over the school. Superintendent Edwards understood his plight and sympathized with Burl's decisions, believing the teenager could succeed after school. To ensure Burl received a diploma, Edwards enrolled him in advanced mathematics courses to make up the credits he needed to graduate.[13] Jane fancied Burl for some time. However, the friendship never materialized into anything further than the two possessing deep respect for one another. "He was a man long before his time, and I admired him greatly," she confided.[14]

It was not just their placement in two advanced mathematics classes that pitted Jean and Jane as, in Jane's words, the "genius" versus the "not so-genius" sister academics. The girls genuinely wanted to own the school in their own way: Jean as the straight-shooting bookworm, Jane as the impulsive, thrill-seeking delinquent of the school. That is why Jane had to swallow her pride when Principal Robert Wolfe announced that Jean earned the honor of being the Class of 1951's valedictorian.

By twenty-first-century standards, being top in a class of thirty-eight seniors would hardly impress. However, in 1951, Riceville's graduating class was on the larger end of the school's recent history. The valedictorian honor meant Jean would receive a partial fee exemption scholarship to the Iowa State Teachers College, presented by the Mitchell County branch of the Iowa State Educational Association. A writer for the school newspaper and band member, glee club, and mixed chorus, the valedictorian received other awards the evening of commencement, including a gold pin representing the Riceville Live and Learn Club's Arion Award recognizing achievement in music, scholarship, and propriety. The school also presented Jean with the Senior American Legion Honors Award and another scholarship to Luther College, which she declined.[15] "[I]t is all right to have castles in the air," Jean wrote in a commencement editorial in the town's newspaper, paraphrasing Henry David Thoreau. "But don't just think about them, work hard towards them, and you will have the satisfaction of reaching them or at least coming close to them."[16]

Reaching for castles in the air would take Jane on a much different flight path—partly driven by the highly charged political atmosphere of the early 1950s. In the early part of the decade, the nation's state was one of ugliness: of Cold War ideological struggles, games of cloak and dagger, and political opportunists like Senator Joseph McCarthy and his staffers stoking fears over values, beliefs, and behavior. Nearly everyone in the Jennison clan seemed to acquiesce to the 1950s' dynamic conservatism and the anti-communist epochal spirit. Jane instead found fascination with the tug of war between prevailing cultural norms and artistic and intellectual traditions new to the landscape. During the era, art became politicized. This presented Jane with an outlet to defy popular opinion and to separate herself from her "super sister," Jean. She almost intentionally placed herself on the ideological opposite end of the aisle when it came to any issue plaguing society. In particular, her niche in high school became comic books, a burgeoning artistic trend and literary phenomenon under attack as the cause of juvenile delinquency.

"Comic books were early television," insisted Jane, who felt, both as a teenager and later as an educator, that comics could help struggling readers gain an interest in reading. "Comic books gave them information, built vocabulary, and also gave people a picture, in color, so they could remember."[17] Her father sometimes returned from town with copies of *The Three Musketeers* or *Superman* as gifts. Once she got her fix, Jane took those ten-cent magazines to school to exchange superhero stories for detective thrillers with friends. Those books were the one thing she possessed that proudly cluttered her room.

While engulfed in a debate inside the walls of Riceville High, she did not quite realize at the time that comic books had become an ideological bogeyman at the center of a culture war gripping the United States. With ambitious politicians as the catalyst, parents, educators, and church groups attacked comics as "lowbrow" art responsible for a surge in malfeasance and insubordination following World War II. However, before television's popularity grew, the years nearly encompassed Jane's freshman and senior years. During that period, local ordinances banned the sale of crime and horror comics in some parts of the country. In public and private school districts in Pennsylvania, public burnings of comic books eerily similar to the undemocratic actions of former authoritarian nations took place in town squares.[18] Iowa school librarians launched "Operation Book Swap," a campaign to convince students to trade ten comics for one "good book."[19] Comic books collected in the swap were eventually destroyed.

As parent-teacher associations deemed comics harmful to learning and destructive to social development, Jane was one of a few in Riceville to speak in defense of the books' educational value. Her opinion was not popular. According to one poll conducted by the *Minneapolis Tribune*, 81 percent of the public in Jane's neighboring state to the north wanted the government to create a committee to review the content of all comics before they were sold. In the same survey, 59 percent of households without children reading comic books and 51 percent of households with children reading comics said most comic book material negatively influenced teenage behavior.[20]

During her junior year, a reporter asked Jane whether educators should punish students caught reading comics. She answered: "Make them read at least five comic books in every study hall and still keep up their grades."[21] Jane's opinion on the issue was predictably alienating. In the same story, her older sister, Jean, suggested that students should receive "Temporary suspensions of privileges." One of her teachers, a man named Mr. Hamilton, said, "Off with their heads at sunrise!"

Despite being in the minority, Jane maintained that comic books generated reading interests and stimulated the imagination in people otherwise disinterested in reading or incapable of reading on grade level. Comics, she claimed, made it easier for struggling readers to understand story structure and plotlines. This youthful crusade to keep comics in the school library helped shape how she later advocated for diversity and inclusion. At a time in the 1950s when social anxiety and McCarthy-era political stunts made victims out of those with unconventional opinions, Jane's classmates assumed she would become a defender of the Othered.

* * *

Events affecting her parents always tugged at Jane's emotional attachment to each family member. In the middle of her senior year, tragedy struck again on her dad's side. On Thursday, October 4, 1951, Jane's paternal grandmother, Lyde Jennison, died at age eighty-two after a four-year battle with an illness that forced her to spend her final years at a Des Moines nursing home.[22] Jane was expressionless upon hearing the news; the emotional attachment to her grandmother, whom she blamed for losing her beloved Grandad Samuel, ended ten years earlier. Thus, in the winter of 1951, Jane remained stoic while she supported her father as he buried his mother next to Grandad Samuel in Riceville's Wayne Cemetery.

The transition from the rural one-room school filled with "runny-nosed" lower elementary pupils instructed by an overworked teacher into a much larger, heterogeneous setting was a healthy change of pace. For one, Riceville High opened Jane's eyes to diverse personalities, lifestyles, cultural trends, and learning abilities. "There were other people to talk to besides your brothers and sisters," she explained. "And there was more than one teacher so that if you got on the bad side of one, maybe you could get on the good side of another."

She often got on the wrong side of Riceville teachers, but not for lack of school pride. Trying to thrive in the wake left by sisters as accomplished and genteel as Mary and Jean would have left most people sorely depleted, but it gave a fighter like Jane a purpose to work harder for better grades and to jettison involvement in her school. In hindsight, Jane was as dutiful as any child in the Jennison brood. Her vitae included the marching band, glee club, vocal sextet, drama club, and journalism club, and she wrote for the student publication

Wildcat Tales. Jane made the girls' basketball team as a freshman.[23] She stuck it out all four years, balancing time between the junior and varsity teams. "That was a joke [. . .]" she admitted about her time on the squad. The coach retained her because she had "sang on the bus going to and from the games." Jane conceded, "I was too short to be on the basketball team, but every coach seemed to think I was good for something."[24] Accessing the school's locker room meant Jane could take showers daily for four years. She said it was a "huge transition" from taking baths in the copper boiler to continue pouring water over her head and body.[25] Jane occasionally made the academic honor roll and served a term as a general member of the student council. For all her work, she finished ranked ninth in her class of forty-one students—down from the cohort's original fifty-two that entered as freshmen in 1948.

As journalist Stephen Bloom writes, she was also "a pint-sized smart aleck" country kid, "outspoken and opinionated," and unaware of her position in the school's pecking order.[26] Indeed, not everyone at Riceville saw her as a model of sophistication. During the 1951 fall semester, she orchestrated a sophomoric prank on picture day for the yearbook by convincing her female classmates to have their pictures taken twice, once with and once without wearing glasses. Teachers in the building realized what was happening when Jane kept loaning her eyeglasses to girls that had never worn spectacles before. When one teacher tried reprimanding the prankster, Jane snapped her frames and quickly pulled the glasses from a friend's grasp.[27]

Because life as a farmer's daughter successfully balancing a liberal arts education with an agricultural lifestyle provided few opportunities to establish a social life outside school, Jane took on roles as an actress in the school theater.[28] She won the lead in the senior play about an abrasive and annoying aunt overly involved in her family's affairs. The drama was titled "There's One In Every Family." Frances Zender, the theater director, typecasted Jane to play the aunt, whom she described as "an irascible, critical, judgmental [*sic*] old aunt who constantly put her relatives in their place by saying whatever she was thinking [. . .] And I didn't even have to pretend for the actors and the audience to take me seriously. I wasn't acting; I was being myself and enjoying it."[29]

In keeping with the peculiar way she navigated public school as a performing artist and someone trying to master critical thinking in the humanities, Jane spent part of January 1952 rehearsing for a regrettable role as Bojangles in a student-produced minstrel show.[30] Jane came to regret the performance, but, at the time, minstrelsy was an inherent aspect of Riceville culture, especially for teenage thespians who never encountered anyone pushing back against the artistic genre. Riceville in 1950 had roughly 940 residents; all were white/ European Americans.[31] For generations, minstrelsy had peppered northern Iowa in places near Riceville, like Kendallville, McIntire, and Cresco. Other small towns bordering Midwestern states put on large gatherings for minstrel theater. Before her birth, the entertainment form was "as popular as a good circus, it appeals to all classes," opined the editor from the *Howard County Times*, which undoubtedly influenced her parents' generation with widespread visuals of "expert dancers, charming singers, and high-class vaudeville."[32]

Blackface art was also prevalent on radio, the dominant form of amusement during Jane's adolescence. *The Harem Scarem Radio Minstrel Revue* invited locals onto the broadcast as it toured Iowa to perform as minstrel singers. Whole-page promotions for upcoming minstrels with burlesque depictions of African Americans ran in the *Riceville Recorder*.[33] High school-aged minstrel troupes performed for elementary and middle school children when Jane attended Jamestown School No. 2. Ubiquitous were reports of Iowa high schools enlisting entire student bodies into Minstrel Theater.[34]

While she would reject attacks on issues about her life, race was not on Jane's conscience or anyone else at her school. In other words, it was not unthinkable to cover oneself in charcoal and dance around in borrowed and caricatured forms presenting depictions of African American culture that spread a false image of white Iowans who never encountered African Americans. So, when asked by her peers, Jane performed minstrel production at a school assembly.

What an irony that Jane Jennison, who had long before adopted a penchant for speaking out against popularized notions of behavior, willfully subjected herself to such evil. Jane's interests in theatrical arts were difficult to untangle at that moment. The issue directly impacted her since acting on stage was a cherished practice. Unlike the fight against the anti-comic book crowd at her school, which was not as personally debilitating, she fortuitously avoided controversies that got in the way of beloved opportunities. Jane was passionate about defending artistic freedom of expression, but her ambition to perform on stage led her to overlook the problematic aspects of minstrelsy. This was despite a lifetime of colorblind indoctrination. It is ironic that Jane and other actors convinced themselves that wearing burnt cork in blackface had no link to racist behavior. In acts of self-reflection later in life, Jane would learn from this experience. Whether conscious or not, she would see dissonance throughout Riceville when townspeople attacked her over the Blue Eyes/Brown Eyes Exercise.

* * *

Not starved for affection, Jane had no time for male counterparts looking for sexual escapades. Apart from natural teenage attractions caused by proximity and familiarity that were well under her control, she had little interest in pursuing a beau. Figuring out that her eldest sibling, Charles, had been conceived by teenagers out of wedlock and wanting nothing more than to prevent a premarital pregnancy, Jane incessantly vetoed potential suitors. Only in the last months of her senior year did she date one of her classmates. Eugene Matthews, a halfback on the football team and the baseball teams' star pitcher, took Jane out a few times. The two agreed to go to the senior prom together. Her decision to attend the prom in the first place was potentially motivated by using the opportunity to defy the school's dress-code policy, which she considered sexist. "I went to the prom wearing a dress that ended just below my knees, even though the code for time was to wear a formal gown, but I couldn't afford a formal gown, and my mother wasn't about to make one."[35] When Jane walked into the school's gymnasium showing off an unconventional amount of skin on her firm legs, she received cold stares from some of her peers and all of the chaperones.

One day that winter, Jane arrived at school wearing denim jeans. She had no time to get cleaned up for school after morning chores on the farm, plus deep snow caused the roads to close. Improvising, Jane and her younger brother, Jim, drove the tractor four miles into school. Though the early morning freezing temperature convinced her to wear jeans on the ride in, she had forgotten to pack the uniform skirt required for all women in school. "Every student who saw me that day was aghast at my daring to do something so forbidden, and before I had gone through one class period, my name appeared on the chalkboard at the front of the study hall, informing me that I was to report to the principal's office," Jane remembered.[36] Principal Wolfe admonished her. Since the roads were terrible that morning, he allowed her to remain at school for the day, but only after threatening expulsion if she ever tested the social boundaries again. Just a semester away from graduation, Jane acquiesced.

It was not the curriculum at Riceville High that enamored Jane. She credits her most memorable learning experience to the Red Cross Home Nursing Program. In the spring of 1952, Jane was one of eighteen high school females that learned the basics of nursing the sick and homemaking from a Red Cross volunteer. Riceville-native Ellen Glee Graves, a school nurse working in Mason City, was just months away from transferring to County-City Hospital in Fort Worth, Texas, to treat polio patients. Sessions met in the basement of Dr. Tink Walker's office twice a week for four months. The course covered a wide range of skills necessary for nursing, including ethics, mattress cleaning, and setting bed sheets into "hospital corners." Additionally, the curriculum included lessons on writing prescriptions, following doctor's orders, making good progress reports, improvising home facilities to use as hospital equipment and other nursing arts required for the care of the sick and injured. The program also advanced home nursing for civil defense purposes. Trainees like Jane, possessing knowledge of nursing fundamentals, could be mustered into the service at short notice when needed in cases of community disaster.[37] Along with thirty-eight adults, Jane and her school-age peers completed the nursing program at a pinning ceremony on Mother's Day night, May 11, 1952.[38]

Unlike everyone in the Jennison clan, making a difference in the lives of others through nursing was Jane's plan. In the days leading up to commencement, she completed registration paperwork and got into the school for nursing at Broadlawns Hospital in Des Moines. Scholarships were available through the Iowa division of the American Cancer Society. First in the United States to set up the scholarship program, the Iowa division hoped $500 worth of tuition, fees, books, and uniforms would encourage young women to enter a field facing shortages across the Hawkeye State.[39] But while pursuing a career in an occupation requiring competent practitioners, Jane felt a familial obligation to obtain a job that could teach her life-saving skills apart from the path in education chosen by Aunt Blanche and her older sisters, Mary and Jean. Pervasively on her mind was how her younger sister, Anne, died. She thought about the home care her Grandad Samuel needed from trained professionals but did not receive. In recent years, Mary overcame pneumonia, asthma, and appendicitis.[40] Afflicting people throughout northern Iowa while studying at Riceville High was polio. She participated in a community-wide epidemic emergency drive that yielded $184.11 for polio patients in and around Riceville. Jane helped by collecting money from local businesses at high school football games, music events, and a house-to-house canvass.[41]

For Jane, there was no greater cause. However, her father, Lloyd, had other plans. As soon as commencement arrived, he persuaded Jane against seeking the cancer society scholarship. The one person providing moral support insisted on looking elsewhere for a career. "I had my papers all ready to be a nurse, but my father said, 'If you're going to be a nurse, I won't help you. I don't want you giving enemas to those dirty old men.'" Lloyd offered an ultimatum: "If you go into teaching, I will help you."[42] Not leaving things to chance, Jane quickly filed paperwork to follow Jean in pursuit of an elementary teaching certificate at the Iowa State Teachers College (present-day University of Northern Iowa) in Cedar Falls.

* * *

Jane enrolled at Iowa State Teachers College (ISTC) in June 1952, two weeks after graduating high school, penniless and with only moral encouragement from her father. She entered this stage of her life with an almost studied indifference to disposable income. She never possessed much, if any, cash. How could someone so disadvantaged and from a large family be expected to pay for college? Forced to take out a $400 loan from the Riceville State Bank and an additional $400 loan from the Riceville Live and Learn Club was enough to pay for Jane's first year of tuition.

There were no self-indulgences. In the summer of 1952, Jane lived rent-free during her first quarter at the home of her Aunt Blanche. Uncle Bryan Hogan, whom Jane affectionately called "Barney" and said could "charm the birds off the trees, just by smiling at them as he walked by."[43] The Hogan household was located on Franklin Street in Waterloo, fifteen miles east of ISTC. She commuted daily to campus, riding the historic Waterloo-Cedar Falls electric trolley through the wooded glen of Cedar Heights and along the Cedar River. Jane had to pick up the trolley at the Waterloo, Cedar Falls & Northern Railroad.[44] Her trolley stop was on the east side of town, which meant walking through Waterloo's predominantly African American neighborhood. This experience, Jane said, was the first time she interacted with people of a different color group. "I grew up in Riceville my whole life, and the only black person we saw was LeRoy Dunn, a football player from Manly High School, that my brother, Jim, played against."[45] Dunn eventually became an All-North Central Conference offensive tackle on ISTC's football team, where he earned a bachelor's degree in education. He later obtained a master's in teacher education with an emphasis on safety education, counseling, and guidance from Michigan State University. Dunn remained in Lansing for his general education and traffic safety doctoral degree. He titled his dissertation "The Development of an Instrument to Measure Knowledge of Traffic Safety Concepts Found to Differentiate Between Violators and Non-Violators."[46]

In the fall, Jane moved into the sophomore dormitory, where she resided for the second and third quarters—the fall and winter terms of 1952. According to her recollections, Jane attended classes until early afternoon, then headed to the Commons Student Center to bus tables and wash dishes. To pay for on-campus housing, she also babysat the children of one of her ISTC instructors. Jane remembered that the experience of that first year at ISTC was unlike anything at Riceville High, where she was involved in almost every curricular and extracurricular program the school had to offer. "I didn't get involved in campus life," she said of ISTC. "I was too busy trying to make some money to pay my bills." Jane put in long days, five days a week, hitting the books and working at the student center. However, all signs indicate that most income she earned went to paying off tuition debts. When she returned to Round Grove after one year of college, Jane had earned enough money to repay loans to both creditors: the Live and Learn Club and the Riceville State Bank. Trying to pave a career without the financial help of her parents presented lessons that Jane never forgot.[47]

* * *

ISTC opened its doors to students in September 1876 as the state's first normal school. During that inaugural year, the college had just four instructors and twenty-seven students. Classes were in a three-story brick building, originally used to house orphans and veterans of the Civil War. Upon Jane's arrival about seventy-five years later, the campus now included 250 acres, thirty major buildings, almost 300 faculty members, and a staff of approximately 220 persons. The college operated by quarters rather than typical semester terms. Almost three thousand students on campus joined Jane. The summer of 1952 was also the first quarter the college enrolled graduate students. College president, James W. Maucker, called ISTC a "dedicated community," striving to produce graduates "dedicated to the service of society through the improvement of one of its basic social institutions—the public school."[48]

Jane would procure that Mauckerian reputation as a bulldog educator dedicated to enlightening communities throughout the United States. Wanted or not, she would take almost a year before warming up to becoming a teacher. "I didn't want to follow my aunts or my sisters into teaching because I was quite certain that I could never become as good a teacher as my Aunt Blanche was nor as my sister Mary was." On the contrary, Jane thought she could hold her mettle against Jean because "Jean was brilliant and didn't have a whole lot of patience with people who had difficulty learning. I knew I could do a better job than she did."[49]

Having found her way to Cedar Falls, enjoying freedom away from Gie's penetrating eye and the confinement of living in the small Riceville area where everyone knew one another's business, Jane was determined to make a mark on the world. But was teaching the answer? It was a question she had been struggling to answer during her first three quarters at ISTC. Finally, in the spring of 1953, she began to answer it.

CHAPTER 4

APPLE OF HER EYE

Jane planned to get her college experience over quickly. Since ISTC offered coursework in quarters, she made a wise choice by enrolling in the teaching preparatory college. By Thanksgiving 1952, Jane was a sophomore. After New Year's, at nineteen, she entered the student-teaching phase of her preservice teaching program. The education department coordinator assigned her to a tiny elementary school in Independence, Iowa, in February 1953, during her fourth quarter at Cedar Falls institution. It had been just two weeks since the inauguration of Dwight D. Eisenhower as the thirty-fourth President of the United States. During that time, Jane found herself student-teaching at a school already in the crosshairs of Joe McCarthy lackeys in a town of 4,800 people, located thirty-five miles east of the ISTC campus. As a nineteen-year-old, stepping into field experience besieged by a McCarthy campaign of misrepresentation, character assassination, and calumny provided little assurance that she made the right decision to go into teaching. Indifferent and sensible, Jane settled into an apartment, a nondescript middle-class enclave near the Frank Lloyd Wright Lowell and Agnes Walter Estate on the acreage of the Cedar Rock State Park, where she would spend the entire spring in the teaching field.

What she saw in Independence was an old-world village surrounded by a medley of cornfields, rolling hills, bluffs, churches, grist mills, and the beauty of the Wapsipinicon River. Settled in 1847 as an alternative to the neighboring town of Quasqueton, Independence was the state's mental hospital site and the nation's most exciting horse, bicycle, and motor races. The town once encompassed a uniquely structured kite-shaped track used for horse and bike racing, which, well before Jane's sojourn, had been turned into pasture ground.[1] With its interurban trolley line connecting the town to considerably larger urban centers in northern Iowa, though lacking in cultural diversity, Independence looked every inch the genteel locale of Riceville and Decorah, though strove for the look of Cedar Falls and Waterloo. In *Everybody's Autobiography*, Gertrude Stein called the people in the region "brilliant and subtle" despite never having stepped foot in Iowa.[2]

Jane was there to learn how to teach. Her cooperating teacher was forty-eight-year-old Hazel Z. Grant, an energetic and remarkably organized principal at Hawthorne Elementary School. The holder of bachelor's and master's degrees from Iowa State College, Grant (who also taught the third grade at Hawthorne) valued ingenuity and structure above everything else. She was contemptuous of rote-learning instruction and considered it boring and indoctrinating. Banking models of teaching made students passive receptacles of knowledge, which enabled teachers to control what students knew and believed about topics taught in schools. In another era, educational critics would criticize the practice as "monological" and "unilateral." Nothing more than what philosopher George Yancy calls a "tool of domination."[3]

Before and after she observed Jane, Grant served as an executive in the Iowa Department of Elementary Principals and as a steering committee member responsible for designing in-service training for elementary principals. Over twice Jane's age, though still as innovative and enthusiastic as a first-year teacher, she was a key figure in the national movement to recruit and retain women educators throughout the United States. She was a member of the Iowa chapter of Delta Kappa Gamma, a national educators' organization that promoted the professional growth of teachers and administrators.[4]

Grant arrived in Independence in 1927 at twenty-two to instruct third graders after teaching two years in one-room schoolhouses near Atlantic—a city of more than 5,000 people in southwest Iowa. As a young teacher, she became known to her colleagues as the one who allowed her eight and nine-year-old pupils to utilize class time by putting on five-string puppet shows. Why? The shows enabled the youngsters to use their imagination by supplementing stories they read in class with visual representations. As she put it, the puppet shows provided "an opportunity for dramatic expression." While the puppet shows often occurred within the confines of her classroom, occasionally, Grant's students performed for other classes in the school. Students picked out their favorite fairy tales. With Grant's facilitation and participation, they composed a narrative for the puppet show. Students would "seldom stay to the script," recalled Grant at her retirement party in 1965. "I tell you, some of it got very dramatic."[5]

Before her promotion to principal of Hawthorne School, Grant held the position of elementary curriculum coordinator. Independence schools had little if any, horizontal uniformity between courses and texts. "We all just went our merry way," Grant said. Crediting the Soviet launching of Sputnik, which caused the federal government to invest funds into education through the National Defense Education Act, Grant trained Independence teachers in hybrid-style pedagogy, blending the teacher's personality with competing interests in the form of active learning tasks. Grant also utilized professional development hours to align the curriculum across the school's grade-level instructors. She wanted common content materials and curricular goals, but Grant never felt that those goals needed to be reached in the same way. She trained her instructors to teach to student strengths, not to those of the teacher. The key to student success "is the teacher and her ability to motivate" the children in the classroom.

Grant taught Jane her pedagogy of cooperative competition. It was an instructional paradigm that fostered an environment and emphasized inter-group competition designed to help children learn and refine self-discipline and leadership while mastering curricular knowledge and skills. The classroom was set up in four rows, and each row separated students into four teams. Four students at a time were selected to be row leaders. Grant would issue points to each row all day, accumulating points throughout the week. Students received a point each for having a clean desk, a sharpened pencil, and a handkerchief. If every student in the row met all three daily requirements, the row received an extra point. Students earned additional points by helping others, cleaning up a mess made by someone else, returning on time to the teacher after recess, and being in an orderly line for lunch. Row leaders shared responsibility with Mrs. Grant for issuing points to their teammates. While winning was important, Grant's award process placed more pressure on the students to not be the one who gets points taken away. "If you didn't behave yourself, you had to take off a point. And woe be on to you if you took off a point. Every kid in the row was angry at you," Jane explained. "The teacher didn't have to do a thing." Due to the system alone, Grant did very little disciplining. The structure of the class was ideal for classroom management.[6]

Grant kept a tally of weekly scores on the chalkboard for students to see. At the end of the week, the row with the most points earned the privilege of retrieving goodies from a grab bag. The grab bag, a simple grocery sack Grant kept in the closet, contained items eight and nine-year-olds found entertaining: erasers, colored pencils, tissues, stickers, folders, paper, and sometimes, a comic book. Jane said, "Kids worked like little beavers to get into that grab bag. And

I watched kids who were behavior problems become saintly in that third-grade classroom because if you behaved yourself, you got reinforced for doing so." Every student had the opportunity to serve as row leader, which would change every week, so students rarely were in the same row with the same students. "It was 'cooperative competition,'" Jane explained. "They cooperated with each other to get what they wanted."[7]

Despite aspects of natural law, free competition, and liberalism prevailing in her teaching style, Grant endured McCarthyite attacks from members of the Independence community. Educators with unconventional styles and progressive beliefs outside of school faced allegations of being Red-ucators, meaning they faced the challenge of proving they were not "joiners" of the Communist Party.[8] The road that led to public allegations that educators like Hazel Grant were disseminating Popular Front dogma in American schools was long and foreboding. However, attacks on American educators began several years before McCarthy emerged as the great treason shouter. The National Council for American Education circulated a booklet titled *How Red Are the Schools?* This carried the thesis that schools were pro-Communist indoctrination centers.

Although sitting U.S. Senators and educators repudiated the paperback as propaganda composed under the guise of fighting Communism, the damage to public perception about schools and teacher loyalty was already done. *How Red Are the Schools?* suggested the removal from public schools all aspects of teaching and learning that did not coincide with personal conservative beliefs.[9] The booklet's author, Allen Anderson Zoll (a known anti-Semite), was the founder of American Patriots, Inc., an extreme right-wing outfit in the 1930s labeled by the U.S. Justice Department as "fascist and subversive."[10] In 1949, the name of his National Council for American Education sounded similar to the respected American Council of Education head, Dr. George Zook. The two organizations and their leaders (Zoll and Zook) with similar-sounding names confused people. As a result, a gullible public found merit in Zoll's claim that educators and pro-teacher legislators were collaborating to communize the public schools through a federal funding system and mixed-sex and mixed-race buildings.

Zoll circulated three additional publications to generate a public frenzy. The first, "Red-ucators at Harvard," claimed that about eight Harvard faculty members, including President James B. Conant, worked to advance the Communist agenda. A year later, the National Council for American Education alleged that the University of Chicago, Yale University, University of California, Stanford University, California Institute of Technology, and Columbia University employed Red-ucators by the dozens.[11] The second and third publications, *They*

Want Your Child! and *Progressive Education Increases Juvenile Delinquency* made public kindergarten through twelfth-grade schools a flashpoint for debate over controlling the content and presentation of information delivered to students. These publications colored Zoll as the defender of public education, with the implied threat that leftist educators were teaching the youth that communism was superior to American republicanism. Zoll wanted every school district to report whether the "schools of your community" have been infiltrated with "so-called progressive education."[12]

The Daughters of the American Revolution found the educational dog whistle a compelling threat. In 1952, conservative education advocate Jessica Payne warned that "most teachers are good Americans, but some are Red-ucators." Owner of a private school in Huntington, West Virginia, named the Work and Play House, Payne suggested that school boards and school officials should "investigate the 'thought and intent' of authors of textbooks and other school materials." She represented a twisted era defined by public calls to "save America" by monitoring educators.[13]

The attack on Progressive educators proliferated further when Zoll and the National Council for American Education circulated a bygone memo written in 1947 and authored by Attorney General Tom C. Clark. It was titled *Attorney General's List of Subversive Organizations*. It deemed approximately seventy organizations and eleven schools as "subversive" communist fronts "which have their knives out for the U.S. republican form of government."[14] Taken together, the Attorney General's blacklist of social organizations bolstered calls to censure teachers during the peak period of McCarthyism. Scholars and public intellectuals were disinvited from speaking engagements on college campuses. Parent groups used the memo and Zoll's publications as evidence that school boards should ban books and fire teachers, principals, and superintendents. Women teachers especially—who were more likely to assume membership in social clubs and equally likely to get blocked from career opportunities—were often charged with becoming Red-ucators. As historian Landon Storrs argued, the Popular Front appealed to feminist ideals: opposition to militarism, civil rights, poll-tax repeal, and reproductive rights.[15] Feminist-owned bookstores and the new generation of young, educated women standing in front of classrooms threatened the traditional way of life.

That duality made Hazel Grant, the paragon of unconventional teaching during ideological intolerance, an easy target. The community's evidence against Grant was her alleged possession of leftist books on the shelves of classroom libraries inside Hawthorne School. Attacks on Grant came during a heated televised congressional hearing led by Senator McCarthy and public calls to expunge government-funded scholarships awarded to professors, scholars, and students with alleged ties to the Communist Party.[16] By the spring of 1953, the anti-communist witch hunts broadened to attack anything that conservative families did not like in schools. The Joe McCarthys and Allen Zolls of the world made Conservatives believe phrases like "new deal," "left-wing press," and "European-minded press of New York" were synonymous with Popular Front attempts to subvert the United States Constitution.[17] Intensified attacks on Grant at the moment of Jane's arrival in Independence to student-teach stemmed from the hullabaloo of the presidential election between Dwight D. Eisenhower and Adlai Stevenson. Educators were a political punching bag during that election season due to the politicized atmosphere where the stakes were high for Republicans to assume control over the executive branch for the first time since the Hoover Administration. Election victory only emboldened and intensified many unfounded attempts to purge progressive educators.

In January 1953, Owen Lattimore, an Asian affairs expert and professor of the history of philosophy at Johns Hopkins University, was indicted on seven counts of perjury related to testimony he gave in front of the McCarran Committee the previous year. Lattimore testified he never sympathized with the communist cause. McCarthy, who was not a subcommittee member, used his popularity to denounce Lattimore as a communist spy and agent acting against U.S. ally Chiang Kai Shek and the Republic of China. The indictment resulted in Lattimore's leave of absence with pay from Johns Hopkins, while his colleagues at the university created a $40,000 defense fund to offset legal fees.[18] When all was said and done, the Lattimore affair (which would result in the exoneration of the professor) served only to stir calls from parents in Independence for book bans and the purging of teachers.

The climate paralyzed many educators, but not Hazel Grant.

According to Jane, a parent group audited the school's library for a children's book titled *The Red Shoes*. They also looked for anything with messages resembling Marxist or liberal creed. While probing the school's resources, Jane said, "Hazel Grant never batted an eye. She let them do it. She didn't argue with them. She didn't abuse the power that she had as the principal in that building to say, 'Get your asses out of here. I don't have to put up with this. If you want to go through my library, go right ahead.'"[19]

Jane was substantially impressed by how Grant kept her cool while in the hot seat. Decades later, when dealing with her own attacks from the public over how she taught her students, she said the memory of Grant's courage during that spring of 1953 kept her strong. "When I did the Blue Eye/Brown Eye exercise in the Riceville schools many years later, I remembered Hazel Grant and how she simply walked through the day, did what she was hired to do, and let it all just slide off her like water off a duck's back. And if you have that kind of example to follow, nothing needs to bother you."[20]

* * *

More than fifty years later, textbook publishing juggernaut the McGraw Hill Foundation listed Jane Elliott as one of thirty influential educators in the field of education. While she laughed off the honor, the traits that got her considered by McGraw Hill primarily resulted from Hazel Grant's influence. Jane trumpeted Grant's impact on her pedagogy and specific strategies until her final day in the classroom arrived in 1985. What shaped her most, she remarked, was the way that Grant's style exposed a difference between teaching and educating.

Today, Jane's concept of education is a fundamental interdisciplinary theory that sees racialized color groupings at the center of what is directly and indirectly taught in schools. In other words, she posits that educational institutions are primarily indoctrination centers because there is a lack of teacher investment in critical assessment of the world. Learning targets as simple as teaching Christopher Columbus first discovered America whitewashes any knowledge that Africans arrived in the Western Hemisphere well before 1492. Her point: stories wherein teachers teach historical misinformation to add up over time and leave students of all color groups clinging to notions of white/ European supremacy. For Jane, bigotry can be unlearned over two generations if schools honestly teach the required curriculum—mainly concerning the humanities and STEM fields. "We can destroy racism with education," she said, "but the system that we currently have has been created to indoctrinate. We teach children to behave a certain way to perpetuate the notion that America is the land of the free and the home of the brave. If truth be told, the people who are free in this country are those who are melanin-challenged (those who we call white). The people who are brave are the melanacious (people of color)— the portion of our society that must be brave every day in a world in which they are despised."[21]

Jane's idea seems too simple to catch on, too fantastical to be widely applicable, and too racially charged to resonate with the mainstream. Nonetheless, she maintained that *teachers* who do no more than repeat what is in the book and do nothing to improve their global knowledge of the subject matter end up teaching students to the insight and values of the dominant cultural group.

On the contrary, an educator, she asserted, "leads students out of ignorance." Teachers should provide students with a pluralistic and inclusionary view of the curriculum and offer space and grace for students to think critically about that information.

Hazel Grant, she said, was "absolutely the person that turned me into an educator instead of a teacher."[22] As Grant's mentee, Jane honed her ability to teach students in the John Dewey approach that challenged teachers to get children to interact with their environment—despite the politicization of education. That spring quarter under the tutelage of Grant at Hawthorne Elementary School made Jane's desire for a teaching career possible. She affirmed: "Mrs. Grant was smart enough to teach us how to teach, and when we proved to her, by doing it, that she'd done a good job, she was pleased. I never saw her displeased where I was concerned. I left that experience knowing that I could handle whatever came my way, in the classroom and with my peers in the community."[23]

* * *

An opportunity to educate young children surfaced for nineteen-year-old Jane soon after fulfilling the student-teaching requirement at Independence. Without the standard elementary teaching certificate and several credits short of a bachelor's degree from ISTC, Jane became the benefactor of a teacher shortage in the fall of 1953 when Iowa granted her an emergency teaching certificate. With a tepid recommendation letter from her high school principal, Robert Wolfe, who wrote, "Jane tends to be sarcastic, but she is smart," Jane received a position that paid her $2,300 to teach the third grade at Randall School. Located in Randall, a tiny Iowan town with a post office, a telephone switchboard, and roughly 300 people, the school sat eighty miles west of Cedar Falls and 120 miles south of Riceville. Randall School became the job of choice despite the distance from her family because nearby was her brother, Jim, who was studying to be a civil engineer sixteen miles away at Iowa State College in Ames. She could, as anticipated, commute home with Jim.[24]

Greeting her at the school was a newly renovated building, which, on Jane's first day on the job, would enroll 180 elementary and seventy high school students. Five teachers were employed at the school for grades 8-12, and six elementary instructors for first through seventh-grade. Visibly new to the schoolhouse was a fully equipped home economics classroom with five new state-of-the-art sewing machines, a new library, and a finished gymnasium floor.[25] When accessing those facilities, Jane and her eight and nine-year-old students engaged in hands-on projects taught to her by Hazel Grant.

That first year at Randall enabled Jane to customize her teaching style by trying novel strategies in front of students, learning from mistakes, and gaining important feedback from her mentor, school superintendent William B. Divine. "The experience was delightful," Jane recalled of her short tenure at Randall.[26] She ventured to try things that blended her personality with activities picked up at Hawthorne Elementary and from her professors at ISTC. Weekends were spent writing lesson plans for the forthcoming week. After class, she filled her journals with notes and observations on how to improve the lesson. Her boss, Superintendent Divine, expected Jane to take risks in her class. Always supportive, the two discussed ways to improve her instruction on rare occasions.

Besides teaching young children, Jane spent much of her life stuck in her head, immune to emotional attachments beyond her career. She rarely made friends, but trying to keep her head above water while teaching that fall helped cultivate an awkward friendship with Mary Parker—an ISTC classmate who had student-taught with Jane at Hawthorne the previous spring.[27] Parker hailed from the small town of Stanhope in central Iowa, with slightly more than 400 people. That fall, Parker, like Jane, obtained her first teaching position. However, Parker worked at an elementary school in Story City. Though at two different schools, Randall and Story City were separated by only a few miles. Besides, Parker continued to live with her parents in Stanhope. As a result, the two occasionally spent time together.

A year older than Jane, Parker looked just like every other first-year teacher: bubbly and ready to change the world, only Parker was more inquisitive than Jane about what existed in that world. Much separated Jane from her new friend; Parker was carefree, charming, curious, and independent. Her appearance veiled a tenderfoot's ambition to succeed as a new teacher and what Jane considered a skill to obtain attention and approval. Jane, meanwhile, was snarky but focused on doing her job well. Parker's choice to create a life of excitement sometimes persuaded Jane to spread her wings by tagging along at social gatherings. One meet-up with Parker took place just three weeks on the job and would change Jane's life.

Although Parker was already involved with a young man, Robert Crum, from a nearby town, she had her eye on an eighteen-year-old produce manager from Boone named Darald Elliott. That September, she devised a perverse plan to have Jane agree to go on a double date with Robert and Darald. Parker hoped an afternoon flirting with Darald would end her current relationship with Robert while sparking up a new one with the young grocer. Jane, meanwhile, agreed to be the bait that would convince Darald to join them on the date. However, when the two men pulled up in Robert's pickup truck, Jane took one look at Darald in the passenger seat and deserted her friend's contrivance.

Born July 30, 1934, Darald Dean Elliott worked as a storekeeper at the National Tea Company's supermarket in Boone. An only child who once dreamt of playing a sport in college, Darald's parents forced him to work for the midwestern grocery chain to help his family financially.[28] Darald was a talented prospect upon entering Boone High School in 1949. However, due to his family's financial troubles, he could only participate in interscholastic sports, which included football, swimming, and track and field, during his freshman and sophomore years. He joined Boone's speech team as a junior, thinking it would be less demanding than playing sports for three seasons. That proved to be unmanageable. "He was working for a living," Jane said of the insistence from Darald's father, Edwin Vern Elliott, a janitor and farm laborer occasionally. Darald's stay-at-home mother, Bertha Ellen Elsberry, didn't bring in an income. "They needed a second income, and he was paying rent to his parents while he was in high school." For Darald, work interspersed with fun was the yin and yang of Edwin's fatherly expectations.[29]

After high school, Darald's parents had less control over what he did in his spare time. He was fetching. While not considered a womanizer, his dark brown eyes, humble charisma, and wavy head of hair naturally pulled women into his orbit. The spat between Jane and Parker is illustrative of his natural magnetism. Upon seeing him at first glance, Jane intimated, Darald, with an appearance resembling Marlon Brando, "was a damned attractive man, who looked about twenty-five years old." She discovered later he was eight months her junior.

Despite never stepping outside the pickup truck he rode in on, the pair only took a moment to hit it off. Just a few minutes into the conversation, he asked Jane on an actual date—just the two of them—to a movie. Smitten, Jane said, "I guess," though she vowed to marry a man with brown eyes. To Jane, she mistakenly thought she had just snagged a dashing older gentleman. "Sure, I'll go to the movies Friday night."[30]

The couple's first date was to see *The Moon Is Blue*, a hundred-minute big-screen adaptation of F. Hugh Herbert's 1951 Broadway play. The movie stirred a significant controversy; it portrayed an indecent love affair between an aspiring actress Patty O'Neill, played by Maggie McNamara, and a playboy architect, Donald Gresham, played by William Holden. O'Neill and Gresham have a chance encounter at the top of the Empire State Building. Later in the film, McNamara's character is introduced by Holden's character to a Manhattan high roller named David Slater. Slater and Gresham spend the night competing and trying unsuccessfully to seduce the virgin, O'Neill.

While *The Moon Is Blue* was initially released in Chicago and other big cities along the East and West Coasts, theater owners in Iowa delayed screening the movie over its crude dialogue and implied sexually suggestive behavior. Condemnation by groups like the Catholic Legion of Decency could not prevent the film's eventual release in the Hawkeye State. When cinematic complexes finally sold tickets for screenings that August, they only did so with clear statements that it was an adult picture treated in an adult manner. Tickets would not be sold to children. The movie was a "test case" for the public to see if movie-goers would tolerate dialogue aimed at adults with lewd and juvenile humor. The Strand, a popular theater in Des Moines, warned matter-of-factly, "This picture is based on an idea by Adam and Eve! The producers of this picture wish to express their thanks to both sexes [. . .] male and female [. . .] without whose inspiration it might never have been made! Let's face it [. . .] if there weren't people like them [. . .] there wouldn't be people like us!"[31]

The film's plot resembles the competition between Mary Parker and Jane Jennison for Darald's attention and affection. Jane never considered whether the onscreen discord reflected her competition over a love interest. Nevertheless, not long after the date, Darald found an anonymous note on his windshield—presumably from Parker—calling Jane "a tramp" and asserting he was "wasting his time." Feeling that he knew Jane well, the sabotage effort hardly bothered him.[32] In any event, Jane's recollection of seeing the movie confirms how controversial it was in the early 1950s. "It was the most risqué movie at that time, and I think they used the word 'virgin' in it." It was, in Jane's opinion, "not the kind of movie you'd want to take your first date to." During the movie, Darald laughed at all the inappropriate jokes. "He wasn't so proper," said Jane of the fledgling young man. "He was having a good time."[33] Darald's infantilism did not bother Jane; the two shared their first kiss at the end of the evening, cementing a lifetime together.

Jane also liked the fact that she made more money than Darald. Commuting from Randall to Boone (where Darald lived) got expensive. Jane used the opportunity to flaunt to his family that her job teaching brought in a higher income than his job at National Tea. Thus, with her fancy salary, she financed their rendezvous for a year so they could commute to see each other.

The only time the couple had privacy was in Darald's car. Jane rented a bedroom inside a home owned by one of her colleagues. Therefore, the two had company whenever they spent time together in Randall. Most of the time,

Jane stayed at Darald's home in Boone. Living at the house, however, were Darald's parents, a grandmother, and an aunt and uncle. His grandmother, Barbara Ellen Flockhart Elsberry, owned the tiny, two-story house and slept in the bedroom located on the second floor. Darald's parents shared the master bedroom with the Johnsons, Uncle Donald, and Aunt Izzy on the main floor while he slept in a makeshift bedroom in the upstairs hallway. Anytime Jane stayed the night, she would get the hallway bedroom, and Darald slept in the same room as Grandma Elsberry.

After eight months together, Jane took driver's education classes at Iowa State Teachers College during the summer of 1954. The couple hoped two licenses and one automobile would be enough to see one another more than just over the weekend. A stylish driver now with her new driver's license, Jane usually took Darald's car to work in Randall and then returned to his parent's place in Boone during the evening. That is, until one night, Jane hit a patch of ice, collided with a truck in the opposite lane, and skidded into Ioway Creek. Jane panicked that it would be the first great challenge to their relationship. However, when Jane thought Darald would explode seeing half of his car in the creek, he surprised her with concern over her wellbeing and indifference about his badly damaged vehicle.

With or without a functioning car, they had no ambition to leave Iowa, let alone tour the country. All they wanted was to be in each other's presence. Spending time together usually meant going to the Ranch Drive-In in Ames, right on the Boone County line, or a picnic at Lake Hendricks in Riceville. "I was absolutely, absolutely totally enthralled with that man," she would say, "and I suspect that one of the reasons I was, was, he was all mine. And I didn't have to compete with anyone for his attention or for his love. And he wasn't used to competing for attention [as an only child], so he was perfectly happy for me to think of nobody but him."

The marriage proposal would not come until fourteen months after their first date. By the fall of 1954, Jane, now twenty, was into her second year teaching at Randall School as a second-grade teacher.[34] While Darald fulfilled his duty with the National Guard the previous summer, she returned to Iowa State Teachers College to finish the official elementary teaching certificate coursework. After teaching for a year, Jane saved up enough and rented a house with three Randall School colleagues. Jane knew then exactly what she wanted in the relationship: marriage, children, and life together. Although Darald, now nineteen, wanted those things too, he was less eager than Jane to begin them. A little reluctantly, he started to proposition Jane for deeper intimacy. Jane responded that they would have to get married if Darald wanted to go "all the way" with her. Darald relented, but not before proposing his ultimatum: he would not marry unless she found a house where they could live free of room-mates and family. They both consented. Jane first found a small house to rent at 421 Crawford Street in Boone. Darald reciprocated with an engagement ring containing one small diamond that Jane called "the most beautiful thing I had ever possessed." Jane later remembered: "I said, 'Well, hell yes! Why not? I thought you'd never ask.'"[35] With her larger salary, Jane paid for the marriage license.

Jane and Darald were married on Sunday, January 30, 1955, in a quick early evening ceremony inside the church office of future Iowa Congressman and real-estate lender Rev. Merwin Coad, thirty-one-year-old pastor at the 1,200-member Central Christian Church at Boone. Attending the ceremony were just two guests—friends of Darald, Don Mueller, and Marilyn DuBois.[36] Jane wore a navy-blue suit resembling a couture allure, a matching hat with a black veil, three diamond studded earrings, and her signature glasses. She carried a bouquet of stephanotis and pink feather carnations encircling a corsage of pink roses. Her bridesmaid wore a brown and white taffeta dress with brown accessories and carried a bouquet of yellow and white carnations.[37] The groom sported a short quiff hairstyle with a side part on the left. The only photograph of the wedding shows the newlyweds flashing polite smiles.

With their wistful demeanor, the young couple returned to Darald's parents' house for cake. No one from Jane's family was present at the ceremony or post-wedding party. After the quaint reception, Jane and Darald honeymooned just a few miles away in Ames. Celebrations finally ended on February 10 when Jane's community of teaching friends at Randall School showered her with gifts at a postnuptial linen party.[38] In the eyes of her colleagues, Jane recalled, she must have been expecting, which was why she got married. "Since we got married in the middle of the year, everyone was quite certain that I must be pregnant." Jane got the impression that her coworkers established an office pool to guess when she would start showing a baby bump.

* * *

On a purely personal level, Jane's view of the world was shaped by, and thus limited to, the Iowa environs. This part of Jane's life is defined as a moment in history when news lumbered across the country, and the culture and social issues transpiring in the ether were rarely felt nor understood close to home. Her career began amid court-ordered school desegregation following the May

17, 1954, *Brown v. Topeka Board of Education* decision, and its May 31, 1955, corollary, *Brown II*. The Supreme Court of the United States (SCOTUS) decree allowing schools to dismantle separate school systems for Black and white students with "all deliberate speed" compounded backlash by parent groups spread throughout the South. Absent a grassroots movement to bolster the SCOTUS decision, segregationists utilized varying strategies to keep schools racially segregated. Some state legislatures delayed integration by passing "freedom of choice" plans, giving parents the right to send their children to schools across district or county lines.

Another popular approach was the "grade-a-year" desegregation plan, starting efforts to bring students of varying colors together in first grade. That approach calmed nervous parents who understood that the plan delayed integration for an entire generation as residential segregation kept elementary schools bound by intra-district borders racially separate. Another approach by many districts was to defy the court order by closing public schools to open segregated academies, leading to the mass departure of white students into private schools.

For Jane, there was no civil rights zeitgeist in 1955. The murder of fourteen-year-old Chicago native Emmett Till that summer and subsequent viral photographs of his mangled face in the national and international press hardly made her flinch. Racial issues of national importance did little to Jane because they did not impact her sphere of influence; she had never taught a student of color.[39] Integration at any level did not threaten the rural Iowan way of life. She was about to start a family and would invest her energy into making decisions concerning the next steps for her growing brood.

That fall, Jane left her job in Randall to teach first grade in Napier, Iowa, a small town twelve miles from Boone. It was a measure of her longing to spend more time with Darald that she left a familiar job where she knew the community and students and had a group of colleagues helping her grow as an educator. Working at Napier made married life easier, as the two saw more of each other throughout the week. She often sat at the dining room table reading until Darald returned from work well after dinner hours. When together, there was steady flirtation and hand-holding. The relationship was stronger for those reasons. As for Darald, he could not help but be aware that his friends and coworkers—envious and surprised—were stymied over his intelligent, witted, and devoted spouse. Everyone in his circle had anticipated a quick annulment of their marriage. In due time, he suspended all skepticism.

Darald was the center of Jane's universe. She treated him like she had seen working women in northern Iowa treat their spouses. She wouldn't consider a major change to her lifestyle until they agreed to start having children. Jane wanted several children; Darald wanted promotions. Darald's wish came first. In mid-1955, the National Tea Company district manager promoted him to assistant manager of its food store at Fort Dodge.

Jane meanwhile tendered her letter of resignation to Napier that December, effective at the end of the fall semester the following month. Not only was she freeing herself to move to Fort Dodge with her husband, but Jane announced that she was pregnant with a due date in August.

The Elliotts had little time to prepare for their new baby in Fort Dodge. After only weeks on the job, the National Tea Company district manager once again transferred Darald to work as manager of the company grocery store in Waterloo. The Elliotts' new home—the third in two years—was in Iowa's manufacturing epicenter with industrial giants John Deere Tractor, Inc., and the Rath Packing Company, which provided jobs to thousands of northern Iowans. Jane spent a summer in Waterloo with her Aunt Blanche and Uncle Barney many years earlier during her first quarter of college, but her relocation there at the end of 1955 was eye-opening.

Like Des Moines, Waterloo possessed one of the largest Black populations in the entire state. Unlike Riceville or Boone, where the lack of racial mixing meant the absence of debate over cultural, political, and economic relations among the racialized color groups, Waterloo's diversity made prevailing discrimination problems hard to ignore. The marker of segregation in Waterloo was the Cedar River. The city's Black residential neighborhood was east of the river, encompassing about 6,000 people, or 7 percent of the city's population.[40] In what was once a colony for Black migrants, bit by bit, whites carved a color line east of the Cedar River, which ran directly through the city center. East of the river to the Illinois Central Railroad tracks north of Walnut Street boxed in Waterloo's Black residents. Financial restraints and the discriminatory practices of white landlords, realtors, and bankers made it impossible for Black tenants to find housing outside the Black ghetto. Opportunities beyond working in one of Waterloo's factories were minimal for Black males in town, as many hiring practices maintained segregated divisions. It was also challenging for Black females to climb higher than a janitor position.

It was on the edge of the Black ghetto where Jane and Darald rented the upstairs of a two-story house on Irving Street that had been converted into two apartments.[41] The spot was ideal since it was within walking distance of the National Tea grocery store on East Fourth Street, a few blocks south of Lincoln Park, near the neighborhood's business district.

After making friends with many of his regular customers, Darald invited five African American friends to go pheasant hunting with Jane's dad, Lloyd, at the Jennison Round Grove farm. Walking through the field with shotguns cradled in the crook of the elbow while sharing hunting stories, Lloyd unwittingly asked, "Do you all hunt coons?" Darald's friends looked at each other, unnerved over a comment that would be taken as a slur in another contextual setting. Saddled with grief, Lloyd took it back: "I mean raccoons. Do you hunt raccoons?" To which someone retorted that he did. Standing in his denim bib overalls, looking up at five men who had just been insulted, Lloyd struggled through his first interaction with African Americans. Not much was said during the exchange, and the men returned to enjoying their hunting experience largely because Darald worked quickly to change the conversation topic. But for Lloyd, it made him think about everything he thought and said about Black people before that moment.

CHAPTER 5

EYE OPENING

Jane and Darald were the original impetus for Lloyd to see the world through a cultured lens. In 1956, however, Riceville was far from accepting people who refused to conform. While hanging out with family in town as Darald and his friends hunted with her father, Jane encountered details about a story that captured statewide headlines. On March 16, Riceville Junior High seventh and eighth-grade teacher Paul J. Richer was fired. Jane's youngest brother, Steve, was a student in Richer's class and recounted the termination issued by Dr. Thomas G. "Tink" Walker Jr. Tink served as the Riceville school board president. After community complaints about Richer's cynicism over the district's educational mission and his method of teaching middle schoolers, he offered the young teacher the pink slip.

At twenty-one, Richer was in the second semester of his first year at Riceville Junior High. He graduated with honors from Iowa State University, winning the Hanser Speech Award—a national intercollegiate oratorical prize earned at a championship event in Cleveland, Ohio. Richer not only possessed astute oratorical skills but also had the compulsion to use them in the theater. He won the lead in T.S. Eliot's The Confidential Clerk during his senior year.[1] A member of Phi Beta Kappa, Richer taught English, reading, social studies, and spelling while also directing school theater at Riceville. At night, he acted at the Little Theater near his home in Mason City.[2] Among the causes leading to his termination was what his hometown paper, The Globe-Gazette, called a "Red Fallacy." Richer created a comparative government unit in his seventh-grade social studies class that incorporated lessons about communism as a form of government. For two-and-a-half weeks, he and the students used a historical lens to discuss

74

communism as it manifested after the Bolshevik Revolution almost forty years earlier. "The kids, themselves, drew the conclusion that communism is a fallacy," said Richer. "That's why I think the unit was successful."[3] In addition to studying various governments, Richer created a comparative religions unit that listed as an anchor text, *How the Great Religions Began* by Joseph Gaer.[4] He also changed the English curriculum by incorporating Shakespeare and excerpts from *Catcher in the Rye* and John Stenbeck's *Of Mice and Men*. Richer said, "The kids could learn this lesson that everybody in this world needs somebody else."[5] His students also studied the family-friendly theatrical comedy *Life With Father*.

Church leaders, parent groups, and war veterans were vocal critics of Richer's critical thinking teaching style, which they deemed too progressive. One unhappy community member asked the school board: "What does my boy need to know Shakespeare for? It won't help him plow a field." The loudest critic, Reverend William Bohi, the seven-and-a-half-year minister of the Riceville Congregational Church, said the examination of religion "was beyond the scope of seventh and eighth graders."[6] Reverend Bohi told the *Des Moines Register* that Richer "was interested in a lot of fool things. He talked to them about mental health. He had them write essays on 'my outlook on life.' Imagine asking seventh and eighth graders that."[7]

Hearing criticism from Riceville's American Legion members brought about Richer's inevitable dismissal. On March 9, Richer directed the high school's one-act play titled *Blackboard Jungle*, a drama about a World War II veteran who accepts a teaching position at an interracial, inner-city school plagued by uncontrollable students obsessed with rock 'n' roll. The play offers a narrative about the nationwide conversation over juvenile delinquency matters. A place without much diversity, Riceville had a history of sheltering its youth from subversive threats from within domestic boundaries. Sexuality, homosexuality, divorce, racial and ethnic diversity, and value diversity found in comic books, films, and other aspects of popular culture could lead to misbehavior and un-American tendencies. Just the talk of the theatrical production turned heads in Riceville. Moments before raising the curtain, Superintendent Donald Johnston and the head of the American Legion, stormed into the theater—the high school's cafeteria—and sought a "parley," Richer told an interviewer from *Pageant* magazine. The play's final scene—a fight between two gangs of students—was to feature a flagpole used to injure another person. They said Richer's play was "desecrating the American flag." Johnston gave Richer the ultimatum of canceling the performance or removing the flag from the scene.

"This play belongs to the students," Richer told his boss. "If these kids think it's appropriate to remove that scene from the play, then that's what'll happen. It's their play, not mine."

"You can't remove the flag!" the students declared, according to Richer. "That's what the play's all about—freedom!"[8]

The superintendent accordingly shut down the play.

In frustration, Richer wrote to the school board announcing he would not return to Riceville at the start of the next school year. In the letter, the twenty-something-year-old progressive unloaded on the community, which vilified him. He said that he never felt supported by the school administration. His words were an indictment of anti-intellectualism from the Riceville community spurred on by the decade's earlier Red-ucator witch hunts. Teaching at Riceville, he said, "is not a creative process, but a task to be performed by a mental puppet."

> Because I have further discovered that within Riceville, the puppeteer is not my principal nor my superintendent, nor my board.
>
> Because I have discovered also that the puppeteer within Riceville is that noisy, misinformed, intellectually corrupt, intolerant segment of a lethargic public.
>
> Because this narrow, noisy few wields such tremendous power and insidious influence that those in position of authority bow to their wishes.
>
> Because these wishes are a compound of ignorance and arrogance and bigotry, and intellectual narrowness.
>
> For these reasons, I request that my name not be considered for a position of employment in the Riceville Public Schools for the school year commencing in the fall of 1956. [. . .]
>
> My decision to leave Riceville is based on one fact—one discovery. That in the middle of the twentieth century, in the middle of the United States of America, there exists a group of people whose chief motivations are cowardice and fear.
>
> I cannot, I will not teach in a mental straitjacket. Thank God. I am not afraid.[9]

Instead of letting the school year run its course and parting ways with Richer in June, the school board fired him during a closed session in the superintendent's office at the high school on Friday evening, March 16. Richer was in attendance. A vote of the board fired him for his "obvious disregard of administrative authority" and his "unwillingness to co-operate [*sic*] with Mr. Johnston and Mr. [Eugene] Orr, and your defiant attitude toward the school board and the community as a whole [. . .]"[10]

Richer asked for a public hearing, but board president Tink Walker said, "There was little point" in granting the request. "I've got to live here," Walker said. "I can't see myself stirring up a lot more difficulty." This was the same Tink Walker that delivered Jane into the world on Thanksgiving Day in 1933. It was true Walker had to live there, and his business depended on how much the people of his community trusted him. The good doctor acted in interest, indeed.

Steve told Jane he was "quite intrigued by [Richer] and found the community's treatment of him disgusting."[11] Many of his classmates also came to Richer's defense after the dismissal. Over the weekend, signs were posted around town. One read, "Christ was crucified; why do you crucify Richer?" Six eighth-grade students tried staging a strike on the first day back to school after the firing. At the start of the school day, Steve watched his peers hang a poster in the school with the slogan "Pursue the Truth" underneath a picture of their slandered teacher. However, the movement failed to convince more classmates to participate, and the strikers were suspended for the day.

Newspapers in northern Iowa ran stories about Richer's dismissal. Most possessed a sympathetic tone. The *Charles City Press* said the young teacher's "only recognizable error" was "a lack of tact."[12] Others writing in various newspapers harkened back to the McCarthy era. One from Manson, Iowa, asked: "Does anyone have the audacity to claim that ignorance will solve the problem of communism? Only a thorough knowledge of communism will ever give us the weapons to combat it." A writer from Mason City proclaimed: "In the past, successful pressure has been brought on educators concerning what material should be presented in classrooms. Why shouldn't one become familiar with the doctrines of communism?" A contributor from New Hampton said: "Now[,] if a teacher is to be penalized for opening the windows of his students' minds and letting the light of truth shine in, we should not wonder why so many young people choose to enter other professions."[13]

Despite the outsider perspective, conformity rang through in Riceville. Speaking on behalf of the Riceville Community School District, Walker said the statewide media outcry was "built up, planned, premeditated" by Richer.[14] Walker framed Richer as a "reformer or a crusader," and many community members called to thank him for acting.

Richer responded to Walker in the *Waterloo Courier*. He said the allegations that he "tried to teach on a college level," as one parent alleged, were taken out of context. There is "to a certain extent," he conceded, truth to the claim that he allowed current events to take over regular lesson plans and brought in resources for students to study. Nevertheless, everything was driven by student queries. "If my social studies class plan called for the study of Washington to Lincoln and my students asked questions about communism, then we discussed communism," he explained. "My students asked questions, and I didn't have the knack of telling them not to."[15]

On March 20, *The Des Moines Register* ran an editorial titled "Is Good Teaching a Crime?" The paper asserted, "No teacher has the right to indoctrinate his students in any point of view. So far as we can tell, however, Richer has not been accused of propagandizing. His "error" seems to have been that he functioned as a great many would want a teacher to function by going beyond the materials in the prescribed curriculum, detecting the real interests of his students and adapting his materials to them, by urging his students to do some creative thinking." In closing, the editor wrote, "If those are not the qualities the people of Riceville want in a teacher, then they have a perfect right to fire Paul Richer." The article made one final poignant remark that predominated the era of McCarthyite hunts for presumed Red-ucators. It asserted that the Riceville board fired Richer because influential community members mounted pressure to act simply because course content contrasted with their personal political beliefs. Once Richer issued his indignation over the allegations against him, the board "felt it had no other choice."[16]

The Paul Richer affair shows that even in small, rural towns across Iowa, attacks on any teacher that challenged traditional banking methods of instruction were part of a broader attack on anything that inexorable communities did not like in schools. It was the latest moral panic coming on the heels of the anti-communist smear tactics associated with Allen Zoll and Joe McCarthy earlier that decade. Ironically, Richer would prove his loyalty to the country when he was drafted into the U.S. Army later that year. He spent the next three years as a private, stationed in West Germany most of that time. From 1959 to 1961, he taught in Nigeria under the auspices of the African American Institute. After some time as a field representative of the United World Federation at Iowa City, responsible for managing the organization in Missouri, Illinois, and Wisconsin, he returned to Mamma, Nigeria, in 1962 to oversee the construction of an elementary school. Ten years after his termination from the Riceville school district, he obtained a teaching job at Kettle Moraine High School in Wales, Wisconsin. After one turbulent year, he resigned to open the area's first professional theater in Delafield, a few miles north of Wales.[17] In Delafield, he built a 120-seat theater out of an old Presbyterian church building.

Jane reflected on the Richer affair years later. In her estimation, the Riceville community wrongfully terminated Richer. But she posited, "Richer was wrong in his description of teaching, 'mental puppets.'" She contended that he should have said, "The teachers were mental puppets and were determined to stay that way."[18] Little did anyone know that her name would be said in the same breath as Paul Richer in twelve years.

* * *

Darald's new job managing his store in Waterloo carried a $45 weekly salary.[19] This new position provided enough financial security for the couple to become enthusiastic about their future. The Elliotts created a plan: after cashing his checks, they divided the money into five envelopes, one each for rent, insurance, utilities, medical, and savings. The eager couple also began preparing for their child's arrival at their tiny apartment on the city's east side. They received the baby bed Darald slept on as an infant, and his mother sewed Jane a wardrobe of maternity clothes.

During the final days of Jane's pregnancy, Darald had to report to National Guard duty at Camp Ripley in Little Falls, Minnesota. Despite her protest, on August 10, 1956, he dropped Jane off at the Jennison Round Grove home on his way to camp.[20] She had little desire to stay with her parents: "It was a house with no running water. No indoor plumbing. And I was eight and a half months pregnant."[21] On the evening of August 15, Gie suggested everyone grab dinner at a nearby festival in McIntire, a town celebrating its founding, about ten miles north of Riceville. It was hectic there, and friends told Jane she should leave because she looked likely to go into labor. Jane awoke the following day before dawn, August 16, 1956, to use the outdoor bathroom. She went into labor on the way. With Gie in the back seat, her sister, Jean, drove her to Tink Walker's medical office in Riceville. Walker was not in, but a locum doctor told Jane she had several hours before delivery and suggested she go to Waterloo's Allen Memorial Hospital—about seventy miles away—to have her regular physician deliver the baby.

"I had seven children; I know what's going on here," Gie said to the doctor, arguing that Jane would deliver the baby at any moment.

"This baby won't be born until five o'clock this afternoon," he replied, having just finished an examination of Jane.

Jane thought to herself: "I'm lying there listening to the expert (doctor) and the real expert (Gie) and thinking, 'You fool.'"

Reluctantly, Jane, Jean, and Gie sped off to Waterloo.

"We got in the car with a bunch of pillows and towels and headed for Waterloo," Jane recalled, as her mom readied to deliver the baby in the car if they did not make it the seventy miles. "I said to Jean, 'Get a damned ticket'" on the way. "I don't want to deliver this baby in this car." Despite the doctor's assurances, Jane agreed with her mother that the baby was coming any minute. Her intuition was right; Jane's sister got to Waterloo at ten o'clock in the morning with labor pains two minutes apart.

Jane delivered a girl, Sarah Jane, thirty minutes later.[22] "She had Darald's eyes and Darald's hair," Jane remembered. "She was just gorgeous." She sent Darald a telegram with news of Sarah the following day. A week later, the hospital discharged Jane. A few days after that, Darald returned from Camp Ripley.

In 1957, Jane was pregnant for the second time. On September 10, Darald took one-year-old Sarah to stay with Jane's parents while Jane checked into Allen Memorial Hospital, waiting for the birth of their second child, a boy. The couple named the boy Brian Dean after Jane's uncle, Bryan Hogan, husband to Aunt Blanche. This time Darald returned to the hospital in time for the birth, but something the doctor said lingered.

The doctor proclaimed: "You got a good one this time."

"What do you mean? I got a good one the first time," Darald replied, shocked the doctor would not consider a girl a "good one."[23]

Apart from the doctor's dispassionate comment, the delivery was uncomplicated, as were the deliveries of their subsequent children. On February 11, 1959, Mary Jean (named after Jane's older sister) was born during a freezing rainstorm that caused the car transporting Jane's mother to Waterloo to drive through railroad gates, colliding with a moving train. Gie survived, but she missed the delivery.

Two years later, on April 13, 1961, Jane delivered a fourth child, a second son, Mark Donald.

The arrival of children marked a peculiar moment in Jane Elliott's life. She was twenty-seven at the time of Mark's birth. Teaching, however, was an afterthought, another lifetime ago. Not working—choosing instead to support a husband that spent almost every moment at his job—Jane's life had become overrun by her domestic responsibility to ensure the kids' safety. She wanted more children. "I would have had a dozen kids if it were up to me," Jane said, expressing the sentiments of an individual from a large family. "Darald, he would have been fine if he only had one." Between 1956 and 1961, Jane described, "All I did was have babies and raise babies."[24] However, Jane's hopes of growing their family vanished when Darald spoke about the financial hardships that would come with another child. While there were health risks to having babies with no break between pregnancies (like anemia and uterine ruptures) for the Elliotts, there were legitimate concerns over being able to feed all their children. "It was too expensive to have that many kids in those days," she conceded.

Soon after the birth of Mark, Jane took a brand new, doctor-prescribed birth control pill, Enovid-10. Nine months earlier, on May 10, 1960, the Food and Drug Administration had approved the use of "the pill." The oral contraceptive had been championed by Margaret Sanger, the women's reproductive rights trailblazer who collaborated with scientists and expert in human reproduction, Gregory Pincus, and the financial support of Katharine McCormick, heiress of International Harvester to bring about the pill's development. Dating back to her 1912 pamphlet *What Every Girl Should Know*, a treatise about birth control published when it was illegal to advocate contraception, Sanger paved the way for the pill Jane would come to take in 1961. Sanger had even been arrested in October 1916 for opening a two-room planned parenthood clinic in the Brownsville neighborhood of Brooklyn, staffed with trained nurses ready to help with reproductive care.[25] Her courage, callousness, and persistence to remain firm on her dream of providing women with safety measures to prevent unwanted pregnancies and seize control over fertility align with the convictions Jane sought in social reformers. For her and Darald, the birth control pill was a means to avoid an accidental pregnancy and to circumvent poverty as they were on the economic lower end now that Jane was not working, and Darald burned the midnight oil.

Indeed, pugnacious debates over civil rights, the war in Vietnam, and widespread drug use among baby boomers overwhelmed households in the 1960s. The pill, however, aroused intersecting interests in the global population, poverty, and morality. National headlines stirred skepticism: "Birth Control Pills: Potentially Harmful,"; "Three Drawbacks Seen in Birth-Control Pills,"; "A Birth Control Pill Poses Moral and Social Questions,"; and "Doctors Question Safety of Birth Control Pills." Additionally, isolated and unfounded stories linking the birth control pill to the mysterious deaths of young women caused greater consternation.

In 1962, *The Charlotte News* reported "6 Deaths Probed for Link with Birth Control." On the West Coast, the *Tacoma News Tribune* simultaneously ran a story about the sudden death of a twenty-two-year-old Los Angeles woman,

Linda Ellis—whose husband told the press she suffered a blood clot after taking Enovid for eight months. Not a single piece of evidence or expert voice substantiated the claim. Nevertheless, the headline, "Woman Who Took Birth Control Pills Dies," elevated the assertion that the pill caused her death.[26] The result was a public frenzy against the unfamiliar drug early in the decade. The American Medical Association (AMA) responded that summer, declaring there was no proof the pill was the cause of blood clots. The AMA insisted that skepticism over Enovid was politically incentivized. In addition, John C. Rock, clinic professor emeritus of gynecology at Harvard University and director of the Rock Reproductive Study Center in Brookline, Massachusetts, released a report stating that the pill did more than prevent pregnancy. After studying couples who wanted to have children but could not, Rock found that Enovid helped the ovaries rest. When the pill was stopped, some of the women in his study became pregnant. Rock called it a "rebound effect" and his scientist colleagues christened the revolutionary finding the "Rock rebound." Rock proved that women who took the oral contraceptive had a better chance of becoming pregnant once they stopped taking the pill.[27]

Jane had her own issues with the pill. While believing that Enovid generated the safest moment in the history of contraception, it gave her excruciating headaches. Taking Enovid, she said, made her "sicker than a poisoned pup."[28] While she paid attention to the national debate over the pill, siding with doctors who considered it a practical means of preventing unwanted pregnancy, she thought: "Why do I have to go through this just so [Darald] could have it easy?" After scrapping the pill, Jane made Darald responsible for his own birth control.[29]

By mid-August, Jane felt well enough to take her children to see *Misty*, a movie based on the children's book *Misty of Chincoteague*. The movie tells the story of two Philadelphia orphans, Paul, and Maureen Beebe, played by David Ladd and Pam Smith, who move to Chincoteague Island off the Eastern Shore of Virginia to live with their grandparents on a pony ranch after the untimely death of their parents. The film sheds light on the practice of auctioning ponies in Chincoteague. The storyline of how the Beebes lose their beloved pony to another bidder, but strive to win Misty back, then release him into the wilderness to live with his kind, only to have the rebel colt return to them in the end, made *Misty* a classic family film.

Walking to the movie theater, five-year-old Sarah (excited to see her first big screen picture) said to Jane, "Look at us, Mom. We are walking on the street just like people do." The comment made Jane feel ill at ease over how the children were raised. "The only time we were out of the house and away from the home was when we'd drive to Riceville on the weekend," said Jane about her failure to expose her children to social opportunities beyond the Jennison and Elliott family circle. Sometimes during the week, she took the kids to Darald's National Tea store after hours. The kids would run around the store where it was safer than having them play in the street, avoiding automobiles and other hazards. "It was what you did," acknowledged Jane. "You raised your kids at home and tried to keep them alive."[30] What worried Jane—who believed the lack of money was not the family's shortcoming—was that the kids rarely spent time with Darald. Thus, she was left alone to do all the parenting. For Jane, it was easier to keep them sheltered at home than to find activities for them to do in public.

Her frustration came to a head when one evening, the kids mistook two men selling burial plots knocking at the door for Darald. Looking through the screen door, thinking they were looking at their dad, the kids yelled, "Daddy's home!"

Later that night, when Darald returned from work, Jane said, "This has gone on long enough. You are gone all day from seven o'clock in the morning until ten o'clock at night. These kids hardly know you." Darald's requirements for managing the National Tea store meant he worked weekends. "These kids have a right to a normal life, but they aren't going to have one as long as you work for National Tea," Jane told him.[31] She was in a lose-lose situation, however. Jane did not want to pressure her husband with ultimatums, especially since his steadfast work for the company earned him a promotion to the supermarket manager position. She spoke her mind to Darald but went on raising the kids while he kept the same work schedule.

Money was Darald's obsession. Years later, she said of her husband: "Most of my life from '52 to '61 was about Darald Elliott; he was more than handsome. He was accepting and supportive and tighter than the skin on a peach and loved me to distraction. But he loved money more. His Scottish background was always in the foreground, and since he was an only child, he really resented the competition he had to put up with from my large, noisy, Irish family. It wasn't a match made in heaven, but it became heaven to us after the kids had grown and left home."[32]

His hard work paid off by way of relative social mobility. Sometime before the end of 1959, the Elliotts saved enough money and moved across the river to a one-floor home on Littlefield Road in Waterloo's sparkling all-white Alabar Hills. The following year, they relocated to a two-bedroom home with a lawn in the same community at 1759 Corning Avenue. Across the river via Route 63, past the John Deere factory, then onto Cedar Falls Avenue, the relocation meant that the Elliotts were far enough away from the Black residential neighborhood. Whatever associates of color the Elliotts had before moving were lost. Alabar Hills residents wanted to contain growing social unrest on the other side of the river for fear of moral decay. The Elliotts did not dare invite their former neighbors from the east side to their new home. Jane said years later, "[Y]ou absolutely didn't bring blacks into your home" at Alabar Hills "if you wanted to be accepted by your neighbors."[33] Maintaining a segregated community was an unspoken agreement among neighbors, sealed by an understanding of town history and soft communication in the form of racist quips.

As long as Darald had to commute to and from work on the east side, there was no escaping the civil rights movement, which had proliferated in Waterloo long before. Led by an African American heroine and labor unionist with a courageous voice named Anna Mae Weems, civil rights efforts in Iowa consisted largely of labor-centered agitation. As a job provider running National Tea, Darald would face the struggle for racial equality in the Factory City of Iowa. The implications of his interaction with Weems would profoundly impact his store and change the trajectory of Jane's life.

CHAPTER 6

AN EYE COLOR TEST

"If you want to go somewhere where there's no racism, die."
—Jane Elliott, Crystal Gardens, Howell, Michigan, 2008

Most civil rights historians have ignored Anna Mae Weems' impact on the civil rights movement. This is because she isolated her work in lightly populated Iowa during the 1950s when the movement dismantled de jure segregation of the South. Yet her work made a difference in the lives of many Iowans, including Darald and Jane Elliott. Weems labored long and hard as a civil and union rights activist in Iowa in general and Waterloo, more specifically, since the early 1950s. Amid organizing sit-ins, corporate boycotts, and rallies, and by leading members of both the National Association for the Advancement of Colored People (NAACP) and the United Packinghouse Workers of America, Weems strove to make Waterloo a more equitable place for African Americans. Today, she is known as an architect of freedom and equality in Iowa.

Born February 6, 1926, in Waterloo, Weems attended Waterloo East High School. As a trombonist who played the oboe and violin, she became the first African American field commander in the school's music department. Throughout her school days in Waterloo public schools, teachers and peers recognized her as a brilliant musician but one who lacked the ambition to make a career of her talent. "I was into the classics," she said of Mozart and Beethoven, which she called "real music." As a precocious teen, she attributed Waterloo's economic and educational disparities to the reality that Black workers received few opportunities to attain anything better than menial jobs. Weems drew inspiration from the *Pittsburgh Courier's* double victory campaign over discrimination in civilian defense industries and against racism abroad during World

War II. She accordingly set out to become the champion of the labor reform movement in her city, hoping efforts would affect a change of conscience regarding racism and institutional changes in Iowa. In September 1944, Weems, then eighteen years old, enrolled at the University of Iowa. The institution's custom was for students of color to live off-campus in segregated housing. Most African American students boarded with Black families in Iowa City. Some found lodging in white fraternities if they agreed to work as housekeepers. While that environment rankled her before stepping foot in her first class, she would not get the opportunity to test the system as a student at UI because the boarding house for which she was to stay burned down a few days before the start of the fall semester. She returned home, instead investing her energy in undoing pervasive inequality in Waterloo's school system, job market, and housing. Coincidentally, UI would desegregate its dormitories in 1946.[1]

In 1954, Weems attained a job at the Rath Packing Company, a meatpacking factory that employed hundreds of skilled and unskilled laborers and office employees in Waterloo. Founded in 1891, Rath emerged by the 1940s as a rival to Iowa's corn, beef, and other soil and breeding products by attracting railroads to the city to export livestock freight—mainly cattle and hogs—to markets across the country. The plant was one of several industrial tycoons in Iowa attracting African American laborers to Waterloo during the Great Migration of Black Southerners. Weems arrived at the Rath plant due to the company's efforts to recruit, retain, and promote Black workers into middle management positions. Before 1954, Rath's policy maintained that a Black woman must work one year as a janitor before being considered for another position.[2] The company's decision to hire Weems as its first female employee of color straight into the sliced-bacon department was an outrageous violation of ethics for the plant's white female workers. The hiring prompted a walkout from those in her department. Historian Marcia Walker-McWilliams reconstructs how Black male coworkers at the Rath plant responded to how the women treated Weems:

> When the predominantly Black male hog-kill department threatened a work stoppage if the plant fired Weems, the white women were told that they could either return to work or be fired. They returned, and Weems eventually became a shop steward in the department for the very women who initially refused to work with her.[3]

Indeed, after a short time packing pepperoni, she bid for a position in the leadership of the United Packinghouse Workers of America (UPWA), Local 46. She assumed directorship duties of the union's Human Relations Committee.

Weems, after that, spearheaded efforts to transform the Iowa Federation of Labor (AFL-CIO) into a more inclusive labor association. "The union should be involved in discrimination in the unions, in the plants where they work, and in the [labor] community," Weems argued. After an African American bricklayer complained that he had been refused membership to the Des Moines bricklayers' union on account of his skin color, Weems embarked on a speaking tour across Iowa. At meetings held by the Black Hawk County Union Council—namely John Deere, Titus Manufacturing Co., Rath Packing, Viking Pump Co., and Tate Cadillac-Olds, Midwest locals, and national union conferences—she indicted the trade union that they were guilty of enabling discrimination within the workforce.[4]

In addition to her work as a union organizer, Weems might be best remembered for her service as president of the Waterloo chapter of the NAACP from 1958 to 1962.[5] She made education, job creation, and housing issues of urban renewal and redlining key focuses of her tenure as chapter president. The Waterloo branch of the association was in its thirty-seventh year when members voted Weems its president. Founded on February 21, 1921, the branch was inundated with the facilitation of Negro History Week commemorations at local middle and high schools while leading moral crusades in the Waterloo community promoting good behavior and civic duty.

As NAACP president, Anna Mae Weems worked tirelessly to arrange a visit by Rev. Dr. Martin Luther King Jr. While still relatively known to the general public, King agreed to visit Waterloo during his national book tour promoting his memoir about the Montgomery bus boycott, *Stride Toward Freedom*. King's tour ended that September in Harlem when a mentally deranged woman named Izola Ware Curry stabbed the paragon of nonviolent resistance, piercing his left chest near the heart with a seven-inch letter opener as he signed books. Police authorities arrested Curry, who was also brandishing a pistol concealed in her dress, outside the Harlem bookstore as she tried to get into a taxicab. "I've been after him for six years," onlookers heard her shouting. "I'm glad I done it."[6]

Thirteen months later, a healthy Dr. King arrived in Waterloo. On November 10, 1959, he spoke to the public (mostly whites) at the East High School auditorium. According to Weems, the local Black clergy portrayed King as a "troublemaker." "He'd been roaming through the land causing trouble," with his speeches, King's naysayers in Waterloo said.[7]

While in the city, he boarded at Weems' home on Oneida Street. A block away, in an empty lot near the Illinois Central Railroad yard, Weems arranged for a "stunt to dramatize King's philosophy of always countering any ill will with love," wrote the *Waterloo Courier*. She placed cardboard cutouts of Ku Klux Klansmen and a replica of a cross burning in the eyesight of every passerby, hanging a sign next to the cutouts that read: "Martin Luther King Says Fight Hate with Love." This act tested the nerve and impulses of Waterloo's east side residents.[8] The next day, King spoke to faculty and preservice teachers at Iowa State Teacher's College in Cedar Falls and the University of Iowa in Iowa City.[9] Several hundred people attended the lecture at all three venues, where he repeated a message about the "Future of Integration": those in the crowd have "a prime situation between two ages," he said, "the dying old and the emerging new." King spoke of the rising problems caused by racial and religious hierarchies in several Asian countries: "Seven hundred million are in China, five hundred million in India and Pakistan, ninety-six million in Japan [. . .] have been exploited by imperialism." King proclaimed that the fight against racism in the United States was linked to the fight to undo the caste system in myriad countries. He argued that the 1955 to 1956 bus boycott in Montgomery existed as a case study to effect global change. He said the success of the nonviolent struggle in what once was the capital of the Confederacy would not have been possible "if it were not for the goodwill of millions of people in other parts of the country."[10] That degree of mass mobilization, participatory democracy, and idealism could change the world.

Inspired by the February 1, 1960, F. W. Woolworth Co. lunch counter sit-ins, Weems launched a series of her own protest demonstrations in Waterloo. On April 22, 1960, Weems placed an advertisement in *The Courier* announcing her own sit-down protest march outside Waterloo's Woolworth's store planned for the following day, Saturday, April 23. She told supporters that "a peaceful picket line will be conducted" in front of the store. "We wish to take this means to emphasize our honest, lawful, and peaceful intent in this moral crusade and to explain the why of the picket line." Citing the need to "demonstrate our full support of the Southern Negro student protest against Jim Crowism in the South," Weems made it clear their protest was not a direct demonstration against the local management of the Waterloo Woolworth store at 601 Commercial Street. She proclaimed, "It is morally unjust and un-American for a large chain operation to practice active discrimination in any of its establishments." Any money raised in the demonstration would fund sit-in efforts in the South.

According to reports, roughly thirty protesters representing the NAACP, UPWA Local 48, and Black Hawk Labor Union Council showed up to picket the store. The turnout was disappointing. At a similar sympathy demonstration in Cleveland a week earlier, 5,000 protesters had attended the NAACP local chapter-sponsored event. Noticeably absent from the picket was Weems. Although she was its lead organizer as head of the NAACP, she was resting at Waterloo's Allen Memorial Hospital, where she had delivered a son a few days earlier. In her place, UPWA Local 48 president, Leo Guynn, led peaceful marchers holding placards as they encircled the sidewalk in front of the store from 11:30 in the morning to one o'clock in the afternoon, a time selected to catch shoppers that detour into Woolworth's restaurant for lunch. One picketer carried a sign that read: "Some Woolworth stores in the South practice discrimination—this is un-American." Another declared: "We don't patronize stores that practice discrimination."[11]

Though Waterloo did not face barriers to Black patrons barred from eating at lunch counters in the city, business owners rarely hired employees of color. Two issues prevailed after rare occasions when a store manager hired a Black job applicant. The first question concerned treating the single, or token, Black worker employed as the business's minority hire. Weems found that over half of the white-owned companies in Waterloo reported having no employees of color. Alarming was the fact that almost 6 percent of Waterloo were racialized minorities. As of 1960, there was no plan to increase minority hiring.

On the other hand, "minority hires" were commonly placed into menial roles, such as elevator operators, janitors, or dishwashers. Department stores like Gamble's, J.C. Penney Co., Inc., Montgomery Ward, and Sears, Roebuck & Co. kept African Americans in the back of the store. This was to keep them away from white customers that might take their business elsewhere if forced to interact with a greeter or salesclerk of another skin color. Weems accordingly made plans to challenge Waterloo's white-owned stores over hiring practices. Her next target was Waterloo's major grocery store chain: The National Tea Company, and its local manager, Darald Elliott.

* * *

West of Anna Mae Weems' home and just three blocks from Waterloo East High School was Darald Elliott's National Tea grocery store. Located on East 4th Street, the supermarket sat between the east bank of the Cedar River and the southern entrance into Lincoln Park, near the center of Waterloo's predominantly Black residential neighborhood. A white-owned grocery store in the middle of the African American community at the ascent of the national civil rights movement presented all kinds of problems for Darald. While friendly to all his customers, including Weems, many of whom he would go on to befriend, he represented a corporation that carried a reputation for poor minority hiring practices. He had staffed only one employee of color while managing the store, an eighteen-year-old East High student named Jim Jackson. But when Jackson went to college in the summer of 1960, Darald could not find a Black replacement.

The Elliotts contended that the National Tea Company tied Darald's hands. When asked why Black storekeepers were not employed at his store, he claimed district management refused to allow him. Management instructed Darald that he could have no more than one Black person employed at any time, no matter the store's location.[12] For whatever reason, his wavering on diversifying his business led to community-wide allegations that he was profiteering from Black customers while giving nothing back to their community in the form of jobs. When the pressure got too hot, Darald contacted Weems for help finding a replacement for Jackson. She declined, eyeing an opportunity to use Darald as a cudgel to make a point to the National Tea Company.

"We are going to picket your store," said Weems, according to Jane's recollection.

Darald responded, "Bring me a black employee."

"No," Weems barked as they debated inside the supermarket. "We're going to picket your store."[13]

Three days prior to Independence Day, Weems announced a boycott of Darald's supermarket. Determined to make the demonstrations indefinite, she borrowed a strategy once employed by suffragists during the late stages of World War I when silent sentinels stood outside the White House for twelve hours a day as they picketed for the vote in 1917 and 1918. She felt that the threat of ongoing agitation on the sidewalk, streets, and parking lot outside the grocery store during the Independence Day holiday (which typically brought in significant business) would garner attention from corporate officers. To expand the movement across the Hawkeye State, Weems worked to mobilize NAACP chapters to lead pickets outside National Tea stores in neighboring cities. She believed widespread protests would do more than tell regional and corporate offices of the National Tea Company that Black Iowans refused to give them their business. She hoped this direct action would match the enthusiasm emanating from the nonviolent sit-in strategy started just weeks earlier, working to combine protests against segregated diners with pickets against discriminatory food providers.

While Weems' level of excitement was high for the July 1 demonstration, the turnout in Waterloo was not. Despite working tirelessly to round up picketers, she could only muster twelve teenagers from East High who were members of the NAACP Youth Council. It was not a total failure. Weems successfully prevented the Black community from patronizing Darald's East 4th Street grocery store during the holiday weekend. In the long run, her community felt the risk was too high. If the protest backfired, closing the grocery store, East Waterloo would become a food desert. With Darald's unwitting help, National Tea Company executives successfully siphoned Black consumers away from smaller, Black-owned food marts in Waterloo. There were none.[14]

Fortunately for Weems, the picket found greater success in other parts of Iowa. After lunch, Darald's bosses, Max Lyons (National Tea's Division manager) and William "Bill" Cook (District Sales Manager), informed Weems they'd allow Darald to hire one Black carry-out boy and one Black cashier at the store. They vowed that the search for the two Black employees would commence immediately and fill in a few days.[15] Weems immediately called off the boycott.

However, Lyons and Cook's promise was a ploy to get Weems to end the demonstration. Not wanting to bother the NAACP and its troublemaker-in-chief, they relocated across the river to the west side of Waterloo, away from the Black residential neighborhood. This location allowed the company to avoid dealing with the demands of African American agitators like Weems.

After two years of planning and construction, the new supermarket opened on August 7, 1962, at the corner of 11th and Washington streets near the Cedar River's west bank. Darald's new store became part of the Black Hawk Village expansion, which included a bargain shopping center along Highway 218. Joining National Tea at the shopping center were Haskell's D-X Service Station, Geary Paint Co., Tire King Tire Store, and several smaller units. The building was gorgeous. It had colored Plexiglass panels, eight check-out lanes, a bakery department unique for the era, and was the only modern meat department in Iowa with $14,000 fully automatic scales that packaged and weighed to the one-hundredth of an ounce and priced meat products—interior walls decorated with hand-painted murals imported from France. Parking facilities accommodated 165 vehicles. The 18,000 square feet supermarket cost the company $260,000.[16]

Despite the excitement over the grand opening, Darald had his doubts. He warned Lyons and Cook that putting the store on the city's west side would mean he would lose all his regular customers, which happened to be Black. Moreover, the decision to place the store on the south side of the street also created problems. The major factories were on Waterloo's east side. People drove to work on that side of the thoroughfare and returned home along the northern route. According to Jane, Darald explained to his superiors: "People won't cross the road to get their groceries at the end of the day, and they certainly won't do their shopping before work."[17] He was correct; the store performed poorly in its new location over the next two years.

As a manager, Darald enjoyed taking home groceries without paying for them. However, when sales plummeted, Darald was warned he could no longer enjoy that management perk. Indignant over how the district office handled the situation following Weems' protest, Darald kept taking food. He was fired in the early spring of 1963.[18] A few years later, the National Tea Store went bankrupt.

Jane offered a sobering opinion on the affair. Speaking of Anna Mae Weems: "She had every right to do that," Jane said about the boycott of Darald's store. "The vast majority of his customers were Black. She forgot how vindictive the owners of that corporation could be. They closed that store because of the NAACP picketing that store. They taught her a lesson,"[19] Jane concluded. She was right. Their relocation to Waterloo's west end, away from the Black neighborhood, effectively made Weems's community a food desert.

"Sometimes racism can cost you a lot of money," Jane explained. "That's what it did for National Tea. It cost them a lot of money. All they had to do was leave that store where it was, hire some Black employees—more than one—and enjoy the riches that racism can bring to you. But instead, they thought they could be racist and rich. It cost them the store."[20]

To that end, Anna Mae Weems' protest against Jane's husband's National Tea store was among the first in a decade-long campaign against the chain store giant. Members of the NAACP could sense Weems was on to something transformative. At the November Iowa State NAACP conference in Waterloo, state president George J. Cooper heralded Weems for her chapter's activism against discriminatory employment practices in Waterloo.[21] Thanks to Weems, the demonstrations materialized into its largest protest march against the company, which occurred at the Chicago corporate office in 1970. Joining protesters were Mamie Till Mobley, mother of lynched Emmett Till, U.S. Representative Gus Savage, and other era icons.[22]

Meanwhile, Jane did not engage much with local or national politics during her eight years in Waterloo. She probably would not have been able to speak confidently about the sit-in movement that led to the protest at her husband's supermarket or known that presidential candidate John F. Kennedy's strong civil rights plank alarmed the Nixon campaign to follow suit. She was not alone in her ignorance of the seriousness of the civil rights struggle throughout the

South. ABC network radio commentator Edward P. Morgan said then: "The so-called leadership of the South has completely refused to grasp the dimensions and the significance of the Negro liberation movement and are treating it with the flatfoot mentality of a country cop."[23] While Jane had some grasp on the brevity of Weems' work in Waterloo, she was more concerned over Darald keeping his job. So, when National Tea inevitably fired her husband for speaking out against Cook's decision to relocate the store and subsequent impropriety, Jane reluctantly engaged in discussions with family members back in Riceville for ways to pay the bills.

CHAPTER 7

A PASSIONATE EYE

"You can listen to lectures on racism, you can learn a whole lot about it in books, but when you experience it, it makes a difference—a considerable difference."

—JANE ELLIOTT, NOVEMBER 1985

Situated on the southeast corner of Woodland Avenue and South Street, near the north end of Riceville, sat the Hotel Burke. Opened in 1902—just a year after a great fire that burned down much of Riceville—the two-story brick building with a basement had been owned first by grain, seed, wool, and poultry dealer John Burke, a hotel entrepreneur described by the *Recorder* at the time of its opening as "one of Riceville's hustling and progressive citizens."[1] The building, called by Dennis Rice, the founder of Riceville, "one of the finest between Minneapolis and Dubuque," stood out as a beauty in the small town. His daughters, Mary and Genevieve Burke, assumed hotel ownership in 1917. The combination of its western style architecture with its signature wide winding staircase and semi-circular wood registration desk made the hotel look like a national landmark. By 1963, however, the owners had had enough of the hotel business and looked for a buyer.

The hotel had become more of a boarding house in recent years. The Burke sisters had long stopped inviting businesses, social clubs, and bridal parties from using the hotel as a ceremonial venue. "It really hasn't been a hotel for a long time," Mary Burke admitted to a reporter writing a story on the hotel's history. "We stopped serving meals in 1917, and since that time, it has been more of a rooming house."[2] The place once teemed with traveling salesmen, school-aged recitals, operas, hunters, and Riceville patrons looking for a hot meal. The quaint hotel had even allowed the town's eye doctor to visit with patients in one of the rooms. However, over time, it slowly became nothing more than a large house inhabited by the Burke sisters. While the building remained pleasant for the townspeople, it no longer held the status of the town's jewel.

The Burkes first told the public they wanted to sell the hotel in 1960. Intrigued by the prospect of owning the facility was Jane's mother, Gie, who had grown tired of living in the family farmhouse at Round Grove now that she and Lloyd were empty nesters. As a child, Gie had been a neighbor to one of the Burke cousins. She adored the Burkes and had her eyes set on owning and living in the hotel. However, Gie did not want to be the one to buy it, nor did she have any idea of how to run a business. More specifically, Gie had no clue how to operate a hotel. She instead convinced her firstborn to invest.

Jane's brother, Charles, agreed to buy the hotel for Gie because he was looking for a way to move back to Riceville. The father of three children, Charles worked as a district representative for Bonewitz Chemicals, Inc. in Rochester, Minnesota. He bought the hotel on June 1, 1963.[3] The transaction had repercussions across the state; the sale of Hotel Burke signified the transformation of a cultural landmark in northern Iowa and the emergence of a new dynasty in Riceville. Being able to own the social heart and soul of the community was important for prestige. Growing the family legacy was, in many ways, as important as turning the hotel into a profitable business.

Despite his vow not to remodel the building, Charles said he would change how the hotel would serve the community. He first confirmed Gie and Lloyd as managers, then made the most notable change. When the paperwork was signed, Charles unveiled the hotel's new name: The Jennison Inn. The branding was a business decision and not a nod to vanity. His grandfather, Samuel, had been an esteemed member of Riceville and a well-respected farmer with property spread throughout northern Iowa. Likewise, Charles' father, Lloyd, whom everyone called "Ginny Gunfighter," an affectionate moniker that evolved from Jennison to Jenny, which became Gennie, then Ginny, to rhyme with his wife's nickname "Gie," was currently deeply admired by Riceville residents.[4] While generally risky to name a business after oneself, he felt the family name was ultra-credible. Even his sister, Mary, was a beloved elementary teacher at the Riceville Community School. He trusted the Jennison name alone would attract business. The previous owner had done it; naming hotels after the owner was common practice.

Right away, Lloyd and Gie retreated from Round Grove and settled into one of the inn's two first-floor apartments. Gie assumed most of the managerial work by making herself responsible for the day-to-day operations, including bookkeeping, staffing, cooking, and cleaning. Lloyd handled long-term planning, repair work, and liaison with the press.

Despite the excitement emanating from Gie and Lloyd, Charles, then thirty-five, expressed regret over the investment after having become exhausted trying to stay organized and maintain a healthy work-life balance between the demands of running a hotel and his day job. Could he get out of the deal as quickly as he became owner? Gie had an idea to capitalize on Darald's termination from National Tea. She suspected that since he and Jane had four children to provide, they could not afford to say no to assuming ownership of the inn, an entrepreneurial endeavor that would make them their own boss.

Never owning the Burke Hotel sounded like a good idea to Jane. It was in mid-summer, however, when she entertained the idea of buying the inn from Charles. Given the paradox of how much Gie and Jane did not get along, but knowing Jane wished to return to Riceville so her children could be closer to her father, there is no way of knowing how much arm-twisting went on. After some brooding, Jane got Darald to agree. Charles sold them the Jennison Inn in September, within three months of purchasing the property.[5]

Before leaving Waterloo, Jane and Darald placed an advertisement in *The Courier* looking for someone to rent their Alabar Hills home. They hoped to maintain ownership of the property. Monthly rent from a tenant paid the bills wherever they ended up in Riceville, and anything earned at the Jennison Inn became disposable income. They also did not rule out a return to the Factory City; renting the place out would make for an easy return, if necessary.

Among the first to telephone inquiring about the home was what Jane assumed to be a woman of color. The caller asked: "Do you rent to coloreds?" Conflicted about how renting her home to an African American tenant would make the neighbors feel about her, Jane answered, "No. This is an all-white neighborhood!"[6] Not only did Jane concede years later that her behavior was racist, but it also cost her family a source of income. They never found a tenant, and the Elliotts put the house on the market before relocating to Riceville by autumn—free of loose ends.

"For a long time after that, I felt like a snake," Elliott told William Peters, director of two documentaries and author of a book about the blue eyes, brown eyes exercise. "I knew what I should have done. I should have said the neighborhood was white but that she could come and look at the house if she were interested. But, of course, I hadn't." She added to the memory, "I had backed away from my principles out of fear of my neighbors' opinion. If we had rented to a Negro family and later wanted to move back, we would have had to face their anger. I saw that when the chips were down, I had not been able to face that. And I hated myself for it."[7]

Thirty-one years later, Jane still cited this phone call as the point when she reassessed her racial presumptions. When interviewed by Canadian columnist and broadcaster Fil Fraser for the *Edmonton Journal* in 1994, Jane said, "I knew I should have said yes. And I swore in that moment that I wouldn't do that again—that I would never compromise my principles again—not for money, not for popularity, not for acceptance, not even for my children and my husband."[8]

Alas, she found herself back in Riceville, a place self-proclaimed as the biggest little town in northern Iowa. Townspeople would soon question whether it was big enough to contain the Elliotts. At the moment, at least, Jane acquiesced to her fate. "And here we are, right back where we started," she said about the 1963 relocation in a 1979 biographical sketch found in the *Jane Elliott Papers* at the Iowa Women's Archives at the University of Iowa. "Four and a half miles," she had moved "in three and a half decades."[9]

* * *

Upon returning to her hometown, the Elliotts first moved into the Round Grove farmhouse, where they had the run of things until they found a house in town. The children—Sarah, Brian, Mary, and Mark, aged seven to eighteen months—enjoyed being confined to the country farm. Jane remembers her children enjoying fetching eggs from the chicken coop, running up and down the rolling hills, and living by unfamiliar rules that hardly matched what they were used to in Waterloo.[10] There was also a remarkable sense of familial obligation. Long ago, Lloyd taught Jane to rely on family as a safety net against life's unpredictable struggles. During family meals or talks around the coal-burning heater in the living room, Lloyd often told her: "If you're going to lie, don't lie to me."[11] It was a message that none of the Jennison children ever forgot. It also meant that if Jane heeded the warning, her father promised to be her insurance. The loving dynamic between Jane and Lloyd was important for her four children to see, despite how difficult it became to operate an inn together.

When Jane moved her family into a house on the corner of S. Pine and W. Eighth streets in Riceville—about eight blocks from the Jennison Inn—her father decided to demolish the Round Grove farmhouse. Jane considered this an affront to the family. To her, it was a structure that endured the turn of the century, two world wars, the Great Depression, and many family misfortunes.

At the time of publication, the property still belongs to the Jennison family, but it has been without a house for almost sixty years. Jane's eyes swelled with tears while conducting a tour of the property in 2021, and she lamented: "I listened to my little sister being born in that house. I listened to my little brother being born in that house. I watched my little sister die in that house. I watched my father mourn the loss of his father in that house. I watched my father mourn the loss of his daughter in that house. And I watched him bulldoze that house, and I was furious. I was born in that house, and I was raised in that house. It was like a shrine to me."[12] She hoped the house would become a shrine to her children. Seeing it bulldozed and covered with dirt only to be replaced by the inn was devastating.

* * *

For about twelve months, Jane was all about the Jennison Inn. Her daily routine consisted of a fast-paced morning spent grooming three children for school and tending to the needs of a growing toddler. Then off to the inn, where she and her mom bickered over the day's work. Darald, largely absent from the inn but contributing to its marketing strategy, worked full-time at the Oliver Farm Equipment Corporation plant in Charles City, Iowa, from the evening shift until eleven o'clock. He earned extra money stocking shelves at a grocery store in Mason City and as a part-time construction worker resurfacing roads in northern Iowa.

The family recognized that the only way to utilize the inn fully was to transform it into Riceville's social clubhouse. In addition to its ten boarding rooms and two apartment suites, the inn contained a large dining room and a basement turned into a conference room—the Elliotts called it the "Sodality Room," a name Gie chose for its roots in the Roman Catholic Church. Within the first week of assuming ownership, the Riceville Quarterback Club held its first meeting at the inn.[13] The local football program also used the inn to locate its post-game meals every Friday in the fall. To attract patrons, Jane sometimes offered specials on oyster soup or "Free coffee for all football Dads."

The QB club was not the only organization to make the Jennison Inn its regular meeting headquarters over the next decade. Many major community clubs, political campaign event organizers, wedding planners, and school officials immediately began paying rental fees to use the dining room or Sodality Room for events. The inn hosted meetings for cub scouts, the parent-teacher association, and veteran's groups in the evenings; the yard served for talent contests, picnics, holiday events, and fundraisers. The inn's Howard and Mitchell

County Homes Gift Giving Drive preceding Christmas in 1963 yielded great success in community participation. Gie brought in a large Christmas tree, and Jane asked Riceville area residents to donate gifts marked for a man or woman. In subsequent years, the drive would garner statewide media attention.[14]

However, these changes to how the Elliotts and Jennisons managed the inn were unsustainable. They needed regular guests to turn a profit. The ascent of the automobile made hotels and inns in small towns like Riceville nearly obsolete. Jane knew it: "In the days when the Burke girls had it and in the days when people went place to place in horse and buggy, that building made money." By the 1960s, she conceded, travelers in cars blew right by Riceville. A fancy restaurant, coffee bar, and meeting venue could not bring in the money needed to provide for four children. In April 1964, a concerned Jane marketed the Jennison Inn as a retirement home. She embarked on an advertising campaign in the local weekly announcing rooms for "elderly people" looking for a "friendly atmosphere" and a "home away from home."[15]

There was another side to this fortuitous endeavor. Allowing community patrons to rent space at the inn left Jane to reckon with the cultural traditions in her hometown at this time. While the building was under her proprietorship, one of Jane's most loyal patrons was the Riceville High School Quarterback Club. Her father and younger brothers, Jim and Steven, were all former halfbacks on the high school team. Darald played for a time at Boone High School. The club convinced fans and parents to dine at the inn every week after football games. Love for the game was in Jennison and Elliott's blood. Accordingly, Jane did not think twice about allowing the Quarterback Club to hold its annual "slave auction" on the property to raise money to pay off the debt owed for the school's new $1,800 scoreboard. During the fundraiser, the team's coach, John Klaudt, and his players paraded like enslaved persons onto the porch of the Jennison Inn. According to reports, the public then bid for one day's work, "doing whatever chores are desired of them, with the time and date of the work being agreed upon by both parties."[16]

Twentieth-century fundraisers that auctioned off people for chores were not occurrences restricted to Riceville. Neither was it a novel practice for the 1960s. Jane and her generation came of age when slave auction fundraisers were routine nationwide. While auctions existed in folk lifelong after the Civil War, it was during World War II that theaters, libraries, schools, churches, and other large venues brought communities together to bid on a "slave-for-the-day" as part of War Bond stunts. The organization hosting any auction would collect tens of thousands of dollars for the war.[17] The practice was promoted as an auction typical of those held in the days of the Roman Empire—a dismissal of the way American enslavers traded enslaved Africans before emancipation. It was common to see the auction begin with a procession of mock enslaved people into the venue, dressed in frayed clothing, or sometimes Roman attire, and a professional auctioneer presiding over the selling. On some occasions, teenage boys and girls were auctioned covered in burnt cork. During the era, coeds at colleges and universities held slave auction fundraisers in blackface.[18] Within a decade of World War II, the chance to sell "a slave's services for one day" to a "master" for anywhere from $1 to the highest bidder became a major moneymaker for public school booster clubs at homecoming rallies and general extracurricular activities. Some schools offered students points for participating in the auction.

It would not be until the 1970s when Black parents and the NAACP raised the issue about school-sanctioned auctions, proclaiming that the practice was "not only demeaning and degrading" for Black students and their families, "but it is unacceptable within the Constitution of the United States."[19] Even then, principals and parents commonly defended auctions as a part of a school's tradition that raised a lot of money, was fun for all, and should be left alone.

At this age, Jane was still naive. Even after the experience at Waterloo, she remained quiet on race matters. A town without a single Black person left her in an unfortunate predicament: Was her position that mock slave auctions were offensive to African Americans a radical one? To think that witnessing the fundraiser would erode the social development of adolescent and teenage children and increase already strained relations among color groups would label her as hypersensitive over the issue. To claim the practice poked fun at a national tragedy that tore families asunder, took lives in various ways, caused physical and mental torture, and was the cause of so many social, economic, and educational disparities might cost her business at the inn. Jane found herself yet again having to choose between calling out the racist antics of her peers or brushing the behavior aside, remaining willfully complicit. She chose the latter, as newspaper reports indicate the community school-related sports teams staged slave auction fundraisers at the Jennison Inn for several more years.[20] It would be the last time she made that mistake.

About a month later, Jane learned that her sister, Mary, and her husband, Keith Yager, were trying to adopt a child. Mary had taught second and third grade at the Riceville community school since 1951. The adoption agency told the couple they could not adopt if Mary worked. Acting accordingly, Mary tendered her resignation letter when the school year ended in 1964. Jane ended up applying for Mary's position. To win the job, Jane had to beat out Ruth Setka, a member of the Riceville Library Board and spouse to a World War II veteran.[21] The community adored Setka, an active Mitchell County American Legion member and substitute teacher.[22] Jane, however, was a Jennison, and the name afforded her social capital. In the interview, the superintendent said, "Well, if we're going to lose one Jennison, if I can gain another one, it'll be all right."[23] Jane accepted the job on the spot. Setka would get a full-time position teaching fifth grade in the RCS district the following year.[24]

While maintaining ownership and accounting responsibilities of the Jennison Inn, Jane turned over all other operations and decision-making to her mother. Jane and Darald would retain ownership rights for three more years before familial squabbles over Gie's business decisions grew too overbearing. After catching her mother taking money from the inn rather than logging it into the books, Jane said to her husband, "Darald, we gotta get out of this." Jane eventually attained a quitclaim deed from a lawyer, transferring the proprietorship to her parents. When the Elliotts and Jennisons finalized the transition three years later, legal records show Jane and Darald received $1000 from Lloyd for the inn. Years later, Jane stated she never received a penny from her parents. Her father, who demanded total honesty from his children, lied about the deed. Owning that hotel "was a dream that my mother had," Jane said.[25] So, she let her have it.

In the end, returning to education was best for her family. In the fall of 1964, after nine years out of the profession, Jane found herself back teaching the children of parents she once knew as schoolmates and others as diners at the Jennison Inn. Ask people anywhere in Riceville whom they want to teach their children to read, write, and do arithmetic. There are few doubts: Jane Elliott, daughter of Lloyd "Ginnie Gunfighter" and Margaret "Gie" Jennison, sister of well-reputed local educators Mary and Jean, and owner of the town's heartbeat—the Jennison Inn. Four years later, she would put that sentiment to the test.

PART TWO

USE

CHAPTER 8

EAGLE EYE

"I think part of education is having a child learning something about living beyond the textbook."

—JANE ELLIOTT, 1970

If the Jennison Inn was where Jane Elliott made herself the center of life in Riceville, the Riceville Community School (RCS) was where she became the most metaphoric. Since the autumn of 1964, Elliott was more than the standard elementary educator earning a yearly salary of less than $7,000 teaching third graders. Her focus became less on the family-owned hotel and more bent on building a teaching career so that she could earn enough money and her family would enjoy a comfortable existence. Simply put, the two men she most loved worked tirelessly. Elliott had had enough. She talked incessantly about the Riceville school, her children's education, and what was best for her community. If Elliott were a spokesperson for any cause in the mid-1960s, it would have been for a better Riceville.

RCS is where that movement began. In addition to teaching the third grade, she volunteered as an executive board member of the Riceville Parent-Teacher Association.[1] She organized trips departing from the Jennison Inn to support local political candidates. Her favorite at the time was Republican State Senator and former co-chairman of the "Citizens for Eisenhower" 1956 re-election campaign David M. Stanley who campaigned on "bring[ing] politics back to the people." Elliott admired how Stanley presented himself not as "these phony [*sic*], packaged candidates" but as one who went directly to the people and looked them "straight in the eye."[2] Perhaps most importantly, she accepted the role of being the one teacher in all of Riceville to be certified in remedial reading: the town had a great need to teach dyslexic children how to read, spell, and write. Elliott's decision to earn a remedial reading certification was completely innocent. In fact, the issue was personal to her.

Walking home from the Jennison Inn one day during the summer of 1966, Marie Nicoll, a parent of a rising third-grade RCS student, caught her attention. "I've asked that my son, Jeff, be placed in your classroom this year," said Nicoll. "Okay. Why?" Elliott asked Nicoll. "Because I know that you're not going to abuse him. He is dyslexic. He doesn't hear words the way they are said. He doesn't see words the way they are written. He is very bright, but because he has trouble with words, he has trouble with teachers." Marie and her husband, Howard, a veterinarian, had decided to take their son to the dyslexia reading center in Rochester, Minnesota, three nights a week. "They will teach him how to read," Marie told Elliott. "All you have to do is read the material to him that he needs to know, but they will teach him to read," she added, to which Elliott replied, "Okay, I can do that."

Their son, Jeff, arrived in Elliott's class as a shy, overly sensitive, and withdrawn young boy covered head to toe in psoriasis. Young Jeff was constantly stressed out, and it caused rashes to consume his body. He would tuck himself into a ball whenever Jane asked him a question. "He was scared to death all the time," Elliott said many years later. Jeff's teachers beat him in kindergarten, first, and second grade. "That kid was accustomed to being struck for not giving the right answers by teachers who didn't know how to teach him. It wasn't that he didn't know how to learn. He knew how to learn, but not the way he was being taught."[3]

The experience of learning about Jeff's struggles caused by dyslexia made Elliott think about her son, Brian. In the fall of 1966, Brian and Jeff were both RCS third graders. Brian was enrolled in the third-grade classroom across the hall from Elliott's classroom in Room 10. He always struggled in school and acquired a reputation as a behavior problem. His teacher often used the trapezius squeeze to get him to sit still. The teacher's lack of patience with Brian rubbed off on the other students. At the end of school, Brain's peers would tell the teacher what Brian did wrong during the day. None of this, Elliott said, "is going to make a dyslexia person hear better or see words better. It's just going to make that person less inclined to raise his hand or to open his mouth in anything but in a way that will get him some kind of attention."[4] Elliott realized her son's emotional and behavioral problems were secondary and an outgrowth of frustration and failure. It took some arm twisting, but Elliott transferred Brian into her class after the first quarter.

Brian was talented in other areas, his favorite being math. He was always fascinated with earth-moving equipment, which would eventually become his life's work. He could intellectually engage with his teachers and peers in discussions outside high-pressure situations, on the playground, and in other social settings. However, conventional teaching methods did not reach him, and anything related to reading was a struggle. As an unassuming eight-year-old, Brian hardly perceived things as they were. He read words like "saw" as "was" and "button" as "nottub." Brian read right to left and wrote letters backward. He was often confused, lacked confidence, and was embarrassed before his classmates. Brian's teachers' short patience only made his aversion to school worse. Elliott, though not until after teaching Jeff Nicoll, realized Brian's teachers weren't reaching her son, not because they didn't know the material they were assigned to teach, but because they didn't know what was going on in her son's mind. They could not differentiate instruction to meet the student's learning differences, and Elliott hated seeing Brian's teachers abusing him.

Dyslexia is a neurological disorder that cruelly tricks children by making it difficult for them to learn to read. Helping students with dyslexia and other reading differences was a top priority for Jane Elliott in her teaching career. Generations of preservice teachers had gone through their respective standard education without ever learning about dyslexia. What was the result? Teachers often labeled children with dyslexia as lazy, immature, emotionally disturbed, disrespectful, and culturally deprived. Inspired by advances made during the civil rights movement, people with disabilities and parents of children with learning differences began voicing grievances against schools and other institutions that excluded or minimized people from their community. At the center of the disability rights movement was the drive to find approaches in schools to better serve the needs of students with learning disabilities. Under Elliott, RCS started to pay close attention to "learning difference," as she preferred to call reading disorders.

Because of her proactive maneuvering to introduce the school to a teaching approach that could mitigate failure and misbehavior from dyslexic students, the *Riceville Recorder* ran a two-column article on the topic. The piece laid out in precision indicators of dyslexic children: "The dyslexic child may be either left-handed or ambidextrous, and there is probably a family history of left-handedness or ambidexterity. Dyslexia is inherited, so a pattern of reading difficulty is evident in the family background of the dyslexic child." The column claimed dyslexia is not a disorder indicating low IQ, going as far as to name Thomas Edison, Sir Isaac Newton, and Henry Ford as examples of successful men with dyslexia. The *Recorder* included statistics showing that 10 percent of all children likely had the disability. Dyslexia was the reported leading cause of juvenile delinquency and school dropouts. "It cannot be cured," the paper reported after speaking with Elliott, "but once a child is diagnosed as having dyslexia, he can learn to read and achieve at a rate commensurate with his IQ."[5]

The idea of educating RCS instructors in strategies to teach dyslexic students came to Elliott in January 1967 after a successful first semester with Brian and Jeff. She went to the principal about bringing to Riceville Paula Rome, the Director of the Rochester Dyslexia Clinic in Rochester, Minnesota. Rome, an expert on best practices, agreed to speak about the institute's reading program for dyslexic children called the Orton-Gillingham approach. The instructional method, named after psychiatrist Anna Gillingham and neuropathologist Samuel Orton and rooted in the medical field, involves teachers instructing small cohorts of students using a card pack. Students are trained to read, write, and spell using a combination of visual, verbal, tactile, and kinesthetic symbols presented in the card pack, as well as instruction in vowels, vowel teams, consonants, consonant blends, and spelling. The teacher begins by having students repeat parts of words, then goes to whole words, phrases, and sentences. Because of Elliott's advocacy, every teacher in the district, kindergarten through twelfth grade, had to attend a workshop held at the RCS Elementary School multipurpose room to listen to Rome's foundational explanation of the remedial reading method.[6]

Not everyone was happy about the professional learning session. One of the high school shop teachers said loud enough for Elliott to hear: "I don't know why we have to listen to this just because one teacher's kid has a problem."[7]

Elliott laughed it off. "That woman was brought in so everybody could look at kids with a new point of view. So, they could see a kid that was obviously smart but wasn't able to read or spell, and say to themselves, 'There is a reason for this. Instead of me calling this kid lazy, or dumb, or not listening, I'm going to see what it is that causes this child to have this problem, and then I'm going to teach to that problem.'"[8]

Elliott believed Rome's ideas could reframe how Riceville's educators instructed children with learning differences. After the meeting, she read the latest literature and decided to train in the Orton-Gillingham remedial reading method. After approaching Superintendent Donald Johnston, Elliott was paid to attend Rome's three-week train-the-trainer certification program at the Remedial Reading Center in Rochester, Minnesota, in July of 1967. Marlene Dillon, a graduate of Luther College and former teacher who previously taught in Los Angeles, California, and Augusta, Georgia, tagged along because of her interest in education and as a concerned parent. The program was titled "Remedial Training for Children with Specific Language Disability." Elliott returned to Riceville at the end of the month and offered to teach the novel approach to her colleagues.[9] She thought giving their colleagues the basics of the pedagogical framework was important. The initiative aimed to identify dyslexic children before emotional problems prevail, which could eventually lead to underachievement and poor behavior. "No longer need the non-reader be shuttled from grade to grade, imprisoned until he is 16 in a world in which he cannot be successful," wrote the *Recorder* of Elliott's work at RCS. "Now, he can be successful if he receives the proper training."[10] Only two teachers signed up for her professional development workshop on teaching dyslexic students.

At the start of the 1967-1968 school year, most dyslexic students were funneled into Elliott's classroom.

* * *

The Orton-Gillingham approach aligns with the pedagogy of active learning that Elliott learned at the Iowa State Teachers College fifteen years earlier. Based on the writings of John Dewey, she held fast to this Deweyan philosophical approach to teaching that aims to cultivate thoughtful, reflective, and socially engaged learners through community-based, exploratory, and hands-on activities that draw upon students' emotional reactions to the world. At the moment, RCS was a battle between two pedagogical education systems. The "traditionalist" group belonged to an old order that classified education through uncritical acceptance of information and rote memorization. Traditionalist beneficiaries learn content, but its opponents believe the method falls short of teaching learners how to think, nor does it empower students to actively participate in the collective learning process. Thus, the Dewey school, or "Progressives," prime learners at all levels to look beyond standard or universal solutions for the world, take the world as they find it, and educate themselves through personal experience and experimentation. This approach sees the world "not as a created one, but as a creative one," as one Dewey scholar put it, and that everyone is one of the world's creators. Indeed, even eight and nine-year-old third graders can thrive in that democratized learning environment. A Deweyan classroom is "a democracy of intellect if you will, and that every human being should have an equal chance of sharing in its benefits."[11]

For these reasons, Elliott considered traditional teaching methods appallingly weak and ineffective for all students, especially for those with learning differences. In Dewey's *Democracy and Education*, one of her anchor texts at the Iowa State Teachers College, she learned that children must not be educated merely with "remembrances of things past" or with "esthetic" conceptions of science, art, literature, and history. Rather, students must react to their environment in order to actively learn how to problem solve. In Dewey's opinion, the world is the object of all learning. The child should be in that world, which becomes the classroom to learn from personal experiences and trial and error, not merely from teachers' lips expounding curricular content. Education aims to teach children how to think, what to do, how to do it best in their environs, and how to do it according to their ability.[12]

Elliott's student-teaching experience in 1952 at Hawthorne School in Independence reinforced Dewey's active learning pedagogy. Her cooperating teacher, Hazel Grant, modeled cooperative competition, a Deweyan byproduct empowering students to challenge one another to execute practical learning tasks while earning incentive points. Grant taught her students the mathematical skills of addition, subtraction, multiplication, and vision. She reinforced reading skills taught in earlier grades while introducing complex and irregularly spelled words. However, to assess learning, Grant allowed her students to create skits, puppet shows, and other projects that entertained or enhanced the learning environment at Hawthorne. Elliott found particularly compelling Grant's method of awarding her students points for personal hygiene, preparedness, organizational skills, leadership, and content learning.

The theoretical study of Dewey and her trial-and-error cooperative praxis as a young teacher enabled Elliott's pedagogics to take root as an elementary teacher in Riceville. She bewildered the school. Some of her colleagues liked her methods, while others demurred. Nevertheless, if she had the support of the principal and district superintendent, Elliott pressed forward in the challenge of education's great myth: learning is not the result of teaching, she believed. Learning is a result of doing.

One describes Elliott's teaching style as experiential pedagogy. This instructional praxis contains four foundational tenets: Wanting to learn is the most important ingredient of the learning process. As such, teachers must possess a practical mind to create a curriculum that meets the needs and interests of students. The second is engaging students in the act of "doing." Because a laboratory is an on-your-feet, mobile research and development process, students must be free to talk with one another to discuss and argue the learning task among themselves. It gets noisy, and, depending on the task, it could get dirty. Turning the classroom into a laboratory grants agency to the learner, thus sparking interest because the student becomes invested in the learning objective. Third, students need to reflect on what they produce. They should probe, study, and adjust as they work. In this sense, the thinking and the doing never stop; the student stays engaged in the activity from start to finish. The teacher is responsible for providing customized performance feedback to make this work. Fourth, students use teacher feedback to make improvements to the learning task. The assessment is not based on students answering questions a teacher wants them to know for a final exam and memorizing that information. Instead, assessments are open-ended, and there is no "right" answer to the important curricular questions in a lesson plan or unit. The more freely students disagree the more knowledge they gain to perfect a learning task.

Elliott asserted that none of this can work if teachers place low expectations on students and deny them the learning opportunities all students deserve. It is common, she contended, to see "teachers and administrators decide as early as the kindergarten level which students are going to succeed and which students are going to fail."[13] Her cardinal rules:

- Do not label students as incompetent, lazy, or disinterested
- Do not let your students get bored
- Find out what your students are interested in and modify the curriculum accordingly
- Do not penalize mistakes
- Apply the learning task to the school community.

She could ensure authentic learning by creating an experiential environment that wrapped students up in their emotions. Students will see that authentic learning occurs only when emotionally invested in the lesson.

This was an early form of social-emotional learning. Elliott was ahead of her time; she primed her students for experiential learning by placing Orton-Gillingham phonics at the heart of her pedagogy. She aimed to get her students reading at or above grade level. Her classroom routine carved out time to give dyslexic students extra attention, including using sound, sight, and feeling associations that helped those children pronounce letters and words properly and to see words correctly. Elliott's primary teaching tool was a card pack manufactured by Orton-Gillingham consisting of ninety-five cards containing the basic sounds of the English language. Elliott's students learned each word sound by articulating a letter or letter combination aloud, then looking at it and using a finger to trace it on the card or in a tray of sand simultaneously. She also characterized it as the "sound-symbol" method. For example, when teaching the letter "a" Elliott would teach the short sound first, then provide a word like "at" so students could associate the sound with a word. She would then move to a long vowel sound, followed by a word: "came." The exercise would end with a broad sound and a word like "about" to match the sound. The repetition would go: "æ," "Ā," "ah," "at," "came," and "about." Students traced each letter and letter combination the whole time, and the word sounded out.

Meanwhile, Elliott was talented at mimicking her student's preferential use of a dominant hand. While right-handed, she often used her non-dominant hand when working with left-handed students. There is a moment in *The Eye of the Storm*, the 1970 documentary about the Blue Eyes/Brown Eyes Exercise with her third-grade students—sixteen of whom were dyslexic—when Elliott draws cursive *W*s on the chalkboard with one of her left-handed students. Since the action of writing on the chalkboard seems insignificant to the film's narrative, the moment is overlooked. However, that interaction is essential to recognize how Elliott thrived at meeting students where they were when providing individual attention. "I have to write the way he does to understand why his writing is different from my own," she said proudly. "If I wrote right-handed, that wouldn't help him at all. He has to see someone write with their left hand in order for him to realize that it's all right to do it, and that he can do it, and that it can be legible."[14]

Elliott's doubters never ceased attempts to discredit dyslexia as a legitimate learning difference. She would counter with her typical cleverness: "If you had a child in your classroom who had only one leg, you would teach him to run in a different way," she illustrated. "But when you have children in the classroom who do not hear words the way they are said or see words the way they are written, you act as if they all hear and see everything the same. It's not fair. It's not right. It's not professional."[15]

By 1978, Elliott was one of the United States' leading proponents of educating teachers to deal with the dyslexic child. She received sustained training through the Rome Remedial Reading Center in Rochester and became a spokesperson for the Orton Dyslexia Society (ODS) of Cambridge, Massachusetts (later renamed the International Dyslexia Association). In her role as ODS spokesperson, Elliott cited research conducted by dyslexia research founding father Samuel Orton. Dyslexia, she told educators, "is not a sight problem. Many people believe it is a sight problem. There is nothing wrong with the dyslexic's eyes. Dyslexia is a physiological problem."

A warning sign for dyslexia in children is having one left-handed parent. Elliott argued that dyslexia is related to ambidextrous children developing a complex called "handedness." She said, "Handedness has to do with which hemisphere of the brain becomes dominant. Language is controlled by one or the other side of the brain. If dominance over language is not established in one or the other hemisphere, it becomes confused. The person's language function becomes jumbled."[16] For these reasons and her personal experiences as a mother of a dyslexic child, wife to an undiagnosed dyslexic husband, daughter to a dyslexic father, and teacher of dyslexic students, Elliott warned that teachers needed to receive training to educate dyslexic children. "These children are required to be in school, but no teacher is required to teach them correctly." She always found that problematic.

* * *

Through the front door of RCS Elementary, to the right of the lobby, down the corridor, and on the left was Room 10, Jane Elliott's classroom—the center of progressive learning for the school's most challenging pupils. Her routine was essential to maintain the structure of the class. She arrived each day by 7:30 in the morning. That gave her one hour to finish grading papers from the previous day before students started appearing. She also used that time to finalize lesson plans, ensuring they were polished and displayed on her desk if the principal visited unannounced. Tired and sluggish students walked into Room 10 at half past eight.

Then came her favorite part of the day: the first matter of business was for row leaders to collect points for having clean desks, sharpened pencils, and a handkerchief. It was the same disciplinary tactic employed by her mentor, Hazel Grant. Moreover, Elliott executed it each day to perfection for her twenty-year tenure at RCS. The rows had to be straight, desks were clean, pencils were sharp, and each child needed a handkerchief. "There's nothing less appetizing or more disruptive than kids who have runny noses at the third-grade level," she said of those students who used their sleeves to wipe the snot from their upper lip. It was almost mechanical: four rows, each with a row leader for a week, who checked to make sure everyone in the row met regulations. The row leader then tallied the points on the chalkboard. At the end of the week, students in the row with the most points enjoyed the gratifying moment when reaching into the grab bag, a paper sack filled with little writing tablets, erasers, pencils, staples, paperclips, and anything else Elliott purchased from the Five & Dime store.[17]

After the Pledge of Allegiance, she led the class in a daily rendition of "God Bless America." Both acts, which she saw as a constitutional violation of the separation of church and state, irked her. Nevertheless, she did them with a smile before issuing out the daily reminder to her students about proper "listening skills." "Good listeners have quiet hands, feet, and mouths," she would begin. "Good listeners keep their eyes on the person who is speaking. Good listeners listen from the beginning to the very end. Good listeners decide to learn something."[18]

Now that everyone was ready to learn, Elliott led her students in poetry reading. By the end of the school year, the students could recite over fifty poems written by Elizabeth Madox Roberts, Ogden Nash, and Joyce Kilmer. Poetry was her way of harnessing a love for the English language.

Next on her daily plan was reading class. She split her class into stations. Students rotated from desk work to the Orton-Gillingham sound pack of cards. The reading lesson lasted about half an hour. Advanced students spent most of the time doing work from the textbook. Her severely dyslexic students were often seated at a reading table of five to seven peers, where Elliott guided them through the card pack. Then it was time for art before recess. After the break, Elliott taught spelling and handwriting. After lunch and another recess, students returned to Room 10 for arithmetic. A third recess was followed by science or social studies. Time was spent executing one of her active learning projects: human-sized papier-mâché dinosaur making, indigenous peoples' material culture sewing projects, Arbor Day tree planting, and more—usually long-term ventures that went on for several days. She designated a segment of the afternoon class for discussion and activities about Room 10's ongoing thematic discussions about the great citizens of the United States that she called "Heroes of the Month." Then students lined up to go home. The day was long but fast-paced. After seven hours with eight and nine-year-olds, Elliott was contracted to remain at school for an hour. She typically used that time to clean the room and prepare for the next day. Sometimes she could get a head start on grading papers.[19]

A former student, Ray Hansen, who became an estate planning attorney in Rochester, Minnesota, confided years later that Elliott's teaching method was "highly exciting, highly energetic." Her patience and skill in working with dyslexic children no one else wanted to deal with engendered a liking for formal schooling. "Imagine someone who now enthuses you about education in a way that you've never been excited before," Hansen conceptualized. "A teacher that shows you that you are as good a student as anybody else in your class—not just your classroom but your class—and does it with lots of participatory learning styles inspires students to give their best effort. She was probably the educator that taught me *I could* [succeed]."[20]

Classroom activities like catching insects brought life to the learning experience. In September, students brought broomsticks, pillowcases, needles, and coat hangers to make insect nets. Elliott instructed them to cut and sew the pillowcase so it would make a cone shape. They then threaded it onto the coat hanger before attaching it to the broomstick. Each student had to go outside to catch as many insects as possible. After placing the insects in a jar, alcohol-soaked into a cotton ball, "put them to sleep," said Elliott.[21] Students would pin the insects according to charts she provided earlier in the day so the bugs could be further studied. In the food unit, students learned the trades of a dairy farmer. Elliott's oldest brother, Charles, a trained dairy technician, often helped teach the children food science technology. Trips to the local creamery were followed by time spent in class learning how to churn cream into butter and make ice cream. A reenactments of Paul Revere's 1775 ride had one student running through the hallway yelling, "The British are coming!" She also created an adopt-a-grandparent program with her students and the retirement home nearby.

A classroom activity met with approval by all of Elliott's students was the clothing unit's Room 10 Store project. For years, timed for the Christmas season, her third graders ran a store out of the classroom "so that the kids could go Christmas shopping for their brothers and sisters and parents," she said. To stock the store, students first donated their used clothing. Soon students not enrolled in her class brought in merchandise for the store, including toys and board games they no longer needed. Elliott did not accept everything the kids—or their parents—wanted to discard. Her policy was that everything needed to be "in good shape, was clean, and had all of its buttons and no tears." The item must be "something someone else would want to buy."[22]

Elliott created Room 10 money as the only form of currency someone could use to buy something from the classroom store. The easy flow of fake currency taught the students lessons about financial transactions. Concerns about students stealing fake money from one another caused Elliott to construct a Room 10 Bank in the corner of the room. Since there was now a bank, she taught the students how to keep a checkbook. When a student brought an item into school to her approval, Elliott would pay them in Room 10 money. She marked up each item a third to gain a return on money to pay overhead expenses. She worked closely with students to do the math to mark the merchandise up a third. Elliott recalled, "We'd put the labels on the clothes, we'd rack 'em up and stack 'em up and set up a store on the side of the room." The principal joined students in a ribbon-cutting ceremony at the store's grand opening. Years later, she reflected on the project:

It was absolutely wonderful because here these kids were buying clothes. These little girls were buying clothes that the taller littler girls had already worn. We put up a cardboard dressing room made out of refrigerator boxes, and kids would try on those clothes, and they'd come out, and they'd say, "What do you think of this, Mrs. Elliott?" And I'd say, "I think that's just great, and it fits you and it really looks good." Then someone else would say, "You look better in that than I did." I was so delighted.[23]

The idea for the Room 10 Store came to her amidst the energy bottleneck following the Organization of Arab Petroleum Exporting Countries' embargo of oil targeting the United States and other countries supporting Israel during the Yom Kippur War. To teach her students about the national debate over the oil crisis and why their parents had to wait in long lines to put gasoline in their automobiles, Elliott thought the Room 10 Store could teach her students one way of alleviating the energy problem. The concept resembled her elementary school experience when, in 1944, she aided the war effort by collecting milkweed pods to manufacture life preservers and aviation jackets for service members. The milkweed drive became a schoolwide competition that carried a monetary incentive. Like her personal experience, Elliott's experiential activity aimed to show her students that they could recycle those still usable instead of discarding used items for something new. The store's motto: "Make it do! Wear it out! Use it up!" modified the famous World War II saying, "Use it Up, Wear It Out, Make it Do, or Do Without."

Much to her surprise, a byproduct of getting her students to problem-solve during the energy crisis led to a collaboration with the management of the *Riceville Recorder*, the town's local newspaper, and the Mitchell County Press News Office in Osage, Iowa. Elliott established a classroom activity that reinforced recycling concepts using scrap paper and leftover felt from both newspaper offices to make decorative gift labels for Christmas wrapping. "[W]e cut out shapes," she remembered. "Christmas shapes: a big black boot, a Christmas tree out of green, a Christmas ball. We pasted the shapes on the front of the card, and the kids wrote haiku poems for the greeting on the inside."[24] The festive Christmas tags were then packaged twelve to a pack and sold by the students to raise money for other classroom projects.[25]

Elliott would tell interviewers years later: "Every year that I taught, we did something that made no sense at all to anybody else, but it made perfect sense to my students because they learned so much."[26] One thing that left her RCS Elementary colleagues bewildered was Elliott's field trips. Over the years of teaching in Riceville, Elliott arranged trips to companies, rural schoolhouses, and farms around town to give students culturally relevant experiences ranging from making cheese to seeing how the printing press works. On a few occasions, she arranged overnight trips to the Jennison Inn to teach her students about constellations. Those trips, according to Elliott, were usually coupled with cooking lessons.

Jane Elliott gained the trust of her students not just with her innovation as an instructor but how she created time and space for students to share their concerns about any issue ranging from something that happened in class to a problem at home. Room 10's mission was to get students reading at the fourth-grade reading level by the end of the school year. However, its mission was also to help those young children manage their behavior and become confident members of the larger school community. Whether students could feel like they belonged anywhere else in the building, she strove to create a sense of acceptance for everyone inside her classroom walls. Accordingly, she proactively addressed out-of-school problems that may affect a child's in-school learning. This is why she came up with the practice of the "Magic Circle."

In the twenty-first century, educators might call Elliott's Magic Circle a precursor to restorative practices. This approach provides a way to build community while intervening with individual problems or classroom issues that surface daily. Room 10's Magic Circle helped students feel comfortable sharing what was on their minds. Elliott, in return, talked *with* her students rather than *at* them. "We did the 'Magic Circle' whenever a problem arose that needed the input from everyone. Whatever you expressed in the moment was acceptable, as were the responses to what you expressed," she recalled. To outsiders, this approach seemed to consume a lot of class time, taking away from curricular learning. For Elliott, the Magic Circle's face-to-face, transparent communication style was needed to build a sense of community inside Room 10 for those low-achieving third graders. She declared: "What was said in the Circle stayed in the circle."[27]

A few years into her career at RCS Elementary, Elliott invented a source of amusement during moments of malaise. Pizzui, Room 10's imaginary gremlin that caused all kinds of spontaneous mischief in the classroom, became her method of generating excitement and intrigue during those inevitable moments of maladaptive daydreaming. When squirrels ran on the rooftop above Room 10, Elliott blamed it on Pizzui. When she misplaced a ruler, the mischievous gremlin took it. When a student became unruly, she used the threat of the omnipresent sprite to summon order.

Elliott was ahead of her time as an educator. However, her teaching style created a dysfunctional work environment. According to her recollection, substantiated by testimonies of former colleagues and students, RCS Elementary teachers contended that her unconventional teaching methods were unprofessional. They also thought she was domineering. One journalist wrote that her colleagues said she possessed an "oversized personality and ego" and that "She didn't seem to care much about getting along with the other teachers." According to RCS Superintendent Dean Weaver, the schism between Elliott and her coworkers was worth it. Weaver told author Stephen Bloom, "She got her kids thinking beyond boundaries, and other teachers got intimidated by her success. She challenged her kids. She'd just go ahead and do things. They were the kind of activities that gave administrators—and custodians—gray hair."[28]

The longest-running curricular activity in Room 10 during any given school year was Elliott's "Heroes of the Month." With an objective to help her third graders discover the history and impact of American heroes, Elliott introduced her students to figures like George Washington, George Herman "Babe" Ruth, Abraham Lincoln, Rev. Dr. Martin Luther King, Jr., and Davy Crockett. Her lessons and activities about overcoming hardships, similar to how the students were overcoming dyslexia, were among the first that introduced them to these figures. One of Elliott's strokes of genius was figuring out that her third-grade students could develop a love of the country's diversity by using the stories of American icons. Elliott would pin the image of each figure to the class calendar at the beginning of the month. Five minutes of class were designated daily for discussing the hero. The objective was to create a stream of biographical profiles that would act as a catalyst, inspiring eight and nine-year-olds to be as interested in the people that shaped the country as they were in Room 10's mischief-maker, Pizzui.[29]

* * *

Room 10's hero of the month in February 1967 was the civil rights icon who championed dismantling of the Jim Crow system in the South years earlier. Each year, she timed the study of Martin Luther King Jr. to the month that observed National Brotherhood Week. That year, "Brotherhood Week" was scheduled for February 19 through February 26 and traditionally marked several days of programs designed to reinforce the message of religious and ethnic tolerance. Elliott sketched a learning activity for the King social studies unit based on something she read in Leon Uris's Holocaust novel *Mila 18*. Elliott considered using eye color to divide her students in a manufactured environment privileging one group while alienating the other as the Nazis had done to Jewish prisoners. In the drafted lesson plan, Elliott would make students with brown eyes the superior group while placing blue and green-eyed students at the nadir of Room 10's hierarchy. She thought the classroom would become segregated, the front of the room zoned for the upper-class, brown-eyed children, and the back turned into a blue and green-eyed ghetto. Elliott planned to give brown-eyed students all the curricular and disciplinary privileges. She eventually decided against teaching the lesson that year.

Deciding against untested hands-on learning activities was not uncommon for Elliott. It is easy to determine why she may have ruled out an idea for a lesson. However, the rumor that she originally planned the eye color exercise in 1967 presents new insight into the origin of Jane Elliott's famous lesson on discrimination. In a discussion with Bertram Verhaag found in unpublished footage for the 1995 *Blue Eyed* documentary, Elliott revealed she planned on doing the exercise with her 1966-1967 third graders.[30] The motivations for the exercise in 1967 were plenty. While it is true that urban riots plagued the country for years before that winter, news about the federal grand jury investigation into the 1964 slayings of three civil rights workers—Andrew Goodman, 20, Michael Schwerner, 24, and James Chaney, 21—predominated the headlines during National Brotherhood Week. While he had not yet given his "A Time to Break the Silence" speech, it was no secret that Martin Luther King Jr. maneuvered that February to convince civil rights leaders to accept a leading role in protesting the Vietnam War. In particular, King pressured Rev. James Bevel, director of the newly formed Spring Mobilization Committee to End the War in Vietnam, to manufacture a coalition between anti-war groups on the East and West Coasts with the Southern Christian Leadership Conference. Though it is unclear how informed Elliott was on these issues then, the stories were all over Iowa newspapers and evening news channels. For anyone who read as much as she did, there was no missing the headlines.

Verhaag failed to probe her revelation in 1995. Maybe she lacked the courage to answer questions from her parents. If too many complained, was she worried about losing her job or tanking business at the Jennison Inn? Alternatively, it may be because her son, Brian, was one of the students in her class. Is it possible she thought the exercise would be too much for dyslexic children?

Unlike every other hero of the month, Dr. King was still alive, but "frustration marked the civil rights front," as journalist Henry P. Leifermann put it. King was among several social justice leaders who drifted from a movement that conveyed a message of harmony among racialized color groups in the United

States toward one that expressed Black pride and called to undo inequality anywhere it existed. That is to say, the civil rights movement of a bygone era was limited to the South, where the prevailing apartheid state separated people by the color of their skin in all public places and transportation. The Black Power movement of the second half of the 1960s, however, targeted housing, jobs, and policing. The nonviolent direct-action shift toward Black Power began after the turbulent Watts uprising in August 1965 and later enhanced in June 1966 following the non-fatal shooting of James Meredith. In the case of the former, Watts residents rejected a visit by Dr. King. Then, after appearing in Mississippi while Meredith recovered, twenty-four-year-old SNCC chairman Stokely Carmichael challenged King to move beyond "love and moral suasion" at a rally in Greenfield, Mississippi.[31] "We been saying freedom for six years, and we ain't got nothin'. What we got to start saying now is black power! We want black power!"[32] Carmichael later co-authored a book titled *Black Power: The Politics of Liberation in America.* Two college students in Oakland, California, founded the Black Panther Party for self-defense a few months later. White anxiety over a proliferating message aimed at empowering Black citizens and where Dr. King positioned himself in that movement intensified the following year.

In 1967, violent clashes between Black citizens and law enforcement officials in more than 150 nationwide cities failed to win over fans of the movement in Riceville. In Miami, police chief Walter E. Headley infamously uttered: "When the looting starts, the shooting starts."[33] Six days of upheaval in Detroit resulted in the bloodiest confrontation since the 1863 New York City draft riots. Governor George W. Romney's order to call in Michigan Army National Guard troops escalated the conflict. Over one hundred square miles of the city and 2,509 buildings were damaged. More than seven thousand people were arrested. Forty-three people in the city died, and another 1,189 were injured. The summer of turbulence in 1967 became known as the "long, hot summer."[34]

That July, a similar degree of upheaval plagued Jane Elliott's former hometown of Waterloo. Between July 7 and 10, parts of the city's east side went in flames as community members vented frustrations over excessive policing and broken legislative and occupational promises. Protesters destroyed property in Waterloo and resisted the mobilized presence of local and state law enforcement. A year earlier, when twenty-three-year-old Eddie Wallace Sallis—a Black inmate arrested on a charge of intoxication—hung himself in a city jail cell, hostilities between the city's Black residents and the police commenced.[35] Black leaders (including Anna Mae Weems) accused authorities of using excessive force against Sallis during the arrest. Compounded grievances against local police were the fact that no motivation ever surfaced for why Sallis took his life. Frustrations also existed in the industrial center of Waterloo. Specifically, the Johnson Administration's experimental jobs training agency, known as the Iowa State Manpower Development Council, failed to act on its promise to collaborate with local unions to recruit Black memberships, which would have made them eligible for contractual work. Unemployment remained high among Waterloo's 6,000 Black residents. Black unemployment was almost four times the rate for whites at that time. Thus, when police arrested a Black resident accused of stealing hubcaps on Friday evening, July 7, the predominantly Black neighborhood east of the Cedar River exploded.[36] Warren Nash, a physician and then president of the NAACP's local chapter, tried calming the crowd but was "pushed around by the police" attempting to establish peace. Other community leaders also expressed that police prevented their intervention efforts to quiet the situation.

There was too much frustration over inaction on "The usual things: housing, employment, right down the line." Nash told reporters. "housing, employment, right down the line." Most of the disturbances occurred near the business district along 4th Street, according to police reports, claiming it was the focal point of "looting, window breaking, and burning and rock throwing."[37] Clashes between law enforcement, numbering upwards of eighty-five officers equipped with riot gear, continued for four days. The worst evening of disturbances was July 9, when clashes between patrolmen and Black residents erupted near Lincoln Park, eight blocks from City Hall. Newspaper reports indicated that eight to ten fires blazed in the area, two cars were overturned, and rock throwers damaged a fire truck. Five persons were jailed, and three were hospitalized with severe injuries.[38] White store owners in the area who opened the following day vowed to use force to protect themselves if threatened. An uneasy truce was settled on July 11 after the mayor announced a curfew for the east side and used police to seal off ten blocks of the neighborhood. Police Chief Robert S. Wright blamed the weekend uprising on "One hundred young hoods."[39]

King's response to the unrest of 1967 was confronting the same problems of housing discrimination, class disparities, and job creation that rocked Waterloo. The aid of Rev. Ralph Abernathy, King, and the Southern Christian Leadership Conference announced the coming of a nonviolent protest in Washington, D.C. It was called the "poor people's campaign for jobs and income." He said the indefinite occupation of the Washington Mall would begin in September 1968. "We are completely restructuring our staff, and the programs the S.C.L.C. and the modern civil rights movement began more than a decade ago as a struggle to end legal segregation in the South," the Nobel Peace Prize recipient stated. "The challenge to us and our battles ahead now looms as a more difficult, long-term struggle for human rights both at home and abroad."[40] (The last part of that sentence was a nod to his recent public condemnation of the Johnson administration's Vietnam policy).

King spoke of an attitude revolution in an open letter on New Year's Day, 1968. "The possibility of full equality for the Negro rests on the ability of the United States to cope with racism," he wrote. Speaking indignantly about "racism running rampant through our institutional structure," King understood that each institution possesses its own culture—a culture that "assumes intense racial overtones" and is established by the people that make up the institution. He contended that once the nation admits African Americans "are in no way responsible for their predicament, and [leaders] determine to deal with poverty, joblessness, slums, and ill health" through government-funded healthcare services, the country could not live up to its founding democratic promise. King believed institutional racism was the prevailing problem on the eve of his death in 1968. However, problems of policy and traditional practice would never change if policymakers lacked respect for persons of color and people with low incomes. His dual approach—linking the treatment of Black people with the poor—and call to conscience was the only formula capable of producing the end of disenfranchisement and exploitation.

> This respect would inevitably lead to fulfillment of the rights to share in the ownership of property, management of community institutions (schools, hospitals, trade boards, transportation authorities, etc.), and representation at every level of decision-making. Mass participation by the poor is an absolute prerequisite for full equality.[41]

Jane Elliott fancied King's concept of an attitude metamorphosis. After reading King's words and studying his movements, and reading books like *Mila 18* about the Nazi genocidal attack on Europe's Jewish population, and Harry Golden's *Only in America* and *For Two Cents Plain*, and after thinking about her treatment as the bastard of the Jennison family, she possessed strong emotions about discrimination.[42] She believed that views about race, like everything else, were due to exposure—that people learn about racism by what society imports. People become living confirmations of that social curriculum.

As a youth, she rarely (if ever) saw a living Black person in her hometown, yet she saw white people in blackface. She had heard the N-word and other racial and ethnic slurs. RCS High School held mock slave auctions. Her colleagues dismissed and sometimes poked fun at young children with learning differences, including those who teased her son, Brian. There were times when she participated in such transgressions. The combination of emotionally investing in the lives of severely dyslexic children while studying and subsequently teaching those same children about the bravery of Martin Luther King, Jr. led her out of ignorance. It was a revolution of attitude, indeed.

When questioned by a documentarian years later, Elliott explained her transformation as such:

> I grew up, and I think many people in my family just grew older. I think when you grow up you give up those childhood myths like Santa and the Easter Bunny. I got old enough and aware enough that the myth of white supremacy is just that; it's a myth. And I read things that those who are technicians and civil engineers don't read. I read things about human relations and human nature. And if you're in a technical field, you don't do that. I think that because of what my profession is, I have to think in ways that are different than ways that my brothers think, who are civil engineers.[43]

While Jane Elliott came out of ignorance, the social revolution beyond her Riceville home found its latest victim. A minute after six o'clock in the evening central time, a single shot fired from a Remington Model 760 rifle rang out from Bessie Brewer's boarding house in Memphis, Tennessee. The bullet soared toward the Lorraine Motel's Room No. 306, where King stood, looking over the second-floor balcony. He had engaged in banter with Ben Branch, a musician-activist scheduled to perform at a rally for striking sanitation workers later that evening. "Ben," King said, "make sure you play, 'Precious Lord, Take My Hand.' And play it real sweet for me." The two men, along with Andrew Young and Revs. Ralph Abernathy, Jesse Jackson, and Samuel "Billy" Kyles were about to head to dinner before the rally at the Monumental Baptist Church.

Precious Lord.

Take my hand.

CHAPTER 9

WITHOUT BATTING AN EYE:
A DARING EXERCISE

"Discrimination diminishes all of us."

—Jane Elliott, April 1968

Jane Elliott spent the last third of the school day on Thursday, April 4, 1968, informing her students about the forthcoming unit on Native Americans. The unit builds upon learning about Indian cultures in kindergarten, first, and second grades. She planned to debunk previously taught myths about Columbus, Sacagawea, and Thanksgiving, followed by short stories, poetry, and biographical profiles of indigenous peoples and the various cultures settled regionally. She had her students confront the truth that there was a very real effort at genocide. Her approach was to challenge the general methods utilized by white instructors to teach white students about the Native American experience. Elliott aimed to tell her students that Native Americans, in their various tribes, made considerable contributions to the country's construction. She especially stressed the importance of a sense of community in tribal customs. She always had students design tepees to hook everyone at the start of the unit.

The previous year, Elliott had her students manufacture a tepee small enough to fit in Room 10 but large enough for groups of students to sit inside together and read stories. In the spring of 1967, she asked students to bring a piece of an old sheet to school. They laid each piece on the floor and sewed them together, then cut out a semicircle and sewed a hem around the top so students could thread a rope to keep the canvas on the tepee's interior. It was this white canvas that her students were excited to decorate. Elliott worked

124

them into a frenzy by the end of the school day. The plan: on Friday, during the Social Studies class segment, students would learn the Sioux prayer, "Oh great spirit, keep me from ever judging a man until I have walked a mile in his moccasins." Afterward, they were going to paint various tribal symbols on the canvas. Over the weekend, she and Darald planned to hike around Lake Hendrick and other spots in Riceville, collecting sticks large enough to hold up the tepee. On Monday, the class would work together to wrap the canvas around the sticks, preparing the tepee for use. Thinking back, Elliott said, "The kids couldn't wait to get into that tepee."[1]

However, the excitement surrounding the tepee project would soon be over-shadowed by the tragic assassination of the nation's leading civil rights leader.

School ended at 3:30 in the afternoon. As usual, Elliott remained in her classroom for another hour to be sure she was ready for the next school day. Her house was only a few blocks away, and she commonly walked to and from work. The Elliott children were already home and playing with the neighborhood kids around the yard. Carrying the teepee home that evening, she planned to wash, dry, and iron the canvas to make it flat for the children to paint the following day. Elliott hardly had enough time to settle inside the house and prepare supper when the phone rang. Her sister, Mary, was on the other line.

"Is your television on?" She asked.

"No," replied Elliott. "What's going on?"

"You'd better turn it on. They shot him."

"Who did they shoot this time?" Elliott asked while thinking about the deaths of President John F. Kennedy, Medgar Evers, and Malcolm X.

"Martin Luther King."

* * *

Nauseated, with tears in her eyes, Elliott put the phone down and readied a cup of tea while sensing guilt for all her inaction on racism. She eventually sat on the rocking chair in the living room, as slack as a rag doll, with one hand kneading at her cheek. The coverage of King's assassination was on television. Even after her children entered the house, she could only stare dully at the monitor. It was apparent to the kids that they would watch the news that night instead of their after-school shows. It made them more willing to go to bed after dinner. She grew upset at some of the comments made by national journalists Walter Cronkite and Dan Rather and local correspondents carried by CBS discussing the outbreak of looting in Memphis shortly after medical authorities pronounced King dead. In particular, she fumed over the line of questioning Cronkite and

Rather posed to leaders in the Black community: "Who is going to keep your people in line," she alleged Cronkite to say. "Don't you Negroes think that you should feel sympathy for us white people during this event because we can't feel the anger that you Negroes can?" she claimed Rather had said.[2]

Elliott wrote in her memoir, "I was appalled at the seeming implication that 'they' and 'we' weren't part of the same society, that 'our' leader (John F. Kennedy) was not 'their' leader, and that the death of Martin Luther King Jr. was seen as a tremendous loss only to the black community."[3]

To steady her emotions, Elliott shoved the couch, wooden rocking chair, and lamp to the side to make space for the tepee's canvas. She ironed it but chose to "roll it up and shove it into the closet" of her bedroom. Elliott was too disillusioned about America and disgusted by the media coverage to get her mind right for that lesson. After putting her children to sleep, she fixated on how she would explain to her third graders why people wanted King dead. Sometime after eleven o'clock, her husband, Darald, returned home from his second shift at the Oliver Tractor Plant twenty-five miles away in Charles City. He placed his lunch pail on the coffee table and asked, "They killed him, didn't they?" though he already knew the answer. Darald had spent the commute home listening to his coworkers in the carpool lauding King's death. The couple drew from past experiences living in Waterloo.

"We know why Martin Luther King Jr. was in the streets. We know how black people are treated," Jane said. "We've seen it. I know what my third graders are learning from their textbooks, and their teachers, and their coaches." She embraced Darald. "Our lesson plan for tomorrow was to learn the Sioux Indian prayer. I'm not going to just teach them that prayer. I'm going to arrange to have it answered for them." She looked up at Darald. Still gripping his shoulders, she said she was no better than the television anchors "indirectly accusing Negroes of being savage and undisciplined."

Jane released him and entered the kitchen to warm up the casserole when Darald asked, "So, what are you going to do tomorrow?"[4]

"I'm going to separate my students according to the color of their eyes."

"This is Iowa in 1968," he cautioned, "and Riceville is just like any other small town in this state. You'll never change these people, and you're going to get yourself into a lot of trouble with this thing. You'd better think it over."[5]

* * *

Jane Elliott's eye color classroom exercise on discrimination grew directly out of her pedagogy of experiential learning. Elliott often tells people the idea for the simulation goes back to her days at Iowa State Teachers College, where she read *Mila 18* and began questioning the racist behavior of her father and fellow Ricevilleans. It is unclear by contrasting recollections if she read that book as an undergraduate from 1952–53 (described in her memoir *A Collar in My Pocket*) or when Elliott returned to ISTC to finish her certification degree in 1974 (as she has told interviewers). "I had read many books that described the Holocaust, when Hitler and his cohorts arrested, imprisoned, tortured, and killed over 10 million people before and during World War II, and I knew that one of the ways they decided who would be subjected to that treatment was eye color."[6] Then she spoke to World War II veterans who shared what they witnessed in the Nazi concentration camps. Her beloved father's uncharacteristic racist comments were bewildering, so she picked up books by Harry Golden and John Howard Griffin's *Black Like Me*.

Since the first exercise, Elliott shared that her objective was to turn her classroom into "a microcosm of society." She designed a learning activity that drew a color line separating those with brown eyes from the blue-eyed. The classroom would become a Jim Crow state. In effect, such a dynamic would create a debate wherein how the authority (Jane Elliott) treated the subclass of students would then embolden those within her same hierarchical group to torment the subclass through words and (potentially) actions. "I was going to pick out a group of people on the basis of a physical characteristic over which they have no control. I was going to lower my expectations of those who had that physical characteristic. I was going to treat them as if all the things I was saying about them were, in fact, true, and when they began to live down to my expectations of them, I was going to use their inadequate performance to prove that all the things I accused them of were real."[7]

Since melanin, or lack thereof, was the chemical that determined skin and eye color. However, no Black or brown students were in her class, let alone RCS Elementary, so she chose eye color as the physical characteristic for which to construct the classroom hierarchy. "I pondered how it would feel to live in a society where your very life depended on having the right color eyes," Elliott illustrated, "and I realized that there were lots of black people [. . .] who could have described explicitly for me how it felt to have your life, and your children's lives, depend on having the right color skin."[8]

What she created that night was not reflected in the kindergarten through twelfth grade RCS curriculum. To Elliott, the exercise touched upon a mandate in the societal curriculum. "I had become [. . .] determined that no student of any age would ever be allowed to express those attitudes or exhibit those behaviors in my presence, nor would they be willing to tolerate that kind of behavior from their peers."[9] It was extremely courageous of the thirty-four-year-old teacher to take on a community that indoctrinated their kids with "all the good things we've done for blacks" by contradicting the messaging of their parents: "Well if it was all that great Martin Luther King wouldn't have been in the streets."[10]

The last thing Darald said to Jane before she went to work Friday morning was a warning: "You know you could lose your job by doing this thing, don't you?"

Elliott: "I know that, but if I don't do something meaningful in answer to this ungodly event, I should lose my job."

Darald asked once more: "Then are you still determined to go ahead with your plan?"

"Is Martin Luther King still dead this morning?" she barked. "Dad has always told us, 'A fair thing's a pretty thing, and a right wrongs no man.' What I'm going for is right."[11]

The lesson plan she created was called Discrimination Day.

* * *

In class on the morning of April 5, 1968, Steven Armstrong was the first to broach the topic: "They shot that King last night. Why'd they shoot that King?"

Those were the first words she heard that day from any of her students. "We are going to talk about that, Steven," Elliott responded, but first, she helped row leaders count points for clean desks, possessing a sharpened pencil and having a handkerchief. Then the Pledge of Allegiance and singing of "God Bless America." At that point, there was no more business as usual in Room 10. Elliott and the twenty-eight students spent the first period discussing King's murder and the ensuing national turmoil. She was unsurprised to hear that many of the students' fathers said "some pretty awful things" about King. That was disappointing. King had been one of their heroes, and she thought the "kids were confused as to who was right" about the civil rights icon. Elliott admitted that the students had hardly "internalized anything they'd 'learned' about brotherhood and respect for others" during February when King was the topic of Social Studies class. She asked them what they knew about African Americans:

"They are dirty."

"They are lazy."

"My dad said you don't need to have them around you."[12]

Since the stories of people of color were largely absent from RCS textbooks, she realized that her students repeated things their environment conditioned them to believe. She could not see how more discussions would enable the children to learn about prejudice and discrimination. She was up against students' social groups of parents, relatives, peers, youth coaches, and past teachers. Informal abstract curricula of the media, music, and local customs presented a goliath barrier to break through. After a lengthy discussion on why King had led protests and why anyone would want to harm him for doing so, she shared her plan to turn the classroom into an environment where half of those present would feel the wrath of discrimination. In contrast, the other half would enjoy the privileges of being in a superior group.

Elliott asked: "Do you kids have any idea how it would feel to be denied a job, or a house, or a good education, just because someone didn't like the color of your skin?" After the students conceded that they did not know how it felt to experience racial prejudice, she asked: "Would you like to do something today that will help you find out how that would feel?" This was an intriguing prospect. To the children, this conversation got them out of the traditional routine of spelling and handwriting. "Yes, Mrs. Elliott! Let's do that!" Elliott suggested: "Well, perhaps we find out what it feels like to be something other than white in this country."

Everyone then discussed what single physical feature they could use to separate the class. After deliberations over sex, weight, height, and hair color, the students came to eye color. Elliott planned all along that eye color would be the feature of distinction, but she wanted her students to think of the idea. "Anything could arbitrarily be chosen as the basis for discriminatory practices by those who wish to identify an enemy," she said. Eye color was the right way to cement a color line in Room 10. Of the twenty-eight children in the class, seventeen had blue eyes, eight had brown eyes, and three had green eyes. She instructed green-eyed children to pass as brown-eyed ones to even out the groups.[13] It became a two-day exercise; brown-eyed students were at the top of the socially constructed hierarchy on the first day, and blue-eyed students were at the bottom. She would flip the hierarchy on day two, which would occur the following weekend, Monday, April 8, 1968. Realizing she had blue eyes, this decision placed Elliott at the bottom of the caste. She told them: "Brown-eyed people are smarter than blue-eyed people. They are cleaner than blue-eyed people, and they are more civilized than blue-eyed people." Seating was arranged to establish a visual stratification in the room, and all blue-eyed row leaders were sent to the back. Brown-eyed students delightedly moved to the front. That's how the privileges began.

Once the classroom was segregated for the exercise, Elliott explained the rules: brown-eyed students would receive extended recess periods, lunch seconds, and more water fountain trips. Blue-eyed students had to get last in line for everything throughout the day. "Blue-eyed people are not allowed to play with brown-eyed people unless they are invited," she explained. "They may not play on the big playground equipment at recess."[14] To drive home the feeling of alienation, she placed green armbands made of construction paper on the blue-eyed students so that the brown eyes might know whom to abuse. She came up with that idea because eye color might not be distinguishable from afar. The Nazis had done something similar thirty years earlier, requiring Jews to wear an armband bearing the six-pointed Star of David. Expressions emanating from her eight and nine-year-old children wearing this badge of shame were "utterly indescribable," recalled Elliott.[15] She caused an immediate shift in position, power, and sense of belonging. Seven boys in Room 10 had dyslexia, and four were brown-eyed. According to her observations, students who struggled all year with printed punctuation marks were "working at a higher level than they ever had before." That day, those brown-eyed dyslexic students were reading and spelling words they could not comprehend days prior.

When reading through the Orton-Gillingham (OG) card pack, the four dyslexic brown-eyed boys exceeded every expectation of them. Elliott said they spelled at least thirty words correctly and could read more than that. Those students had zipped through the OG card pack in record time. Her trick: she created a myth to make the hierarchy work. She guaranteed their success. She praised them when they made a mistake in the card pack, having never mentioned they made mistakes. When brown-eyed kids misbehaved, she said nothing. The system was working just as she had planned.

Later that afternoon, after noticing Elliott failed to return written spelling tests, brown-eyed Billy Thompson anxiously asked, "Where's my spelling paper?" With tears of pride swelling in his eyes, he continued, "I wanna take it home and show it to my mother. She thinks I can't spell, and I can."[16]

On the contrary, the blue-eyed students struggled to learn anything that day. The "blueys," as Elliott called them, were given an exceedingly difficult learning experience and judged by an unreasonable standard of behavior. She slowed the situation by forcing the students to do everything precisely as she dictated. Even with the slightest mistake, she made insults, told them they could not learn, and forced the students to repeat the task until they did everything correctly. When one blue-eyed student folded the corner of a page in the reading textbook, Elliott plucked the book from his grasp and admonished him in front of the class: "Do blue-eyed people take care of the things they are given?"[17] One of the blue-eyed third graders named Carol Anderson—a blond-haired standout pupil who could read at the sixth-grade level and never made a multiplication mistake—became a shell of herself before lunchtime. Carol had transferred into her class mid-year and quickly became an accelerated learner. "She had a steel trap mind, could attain and retain information like no child I had ever encountered before," Elliott described. "I watched that child disintegrate before my very eyes."[18] On one occasion, Carol was bullied to tears by three brown-eyed classmates at recess.

Elliott's lesson on discrimination exposed a problem that social psychologists would later classify as a stereotype threat. She discovered that students performed poorly on that first day because of social pressures driven by negative stereotypes. In the context of Room 10, her blue-eyed students struggled to listen, learn, and execute targeted skills because they felt extra pressure brought on by the widely held expectations that they were not going to do well because of their physical appearance. On the contrary, the same could be said for high-performing students. Being part of the dominant group granted boosted confidence and emboldened bigoted behavior.

Without a bachelor's degree, Jane Elliott figured out that how one thinks others see them shapes their behavior and proved that a vulnerable, self-defeating attitude becomes a self-fulfilling prophecy.

The environment at RCS Elementary was ripe with ugliness. At lunch, she asked some colleagues whether to cancel the exercise. One proclaimed that she was wasting her time; of course, she should end the exercise. Another praised the killing of King: "I thought it was about time somebody shot that son-of-a-bitch." No one in the teacher's lounge repudiated the statement. Most laughed or nodded.

Aghast, Elliott returned to her classroom determined to challenge any student with the same feelings as her teaching colleagues. "No student of any age will ever leave my presence with those attitudes unchallenged," she soon told the audience. "I may not be able to change people's attitudes, but I can challenge them." From then on, Elliott avoided attaching herself to any faculty member at RCS Elementary. That kind of talk from church-going people who taught adolescent children is where she drew the line.

The browbeating at that teacher's lounge was a springboard for Elliott. However, the blue-eyed students slugged through the remainder of the day. At one point, she pulled down a roller map showing the United States during Social Studies class and lost grip on the ring, and the map flung around the roller backboard. Even though Elliott had a habit of doing that, one of the Debbys who had bullied Carol on the playground said aloud, "Well, whaddya expect? You've got blue eyes haven't cha."[19] One student, a bluey like Elliott named Alan Moss, came to Elliott's defense. "Her eyes ain't got nothin' to do with it; you know she never has been able to do that right."

Elliott thanked Alan for defending her with a wink and a nod, a sign of blue-eyed affinity. That was the only sign of strength from the blue-eyed cohort during the day. Elliott no longer needed collars to distinguish one student from the next. "I could tell simply by looking at them. The brown-eyed children were happy, alert, having the time of their lives. And they were doing far better work than they had ever done before. The blue-eyed children were miserable. Their posture, their expressions, their entire attitudes were those of defeat," she said. "[. . .] they looked and acted as though they were, in fact, inferior."[20]

Her students were eager to go home when the dismissal bell rang at 3:30 that afternoon, but not before Elliott reminded them that the exercise would reverse come Monday. However, she remained uncertain: Would her Code-a-Phone answering machine at home contain messages from upset parents? Perhaps the superintendent would ring her that evening to understand what happened in school that day. She did not want to know, and the Jennison Inn was the first place she visited after work to delay what she thought was inevitable. Although exhausted, Elliott sincerely wanted to talk to her parents about the exercise. Gie was the only person at the inn and told her daughter the exercise sounded insane. "You'd better be careful, Jane," She warned. "You don't want to end up where Aunt Eunice did."[21] Gie's Aunt Eunice, a family member for whom little is known, was committed to a mental institution.

That was enough. Elliott went home and prepared her kids for a family picnic with friends, the Schwarks, at Lake Hendricks. As they were loading the car, the phone rang. The Schwarks, whose son Elliott once taught and was good pals with Brian, called to ask for a rain check because one of their kids was sick. When the Elliotts arrived at the lake, they discovered their friends sitting at a picnic table with another family.

"Look who's here," someone said, "I hope they brought the watermelon."[22]

Looking at their children, Darald and Jane decided to avoid confrontation. They walked to a different location along the lake when young Brian joked, "We should cut them up and use them for bait."

"Yeah, I'll bait the hooks," said eleven-year-old Sarah.

"Leave it alone!" Darald said.

The episode spelled the end of that friendship, the first fatality of the aftermath of the eye color exercise. It was also when Elliott first thought about how the community would treat her family. Elliott suspected students went home and told their parents about the exercise. Then parents got on the phone with one another. She also believed her teaching colleagues were already plotting how to get her fired.

At the Jennison Inn, men were talking over coffee about the exercise. Elliott's sister, Mary, and her husband, Keith Yager, were at the inn and overheard the men talking. "Why is she doing this in Riceville?" a man asked. "We don't have any racism in Riceville. We don't have any [N-word]s." Keith said that was when he learned it was best to keep his mouth shut and avoid identifying with Elliott.[23] In a few hours, she had become the town's residential pariah. After that April 5 school day, no one would get caught speaking to her one-on-one.

While delighted that her students' parents did not call to complain, neither did the call come announcing the location of the weekend's bridge club meeting. Elliott was next cut off from her bowling team and quickly became the bane of existence for many people in Riceville. In interviews about the first lesson on discrimination, she regularly compared herself to Typhoid Mary, a nineteenth-century cook named Mary Mallon accused of having served families with typhoid fever. Mallon had complained so much about her working conditions that health officials in New York tested her for typhoid, claiming that she might be the cause of the typhoid epidemic. Authorities discovered typhoid in her feces and arrested her as the cause of the outbreak and culprit of a years-long string of typhoid epidemics across New England and the Mid-Atlantic. Similarly, Elliott saw herself as someone accused of spreading racism while trying to undo it at the root.

On Monday, Room 10's blue-eyed students arrived at school excited about the opportunity to be at the top of the classroom hierarchy. Brown-eyed students came in "dejected," Elliott said. Blue-eyed students took solace in becoming row leaders. It allowed them to get even with their counterparts at the start of the day by awarding one another points without awarding a point to the brown eyes. She did notice, however, that the viciousness was much tamer that day. She surmised that the treatment was so bad on day one that the blue eyes could not bring themselves to mock and bully their peers.

These kids were transforming before her blue eyes.

Elliott finally ended the exercise at the end of the day. She instructed students to remove their armbands and embrace one another. The students were elated that it was over. Though it pleased her to see the students laughing and playful once again, she told them there was more work to do. She announced they would discuss the exercise the following day and get to the bottom of the problem of discrimination through the lens of being people treated as dehumanized individuals for a day.

Not everyone was relieved to see Elliott's students affable again, however. The looting that occurred in the wake of King's death had personal consequences on a business owned by the son of a fourth-grade teacher at RCS Elementary. "I hope you're happy!" The colleague lambasted her, spittle flying from her mouth. "Look at what your Blacks have done to [the business owned by] my fine young son."[24]

*　*　*

On Tuesday, April 9, students were asked to write a four-paragraph essay responding to four questions: What is discrimination? How did you feel on Friday? How did you feel on Monday? Who was Martin Luther King, Jr.?

After finishing their essays, the students and Mrs. Elliott gathered in Room 10 Magic Circle, the classroom's collaborative space where everyone spoke honestly about issues that arose in class. Elliott directed the first question to blue-eyed students: Why didn't they get even with the brown-eyed kids?

"Because we knew what it felt like to be on the bottom, and we didn't want to make them feel that way." Someone said.[25] Debbie Hughes and Kim Reynolds said they felt like dropping out of school. Debbie Anderson said she "felt dirty," while Sindee Hockens said, "I was sick." Billy Thompson admitted to "crying" over his mistreatment. Theodore Perzynski said he "felt like kicking a brown-eyed person."[26]

The students divulged that when members of the inferior group used time on the playground and in the restroom to discuss hurting Jane. "It ranged from throwing things at me to killing me," Elliott said. She admitted she was clueless about how "destructive a feeling of inferiority" the exercise would levy on the students. "[I]t can literally change a personality, [and] destroy motivation."[27]

Debbie Anderson described how she felt "mad" on Monday when she was on the bottom and how she "wanted to quit school because [the blue eyes] got to do everything first, and we had to do everything last." She said she felt "dirty" and "did not feel as smart as she did on Friday." Brown-eyed Billy Thompson admitted, "I felt good inside" when he ordered around the blue-eyed group. However, "I felt like crying on Monday," he confessed. "Martin Luther King died trying to save colored people from discrimination. White people at least could treat colored people like any other person." Blue-eyed Alan Moss spent Friday feeling like he "wanted to hit the brown-eyed people."[28]

One student expressed confusion over what his cherished teacher tried to teach him due to his father's comments. "My dad says you're nothing but a [N-word] lover, and you're wrong. He's been around [N-word]s, and he says yer wrong."

"Well, Tommy," she replied, "either your dad is wrong, or I am. Only time will tell, which it is, but in the meantime, because of the experiences you've had in the last two days, perhaps you won't make the same mistakes that your dad and I have where racism is concerned."[29]

Before the day's end, students wrote condolence letters to Coretta Scott King as Elliott put King's funeral on television. Reflecting on the students' responses, Elliott said, "If I could get this message to white people in the United States of America, maybe they could understand that once you've been through this crap, you don't want to do it to another person. There must be a way for other teachers, for preachers, for lawyers, or doctors for God's sake, for people in delivery rooms, for patrolmen, for policemen to find out. Once you've been on the bottom, you don't want to get even; you just want what the Constitution promises you, which his equal treatment under the law. That's all the blue-eyed kids wanted the first day. It's all the brown-eyed kids wanted the second day."[30]

The group gleaned ten lessons from the exercise.

1. The way marginalized people—women and racialized minorities—behavior is driven not by a "weakness peculiar to their genes" but by dominant groups labeling them with inferior traits based on their physical appearance.

2. The anger excused by people of color is not a racial or ethnic trait; it is a reaction to treatment experienced throughout their lives and how systems and institutions have unjustly worked for people that look like them.

3. They recognized that almost every student wrote in their essay that they wanted to inflict violence on the dominant group but chose not to because it could have brought more violence to them and the people in their group.

4. The exercise teaches about the feeling of inclusion. Elliott said, "The students agreed that they wouldn't be interested in coming to school if they knew they'd be mistreated on the basis of their eye color every day." They gained empathy for the experiences of Black people in predominantly white spaces.

5. The group learned that people of color do not need to live in Riceville for people in town to hold racist points of view and behave in racist ways. The conversation exposed students' racial presumptions acquired through a lifetime of hearing and seeing racist comments. Without African Americans living in Riceville, racist stereotypes pass through generations.

6. With that in mind, the sixth lesson suggests that Room 10 students learned that no one is born a racist. Since eye color was the physical feature for inventing a caste system, students realized they had never possessed an eye color bias before Elliott said so. Since racism is learned, it can be unlearned.

7. Because the teacher's behavior has such a profound impact on the viciousness of the students, the group learned that discrimination causes prejudice, not the other way around.

8. Twenty-eight students shared the responsibility to make the exercise work. The activity would have fallen apart if there had been just a few resistors.

9. The group at the bottom was in a powerless dilemma. If they quit or walked out of the room, that would only confirm stereotypes Elliott was already saying about them—that they were "weak," "lazy," and "cowardly." The options were limited: either continue with the exercise and endure the abuse or attempt to disrupt it. That, however, ran the risk of being labeled confrontational, uncivilized, undisciplined, or violent.

10. The phrase "sticks and stones may break my bones, but names will never hurt me" is untrue. Elliott said, "We told people they were superior or inferior, and they reacted to what we said."[31]

* * *

The Discrimination Day lesson was a consequence of Jane Elliott's teaching style. She would not walk into her class on the morning of April 5, 1968, and discuss with her students why someone murdered one of Room 10's heroes of the month. That was not how she taught. In her view, the type of education that expects students to sit idle while a teacher deposits information into their brains was not sustainable learning, nor was it transformative. Enlightenment does not occur in that sense. The exercise was designed to be an experiential learning activity for the sixteen boys and twelve girls in Room 10, so they could understand what King meant when he said, "Privileged groups seldom give up their privileges voluntarily."[32] She might not have repeated the exercise in subsequent years if not for capturing local and national media attention. It was too ugly of an episode for everyone involved, and it broke her heart to see her young children behave like monsters over two school days. "If I had known how well it would work, I probably wouldn't have done it," Elliott conceded. "That was the worst day I had ever spent in the classroom."[33]

Nevertheless, *The Tonight Show* came calling in a month, and Jane Elliott's life would never be the same.

CHAPTER 10

THE EYES HAVE IT: THE BIGGEST LITTLE TOWN IN NORTHEAST IOWA

"Every American child should have a gifted teacher like Jane Elliott. For education to match, the challenge of our times calls for more than money. It calls for the imagination of our brightest people. Yet, Mrs. Elliott is the exception, not the rule. And will be until we again give priority to the education of our children."

—Box Elder Education Association (Brigham City, Utah), April 1975

It did not take long for word about Elliott's Discrimination Day lesson to reach the town's newspaper, the *Riceville Recorder*. Upon hearing what Jane had done with her students, Gie felt compelled to protect her daughter and impulsively leaked the story to Merritt E. Messersmith, the paper's editor. On Tuesday, April 9, 1968, Elliott shared her students' Discrimination Day compositions with her parents. While everyone in town admonished Elliott, Gie thought the essays could potentially become Elliott's saving grace. If only the community could see how the perspectives of these eight and nine-year-old children changed because of the exercise, then they should be able to accept her daughter's efforts. Gie asked if she could keep the essays overnight to do a closer reading. Instead, she stuffed them in an envelope and ran them over to Messersmith's office a few blocks from the Jennison Inn.[1]

After reviewing the essays, Messersmith later wrote that the letters reflected "a feeling of dejection, bitterness, and violence" and asked Elliott to print the students' words in the paper.[2] Surprised about what her mother had done, she told him, "There are no secrets in my room other than what students tell me

138

in confidence." After she received consent from her students and their parents, who thought "it would be exciting to have their essays in the paper," Elliott approved Messersmith. She sent him a note: "Discrimination diminishes all of us, those who practice it against others, as well as those against whom it is practiced. Discrimination limits the numbers of our friends and experiences and thereby limits our education. Discrimination discourages the second-class citizen and so prevents him from doing his best, and it creates in the first-class citizen a false sense of security which makes him feel it unnecessary for him to do his very best."[3] Messersmith printed the essays in five columns on page five of the April 18 edition under the headline "This Is How Discrimination Feels."[4]

No metric indicates the students' letters' impact on the total Riceville 898 population.[5] People remained angry. However, one Riceville resident, Charlotte "Char" Button, found the essays inspiring. Button, a pianist and professional photographer, tucked the April 18 *Recorder* in an envelope along with a note and mailed it to both the NBC offices of Hugh Downs from the *Today Show* and Johnny Carson, host of *The Tonight Show Starring Johnny Carson*. Button struck out with *Today's* Downs. In a letter from staffer J. James Rathnam, Downs expressed, "Our programs are scheduled weeks in advance" and were accordingly "unable to honor viewers' requests for including additional features at a short notice."[6]

Button had much better luck with Johnny Carson. Earlier that February, Martin Luther King, Jr. appeared as one of the show's guests (although actor-activist Harry Belefonte substituted as host during February 5-9 while Carson was on vacation). King's appearance on *The Tonight Show* still resonated with Carson's audience after the civil rights leader's death. Profound were King's words that the civil rights movement's victories, specifically the civil rights and voting rights bills of 1964 and 1965, respectively, "did very little to improve" the condition of African Americans living in the North. He lamented to Belefonte that those pieces of legislation "did little to penetrate the lower depths of Negro deprivation in communities all over."[7] When Button heard about what Elliott did in her classroom as a reaction to King's death, she utilized her media connections to ensure Carson's office read her correspondence.

Button, whose maiden name was Wilkens, was born and raised in Chicago before she arrived in northern Iowa. She married Donald "Don" Button, the *National Livestock Producer* magazine editor. Her husband's roots, however, were in the Hawkeye State, where he grew up on a horse farm west of Riceville. In 1961, the Buttons left the Windy City for small-town Iowa. They settled on Donald's father's farm while his parents moved into a home in town on East

Fourth Street. In 1966, Charlotte and Donald started a youth photography education program through Riceville's school-to-community connections mission called the 4-H youth program.

In rural communities, 4-H youth programs supported schools by providing supplemental curricula for students in enhanced vocational training. Generally, 4-H programs offered club experience in agricultural trades pertinent to the local community since community leaders were the ones who volunteered to design and instruct each program. Club offerings generally involved gardening, clothing, farm safety, home improvement, leadership, and livestock production. The four-leaf clover served as the emblem of the 4-H organization, with each leaflet bearing the letter H. The four Hs represented essential life skills required for youth development, namely *head* for thinking and managing, *heart* for relating and caring, *hands* for working and giving, and *health* for being and living.[8] Club leaders taught the curricula for the various 4-H clubs outside the school setting. The Buttons' 4-H photography club trained teenagers on the basics of choosing the best photography technology, using a camera, lighting, perspective, and concepts of background, foreground, and visual tension. Several of the Buttons' students ended up winning prizes for their pictures at state fairs across the state of Iowa.[9]

Button, who died of breast cancer two weeks before Elliott's thirty-ninth birthday in 1972, befriended her in 1965. Elliott's daughter, Mary, and Charlotte's son, Bradley, attended RCS Elementary together and were regularly placed in the same classroom. As they got to know each other, Elliott allowed her children to visit Charlotte and her husband at the Button farm, sometimes taking photographs of the livestock. "She had a great eye for telling a story with a picture," said Elliott of her friend. "You didn't need words when you looked at [Charlotte's] photos."[10]

Johnny Carson's willingness to answer Char Button's letter changed Jane Elliott's life. On May 21, 1968, a representative from Carson's office first reached out to Messersmith at the *Recorder* to investigate Elliott, her exercise, and the town. According to how Messersmith described the correspondence, Carson's people asked three questions targeting the demographics and culture of Riceville, the RCS school system, and "whether or not Mrs. Elliott might consider appearing on *The Tonight Show*."[11]

Two days later, Carson's people touched base with a stunned Elliott. The phone call came in the middle of the school day. Elliott and her students thought it might be Coretta Scott King. After making her way to the front office to take the phone call, Elliott grabbed the receiver but held it a few inches from her ear so the receptionist could listen. The show's producer, John Carsey, was on the other end. He issued Elliott a formal invitation to be one of Carson's guests. She agreed, and everyone in the office erupted in excitement. Students in Room 10 did not share the same level of enthusiasm.

"Kids," Elliott began, "it wasn't Mrs. King. It was Johnny Carson."

"Who is Johnny Carson?" The kids responded.

"He's got a late-night talk show. He's on when you go to bed at night."[12]

The *Recorder* ran a front-page story with a large photograph of Elliott announcing her scheduled appearance on the show. The article led off with the hook: "When Mrs. Jane Elliott, third-grade teacher in the Riceville Community Schools, used the division of her students to explain the meaning of discrimination, she had no idea that the example would carry to the point where she would appear on a nationwide television show." It described Elliott as an educator with "a great interest in helping children with speech defects."[13]

The rising stardom seemingly made some of Elliott's closest friends jealous. Don Button, husband to Charlotte, perhaps frustrated that his wife did not receive much attention for her role in arranging the appearance, poked fun at Carson's invitation. "Red Alert," he wrote to a like-minded audience. He said the "eyes of the world" will again zoom in on Riceville and its "nationally recognized school system" thanks to Jane Elliott. He said mockingly, "She will be discussing the recent race riots which broke out when a Black Angus Cow tried to move into the same pen with a White Shorthorn Steer at the local stockyards." He signed the correspondence: "The Riceville Committee for Easing Racial Tensions in the Greater Riceville Metropolitan Area."[14] Though Elliott got her hands on Don's letter, all signs indicate she brushed off the slight. "Never let people see you with your head down" became her mantra to live by in such moments of betrayal.[15]

Elliott's appearance on *The Tonight Show* was scheduled for Memorial Day weekend, which fell on Monday, May 26, but was set to air on the last day of the month. This meant she had only a few days to buy a new sleeveless dress, board a plane to Manhattan (her first flying experience) and prepare for the national spotlight. Johnny Carson's people put Elliott and her husband up in the Warwick Hotel, located five blocks north of 30 Rockefeller Center and just beneath Central Park.[16]

Carsey prepped Elliott with Carson's interview questions. She felt comforted when he informed her that Carson was born in Corning, Iowa. He then told her not to say anything thought-provoking. "The people who watch the Johnny Carson show don't want to think," Carsey instructed, "Don't say anything depressing. The people who watch the Johnny Carson show don't want to be depressed."

"Then why am I here? I can't think of anything that isn't depressing about racism." Elliott replied.

"Don't worry. We're going to punch it up." Carsey said.

"I'll stay then," Elliott said. "I've never seen racism 'punched up.'"[17]

Carson's makeup team had to "rebuild my face," she remembered. The actor James Garner, who had launched his promotional tour for the upcoming film *How Sweet It Is!* co-starring Debbie Reynolds and Maurice Ronet, was in the green room with Elliott. Somebody asked Garner if he needed any make-up. He responded, "I could use a little powder." She laughed audibly and jokingly said, "He could use a little powder, and I'm getting remade. My God, James Garner doesn't need any powder. He is gorgeous."[18]

Alex Chitlin's band, the Box Tops, had one of the Top 10 LPs that spring, "Cry Like a Baby," which peaked at No. 2, was Carson's musical guest that evening. The band had been on tour the day Martin Luther King Jr. was assassinated. It would have upset Elliott to know Chitlin's response about King's death was: "In many ways, I was just too busy for 1968 [. . .] I could look over and nod and say, 'Okay, that's happening,' but I didn't have time for it."[19] Elliott found the entire experience "silly." She described her invitation as facetious, claiming many guests like her were tongue-in-cheek additions to the show. She got that sense during her four minutes on stage. Carson, looking older than his forty-three years, never looked her in the eye. She later asked John Carsey about Carson's behavior. He explained that Carson always looked at the potted palm tree beyond her eye line, which was how the camera captured the host's good side.[20]

The Tonight Show did not air in Riceville or elsewhere in northern Iowa and Minnesota the evening they recorded. Television stations chose instead to broadcast the Minnesota Twins harrowing walk-off five to four victories over the Boston Red Sox. After Boston took four-to-nothing leads in the fourth inning, the Twins scored two in the sixth, a third in the eighth inning, and two in the bottom of the ninth. Elliott's appearance on the show finally aired locally on KROC-TV Channel 10 in Rochester, Minnesota, and KWWL-TV, Channel 7, Waterloo, Iowa, at 10:30 p.m. on May 31. When it was time, she and Darald climbed into bed to watch her performance. Unhappy with the line of questions, which barely scratched the surface of the exercise, she called the show "a waste of time."[21]

"I was lucky in that respect because some of [Riceville's residents] went to bed, so they didn't have to see it. The problem in Riceville was that everyone knew everything about everybody. So, everybody knew what they thought about that experience and how I dared to do that. And some of them said, 'Well, she has a lot of courage.' Some of them said, 'She doesn't have any brains.' And some of them said, "She's got to be fired.' And some of them said to the superintendent, 'You need to fire her.' And he said, 'No, I don't.' And school board members got elected on the platform that they'd get rid of the town's only [N-word] lover. And he would say at the beginning of the first school board meeting of the year, 'You are not elected to hire and fire teachers. I am hired to do that.'"[22] What follows is how Elliott remembered the public's reaction to her fifteen minutes of fame.

> We didn't "punch up" racism, but I learned a lot about Johnny Carson's audience. Over thirty percent of the letters I got after the show were so vicious and obscene that I didn't want to share them with my students. I didn't share the worst of them. On the other hand, the other letters were so appreciative and warm, and thoughtful that they really helped to get me through some of the unpleasantness that followed.[23]

Elliott received harassing phone calls and letters for weeks following her first small-screen appearance. Public critics called the exercise "a laugh of the year" and that she was "talking in an area [she] know nothing about."[24] Condemnation was so nasty that it provoked a letter to the editor from Peter J. Children of Mason City in her defense. "I can well remember 12 years ago when a classmate of mine was discharged from the Riceville school system for trying to teach his students some of the same things that Mrs. Elliott is trying to do now. I refer to Paul Richer." Children wrote.

Paul J. Richer was a twenty-one-year-old junior high teacher terminated from the RCS district in 1956. This was after the superintendent and school board buckled to community complaints over his teaching about the communist form of government and for introducing popular humanities texts into the curriculum (discussed in detail in Chapter Four). Children noted Richer's termination from RCS "brought nationwide attention to this same Iowa village that now basks in the national spotlight." He challenged the Riceville school board to protect Elliott rather than levy the same treatment his friend received.[25] The two were similar in how they each found support from the public beyond Riceville's limits and became persona non grata in Riceville. The difference between Mrs. Elliott and Mr. Richer was that the former was homegrown and deeply invested in the community. Unlike Richer, there would be no running for the diminutive woman with titanic confidence and an imperviousness with roots all over Riceville. Her parents were trying to run a business in town, and her children were already in the school system.

Jane Elliott was there to stay.

* * *

Widespread attention meant Elliott would have to make crucial decisions over whether she should continue to conduct her Discrimination Day lesson at Riceville Elementary. It must have been something she debated internally after appearing on *The Tonight Show*. If she wrestled with the idea of repeating the eye color exercise, two events at the end of the year convinced her to give it another go.

In the late fall, Scholastic Magazines, Inc. asked Elliott to contribute an article for its education-centered publication *Scholastic Teacher*. She penned an article titled "Exercise in Discrimination" explaining the eye color lesson, including some students' essays. Impressed by her explanation for what motivated her to challenge the status quo in Riceville, the magazine's editor, Loretta Marion, entered the article in the *Scholastic Teacher's* Promising New Practices in Education Contest.[26] Elliott's entry went on to win first place, which carried a $25 prize and a note from Marion stating the piece "merits national attention as an innovational practice in education."[27] The combination of her first publication and the visit to *The Tonight Show* presented Elliott with several reasons to improve upon the Discrimination Day lesson exercise at RCS Elementary and to enhance her knowledge of American race relations.

Another factor that convinced Elliott to continue with the Discrimination Day lesson was to see whether it had the same results on adults. On Tuesday, August 20, Elliott accepted an invitation to be the luncheon speaker for the Osage Rotary Club.[28] While they wanted her to talk about Johnny Carson, Elliott used the opportunity to discuss gender discrimination. Her held stereotypes about local Rotarians troubled her from the outset. She felt the Rotarians censured women who were seldom invited to speak at the club, nor were they allowed in its membership. In a defensive mood, Elliott told the event organizer Wes Birdsall that she would accept the invitation only if she could put the men through the discrimination experience. She thought the exercise might teach them something about sex discrimination.

The standard rotary club gatherings lasted sixty minutes. Meetings traditionally began at noon, when the members had lunch before discussing old and new business, followed by the guest speaker's ten to twenty-minute presentation. As she planned, there would be no talk about *The Tonight Show* this day. She designed a program that would take up the entire hour with a modified version of the exercise. Brown-eyed Rotarians were at the top of the hierarchy; they were served lunch first and could choose seats at the front of the room. Elliott planned to treat those with blue eyes rudely. While the brown eyes got their food, the blue eyes were told to stand and wait. The tables and chairs for the blue-eyed Rotarians were folded against the wall, and Elliott told them to make the tables, which included setting the tablecloth and places. She ended up making half of the room angry at her. One man, whom Elliott described as "Mr. K." came close to hitting her when she allowed a brown-eyed Rotarian to cut in front of him in the food line. During lunch, several people in the blue-eyed group made a sign out of the tablecloth: "Elliot [sic] Go Home!" After everyone ate, she began her remarks; most blue-eyed members walked out. Many others with blue and brown eyes stayed in the room chatting with Jane until half past two o'clock.[29]

Instead of a bunch of Rotarians out for blood, Birdsall proactively asked Elliott to partner with the club on its nineteenth annual initiative, which arranged for international students enrolled at the University of Iowa (UI) to stay with a host family for three days over Thanksgiving vacation. Since most UI students returned home over the holiday, the program gave about thirty international students a place to go for the semester break and to see how people in Iowa celebrated Thanksgiving. That fall, Elliott assisted the Osage Rotary Club in finding placement for thirty-two international students from Wednesday, November 27 to Saturday, November 30, and hosted a UI graduate student from India and his wife and toddler daughter.[30]

To the dismay of some Rotarians, Elliott was gracious enough to be the keynote speaker at a program held at the Osage Municipal Building the day after Thanksgiving. It was a dual celebration. On the provisional stage—an area that was more of a dance floor than a stage—she felt the glares from Mr. K seated behind her. In the middle of her remarks, she turned around and said, "Uh, you want to go sit someplace else? I don't think I can trust you behind my back."[31] For her part, Elliott felt it was wrong for cynics to menace her at festive events that had nothing to do with the eye color exercise. She won the room with a few jabs. First, she concluded her remarks by praising the international students. Everyone honored the presence of students from India, China, the Philippines, Sweden, Egypt, Ghana, Ethiopia, Lebanon, Hong Kong, and Venezuela while also recognizing Elliott's thirty-fifth birthday. Second, she accepted an invitation to be interviewed by KGLO-TV in Mason City, becoming the face of the Osage Rotary Club's international exchange program.[32] Elliott sustained her involvement in this program for several years.

* * *

Elliott wrote in *A Collar in My Pocket* that she intended to do the exercise with her 1968-1969 third-grade cohort. She may have reconsidered, thinking instead of focusing solely on the standard curriculum and getting on with her life if it was not for the event with the Osage Rotarians. It is also possible that an unexpected phone call from Ontario cemented her second attempt to subject her third graders to the discrimination exercise.

Before the school year started, Canadian Broadcasting Corporation (CBC) newsman Stephen Banker telephoned Elliott requesting a visit to Room 10. He wanted to film a documentary about the exercise. Banker explained how discrimination thrived in Ontario: Canadian Inuits were victims of personal and institutional discriminatory treatment. He felt a film showing how Elliott's exercise transformed her adolescent students in forty-eight hours would lead to reform in Canada. Her acceptance of Banker's proposal would eventually yield greater attention and eventual changes to conducting the exercise.

After the RCS school board approved, she told Banker they could film her class.[33] Elliott intended to do the exercise in the fall "so that we could build on what we learned the previous year for a longer time in my classroom."[34] However, she had cause for concern before the first day of school when the principal, Dinsmore Brandmill—a World War II veteran who survived Okinawa—told her that "twenty percent of the parents" refused to enroll their children in her class. Parents did not want to subject their children to a lesson about "them [N-word]s," Brandmill told her.[35] One father wanted to shelter his child from race talk but conceded Elliott was the best third-grade teacher in Riceville. He told the school, "I don't want my kid in that [N-word] lover's classroom, but I want him to learn to read, so put him in there, anyway."[36] Whether the parents liked it or not, Brandmill placed twenty-one students—fourteen boys and seven girls—in Elliott's class that fall.

A time later, Brandmill's grandson, Michael Judge, confirmed Elliott's account of that moment. Writing for *The Wall Street Journal* near the fiftieth anniversary of the Blue Eyes/Brown Eyes Exercise, Judge explained that as principal, his grandfather "faced more than a few irate parents and school board members calling for Ms. Elliott's resignation." Despite the firestorm against Elliott, Judge championed her work, "telling her to continue with her lesson–that he, in effect, had her back."[37]

The timing of the CBC documentary was unsettling in some respects. Banker and his film crew arranged to spend four days in town, September 17 through

September 20. Three days would be spent in Elliott's class, one of which was to get students comfortable with a camera crew documenting their lives. Filming for the documentary was scheduled for September 18, when the blue-eyed students were at the top of the social ladder, and September 19, when the students with brown eyes became the privileged group.[38] The crew was slated to take shots of the happenings and sites that Riceville had to offer on their last day in town. However, a few days before Banker and Elliott connected, racially charged violence erupted in Waterloo between police and the city's east side members.

On Friday, September 13, physical clashes began during halftime of the Waterloo East High football game against St. Joseph High of Winchester, Illinois. Fighting between law enforcement and townspeople continued throughout the night as skirmishes erupted well beyond the football stadium and into the Black residential neighborhood. Waterloo's Shepherd Lumber Company and three homes adjacent to the store were set ablaze during the turmoil. Waterloo Fire Chief Harold Smith indicated that someone also attempted to set fire to East High School. A small fire destroyed at least one classroom.[39] The violence ceased once the National Guard arrived Saturday morning.

Turmoil in Waterloo was precipitated by the violence that swept the city the previous year. After the disturbances of 1967, Black students and adults pressed the Waterloo School District for changes. Their patience grew thin after Martin Luther King's death. At the start of the new school year, Black residents sent the Waterloo School Board a list containing twelve demands. Those making demands insisted that the school create a Black history course, hire more Black teachers and counselors, and dismiss prejudiced teachers.

Similarly, they wanted the school board to create a teaching standard that would otherwise punish faculty who discouraged Black students from attending a college of their choice. They wanted an equitable disciplinary system that removed bias in punishing Black and white students. They also asked that scholarships and awards be made available to Black students and that the students be allowed to form a Black Student Union. They no longer wanted to tolerate being called "Negro". Instead, the terms "blacks" or "Afro-Americans" should be used by teachers. Finally, they demanded the removal of police officers from the high school.

The school board vetoed the idea of a Black Student Union. It claimed uniformed resource officers were not "regularly assigned" to the school and would be summoned upon any threat of violence. While the board did not address the issue of recruiting and hiring Black staff, it voted to create a one-semester Black history and culture elective.[40]

The board's response to the demands divided the school building, which was about 45 percent Black. On Monday, September 9, a community group led by Charles Derden, a twenty-one-year-old East High graduate, and former valedictorian, arrived at the school to inquire about the Black history curriculum. According to reports, Derden, a pre-law major at the University of Iowa, and forty Black students "walked out of their classes, and several teachers threatened to leave their jobs," in response. Before the situation became too unruly, the superintendent canceled classes that Thursday and Friday while allowing the school's district powerhouse football team to play its game as scheduled.

Waterloo was a ticking time bomb on the cusp of exploding that weekend. While largely due to problems in the Waterloo school system, the previous week's disturbances were also part of broader transformations in response to urban riots following King's murder earlier that spring, plus the ugly four-day disturbance in Waterloo the previous year. There were also protests over academic inequity on college campuses across the country. Black athletes threatened to boycott the October Mexico City Olympic Games. Seeing the government wage a bloody campaign in Vietnam added to the contentious climate in town. Ultimately, the decision to play Friday's football game allowed the powder keg to erupt.

The disturbance began during halftime when police struggled with a Black teenager outside the stadium. The scuffle became a brawl when other Black teens rushed to the scene to resist the police. "Several other Black youths inside the stadium climbed over the fence [. . .] and joined in the struggle," the *Des Moines Register* reported. Another fight between a police officer and a Black teen erupted in the East High student section near the game's end. After the game, police struggled to get the crowd to leave the stadium. A rock was thrown at a line of officers when twenty-five Black high schoolers were instructed to go home. The police wielded batons and sprayed mace before charging the group of teenagers. Later that night, roughly two dozen Black community members went to the police station to "voice protest about the police beating and the use of chemical Mace on Blacks." A fight almost broke out inside the station when the officers justified using force "when it's necessary." Most clashes between police and Black community residents (including gunfire and Molotov cocktails) occurred up and down East 4th Street through the night.

While Banker and the CBC network wanted the film about Elliott's exercise to serve as an impetus for change in their country, she had other plans. Considering what recently occurred in Waterloo, she hoped that if the exercise were viewed in the United States, it could be used as a key resource in the

debate over racism and Black progress since the end of the civil rights movement dismantled the South's Jim Crow laws and customs. When completed,
Banker produced a thirty-minute black-and-white feature shown on Canada's
public affairs program, *The Way It Is*. It premiered on October 6, 1968, in the
middle of an hour-long episode about the discriminatory treatment of Ontario's
Eskimo population. Elliott appeared tyrannical. Aside from a few voice-overs,
it did not help that Banker's production failed to humanize Elliott with commonly used short confessional interviews. On day one of the simulations, she
placed the blue-eyed students at the top of the social hierarchy. The exercise
opened with her patented lines: blue eyes are smarter, cleaner, and better behaved than their brown-eyed peers.

It was clear Elliott cared to unveil how prejudicial beliefs turn into discriminatory behavior, destroying the spirit and self-esteem of those at the bottom of the social caste than viewers would feel about her. Moments into the
film, Elliott called brown-eyed students to the front of the room, where they
had to recite their names for the cameras as she placed an armband around the
right bicep. She taped small signs proclaiming "blue eyes only" and "brown
eyes only" onto the classroom's drinking faucets to segregate access to water
and took away playground and lunch privileges. Banker's cameramen focused
most on the students, capturing dejected expressions as Elliott found reasons
to mercilessly correct the blue eyes on day one and brown eyes on day two.
After switching roles on day two, blue-eyed Todd Brandau (who thrived the
previous day) shared that a classmate had bullied him, an incident cut from
the film. Brandau and other blue-eyed students appeared broken. The eight-
year-old boy repeatedly fought tears when expressing his feelings about the
experience.

Elliott stayed in character, withholding any show of sympathy. She pounced
further on Brandau for stuffing a pencil into his armband and harangued other
blue eyes who complained that the armbands felt too tight. "I didn't hear any
brown eyes complaining about the armbands yesterday. Blue-eyed people are
weak," she declared. [41]

While the unscripted performances of Jane Elliott and her students were
on a lower level than what would be seen in future documentaries, this film
was needed. Old stereotypes prevailed in the Ontarian populace, character-
izing Eskimos as fat, nose-rubbing inhabitants of igloos, affecting their overall treatment and ability to secure housing and employment. The goal of the
broadcast was to dispel Eskimo myths by showing how little was known about
them in the first place. This seemingly condensed program provided the right

juxtaposition, pushing viewers to reconsider presumptions about majority and minority populations in the Canadian province.

Mary Carpenter, an Eskimo from the Northwest Territories, accused the Canadian government of treating Eskimos as "a kind of new [N-word] with a parka." That phrase echoed how Banker described the Inuit situation to Elliott. A second-year history and journalism major at the University of Western Ontario in 1968, Carpenter organized a movement against the government's support for the Panarctic Oil project, which exploited native lands and aimed to expose a media bias toward the government's view that "the rape of the north" was good for the Eskimo. "I don't wish to alarm you, but the facts are that the federal government is doing exactly to my people [. . .] what the whites have done to the Negroes of the United States," Carpenter told members of the Indian-Eskimo Association of Canada. "They are making us into service-class people or slaves."[42] Because of its message, viewers sympathetic to the Inuit's cause voted *The Way It Is* the best television program on CBC the week it aired. As a result, the station aired the program a second time on the show *Pick of the Week*.[43]

Returning to the first time she put her students through the Discrimination Day lesson earlier that year, Elliott and her father Lloyd, discussed the exercise. Despite Lloyd's willingness to hear the reasons justifying why she did this, Elliott had yet to feel affirmed by her father. *The Way It Is* enabled Lloyd to do more than listen to the exercise descriptions. Now, he could watch his daughter interact with her students. The fact that Jane's students were the children of many of his friends and Jennison Inn patrons compounded his emotions during the screening. The CBC film allowed him to see growth and transformation occurring in his daughter's classroom. It challenged him to consider how he lived in a state of willful ignorance in his interactions and opinions about those of different cultural groups. "I wish I'd been put through that when I was a boy," Lloyd told Jane, choked up after watching the program.[44] Those words boosted Elliott's spirit. She needed them to alleviate doubt that what she was doing was righteous.

* * *

Not long after the two airings of *The Way It Is*, the caviling reigned down. The corporation was the first to field critical opprobrium. Letters from irate viewers already upset by the program's incessant content promoting progressive stances on social justice landed on the desk of corporate executives. Public criticism called the episode "trash" and "sickening." Elliott, of course, was at the heart of the firestorm. One viewer wrote, "It's such teachers [sic] as this that spoils our young people."[45] Another asked, "Please would someone explain to me why that teacher was frightening these very small children about blue-eyes & brown-eyes," questioning what the exercise ultimately accomplished. "What did it all mean? Why should young children be almost brought to tears, as one small boy was [sic]."[46] The writer's query cited blue-eyed Todd Brandau, who wrote in his final reflection: "I felt very good on Wed. I felt that way because we had five minutes extra recess. I felt very sad on Thurs. I felt [sic] that way because [sic] we did not have five minutes extra recess [. . .] I think we learned that we are all the same."[47]

Not every letter arriving at the CBC studio was negative. It was mostly educators who authored several favorable correspondences. Sister Judy Richardson from Kamloops of St. Ann's Academy in British Columbia called the show "technically innovating, intellectually stimulating, and creatively captivating." Watching with her students, Sister Richardson confessed that the film profoundly impacted those enrolled at St. Ann's. Classrooms across campus "buzzed," she wrote after the show's debut the following day. "We had a vibrantly alive Monday,"[48] A history teacher from Scarborough wrote to the station requesting a film copy.[49]

However one viewed the program, no doubt the Ontario public debated Elliott's approach to teaching children about discrimination. To capitalize on the excitement, a CBC station representative invited Elliott to visit the studio in Toronto to discuss why she does the exercise with her third-grade students. "It seemed their switchboard had nearly blown a fuse as viewers across the country had called in demanding to know what in hell was going on with those poor little kids in Riceville, Iowa," she said. Elliott's recollection of the event was largely accurate. Elliott arrived at the CBC studio and instantly felt like the whole thing was a "setup." She was told to sit in the middle of the studio's auditorium surrounded by about two-hundred angry people. The audience took her to the woodshed for four hours.

"Don't you think you could do great psychological damage to a child by doing that exercise with them for a day?" said a woman in the crowd.

"Yeah, I suppose you could. And if you're concerned about what happens to a white child with that exercise for a day, you must be absolutely infuriated by what happens to colored children."[50] Elliott replied, adding, "I was more concerned with the damage that is done to people with whom we do this exercise based on skin color every day."

Woman: "That's different. They're used to it; they can take it."

Elliott compared this exchange to the one she had in the teachers' lounge at RCS Elementary the previous spring. There would be no teaching these people unless they agreed to participate in the eye color exercise, which she felt was a long shot.

A second exchange frightened Elliott further, but in a way that became affirming.

"I came here to tell you how much I hate you," A second woman began. "I am Jewish. I was born and raised in Germany." She went on to explain how the headmaster of her school forced everyone to salute and say "Heil Hitler." "I watched those who value their faith more than life itself continue to bow and say, 'Good morning, Herr Headmaster.' They disappeared, and we never saw them again, but we know where they ended up." The woman paused, then said, "Your students are very fortunate. They will never allow what happened in our society to happen in yours; they'll see it coming and put a stop to it."[51]

Back in Riceville, a few high school kids teased Elliott's students for participating in the Discrimination Day lesson. "You're the kids who have that [N-word]-lover for a teacher. You must all be [N-word]-lovers in that class!" said at least one teenager.

To set the record straight, Elliott tried taking the exercise directly to the people of Riceville. At a meeting of the Jenkins Township election council chaired by Donald Button and held at the Jennison Inn on December 9, Elliott facilitated a screening of CBC's *The Way It Is*. After the video, she fielded questions in a manner like a forum she'd been trapped into doing in Toronto a month earlier.[52] Except for this time, she was her own moderator. She used that privilege to interject her questions to get the audience to think deeply and critically about their racial presumptions. Some of the feedback was affirming. One commenter said she'd like to send her husband through the exercise for fear that her kids would grow up talking and thinking the way he does. That comment aside, Elliott struggled to make inroads with the masses in Riceville.

In another part of the country, in the D.C.-Maryland-Virginia metropolitan area, one middle school proved to be where Elliott might belong.

* * *

On February 19, 1969, the first day of National Brotherhood Week, the Cabin John Junior High School in Bethesda segregated the entire building by the color of students' hair. Under the dry but chilly forty-three-degree temperature of the Chesapeake, students walked off the bus only to encounter brunette-haired students blocking the main entrance and signs proclaiming, "Blondes use side door." In other places throughout the school, "No Blondes Allowed" placards segregated drinking fountains, restrooms, lunch tables, and stairways. A clear minority, roughly 120 of Cabin John's 800 students, was blond.

"It's stupid," yelled a blond female student at lunchtime. "People are learning to discriminate." She and her underprivileged peers encountered a much more uninviting environment than Jane Elliott's classroom; every inch of the building was segregated. "I was really thirsty," said a blond, "and I had to look all over [the school] before I could find a fountain I could use."

Days before the exercise, dark-haired students and faculty advisors published a newspaper called *The People's Guardian.*[53] The pages were filled with stereotypes commonly applied to Black Americans.

"I don't want a blond family living next to me. They all put trash in their yards."

"Blondes will take every opportunity to try to gyp you out of money."

"Blondes are cons!"

"Ho Chi Minh is a blond."

At a point, a one-skit drama broadcasted over the loudspeaker ridiculing blondes as dense and scatterbrained interrupted learning. Some blondes reached a breaking point and revolted by creating "blond [*sic*] power" signs. Two students dyed their hair brown so they could pass as dark-haired students.[54] Interviewed fifty years later, then eighth-grade blond student, Jan Shipe Brown, told a reporter from the *Washington Post*, "I have never forgotten that week. It was a seminal event in my life."

At the time, however, the exercise on discrimination generated parental protests and national news coverage. Walter Cronkite produced a feature on the exercise for "CBS Evening News." The idea was that of Cabin John Principal Tom Warren. Realizing the exercise might be problematic for the school's Black students, Warren and his cabinet went with hair color. A warning sent to parents a few days before the exercise explained that a multi-day program on discrimination would kick off National Brotherhood Week. Warren's theme for the nationwide observance of tolerance was "Togetherness and Brotherhood."

Similar to Elliott's exercises, newspaper reports from the time and a fiftieth-anniversary story about the exercise showed that the brunette, black, and red-haired students became bullies, particularly the hall monitors who enforced the designated bathroom and water fountain for blondes. A ninth-grade brunette, Chuck Sullivan, said the "tough guys had free rein to harass people." His brunette peer, Mark Walston, called the hall monitors "neo-Nazis" who "took their job just way too far." Cindy Minter later said, "I remember some kids getting beaten up and pushed around [. . .] It was just bringing out what African Americans were going through all of the time."[55]

At the end of the three-day exercise, blond students were told to give short speeches about their experiences. "Discrimination is stupid," said a seventh-grade girl. "It is learned, not inborn. And it is a singularly cruel thing to direct against another human being. It hurts, and it hurts deep."[56]

Principal Warren never mentioned Jane Elliott to reporters; at least, the journalists who documented the story made no connection to the woman whose appearance on *The Tonight Show* inspired educators across the United States and Canada. In any event, the case study of Cabin John's exercise generates hypotheses about ethics and participatory learning; it begs the question of how and where Warren came up with the idea. With all its dazzle, the fleeting coverage of Warren's anti-discrimination approach left onlookers with doubts over community reaction and how many times Cabin John Middle School attempted it in the following years.

During the summer following the Cabin John exercise, Northwestern University hosted a seminar for educators that separated attendees by hair color. Educators with blond hair were the victims of discrimination. One of the participants was browned-haired Beth Greenberg, an employee at Niles North High School in Skokie, Illinois. Greenberg took what she learned at the Northwestern workshop and created a "discrimination test" for the students and staff at Niles North. Her attempts to create a social order by positioning blondes at the bottom through segregated classrooms and mistreatment in school facilities fell flat as an insipid 20 percent of the students chose to participate in the optional exercise. "An experiment such as this can't be entirely successful unless everyone cooperates," Greenberg said.[57] One blond student dyed his hair brown to pass over to the superior group. When the day concluded, students and staff complained most about real cases of social discrimination existent at the all-white Niles North High School.

Therein lies the predicament Jane Elliott created for herself. Even as copycats took and modified her eye color exercise, she questioned whether it harmed students by making them vulnerable to ridicule. Or did she do them a favor, as she believed, "by making them aware of what racism really looks like and how all-pervasive it is in our society?"[58] This was the pressure swirling around Elliott heading into the new decade. This period was unlike any before as school leaders searched for new ways to prevent clashes that might materialize in America's diversifying schools and educate monolithic student bodies about issues of cultural diversity before heading into the real world. Elliott and the exercise made people think about a new system of ethics in which decisions about right and wrong are made on the merits of a specific situation or context rather than rigid school codes. This context is crucial to understanding why she did the exercise repeatedly. Half a century later, it was a decision that still defined Elliott, whether she liked it or not.

CHAPTER 11

EYE OF THE STORM

"Riceville, Iowa, with a population of a little less than a thousand people, sees the turmoil and hears the angry voices of the times only in television. It has no ghetto. It has no campus. No riots. No demonstrations. No Negroes. Its people are all white and all Christian. It's a relatively poor town surrounded by large cornfields. It is so far removed from the anguish of the cities that it's often hard for the people here to understand the forces that are dividing the United States today until a teacher at the town's school deliberately provoked an incident of discrimination based on color. It happened at the community elementary school in Riceville, the town's finest building."

—BILL BUETEL, *THE EYE OF THE STORM*, MAY 11, 1970

If her 1968 visit to *The Tonight Show* marked the moment that transformed Elliott into the most divisive person in Riceville, the forthcoming appearance of her third-grade students in an ABC documentary in 1970 made her a highly sought-after catalytic agent in the fields of anti-racism, mental health, and education. During the summer leading into the 1969-1970 school year, she received a request from freelance documentarians William "Bill" and Muriel Peters to film a documentary for the ABC network about the Discrimination Day lesson. "Oh, God. Here we go again!" Elliott thought at first. She questioned the Peters: "Aren't there more exciting news stories out there?"[1]

"Out of twenty years of reporting on civil rights," Bill Peters explained to Elliott and again later to the *Riceville Recorder*, "the lesson in the Riceville

Elementary School in prejudice and discrimination is the most original that I can remember."[2] The comment was quite the approbation to her work in experiential learning. Bill was an accomplished freelance documentarian at that point in his career. In 1956, he wrote a landmark essay published in *Redbook* magazine about Martin Luther King Jr. titled "Our Weapon is Love."[3] With direct quotes and personal notes mailed to him from King, Bill's exposé documented the twenty-seven-year-old civil rights icons' behind-the-scenes decision-making during the Montgomery bus boycott. King told Bill, "The spirit of passive resistance came to me from the Bible, from the teachings of Jesus. The techniques came from Gandhi." Years later, when Coretta Scott King shipped her late husband's papers off to Stanford University, the individual responsible for handling the documents, Clayborne Carson, described Bill's article as "an important source for tracing King's intellectual development."[4]

Bill Peters himself was an important source for tracing the development of the civil rights movement. Born in 1921 in San Francisco, he served as a first lieutenant pilot in the Army Air Force during World War II, where he was based in England with the 8th Air Force, 351st Bombardment group. He flew B-17s. During one mission over the Dutch coast, German fighters shot down his plane, killing his navigator and knocking his bombardier unconscious. According to reports, the plane crashed into the North Sea at 125 miles per hour, bouncing back and down again, and sank within forty-five seconds.[5] Bill and his co-pilot climbed out of the aircraft through the co-pilot's window. The rest of the crew escaped through the radio hatch. Nine men total floated on rafts for forty-five minutes until they were rescued.

Peters earned a degree in English from Northwestern University two years after the war. According to one obituary, he "resigned from his fraternity in protest after it refused to admit a black student."[6] After college, it took Bill little time to attain publication deals with *McCall's Magazine*, *Redbook*, and *Good Housekeeping*. His articles seemingly generated "a strong female readership" during that time. His byline included pieces on interracial marriage, discrimination in private social clubs, and a hate crime committed against a Jewish couple in his hometown of San Francisco. His first book, published in 1959, two years after the crisis of the Little Rock Nine at Central High School, was *The Southern Temper*. In the volume, printed by publishing tycoon Doubleday & Company, Inc., Bill uses the voices of pro-integration Southerners to argue that racism could not be legislated out of Southern culture. As expected, Southern reviewers were largely negative, citing dereliction as a journalist to include the perspectives of those Bill ascribed as unwavering segregationists.[7]

In 1962, CBS hired Peters as the station's race relations field journalist. His breakthrough assignment was an investigative report on voter disenfranchisement in Hattiesburg, Mississippi. The documentary *Mississippi and the Fifteenth Amendment* aired on September 26, 1962. He then produced two of three parts of the Peabody award-winning documentary *Storm Over the Supreme Court*, about the contentious debate over religion in schools.[8] In 1967, he helped Myrlie Evers, widow of the slain president of the Mississippi chapter of the NAACP Medgar Evers, write her memoir, *For Us, The Living*. He moved to ABC News that same year to assist on several projects, including another Peabody award-winning production, *Africa*. While working in Africa, Bill met his second of three wives, filmmaker Muriel Neff, who would act as associate producer on the documentary about Elliott's eye color exercise.

Living in Montauk, Bill and Muriel Peters first discovered Elliott and the exercise. Bill had read an *Associated Press* article about the Ricevillean in *The New York Times*. The timing was right, as he and Muriel were searching for the topic of their next film. After finishing the article, Bill proclaimed he had found their new project, according to Muriel's recollection.[9] They wanted to make an hour-long documentary in his initial pitch to ABC, who, according to Muriel, "weren't terribly interested" in the topic. Nevertheless, the station was "interested enough" to offer the Peters' a small contract to make a thirty-minute documentary for its new Monday evening docuseries titled *NOW*. The network's *NOW* program offered short films on matters of national importance every Monday beginning in March and running through September 1970.[10]

After an initial telephone call to Elliott, the Peters flew to Riceville to prove how serious they were about making the film. They won her over by the end of dinner at Elliott's house. Though convinced, she insisted that no work on the film would begin until Principal Dinsmore Brandmill and Superintendent Donald Johnston green-lighted the project. In the meantime, Elliott had to wrestle with the fact that almost all her eighteen students that year were "moderately to severely disabled readers." Could she put those children through the exercise before a national audience? Would they be able to control their behavior in front of television cameras? If the parents approved, Elliott reasoned that she would do it. To her surprise, only one parent was uneager to sign the waiver granting ABC permission to use the footage "how and when they chose to" and to state that they expected no remuneration for having their children in the film. While the parent eventually signed the form, his grievance was not about how his child would look on television but about his dislike for Black people.[11]

To incentivize students, parents, and the school's administration, Elliott convinced Thomas H. Wolf—ABC Vice President and Director of Television Documentary Programs—to pledge gifts to the students to learn about filmmaking. In a letter to Elliott, Wolf promised that the Peters would bring "whatever we can provide in the way of still photographs of behind-the-scenes film, tape, and live production for use with your students."[12] He also confirmed that ABC would provide the school with a 16 mm print of the film's final cut. It was all set; ABC chose National Brotherhood Week, February 22 to 25, 1970, as the days to make the movie.

As with everything surrounding how Elliott administered instruction in Room 10, she designed a unit on photography. In addition to putting cameras in their hands so they could enjoy snapping pictures of one another, her objective was to acclimate students to the reality that fourteen hours of their lives for two school days were going to become a television show with spotlighting, boom mics, and large cameras filming from multiple angles. She used cameras that Banker and the Canadian Broadcast Corporation gifted the school after filming their 1968 documentary, *The Way It Is*. Her friend and professional photographer Charlotte Button appeared as the unit's guest instructor. They even planned a field trip to Button's home, where students saw their first darkroom. She recalled, "We put cameras in the kids [*sic*] hands, and they took pics of one another."[13] Elliott financed the development of the students' pictures. "By the end of January, those kids were lookin' and feelin' and doin' good," Elliott wrote in *A Collar in My Pocket*.[14]

Talk about the film turned into action when members of the ABC team started arriving in Riceville as early as February 19. Guaranteeing that one camera documented Elliott's every move with the other glued to the students, two small crews made up of ABC personnel flew in from New York and Chicago. In addition to Bill and Muriel, nine individuals made up the crew, including two cameramen, three sound technicians, two electricians, and two assistant camera persons. They arrived Sunday, February 22.[15] After checking into the Cresco DeLuxe Motel, the crew went to Riceville Elementary to set up the equipment in Room 10. At the same time, the Peters' met with Elliott, Brandmill, Johnston, and the parents of students.

Monday, February 23, the day before the exercise, was used to adjust the students to the lights, camera, and crew. Muriel called it a necessary "fake shoot" since the students could not take their eyes off the equipment or the personnel mulling around Elliott's diminutively sized classroom. At the same time, their teacher instructed them on spelling, handwriting, and mathematics.

They were particularly distracted by the two soundmen, Morgan Smith and Jack Brennan, both African American. "This was astonishing to the kids because they had never seen a Black person before," said Muriel years later, who had watched in amusement from a tight corner in the room. "[. . .] those kids couldn't take their eyes off these guys for an hour or two."[16] Since the commotion from Room 10 created minor distractions elsewhere in the building, the film crew invited students from neighboring classrooms to Elliott's room to see what was happening.

Elliott tried to make it "business as usual" by counting points, saying the Pledge of Allegiance, and singing "God Bless America." She then hooked the students into learning with a chorus of Frank Sinatra's 1959 Oscar-winning song "High Hopes" from the movie *A Hole in the Head* with child actor Eddie Hodges. A few minutes into the morning, a student asked why the television people were in their classroom. She told the class: "They were looking for the greatest group of third graders they could find; why wouldn't they come to my classroom?"[17] She did not indicate that the class would soon be divided by eye color. During a break in the day, first cameraman Vincent Gaitto allowed the students to play with the television cameras.

The faux shoot was essential for ensuring that external forces would not contaminate or disrupt the fidelity of the exercise. With help from Peters and Charlotte Button, Elliott designed an unscientific metric to demonstrate the impact of discriminatory treatment. Button was present in the classroom to document the entire exercise with her equipment. She made sure to take before and after pictures of each student. The photographs would be collated and used as anecdotal evidence of how the experience impacted the emotional well-being of the children through abnormal posturing and facial expressions.

Moreover, Elliott created a multi-step "semantic differential" test to measure how students felt before, during, and after the simulation.[18] Twice during the exercise—once on day one and again on day two—she asked the students to rate their present feelings about the school (scored from bad to great), Room 10 (miserable to happy), Mrs. Elliott (horrid to wonderful), and television (hateful to fun). On each day during art class, Elliott had the children draw self-portraits based on their feelings. At the end of each day, they were told to list the names of three people who were supportive friends during the exercise. Elliott also administered a spelling test to measure academic performance on days students were mistreated versus privileged. These materials are buried in the University of Iowa archives; however, they do not appear in Peters' finished documentary about the Discrimination Day experience.

Elliott seethed a bit, thinking that little learning had occurred during the fake shoot. It was an "intrusion," she recalled, adding, "but the kids enjoyed every minute of it because they were experiencing something they had never experienced before." She understood it was important to get the children accustomed to the cameras to ensure the authenticity of the discrimination exercise. "I wanted them to pay attention to the exercise and not to the cameras."[19] She left them with one final thought before boarding the buses home; it was National Brotherhood Week and reminded the children of the annual tradition's significance, which began in the 1920s to mitigate xenophobia, anti-Catholic, and anti-Semitic sentiments. These emanated during an era that witnessed the second founding of the Ku Klux Klan and politically incentivized debates on Capitol Hill over immigration restriction. Leading up to that week, President Richard Nixon told the public that "Brotherhood begins with respect."[20] Elliott intentionally repeated such messages that day so she could use them as the hook to begin the Discrimination Day lesson.

Indeed, on Tuesday, February 24, after row leaders counted points and the customary recitation of the pledge and "America the Beautiful," Elliott began class by asking her students to explain the meaning of National Brotherhood Week. She guided the children's answers with the golden rule: "Treat everyone the way you would like to be treated. Treat everyone as though he was your brother."[21] She then asked the students to name groups of commonly mistreated people and explain why that mistreatment exists. "It might be interesting today to judge people by the color of their eyes. Do you want to try this?" A chorus of yeah's rang out from the students.

As was commonly done in the early years of the exercise, Elliott placed the blue-eyed children on top that first day. In later years, she would place the brown eyes on top the first day of the exercise.[22] She explained the reasons why people with blue eyes are superior. "It's a fact. Blue-eyed people are better than brown-eyed people," she said as many brown-eyed students sank into their seats, dumbfounded that their beloved teacher said such things. Brian Saltou rejected every word, becoming one of the most memorable students to appear in the documentary.

As soon as Elliott finished explaining how the class would be divided by eye color, she allowed the blue-eyed students to place collars around the necks of their counterparts. Desks were rearranged to position those with blue eyes at the front of the room. Then the instruction began, with Elliott commenting, "We spend a great deal of time waiting for brown-eyed people." Within thirty minutes, the blue eyes became "arrogant, condescending, judgmental, accusatory." On the contrary, the brown eyes grew "timid, shy, retiring, frightened."[23] Elliott felt things started occurring that would not have happened had she not forced the exercise on the students. To gain approval from his "demigod," blue-eyed Raymond Hansen told Mrs. Elliott to use a yardstick to whack misbehaving brown-eyed students. Hansen also instructed the cafeteria staff to bar brown-eyed students from seconds of lunch.[24] A brown-eyed student, Sheila Shaefer, got into an accident on the playground, causing swelling on her forehead. As shown in *The Eye of the Storm*, John Benttine punched Russell Ring because the latter called him "Brown Eyes." Later in the day, Ring was rushed to the hospital seventeen miles away in Osage after swallowing the straight pin used to keep the collars fashioned around the necks of the inferior students.[25]

"We didn't like each other by the end of the day," Elliott told Bill Peters during the confessional interview after recording. In fact, on the bus ride home from school that day, Elliott's daughter, Mary, a fifth grader at RCS Elementary, heard one of her mother's blue-eyed students, Rex Kozak, say to a friend, "She can't sit with me, she has the wrong color eyes." Mary later explained that her mom had given Kozak a "license" to behave that way, even after school hours. "He was running with it."[26]

"Being blue-eyed, I was on top of the world because my eye color was the dominant group," writes Kozak more than two decades later as a special contributor to the Cedar Rapids *Gazette*. Among the shortest in the class, he was in his element that first day of the exercise. "I couldn't do anything wrong," he said, affirming Mary's interpretation of his behavior. "I took this superior feeling home." His older siblings were having none of it. They warned Kozak that his dear blue-eyed teacher would switch roles tomorrow.

For all the doom and gloom experienced on day one, all the students returned for more the following day. Kozak's recollection of the sudden turn of events provides a particularly compelling snapshot into the minds of the blue-eyed children. "After being on a high all night, I was looking forward to going back to school the next day. I let people know I was superior all the way to school," Kozak said.[27] But then, Mrs. Elliott reversed positions. She suddenly started insulting the intelligence and behavior of the blue-eyed children. She goaded the brown-eyed children to do the same. Kozak's condition made him think only about being shamed by his peers and siblings, who told him this was coming. The collar was equally humiliating. "I felt terrible," he recalled. "I remember tears building up in my eyes, not only because I was going to be in the down group but because the person I believed in had turned on me."[28]

The confidence of those with brown eyes increased when Elliott would say things like, "Boy, brown-eyed people learn fast." A segment of *The Eye of the Storm* showing Elliott with the brown-eyed students at a small table working on the Orton-Gillingham card pack is among the most revealing scenes of the thirty-minute episode. The part reveals how quickly students could read through the card pack compared to their poor performance the previous day. What was the difference? "We just kept thinking about those collars," said the children. Meanwhile, the blue-eyed cohort's score was a minute and eighteen seconds slower than the day they ruled the classroom.

A touching moment occurred at the end of the day. Elliott had gathered the class in a circle at the end of the day to announce that the exercise was over and that she had lied to everyone. One girl, Sheila Schaefer, was so relieved she cried. Hugs were shared copiously. Elliott suddenly felt compelled to lead the group in the song "The Paw-Paw Patch" with a twist. As an alternative for "Where, oh where, is dear little Jimmy?" she changed the lyrics to "Where, oh where, is dear little Sheila?" Bill Peters described the end of the exercise as such: "The tensions of the two-day exercise broke like a dam giving way to a flood, and she laughed with them, comforted those who cried with relief, and nearly cried herself at the sight of boys who had been separated by the color of their eyes wrestling happily together, of girls, eyes wet with joy, hugging friends they had thought forever lost."[29]

After filming, Elliott invited the film crew to the Jennison Inn for supper. Gie cooked dinner while Elliott prepared dessert—two apple pies, one of which slid off her car's front seat when driving from her house to the inn. No one seemed to notice its battered appearance. While enjoying a piece of Elliott's pie, cameraman Vincent Gaitto, who listened to Riceville teachers lambaste Elliott's work earlier that day, told Gie, "She's got a bear by the tail," and he was surprised someone would "take on such a topic and in such a forward way."[30]

Bill Buetel, the London correspondent for ABC working as the documentary's narrator, arrived in Riceville after the shoot. His job was to open and close the episode in an outdoor location with short contextual monologues written by the Peters about the Riceville community and the impact of the eye color exercise. Indeed, the script enabled Buetel to offer an acute observation. Riceville, he said, "is so far removed from the anguish of the cities that it's often hard for the people here to understand the forces that are dividing the United States today until a teacher at the town's school deliberately provided an incident of discrimination based on color."[31]

Both Buetel and Giatto were right. However, the firestorm would not come for another three months. The show was tentatively scheduled to air on late-night television near the end of the school year. That gave the Peters' two months to produce their film. Writing a few days after leaving Riceville, Muriel Peters told Elliott, "[. . .] what you're doing is so illuminating and courageous that it will make itself felt even if we don't do you justice. But I think we shall. I know we'll try."[32] In a subsequent letter, written March 13, a few days after cutting the film, Muriel remarked: "You are just marvelous, by the way, in your interview sequence."[33] Her only regret was that she and her husband had to cut out interviews with Elliott's teaching colleagues and the older RCS students. "I'd like to do a half hour on Brian [Saltou] alone," she quipped. "What an actor!"[34]

* * *

The town was still spinning after the ABC crew left as parents and colleagues debated whether Elliott not only tormented those children but if she had wasted three days of taxpayer-funded instruction time. Principal Brandmill calmed concerned citizens when he told the local paper the students had a "normal" reaction to the television lights and cameras, adding "regular schoolwork" continued "in the class throughout the filming."

There is plenty of first-hand evidence that the standard curriculum was effectively taught during those two days without distraction from the ABC crew. Muriel Peters revealed later that people often asked her if the children were paid actors since they seemed so relaxed and comfortable on television. "We were gone," she said, suggesting that Elliott's talents as an educator made students feel as if there were no camera personnel filming the class. "They were so into what she was doing. They had had a day of us around. They were used to us; we were no longer things in their lives."[35] No script was necessary, said Room 10 student Donna (Reddell) May in an interview marking the thirtieth anniversary of the Discrimination Day lesson. "You ended up living in your role," she said, explaining that feelings of depression and defeat took hold of her body when wearing the collar.[36] Classmate Raymond Hansen confirmed that assessment: "Once we got into the exercise, [the camera crew] might not have even been there. There was no one performing for the camera," adding, "except for maybe Brian Saltou. But everybody else was so engaged in what was going on that I don't remember them being there."[37] Hansen offered another conciliatory statement, a homage to Elliott's experiential pedagogy that spoke to the authenticity of the discrimination simulation. "What she did as far as the instructional system of the day was consistent to what we did every day. It wasn't that she did some extraordinary training. It was normal stuff."

All sides agreed on how extraordinary it was, just two years after Elliott helped introduce small-town Riceville to the country on *The Tonight Show*, that a farmer's daughter from the Midwest was an integral voice in the race conversation across America. The *Riceville Recorder* plastered Elliott's picture on several editions, making her better known than when she owned the Jennison Inn.

Nearly every adolescent and teenager in Riceville knew about the third-grade teacher who subjected her students to isolation and torture for two days to teach a lesson about discrimination. Stories about Elliott and the Room 10 students started appearing in newspapers nationwide to help promote the upcoming airing of *The Eye of the Storm.*

The Peters initially wanted to title the documentary "The Anatomy of Prejudice." After deliberations, however, the duo settled on a metaphoric moniker. Why? A racial tempest had already engulfed larger cities like Chicago, Minneapolis, Waterloo, and Des Moines, which surrounded northern Iowa, where calm seemingly encapsulated the small town of Riceville. But the Peters planned to challenge viewers to contemplate how deeply responsible white parents and white educators were in sustaining a culture of racial indifference by ignoring policies. Were white realtors and bankers responsible for urban congestion? Should white teachers be blamed for shaping a school system that steered Black students into menial occupations? Did white doctors sit passively by as the healthcare system did little to stymie lower life expectancy rates for people of color? What onus do whites carry for enabling law-and-order initiatives that target communities of color? Were homogeneous towns guilty of perpetuating a great mythology? Did such communities cause more harm to society by teaching children to deny that racism exists or that there is something innately inferior in people of color? The heart of racism, they argued, was in communities like Riceville that placed fishbowls around their young ones while allowing the cyclone to wreak havoc on neighboring Black communities.[38]

Life magazine ran a TV Review feature titled "Ghetto for Blue-eyes in the Classroom" in its May 8 edition. The article's author, novelist, and *New York Times* book critic John Leonard rubber-stamped the exercise. "Unfortunately, not every elementary school is full of Mrs. Elliotts," he wrote.[39] It was a comment that must have aggravated Elliott's colleagues.

Meanwhile, in her household, Elliott optimistically believed "that once the people in the community realize how great the learning had been and how important the concepts were, they'd be proud and impressed with what was happening in this little rural community, rather than being angry and threatened."[40] Hearing that ABC executives reacted with adulation to the finished product bolstered her hope. Associate producer Muriel Peters recalled: "We had a private screening for the head of ABC News and the head of ABC Documentaries, who had been kind of skeptical and not very interested. So, we had this little screening in a very little screening room, and the lights were out, and when the lights came on, they were both in tears."[41]

ABC aired *The Eye of the Storm* on May 11, which fell near the end of the twenty-six-week-long *NOW* series. The fact that the *NOW* program regularly came on television at half-past nine o'clock in the evening in Iowa and at 10:30 p.m. on the East Coast produced mixed reviews for the ABC series. One critic, Ray Bennett, called the Monday night news program "glossy and shallow" and said the longer it ran, the more frequently it "failed to get to grips with some pretty important subjects."[42] *NOW* producers created shows on race, gender, culture, religion, and politics. One of the earliest episodes gave viewers insight into income taxes. Most, however, explored contentious cultural conflicts plaguing the country then.

The series included a feature titled "The Panthers," which reflected on how much influence the Black Panther Party had on Black Americans. In "No Deposit, No Return," the program explored the beauty of the North American continent and how that beauty was being destroyed by "negligence" and disrespect of indigenous land. Other stories concentrated on the impact Vietnam War casualties had on small towns in America and the emergence of the women's liberation movement. The series also featured an episode titled "Black Mayor in Dixie," which documented the election of Charles Evers, the first Black mayor of Fayette, Mississippi, and the brother of the late Medgar Evers. This episode aimed to explore the increasing political consciousness in communities that were disenfranchised before the passage of the 1965 Voting Rights Act. Of the twenty-six episodes aired by ABC, however, Peters' feature on Jane Elliott received the most acclaim. It eventually won a Peabody Award.

The exercise, as seen on television, had immediate ramifications for Elliott's family. One night, a crank call came at three o'clock in the morning. "After listening to him for a while [sic]," she told a reporter from the Mason City *Globe-Gazette*, "I just put the phone down, and every fifteen or twenty minutes, I'd pick it up and say something like, 'that's right, sir,' and then put it back down again. I hope he got some satisfaction out of it because it sure cost him a lot of money."[43]

Residents of Riceville saw the show as a community touchstone by which racist communities should be judged. The day *The Eye of the Storm* aired, Gie and Lloyd sold out of their lunch and dinners—a Riceville tradition for two dozen regulars. To those welcomed guests, the Jennisons set up two long tables in the dining area and served the meal family-style. But on May 12, they sold none. To further shame her parents "for raising the town's only [N-word] lover," Elliott recalled, the community regularly parked in front of the hotel and walked in the eyesight of Gie farther down the road to Petit's Cafe.[44] The Jennison Inn would remain under Gie and Lloyd's ownership for decades. According to her mother, however, the inn's abject condition in the years to come was Elliott's doing. Meanwhile, Petit's Cafe became the nexus of rumors about the possibility that Black families would soon move to Riceville.[45] They resented Elliott for the facile threat of Black encroachment—a theory later described as the "great replacement."

Malignity in Riceville notwithstanding, outside reception toward Elliott's performance was much more flattering. Muriel Peters wrote to Elliott on May 12, the morning after the premiere, "Literally everyone who has called [ABC] has said, 'What a wonderful woman the teacher is,' so maybe you should run for president while the iron is hot."[46] The film, in her estimation, was delightful.

The world's largest educational organization, the National Education Association (NEA), highly endorsed *The Eye of the Storm* to its more than one million members, composed of elementary, secondary, and postsecondary educators in all fifty states. The NEA first persuaded ABC to make "non-theatrical, direct exhibition" screening reels of the documentary available for educators in sixteen-millimeter format. It then advised its members to use the video in classrooms for its "educational and instructional value."[47] The idea prompted the corporation's marketing department, ABC Merchandising Inc., to begin a "new service to the educational community." In his announcement, ABC Merchandising's vice president, William Dennis, called *The Eye of the Storm* a "topical and most relevant film." ABC wrote up a teacher's guide to go along with the video. Distribution to educators began later that summer.[48]

Acclaim over the show convinced the station to rebroadcast *The Eye of the Storm* on August 10 ahead of the new school year. "ABC News is pleased to repeat *The Eye of the Storm* to meet the hundreds of requests we have received from around the country," announced Thomas Wolf, ABC News vice president and director of television documentaries. "This program is an example of documentary programming at its best. The story of Jane Elliot [*sic*] and her class of third graders is appealing, moving, and enlightening. And the program's message needs no further elaboration. It is concise and self-contained."[49]

Reading such remarks provided assurances that have stayed with Elliott her entire life. Kinship with Muriel Peters and affirmation of a job well-done from the NEA was especially important since a torrent of love and hate mail arrived rapidly at her personal P.O. Box and teacher's mailbox at Riceville Elementary. While accepting praise was easy, living with ugliness was more difficult. "What I was doing wasn't wrong," she told an interviewer some years later. "It was different, it was challenging, but it wasn't wrong. I honestly believe that to this day, and I will to the day I die."[50]

CHAPTER 12

MORE THAN MEETS THE EYE

We all exist in our own selfish worlds. It is always easier to participate physically than it is to participate mentally and spiritually. But when we are able to shift our focus from ourselves and center it on others—on human beings and human conditions—we will probably begin to understand what it truly means to be in community with others.

—Jane Elliott, unsent letter to Wilda Wood, June 4, 1970

It is nearly impossible to capture the range of emotions Jane Elliott experienced in the days following the May 11, 1970, premiere of *The Eye of the Storm*. The composite praise heaped upon Bill and Muriel Peters was something Elliott enjoyed occasionally. While she enjoyed receiving letters expressing admiration, condemnation was levied upon the Jennison family. Threats were made to boycott the family hotel and restaurant, verbal and sometimes physical altercations occurred with her kids at school, and the occasional death threat was expressed in phone calls and postage. These accounts are well-known to followers of Elliott's life. The story of a letter that arrived in her family's P.O. Box on May 14 is less known.

Elliott noticed that the remarks were usually tenderhearted and reassuring when receiving letters from educators, whether from classroom teachers or school administrators. The May 14 letter, however, was composed by schoolteacher Mary Carroll of Pine Valley Elementary School, an academy serving the children of Air Force cadets in Colorado Springs, Colorado. In eight sentences, Carroll accused Elliott of plagiarizing the eye color exercise from one of her colleagues,

Wilda Wood, who had conducted a similar project on discrimination at Pine Valley for at least three years. Carroll called the content of Elliott's classroom simulation an "extraction" of Wood's curriculum called "Project Misery."

"Your failure to give credit to Mrs. Wood and her class for their efforts, initiative in planning, and implementation of ideas was at best, grossly unfair," declared Carroll, an apparent former Colorado Education Association division officer (CEA). Out of a "responsibility for integrity," she notified Elliott that she was filing complaints with the CEA and the National Education Association.[1]

A teacher of almost two decades, Wilda Wood, conceived the idea for Project Misery in 1965 while taking a human relations course at Colorado College. A student of Morton Sobel (not to be confused with the Soviet spy imprisoned for espionage in 1951), Wood's term paper offered a classroom simulation to make young students understand the social and psychological impact of legal segregation.[2] After her professor awarded an A-plus for the paper, Wood presented the idea of testing the project in her sixth-grade class to Pine Valley principal Roger Thorson and school superintendent Howard Dunning. Both gave stamps of approval. Wood performed Project Misery once a year, each lasting five school days, from 1965 to 1967. The project was voluntary, and she received consent from the students' parents in advance. Unlike Elliott's Discrimination Day lesson, Project Misery was not an eye-color exercise. It appears all of Wood's students were placed into an underprivileged group, segregated from the rest of the student body. The Pine Valley simulation was quite the production.

Before the project began, Wood asked that students bring in newspaper and magazine clippings about civil rights topics occurring in the news. The articles discussed terms like prejudice, second-class citizenship, discrimination, and segregation. The mistreatment of Wood's students grew more severe as the week progressed. On Monday, the same day as the current events discussion, the students faced discrimination in the lunchroom by being forced to eat at a separate table marked with a sign. This occurred all week. On Tuesday, Wood's students had to ride in the back of all public transportation, step off the sidewalk when others passed, and converse only with students from their class. Discriminatory treatment continued for the remainder of the week. On Wednesday, school jobs—ranging from teaching assistant to student council and bookstore clerk—were given to students in other classes. The blacklisting continued through Friday. On Thursday, Wood's students used outdated books, science equipment, art supplies, and audio-visual materials. They could not attend band, physical education, and other popular elective classes and received poorly planned busy work.

The arrival of Friday meant Wood's students faced restrictions on what they could wear to school. Anyone wearing blue jeans had to segregate from the rest of the student population. None of the students were permitted to speak about an academic subject without first getting approval from their peers enrolled in other classes. Additionally, no one was allowed to write a paper on politicized topics. During the 1967 project, Wood brought in James Reynolds, head of the Colorado Civil Rights Commission, to stage a mock civil rights investigation of the school. He inspired the students to stage a sit-in protest, which lasted one class period. Others distributed copies of the U.S. Constitution.

Project Misery did receive national coverage in 1966 and 1967. In 1966, ABC's Piere Anderton and CBS's Terry Drinkwater provided stories about the work undertaken by Wood.[3] A featured story by Jim Gibney about Wood's project made its rounds through the *Associated Press* that same year. Additionally, Pine Valley's Principal Thorson published an essay about the success of Project Misery at his school in the February 1966 edition of *The National Elementary Principal*. Also, in 1966, the *NEA Journal* described Wood's work in its column "Idea Exchange." The *Colorado School Journal* featured an expose on Project Misery that same year. In 1967, details about the project appeared in *Education Summary, ADL Bulletin, Craft Educational Service, SRA Newsletter,* and *School Management*. The popular advice columnist and psychologist Dr. Joyce Brothers referenced Project Misery and Wilda Wood in a February 1967 response to teachers seeking strategies to better engage students in diversifying kindergarten classrooms.[4]

Wilda Wood also wrote a letter directly to Elliott. Written the same day as Mary Carroll's correspondence, Wood used the opportunity to explain how popular Project Misery was among the nation's teaching population. Wood explained, "large numbers of teachers were reached via the printed word" and that educators had written to her requesting Project Misery training resources. Wood said she happily compiled a packet of material to help educators customize the project for personal use. The Pine Valley teacher noted that an exchange of views generated "clever ideas" for teaching about bias and discrimination, such as "poorly dressed vs. well-dressed; boys vs. girls; blondes vs. brunettes; class vs. class, etc." Before her complimentary closing, Wood saluted Elliott's third-grade students for their performance on the silver screen. "They were superb," she admitted. "They came through as intelligent, impressionable youngsters," then added: "Let's hope they will always be guided by conscientious, scrupulous teachers."[5] Wood then demanded a response.

While Elliott did not take kindly to the allegation, she refrained from sending Carroll and Wood an irrational response. Alternatively, she welcomed an ethics investigation. It is unknown whether Elliott first notified the National Education Association (NEA) or the grievance of Carroll and Wood landed at the association's Washington D.C. office. Documents show, however, that Elliott was in communication with ABC Director and Vice President of Television Programs Thomas Wolf, along with Bill and Muriel Peters, about the accusation against her. Elliott also presented her side of the story to the associate secretary for ethics at the NEA, Donald H. Morrow.

Following a two-week investigation, on May 28, Morrow wrote to Wood's boss, Principal Thorson, clearing Elliott of any impropriety. Conceding that Wood "was widely recognized in 1966 and after that for the activities of her class in a project on discrimination," the ethics official explained that that recognition presented Wood with "no special rights" over the project. Moreover, Morrow proclaimed, "Similar projects have received news attention since that time." He questioned whether Wood could provide copyright over the school-based exercise. Additionally, Morrow demonstrated that the ethics committee's interrogation of the stenographic transcript of *The Eye of the Storm* proved the defendant never claimed that she "originated the idea" or misrepresented any facts about when she began the exercise in 1968. "The matter of origin of the idea is not spoken to in the transcript in any way, only the expression of Mrs. Elliott's concern that the children be involved in feeling the effects of discrimination."[6] In the end, Morrow said the NEA could not find cause to prosecute Elliott for unfairly treating or appropriating Wood's project.

After consulting with Morrow, the Peters, and Wolf at ABC, Elliott finally wrote to Wood on June 4. "I was happy to learn that you received so much recognition for your 'Project Misery,'" she said. "I wish I had seen some of the publicity and thus been aware of your work prior to my Discrimination Day exercise, as I am certain I would have benefited greatly from your experience." In an early draft, Elliott entertained asking Wood for a Project Misery resource packet. Instead, she safely chose to add, "That there are similarities is not surprising since the characteristics of discrimination are analogous in most discriminatory situations. It is surprising to me, however, to receive an extremely vituperative letter from one of your colleagues (Mrs. Mary Carroll) at the Pine Valley Elementary School in which, among other things, she censured me for plagiarizing [sic] your idea and presenting it as my own. It is unfortunate that she [. . .] made these unfounded accusations before determining the facts." Elliott expressed a willingness to keep the lines of communication open and expressed a "fervent hope" that their respective work could "be construed as they were conceived—for the purpose of furthering understanding among children, thereby lessening misunderstanding among future adults."[7]

When asked to recall this incident more than fifty years later, Elliott praised "the educator" for trying to undo racism. Education is a field where ideas are shared, coopted, advanced, and customized to fit a specific context. Wilda Wood and her Pine Valley colleague may have been right to be unsettled by their suspicions of Jane Elliott's actions. Consciously or not, she may have adapted Project Misery, at least partly from discussions about improving racial and cultural understanding among America's school-age population. If so, her likely resource would have been creating a more welcoming school climate for dyslexic students. Professional learning sessions at the Dyslexia Reading Center in Rochester, Minnesota, bred opportunities for novel approaches to multicultural education.

Despite the conjecture, no evidence indicting Elliott of infringing certain aspects of Wilda Wood's anti-discrimination pedagogical blueprint has surfaced. No matter how one looks at it, both educators presented a case for making the future of education based on virtue diversity. Elliott wrote to Marylin "Mickey" Alcorn, a dear friend from college: "Too much emphasis on Reading, Writing, and Arithmetic and too little emphasis on Reason, Rights, and Responsibility." She said empathy "is more effective than empty sympathy, and I want my children to empathize."[8] In other words, her experiential pedagogy indeed morphed into that Sioux prayer: "Keep me from ever judging a man until I have walked a mile in his moccasins."

* * *

At Sacred Heart School, LaSalle in Windsor, Ontario, twenty-eight-year-old teacher Frank Kapasi was so moved by Jane Elliott that he designed his own lesson on discrimination for his eighth-grade students just days after *The Eye of the Storm* debut. Kapasi used Elliott's exercise as a template to create a similar experience for all 100 of his middle schoolers. With a subtle modification, his exercise kept those with blue eyes at the top of the hierarchy for both days. When a journalist asked about his two-day activity a few days later, Kapasi conceded it was easier for Elliott to switch superior groups since she had her elementary students in the classroom for an entire school day. On the contrary, he had his pupils for a portion of the day before a new cohort of eighth graders arrived. He arranged for the superior blue-eyed group to sit in front of the class. They received extended recess and could arrive at class a few minutes late and leave five minutes early. Kapasi let the blue eyes leave class for a drink of water anytime they pleased. He said it was up to the blue-eyed students to speak to the brown-eyed students. The students were praised for completing simple tasks and were never corrected for mistakes. When teaching, Kapasi instructed the brown-eyed students to teach themselves the lesson from the textbook. He spent the period working closely with the blue-eyed pupils, "encouraging them and being friendly and warm."[9]

As a teacher of eight years, the sudden change in the personality and behavior of the students shocked Kapasi. He said it was fifteen minutes before the blue-eyed students took learning more seriously and improved their classroom behavior. "They were proud to be superior, and their confidence increased," reported *The Windsor Star*. Brown-eyed students, meanwhile, became angry and irritated.[10] Only 5 percent of the brown eyes earned perfect scores during a spelling test.

In comparison, 30 percent of the blue-eyed students had perfect marks. On the second day, he administered a timed grammar test. Most blue eyes finished within ten minutes, against less than a third of the brown eyes.

Kapasi acknowledged having difficulty trying to behave "purposely bad" and "had to work to keep a straight face."[11] Nevertheless, when he referenced specific events in class during the school year, he convinced the students that he was serious about people with blue eyes possessing superior traits. Some were petty samples of brown-eyed misbehavior, like chewing gum against school policy or speaking out in class. Kapasi anticipated fights breaking out among students. His classes experienced "an inordinate amount of teasing, a near brawl and genuine belief in the manufactured biases." Like Elliott's students, the performance of those labeled inferior dropped off, while the labeled superior group excelled.

"Sir, you know what you're doing—you're making it just like it was black versus white," said one of his students.[12] Kapasi disagreed, sticking to his myth that blue-eyed persons possessed superior traits.

Kapasi sat blue-eyed and brown-eyed students across from one another at a table set up at one end of the classroom to end the exercise. He led a short debrief, then ensured everyone shook hands and understood this was just an exercise. "I did it as an experiment only," he asserted. "I just wanted them to get a small bitter taste of what discrimination was like." Blue-eyed thirteen-year-old Diane Meloche said the lesson "made me feel more intelligent." She also admitted to teasing her inferior-labeled peers. Fourteen-year-old Rick Reaume, also with blue eyes, was one of six students that bullied a brown-eyed patrol boy. The patrol boy was fourteen-year-old Gilbert Forster. "I couldn't fight back" because Reaume was much bigger, he said. Chris McKinnon, age thirteen, with blue eyes, teased a group of brown-eyed students because he felt emboldened by his teacher. His teasing almost led to a playground fight. It appeared that four of his students took too much of a liking to be on top of the hierarchy. Kapasi met with students the day after the exercise to clear up the situation. "It showed that prejudice, once taught, can linger," wrote the local newspaper.[13]

Kapasi's exercise is one of the most revealing pieces of evidence showing that Jane Elliott's influence stretched beyond *The Eye of the Storm*. But it seems that it wasn't Peters' film that served as Kapasi's muse. If anything, it would have been the Canadian Broadcasting Company's 1968 *The Way It Is* segment that ignited discussion in Ontario about the Inuit population that inspired Kapasi to create his custom-made anti-discrimination simulation. This is important to note, considering the Project Misery plagiarism allegations. Elliott was also about to face her most prominent public critic since she first taught the discrimination exercise.

*　*　*

Another significant measure of the eye color exercise was the criticism opponents leveled against it. Nowhere was that criticism on greater display than in a nationally syndicated column, "Dr. Max Rafferty," which condemned the exercise as "educational malfeasance." Accusing Elliott of "bad reasoning, bad analogy, and bad teaching," Max Rafferty told readers that taxpayers did not expect teachers "to plant her own ideas about political and sociological problems" into the minds of students or to "frighten youngsters or torment them to make them feel inferior." The outgoing Superintendent of Public Instruction in California and author of several books on education, Rafferty called Elliott's reason behind the inspiration for the exercise misinformed, simple, and "atrociously non sequitur logic."[14]

An editorial of this nature was consistent for Rafferty. However, some contextual items must be understood to grasp why he would attack a woman from an all-white all-Christian town of less than a thousand people. Three weeks before his words went to press, Rafferty lost his superintendent re-election campaign to Wilson Riles, the first African American elected to any statewide office in California. During his lame-duck period, Rafferty pursued (and eventually obtained) a job as Dean of Education at Troy University in Alabama. The breaking point came when he read the *Life* magazine article about Elliott sometime after its May 8 publication date. The article's opening irked him: "For the third year in a row, Jane Elliott has introduced a little terror into the classroom." Rafferty responded, "Whenever I read a sentence like the one above, I wince. When it's used to kick off a *Life* article, I add a good, solid cringe to the original wince." He pilloried Elliott's method of using eye color to separate students into superior and inferior groups. "Shades of old Adolf!" he charged, adding that her connection between eye-color bigotry was "hogwash" in comparison to the reason why Martin Luther King Jr. had been assassinated two and a half years earlier. His intimations that he didn't "know what motives" caused James Earl Ray to murder King or that "Race usually has little to do with assassinations" are puzzling.[15] And, in the case of the murdered American civil rights champion, his words come off as if he aimed to gaslight the public.

Elliott was distraught, admittedly feeling "alone" sometimes. It was one thing for critics to call the exercise unethical that a mother might become "unhappy" about how her child is learning the implications of a racialized culture sculpted over time to privilege those with pale skin and a Christian upbringing. Even then, Elliott conceded in a letter to a fifth-grade teacher from Winona, Minnesota, Don Walz Jr., who received a complaint from one unhappy parent after conducting a similar anti-discrimination exercise in his class a year earlier.[16] Writing a few weeks after the publication of Rafferty's editorial, she assured: "Well, you can't change this mother's mind." If Elliott continued with the exercise, teachers around the country, like Walz, could continue to emulate the lesson.

Moreover, to sustain the educational turn to make school curriculums more inclusive, Elliott would be forced to develop a response to public faces like Max Rafferty. In her distress at the mounting public criticism—such language was no longer levied at her in private correspondences—Elliott began crafting a figurative statement conveying the exercise as a "preventive medicine." She wrote to Walz on November 30: "We all have our children inoculated [sic] against diphtheria, tetanus, and polio on the off chance that they might be exposed to one of these diseases someday. Now, the inoculation [sic] is painful and makes some children quite ill, but we do it 'just in case,' anyway. Why, then, shouldn't we do an exercise like this one?" This was an argument that resonated with supporters later. "After all, there is the absolute certainty that they will be exposed to prejudice and discrimination! How dare we send them out unprepared for this kind of disease [. . .] [it is] much more widely spread. And we're a long, long way from developing a cure!"[17]

The list of public figures who followed Rafferty's path in attacking the merit of the Riceville educator's exercise grew to include anti-feminism activist Phyllis Schlafly and future second lady Lynne Cheney. But in the final days of 1970, Elliott found herself "absolutely shocked" that a state superintendent of schools would call her "like Hitler" and "one of the worst things that ever happened to education." At first, Elliott thought Rafferty's column would lead to her termination. As time passed, she reminded herself that Rafferty had never contacted her.

In her view, he thrived on "trading on his ability to inflame an angry populace." It was a smear that "appealed to our lesser instincts."[18] After wounds caused by the column healed, Elliott could make sense of Rafferty's motives.

> And then, I looked at what those children were gaining as a result of what I had done. And I said, "Wait a minute, Max Rafferty doesn't know anything about me; he doesn't know what I'm doing or what I've learned from doing this exercise." [. . .] I had to remember that Max Rafferty didn't know as much about racism as my nine-year-olds did. [. . .] My nine-year-olds are wiser in this area than he will ever be because they learned it at the age of nine. And I compared him and his reaction to something that he didn't know other than what he saw on the Johnny Carson show, maybe, or saw in *The Eye of the Storm*, maybe, . . I don't think he had any idea of the importance and the real educational value of that Blue Eye/Brown Eye Exercise. I think he knew full well the effect that racism was having on children of color, but he had no idea of the negative effect of racism on what we call white children. I think it never occurred to him if he had been in my classroom when he was nine years old that, he would have learned more about the human race and racism and to advocate for a fair and just society than he knew as a fifty-two-year-old man. My third graders knew more than he did. And it wasn't because I stood in front of them and lectured. And it wasn't because I forced them to read books about it.[19]

The bitterness of protests against her exercise, whether emanating from Riceville or beyond, was evidence that Jane Elliott had successfully challenged the country to deal with the collision of values, attitudes, and beliefs in areas previously insulated from cultural diversity. She waited for the day when someone in the educational world would say, "The damage we are doing to people of color is being done equally to colorless children. We are damaging [white children] every day by miseducating them in the area of race. We are inhibiting them in their relationships and limiting them in their humanness."[20]

* * *

After watching *The Eye of the Storm*, Michael Jay Weiner and Frances E. Wright, two psychology professors at the University of North Carolina, Greensboro, put Jane Elliott's eye color exercise through an academic study of their own. The psychologists aimed to evaluate whether her classroom technique of making students experience and exude discriminatory treatment lessened discriminatory behavior while exposing how oppressive environments cause detrimental performance. The study, published in the *Journal of Applied Social Psychology*, asked if Elliott's discrimination simulation was merely subjective speculation.

Over four class meetings (three consecutive days and a day two weeks later), the study divided third-grade children enrolled in an elementary school near Winston Salem into two classrooms: an experimental cohort and a controlled cohort. The experimental class contained fifteen white males and sixteen white females, while the control class contained fourteen white males, one Black male, and sixteen white females. Both classes were taught by white females.

During the study, instruction went on as usual for the control group. On the contrary, the teacher of the experimental class divided her thirty-one students into a superior orange group and an inferior green group. Like Elliott's Discrimination Day lesson, the teacher forced the labeled inferior students to wear armbands. The teacher labeled the orange students "smarter, cleaner, and better behaved" than the green students. The orange group received classroom privileges, including lunch, dessert, and the chance to serve as line leaders, door holders, and book distributors. Orange students were also first in line to go to lunch, recess, and the bus at the end of the school day. The teacher praised the orange students throughout the day while shaming the green students. On the second day of the experiment, the teacher reversed the two groups' statuses, granting green students privileges and praise.

On the third day, students in both experimental and control classes completed an anonymous survey. The survey encompassed two hypothetical questions measuring student willingness to interact with Black people. The first question asked: "Next Saturday, there will be a picnic near school with some third-grade Black children from another school. Would you please say if you would like to go with them?" The second question asked: "Next year, there will be two new teachers, a Black teacher and a white teacher, teaching at this school. Would you please say which one you would like to have as a teacher?" Seven Likert scale questions appeared on the survey, which assessed the students' prejudgments about children and adults of color on a scale measuring "agree strongly" to "disagree strongly."[21]

When comparing survey results between the two classes, Weiner and Wright found that the simulation on discrimination countered discriminatory beliefs and behaviors among the thirty-one students in the experimental class. To this degree, the study affirmed the result of the Discrimination Day lesson. However, the researchers found that the manipulation did not impact academic performance.[22]

CHAPTER 13

A BLACK EYE: ANATOMY OF PREJUDICE

"I feel sorry for those who were damaged in a half hour. Prejudice has been causing damage for 200 years. Half an hour is unfortunate. A lifetime is criminal."

—JANE ELLIOTT, 1975

President Nixon declared, "Never has this White House Conference come at a time of greater national questioning." The "conference" that Nixon referenced was the decennial White House Conference on Children and Youth (WHCCY). Established in 1909 by Theodore Roosevelt's administration, the WHCCY historically welcomed the country's authority figures and experts on the nation's most critical issues. It also operated as a fount of social change for children and youth from birth to twenty-four years. At that inaugural conference, Roosevelt warned, "When you take care of the children, you are taking care of the Nation of tomorrow."[1] In 1970, the conference fell in the wake of the swinging 1960s and two biting studies—the 1965 Moynihan Report titled *The Negro Family: The Case for National Action*, and the 1968 *Kerner Commission Report*—that offered windows into the lived experiences of African Americans. Coupled with student unrest, a costly war, and debates over the source of juvenile crime, Nixon's announcement for the conference warned of the fall of democracy. He described the moment as a precipice that needed answers to questions concerning "family planning, pornography, health services, school curricula, sex education, family structure, drug abuse, moral standards, governance of higher education, responsiveness of government."[2]

The president left the daunting challenge of planning the conference to his deputy assistant of urban affairs, Stephen Hess. Hess's first move as national chairman was to divide the conferences. There would be one for children (birth to age thirteen), planned for December 13 through 18, 1970, and one for youth (ages fourteen to twenty-four) scheduled for February 1971.

Back in Riceville, *The Eye of the Storm* had already generated interest for Elliott to be a guest on several daytime talks and radio shows. She also found herself at the center of countless newspaper articles about mental health and education. Her first noticeable invitation to appear in front of a national audience following the documentary's summertime rebroadcast occurred at the *Virginia Graham Show* on September 29. As the former host of the daytime popular culture celebrity gossip show *Girl Talk*, Virginia Graham's new program launched in the fall of 1970 to engage the populace in discussions about political and social issues of the day. Elliott was pleased to be invited on the show as one of Graham's first guests. It meant the public expected her to serve as a leading voice on educational matters. She appeared that way, too. After showing highlights of *The Eye of the Storm* to the audience, the passive host allowed a white male doctor to confront Elliott over the ethics of the eye color experience. Unnerved, the teacher from Riceville remained steadfast: the documentary displayed that her students grew into more inclusive-minded people.[3] She maintained that no other evidence would need to be provided to the doctor. Elliott hoped to describe "object lessons" or myriad forms of the societal curriculum—messaging emanating from peer groups, family members, churches, occupations, and, among other factors, mass media that seemingly perpetuate stereotypes about marginalized communities.[4] While the audience seemingly bought it, there was no telling whether she convinced the host or other guests.

That same fall, an unexpected invitation from Washington D.C. buzz around this diminutive teacher from northern Iowa captured WHCCY chairman Stephen Hess's attention. Hess telephoned Elliott and said: "We've looked high and low, and you're the only classroom teacher we've been able to find who's doing anything meaningful in the area of reducing prejudice in children."[5] Hess found the moment prime for classroom instruction on prejudice reduction. This was just a generation removed from court-ordered desegregation and the start of school busing initiatives to achieve greater racial balance.

Humbled and confident that she could offer value to any program designed to dispel myths about race and reading literacy, Elliott sought approval from Superintendent Johnston to miss a week of school before Christmas break to attend the White House Conference on Children.

"What house conference?" Johnston asked.

"The White House Conference in Washington D.C.," Elliott explained.

"Oh, that house," he quipped, seemingly stoic. "Yes, I guess that'll be alright."

Hess later sent Elliott a formal invitation. Accepting the bid meant she would join 4,000 social scientists, clergymen, businesspersons, health practitioners, lawyers, parents, and students collaborating on finding root causes and solutions for the overlapping issues affecting children that Nixon mentioned in his announcement of the WHCCY conference. Additionally, the attendees, who harbored suspicions around President Nixon's commitment to implementing their recommendations into an administrative policy, planned to challenge the White House on "reordering national priorities."[6]

More particularly, Elliott agreed to serve as one of twelve members of a forum committee titled "Children Without Prejudice." The committee included some of the most influential people in psychology and education, some of whom would have difficulty working with her over reasons of prestige and (in her view) personal pride. The committee's charge was to "consider the consequences of adult behavior and actions upon the attitudes of children" and "to seek to identify not only how prejudice is acquired by children, but its impact on their healthy development."[7] Elliott did not anticipate being in the twelve-member committee's leadership. Nevertheless, with all the attention given to her discrimination simulation, she had no problem taking directives from those she found to be the most spirited leaders. She admired Jeanne Spurlock, award-winning chief of the psychiatry department at Meharry Medical College and chairwoman of the Children Without Prejudice Committee. Elliott also liked Ada Deer, the director of Upward Bound at Stevens Point State University and committee vice chair, and K. Patrick Okura, former president of the Japanese American League and an administrator at the University of Nebraska College of Medicine. It took Elliott some time to establish a rapport with Piri Thomas, author of *Down These Mean Streets*, about his rise from crime and drug addiction.

The group was responsible for designing an educational panel for almost two-hundred people that signed up for the Children Without Prejudice forum. At one of the committee's pre-planning meetings in Chicago, Okura suggested that instead of a panel discussion on their prejudice-reduction work with children, they should put attendees through Elliott's discrimination exercise. Despite feeling the pressure that the attendees at the conference were "educated, intelligent, expert individuals" with proven records of "improving the lives of children throughout the U.S.," she wrote in her memoir, Elliott consented to do the exercise. In a moment of doubt afterward, she wrote to a friend, "Can you feature a hundred-and-sixty angry delegates all yelling at me?"[8]

Elliott saw this as an opportunity to do something she had long desired: to test her theory that the exercise could transform adults like it had the students in her class. The prospect of facilitating the exercise in Washington D.C. begged the question: how would the Discrimination Day lesson work on a group of adults numbering almost two hundred? She brainstormed new logistics for the session and came up with a carefully designed workshop—nothing like the abridged session she had attempted with a few Rotarians over the lunch hour two years prior.

She leaned heavily on Okura and Spurlock to brainstorm new ideas and tailor the exercise for adults. Among the most crucial needs was to plant a mole within the inferior group to keep her and the superior group informed about their reactions and any plots. They also thought to plant people amongst the brown eyes to "initiate aggressive behavior if response fails to materials." She noted that it "May not be necessary," but she had no experience to glean. Elliott also planned to constantly interrupt blue-eyed speakers and call on the brown eyes more frequently.[9]

Elliott incorporated the standard privileges. Inside Forum 18's conference room at the Sheraton Park Hotel near the White House, she placed the brown eyes at the top of the hierarchy for the first time. They were immediately welcomed into the meeting room and enjoyed seats at the front while blue-eyed participants had to stand against the wall for half an hour before registering. Elliott had previously assigned roles to the committee members; she made Manuel Ortiz—an elementary school principal from San Antonio—the program's greeter tasked with welcoming brown-eyed participants with affection. Okura would also be a greeter, but his job was to stoke anger among the blue-eyed group. Piri Thomas acted as a security guard. The actors did a fine job irritating the blue-eyed group with comments such as "Get over there with the rest of those Blueys," and "You, you Blue-eyed people—always late," or "Can't you see you're blocking the way of this Brown-eyed person," along with commands to quiet down and stop complaining. Elliott informed the brown-eyed group about the exercise inside the meeting room and insisted on their cooperation. The blue eyes were processed with armbands instead of the collars she had used on her students.

Additionally, she made arrangements to zone out the conference room into segregated sections. In one room, the brown-eyed group sat comfortably in seats at the front, and in the back, there were only enough seats for half the blue-eyed group. Once the blue eyes started grumbling amongst themselves before any formal presentation began, Elliott started labeling them as "aggressive, belligerent, anti-social, ignorant, uncivilized, and unclean."[10]

In her memoir, Elliott makes the session sound like a tumultuous affair. From the beginning, blue-eyed participants behaved belligerently. One woman led her peers in a rendition of "We Shall Overcome." When the larger pack of brown eyes drowned them out with "Beautiful Brown Eyes," several blue eyes tore down posters and pictures hung on the conference room walls. One woman led a sit-in at the front of the room. Their unruliness allowed her to reiterate blue-eyed stereotypes. "Each statement they uttered, and each behavior they exhibited was further proof that we had not stereotyped them unfairly," she announced with contempt.[11] "We hope *you* people can behave yourselves [. . .]. *You* people will have to be quiet [. . .]. *You* people get us some more chairs."[12]

When one older, brown-eyed woman gave up her seat to a younger blue-eyed woman, a blue-eyed person yelled out, "Look at that! She gave her chair to a blue-eye! See? Not all Brown-eyes feel the way you do!" Elliott responded, "Yes, that older, brown-eyed woman was kind enough to offer that Bluey a chair, and she, even though she's much the younger of the two, took it and is letting that older female stand. What does that tell you about blue-eyed people?" The comment left everyone stammering or speechless. When it came time for breaks, she held the blues outside only to resume the session so that the browns could blame their tardiness on their eye color.[13] There was no way Elliott would give an inch.

At lunchtime, she dismissed the brown-eyed group first. She insisted that the blue eyes had to wait, and when someone asked why, Elliott responded, "Because you might vandalize the other areas of the hotel if you're allowed to wander off!" That caused an uproar, and the blue eyes rushed through the door as Ortiz, Thomas, and Okura failed to prevent them from escaping. The hotel staff had had enough of the commotion and called security to the Forum 18 room. While some blue eyes left entirely, those who remained to participate successfully negotiated with Elliott's committee and hotel security to relocate to a new room after the break.[14]

A frenzied morning eventually settled into an earnest and poignant afternoon once the ugliness of prejudice and discrimination were out of the way. Elliott led the large group in a moment of healing before dividing everyone into smaller groups for a long debrief session where personal experiences were tied to incidents of the exercise. The discussions, led by members of the Children Without Prejudice panel, in her estimation, were "frank and open [and] honest." The experience of enduring mistreatment, on the one hand, and levying it, on the other, provided much-needed windows into the lives of others. They considered the impact of labeling on the feeling of helplessness. "It was compelling, frightening and sometimes musing journey into discrimination for us Blue eyes," wrote Toni House of the *Washington Star*. "It was a quick lesson in second-class citizenship." Knowing in advance that the exercise was "a game" that they willingly signed up for didn't prevent emotions from taking over when that feeling of exclusion surfaced. That simple notion was revelatory. As early as registration, House said, "group personalities [began] to form."[15]

Not everyone was as moved as House. One individual, a person of color, called the exercise a waste of time. When he charged white women with being able to "jump in and out [but] Black children can't," no one disagreed. However, many blue-eyed white people said they had learned from the exercise. Elliott's objective, alas, was to change the minds of the white folks in the room. The only question remaining was whether the eye color exercise did anything to help the children.

To what extent did Jane Elliott and the Forum 18 Committee accomplish the Children Without Prejudice objective assigned to them by conference director Stephen Hess? One participant seemed to concede everything she had argued about the exercise: "We all knew better," the participant said about their childlike behavior, "but it seemed like we couldn't help ourselves. I've learned first-hand that racial discrimination is a cruel and dangerous thing."[16] In an interview many years after the conference, Elliott insisted the WHCCY organizers' decision to prioritize prejudice was like putting the cart before the horse. "Prejudice isn't the problem," she said. "Discrimination is the problem. Prejudice is an attitude. It can't hurt you. Discrimination is a behavior. And because of our discriminatory behaviors toward people who are different from ourselves, we are encouraged in our prejudices. We create prejudice by discriminating. We've got the axiom wrong [. . .] And until discrimination is stopped, we will not do away with prejudice when skin color is concerned. "[17]

After the Discrimination Day lesson, the Children Without Prejudice Committee composed a ten-page document challenging President Nixon to "immediately and unequivocally" create a doctrine that would "rear a generation of children without prejudice." This issue, they assailed, should become the Nixon administration's top priority. Elliott's group gave additional recommendations to the U.S. Congress by insisting that national lawmakers remove funding barriers to impoverished schools. They challenged state directors or superintendents of instruction to require that educators undergo training on the history and cultures of America's marginalized groups. The committee also insisted on diversifying school curricula at all grade levels.

Elliott's language is all over the report's introduction. When discussing prejudicial attitudes, the report states, "Usually, the emphasis is on the minority group child, and this may be why so many Americans feel that the problem is of no concern in their community or to them as individuals." The report cites two crucial perspectives when explaining the effects of prejudice on majority group children. One is Dr. Kenneth Clark, a social psychologist known for the Baby Doll study that vividly explained the emotional impairment caused by segregation on the development of Black children. By the late-1960s, Clark was an outspoken critic of handling school integration; in particular, he found that almost 90 percent of American children still attended segregated schools a decade after the *Brown v. The Topeka Board of Education* decision ordering schools to desegregate. As a result, he affirmed that education provided to children in less privileged schools was of lower quality. He argued that the system was designed to make parents of those children powerless to affect any fundamental changes to school conditions. As it related to the surfacing of prejudicial behavior in white children, Clark claimed that "institutions fostered racial discrimination upon children of the majority groups." However, institutional conditioning of anti-Black prejudice is "less obvious."[18]

The second voice used in the report to speak on the effects of prejudice on majority group children is Jane Elliott's. While not quoting her directly, the report describes in detail that the annual use of the eye color exercise on her elementary students generated the same results: "The children's reactions to being the object of discriminatory attitudes were immediate and frightening. Within fifteen minutes, the children became what the "power structure" had accused them of being. Each child, on his day of inferior status, showed a drastic drop in academic achievement, whereas, on his 'superior' day, academic achievement soared." In a way that elevates Clark's assessment, the report suggests, the result of the exercise makes it seem "certain that such psychological patterns breed the alienation and hostility of our youth."[19]

All 4,000 attendees at the conference agreed with the forum report composed by Elliott's committee. When Hess asked all delegates to state the six most important recommendations from the conference, redesigning education to "achieve individualized, humanized, child-centered learning" came in second.[20]

A drained and guarded Jane Elliott returned to Riceville wondering if the Nixon Administration would implement any of the recommendations produced at the conference. She resolved the theory that the eye color exercise works with adults. Writing to friends after Christmas, she claimed, "Over a hundred so-called 'mature, educated, civilized' delegates to the WHCCY proved how damaging discrimination can be. Elliott expressed regret that the session was not recorded, as she thought it would offer the perfect behavioral juxtaposition shown alongside the third graders in *The Eye of the Storm*. Elliott stated that she had "never been so delighted."[21]

Elliott also learned that there were serious issues taking place in her home.

* * *

Jane Elliott's world was rocked almost as soon as she returned from the White House Conference on Children. She had been so wrapped up in attention over the Discrimination Day lesson that she failed to notice that her children were victims of town gossip. Fourteen-year-old Sarah finally drummed up the courage to tell her that relations with peers at school were falling apart. While away in the nation's capital, Sarah's friends started rumors that her mother was having an affair. Later that winter, Sarah took her brand-new purse to school, gifted by her parents. When she was not looking, several bullies cut off the strap and used Sarah's lipstick to write "[N-word] lover" on the bathroom mirror. Sarah was accused of staging the incident when she showed it to the principal and thus resented her mother for the dark cloud that hung over the family. Elliott's other daughter, Mary, in sixth grade, was once surrounded by her classmates as they taunted her with stories proclaiming it was only a matter of time until Elliott "was sleepin' with those [N-word] men."[22] Sometime later, a pack of bullies jumped Sarah and Mary on the way home from school. Sarah recalled one bully flinging "a big, metal buckle coming at my head."[23]

Elliott's eldest son, Brian, was gripped by worry after listening to his sisters share those stories. Since 1968, he bore the brunt of the town's rancor. He was the first to hear his mother called the N-word and endure playground teasing that his mother was an N-word lover. As an upper elementary student, Brian was bullied by high school kids on the bus. A few days after her appearance on *The Tonight Show* made the local newspaper, Brian fought a kid who said, "Your mom's going to New York so she can fuck [N-word]s."[24] At least one time, bullies jumped Brian in the locker room. "Two, three on one," Brain recalled.

"Nowhere to go. 'Fuckin' [N-word] lover!' Take cover!" said one teenager.

He kept how he had been bullied a secret from his parents for several years. "Every break between class, I was fist fighting," recalled Brian.

Brian once told an interviewer that when Darald called the parents of one of the other kids picking on him, the father said, "Your son got what he deserved." Upset, Jane jumped on the call to question the father on how he was raising his son. The father retorted, "You should have thought of this before you did that eye thing."[25]

Journalist Stephen Bloom described one "nasty rumor" that Darald had not fathered two of the Elliott children. "The whispers multiplied and morphed," Bloom wrote. "Sarah heard them, and so did Brian, as did scores of others in town." The suspicion was: "Sarah and Brian had darker complexions than the other kids in Riceville."[26] The father was alleged to be a Black man from their Waterloo neighborhood, though the timing does not align.

"I hated my mother for a long time," admitted Sarah. "When [my] mother took away all [my] friends, and when she took away all of Brian's friends, it's hard to get over."[27]

At first, Elliott tried to teach her children about ignorance, but she also dug deeper into investigating whether the schools were taking measures to protect her children. She found no satisfactory evidence, choosing instead to heed the advice from friend and Riceville middle school teacher Ruth Brandmill, wife of the principal at RCS Elementary, who suggested Elliott get her kids out of RCS schools. "These teachers are going to ruin your children," she warned. Acting accordingly, Jane and Darald put their house up for sale.[28]

The Elliotts found a new place to live eighteen miles outside of Riceville. They settled on what used to be a schoolyard located northeast of Osage, Mitchell County, a year later, in August 1971. Their new home used to be a one-room schoolhouse built in 1929, formerly known as Burr Oak. The estate was familiar to Elliott; she played softball there as a child. She and Darald would turn the spacious classroom into a dining and kitchen area on one side and the living room and bathroom on the other. They added two sun porches to the residence's exterior.[29] The four children enrolled in the Osage Community School District while Elliott remained a teacher at Riceville Elementary. Darald found full-time work as the manager of the Red Owl grocery store in town.

The relocation meant Jane Elliott came to terms with where she fit in (or not) at her hometown of Riceville. An urge to help shape a more inclusive worldview for future generations proved an uphill climb. It was too costly for her family. Her new Burr Oak home became a sanctuary in many ways, but none more than a way to protect her family.

CHAPTER 14

EYE TO EYE OR A CLASS DIVIDED?

"What started out as originally a two-day exercise in a classroom could well turn out to be an experience designed to last a lifetime."

—CAROLYN DECELL, THE DEER CREEK PILOT, SEPTEMBER 1980

At a conference of the American Psychological Association (APA) in Washington D.C., professor of engineering science at Stanford University, Dr. William Shockley, argued that intelligence is an inheritable trait; Black intelligence is lower than white. Winner of the 1956 Nobel Prize in physics, Shockley maintained that it is not one's social environment that influences human performance and behavior but genetic characteristics. At the APA conference, he asked the National Academy of Science to conduct a "full-scale investigation" to confirm or refute his claim.[1] As for his actual findings, Shockley presented a mathematical model showing a "bell-shaped error function" that living conditions, attending impoverished schools, and whether one comes from a low-income household had little to do with performance. "I submit that the Negro [-] white difference in [test scores] may be evidence for racial genetic differences in neurological organization rather than due to environmental differences," Shockley noted. He proposed "Giving a bonus to low IQ groups that do not reproduce."[2]

Contrary to how it sounds, Shockley's thesis did more to stoke the flames over racist science rather than advance evidence in the IQ debate. He was a physicist, not a psychologist. His biographer Joel Shurkin contended he "did very little original research." Instead, Shockley based his APA paper on the work of Arthur Jensen—an educational psychologist from the University of California, Berkeley. In the 1969 *Harvard Educational Review*, Jensen wrote that while children with low IQ scores were both genetically and environmentally challenged, genetic factors accounted for most of the variation in intelligence. That being the case, Jensen's work suggested any effort to raise an IQ through education was ill-fated and that academic achievement was predetermined by genetics. Jensen was the first to revive the pre-Holocaust nature versus nurture debate linking intelligence with race. Eugenicists once championed this idea, thus countering post-war theses set forth by social scientists claiming problems in African American achievement and behavior were caused by slum conditions and historical economic disadvantages. Shockley's name alone advanced Jensen's theory.[3] "He mainly did new statistical analyses of other people's data," writes Shurkin of Shockley's advocacy for making Jensen's theory a curricular requisite.[4] While he had little respect in scientific circles, the Nobel Laureate's words garnered much attention in the national press.

The revival of racist science certainly had Jane Elliott's attention. Even if it slipped past her, the media (which had become enamored with her eye color exercise) had no problem juxtaposing Shockley's pseudoscientific theory with her non-empirical experience in discrimination, stereotype threat, conformity, and social conditioning. Two publications in 1971 accompanied the eye color exercise in the constellation showing intelligence as a byproduct of social factors.[5] George W. Mayeske of the U.S. Office of Education and Jane R. Mercer, professor of sociology at the University of California, Riverside, found in two separate studies that little difference in academic achievement test scores existed among racialized groups and white students when social and environmental factors were considered. Dr. Edward J. Casavantes of the U.S. Commission on Civil Rights called the work of Mayeske and Mercer "the strongest ever presented documenting that environmental and social factors affect IQ and academic achievement test scores." Mayeske examined school achievement testing data from 123,386 elementary school students of various racial-ethnic groups initially gathered by the U.S. Congress in a 1965 Educational Opportunities Survey. He found that when "environmental and social factors" were statistically disaggregated from such test scores, Puerto Rican, American Indian, Asian American, Mexican American, African American, and European American student achievement was virtually identical.

In "Pluralistic Diagnosis in the Evaluation of Black and Chicano Children: A Procedure for Taking Sociocultural Variables into Account in Clinical Assessment," written for the *Chicanos: Social and Psychological Perspectives*,

Dr. Mercer found the same results in an eight-year study of white, Mexican American, and African American children in Riverside when looking at IQ test scores. Mercer's research on classifying children began when studying the epidemiology of mental retardation in Riverside, California. He found that Mexican Americans and African Americans with the highest IQs came from two-parent homes with fewer children, at least one white-collar breadwinner, and familial emphasis placed on education.[6]

The impact of Jane Elliott's eye color exercise on the performance of dyslexic children shows in a few minutes what Mayeske and Mercer documented in two comprehensive studies: assigning a child to a stereotype and treating the child per the ascribed label will result in altered behavior that lends validation to the stereotype. Expectations determine performance, Elliott would go on to claim. Once a child is labeled inferior, especially when the surrounding circumstances are debilitating, there is little chance for high achievement.

When conducting the exercise with third-grade children, Elliott's objective was to teach about discrimination solely to help those adolescent children learn how to recognize and effectively disrupt prejudice. While the approach for adults was similar, her concerns were over convincing people already stuck in their way to concede that they harbor bias and use that knowledge to educate their children in a way that acknowledges and respects diversity. Therefore, Elliott took every opportunity to speak with adults about the eye color exercise. On April 22, 1971, she was the keynote speaker at a Parent-Teacher Association event in Winona, Minnesota, near Rochester.[7] She was intrigued by the apparent wealth of interest from educators and parents and soon became a moderately sought-after speaker at schools, businesses, and institutions in the Midwest.

Her time as a public lecturer that spring coincided with the announcement that *The Eye of the Storm* documentary won the George Foster Peabody Award for Television Education. Thomas Wolf, ABC News vice president and director of television documentaries, accepted the Peabody at April's luncheon.[8] Elliott was invited but declined due to swift-approaching final exams at RCS Elementary. The film's two producers, Bill and Muriel Peters, joined Wolf but later intimated the event was "anticlimactic." In a letter to Elliott that June, Bill Peters said Wolf accepted the award and was responsible for giving the acceptance speech. "Mike and I," he wrote, referring to Muriel by her nickname, "alone among the real winners, sat at a table and watched Tom Wolf receive the award." Peters conveyed indignation toward ABC, calling them cheap "compared to the other networks (or should I say the real networks)." He attributed Wolf's monopolizing the award recognition to the fact that *The Eye of the Storm* produced ABC's "only Peabody award," while the rivals, NBC and CBS, he said, "each copped several."[9]

Elliott received her Peabody by mail as a certificate. While she placed the parchment in a drawer and no one in Riceville (including the weekly *Recorder*) said much about the accolade, newspapers from more populated centers in Iowa ran stories about the Peabody news. Cedar Falls resident, Rody Spreitzer, applauded the honor as "only the beginning." Spreitzer praised Elliott and the Riceville Community School District "in allowing and having such a capable teacher on its staff [and] for encouraging this thinking in teaching methods."[10]

The Peabody was followed by Elliott's first request to be a diversity consultant. In August, Paul Retish, director of the Desegregation Institute at the University of Iowa (UI), asked Elliott to deliver the eye color exercise at a workshop for faculty, staff, and elementary school educators. For the second year, the Department of Health, Education, and Welfare awarded Retish's institute an $86,000 grant to hold two two-week workshops and five weekend training sessions on multicultural education. Retish brought Elliott in for half a day during the first two-week workshop, which provided presentations, exercises, and seminars for educators working in schools with changing student demographics. Much of the program was dedicated to helping participants interrogate their attitudes about students from diverse and non-dominant populations.

On June 21, 1971, Elliott designed a jarring experience for approximately ninety teachers, counselors, and principals from twelve Iowa school districts enrolled in the UI workshop series. As intended, neither Elliott nor her exercise was listed on the agenda. After the morning sessions (which she did not attend), participants returned to the Iowa Memorial Union, where the workshop was held, and were told to re-register. With help from Retish, along with Hal Adams, program coordinator; Henry Tanners, administrative assistant; and six institute instructors, Elliott segregated the educators by eye color. Like the program at the White House Conference on Children a year prior, the blue eyes were placed at the bottom of the hierarchy and forced to wait in a holding room.

In contrast, the brown eyes went through registration and received the details on how Elliott would administer the exercise. Elliott used the informational session to give the brown eyes the scoop about how the blue eyes would be treated and to give an out to any brown-eyed participants who felt they could not participate in such dogmatic behavior. When the blue eyes were invited to go through processing, they were given green collars and told to sit on the floor in the back of the classroom. Elliott hung hand-drawn placards on the classroom walls: "If I Have But One Life, Let Me Live It As a Blonde," "Would

you want your daughter to marry one?," "Eenie, meenie, minie, moe. Catch a
Blue-Eye by the toe," and "If they don't like it here, why don't they go back to
where they came from."[11] Whereas the brown eyes sat quietly and respectfully,
the blue eyes almost suddenly started misbehaving. They spoke, sang, and threw
paper airplanes when she was speaking.

At one point, Elliott explained that the insubordination emanating from
the blue eyes was typical behavior from those possessing that physical characteristic. They were "inferior in every way," Elliott said. Her labeling of the
Blueys rubbed off on the brown eyes. One brown-eyed attendee pointed to a
person sitting in their section of the room wearing sunglasses, alleging that the
educator was "passing for brown." Another educator with green eyes sitting
in the blue-eyed section tried to switch to the brown-eyed group. In twenty
minutes, the blue-eyed group engaged in "Mob action," as one Iowa newspaper
reported. Elliott brought in campus police to read the blue eyes the "riot act."
She suggested to the officers that some people in the blue-eyed group were "il-
legally assembled" and had no right to be there. One of the officers insisted on
taking photographs of the blue eyes so they could be cross-checked as registered
participants in the workshop. While pictures were taken, three blue-eyed people
had enough and snuck out of the room. While this was going on, Elliott took
the brown eyes to a different classroom. At that point, members of the blue-
eyed group piled furniture against the door, trapping the brown eyes and Elliott
in their new facilitation room.[12] Others ripped Elliott's posters down from the
original classroom.

Despite the violent scene, Retish was happy with Elliott's session. "What
was important was that both sides [. . .] really felt mob emotion, whether as
ruler or the persecuted; they discriminated and reacted blatantly without thinking about it first. It's that kind of human injustice we're trying to cope with in
the institute—whether the discrimination is couched in racial, sexual, or some
other terms. Teachers must be aware of their own feelings and those of people
who discriminate outside workshops. Otherwise, we never will control hate."[13]

* * *

Later that summer, details about Elliott's exercise appeared in book form. The
laborious effort of storyboarding, scriptwriting, and editing to produce *The Eye
of the Storm* along with his wife, Muriel, was among Bill Peters' most revered
projects in his filmmaking career. He also had an appetite for writing about
some of the most harrowing moments in American civil rights history—a passion he developed after serving in World War II. Discovering Jane Elliott was

like striking gold for a documentarian. The Riceville schoolteacher and her exercise as content material for a curriculum on social justice came about during a time of great peril: schools were slowly desegregating, the death of Martin Luther King Jr. and the looting that followed brought about discourse over issues of police brutality, economic inequality, and de facto segregation. The lesson in discrimination challenged educators to decide whether schools were responsible for leading children out of racial ignorance.

Additionally, Elliott's pedagogical approach was controversial enough to engage the nation in a debate over her ethics. This was the recipe that could give Peters instant cachet. She could open new horizons for his career. Acting opportunistically by capitalizing on the Riceville teacher's fifteen minutes of fame, Peters attained a book contract with a familiar printing house, Doubleday, publisher of one of his earlier tomes, *The Southern Temper*. He set about to turn *The Eye of the Storm* into a book about the eye color lesson.

Elliott was not the wiser. Innocence and naivete overshadowed her signature wit and aggression. She had yet to seek out a manager or a lawyer to counsel on business decisions. No matter how high she rose to stardom, Elliott genuinely thought the attention would soon end. On the contrary, Peters aimed to exploit Elliott until the day she stopped agreeing to his requests. He had business control over her, suggested Peters' second wife and production partner, Muriel. Indeed, she would say many years later, "He took over [Elliott's life]."[14]

Correspondence between Elliott and Bill Peters suggests she had little influence over the book's portrayal of the Discrimination Day lesson. In a letter penned on November 16, 1970, Peters informed Elliott he was taking "a few liberties with specific quotations [. . .] and your thoughts."[15] She ultimately consented, though when asked, she regularly told people her biggest grievance about the publication was the first chapter, where Peters perverted most of her on-record words. In the same letter, Peters agreed to concede one thing about the book's scope: "I'm trying to avoid the use of the word 'experiment,' which I know you disapprove." This battle over framing the eye color simulation as an exercise or experience, not an "experiment," would become a lifelong battle for Elliott.

Adamant that the future publication does not portray the exercise as a scientific undertaking complete with hypotheses and human experimentation, Elliott insisted her simulation be framed precisely how she wanted. "This may sound like 'semantic antics' to you, but I wasn't trying to discover how my students would behave under these conditions—I wanted them to acquire some insights into why people who live under these conditions behave as they do," she expressed in a separate letter to a third party, a woman named Susan.[16] Titling the book became the first battleground, of sorts, in the struggle to control how the media characterized the exercise of discrimination for school children. Eight months before publication, Peters wrote to Elliott complaining about Doubleday's insistence to name the book, *The Blue-Eyed Experiment.* He asked Elliott if she had variants to suggest. Records indicate that she could offer nothing through a marketable alternative, but Peters would eventually counter with *A Class Divided.*[17]

Of course, the book brought more attention to Elliott and the town of Riceville. This meant an already engaged public would spend $4.95 to learn more about one of the most controversial teaching activities and the towns-people ever documented on television. Little effort went into writing the book. Peters composed a one-hundred-page narrative about the first three times the RCS Elementary students experienced the Discrimination Day program. He used three sources: Elliott's recollections, the first group's post-exercise essays, and *The Eye of the Storm* documentary footage. He wrote nine chapters and attained social psychologist Kenneth Clark to write the foreword. Clark's name attached to a book about an unscientific study of children's behavior boosted the project's profitability. The book would subtextually address whether impos-ing discrimination on young people would impair children in any way. As such, Clark's Foreword provided an affirmative endorsement of the Blue Eyes/Brown Eyes Exercise. "My wife was on a television program with Kenneth Clark, the Negro psychologist who had so much to do with the 1954 Supreme Court desegregation case," Peters explained. "Clark was tremendously impressed with Mrs. Elliott's ability to think of this idea. He worried in the beginning as to whether she might be doing damage to these children. Then he realized that there are twenty million American Negroes to whom this is a daily experience."[18] When published in the summer of 1971, the book was titled *A Class Divided,* with a cover design showing third graders Greg Johanns and Verla Beels.

Neither a hagiography nor *A Class Divided* did anything to humanize Elliott for those questioning her teaching methods. Peters wrote for an audience that wanted to recount the details of the exercise. Before the book's publication, some people refused to see Elliott as a woman and mother of four children who genuinely tried to view the world without bias. Then, after the book was published, the same group still saw her as a contemptible wanna-be educator who deserved to be blamed for traumatizing her students. There was nothing on the pages regarding classroom policy and pedagogy to help educators improve their praxis and minimal author commentary for the public to understand how silence empowers racism. In other words, the book did not make anyone consider their degree of humanity. To Elliott's critics, she would remain a monster.

Reviews in *Parade* magazine and *Reader's Digest* generated interest a month before publication.[19] When the UI Desegregation Institute workshop concluded, Elliott joined Peters on three high-profile promotional events in the Midwest and New York City. The first was an appearance on NBC's *Today Show* on August 6, 1971.[20] In New York, they additionally appeared on local television and spoke with reporters from the *New York Times* and the *Associated Press*.

This was Elliott's first sustained interaction with Peters; they traveled on airplanes and in taxi cabs for long periods, getting to know one another more personally. While Elliott always respected his work, she was troubled by Peters' character and temperament. In particular, she grew tired of Peters dominating all questions related to the exercise. His comments about Elliott's segregation exercise were glowing publicly: "[The exercise] sounded like a fantastic means of teaching about discrimination. But more than that, it seemed to have an enormous teaching potential for adults. It seemed to me that we had an almost test-tube laboratory for showing what happens when a group is discriminated against on an illogical basis. People could not help but see this in third-grade white children." He would tell other interviewers: "On an intellectual basis, they learned a lesson. On an emotional level, who knows? Maybe it'll be a sort of long-term result. When they come into a situation years from now that smacks from discrimination, they'll back off. I don't have any illusions that it'll turn them into any stalwart civil rights activist, though." In private, he unveiled a degree of contempt over her confidence. Fundamentally, he had trouble taking a back seat to a woman.

While Peters fielded queries about the eye color exercise, Elliott took questions about Peters' book. "Yes, I'd call it a good book," she told a reporter. "I wasn't crazy about the rough draft, and I still don't like the first chapter much, but after you get past that, it's good." She was also very clear about not earning a penny for the book. "I'm getting nothing out of Peters' book in a monetary sense. In fact, this is all costing quite a bit of money, with the new clothes and all."[21]

The pair traveled to Ohio from New York to appear on WNBC's *Phil Donahue Show*. Thinking back years later about her moment on the *Donahue Show*, Elliott noted a blistering exchange with Peters. One audience member asked Elliott to explain the purpose of the exercise. Peters interjected before Elliott had the chance to speak. He did it a second time and a third time. She finally retorted: "I can answer my own questions, Bluey!" While the audience laughed, she intended it to be a personal jab. The riposte had the effect she hoped when she saw that Peters' face turned red. Tension mounted between the two on the cab ride to the airport, where they were to catch a flight to Chicago and were due as guests on *The Howard Miller Show* the following day. Peters told her, "I'm going to do the blue-eyed, brown-eyed exercise on you."

"Go ahead," said Elliott. "If you do, I'll take all the blue-eyed camera people and walk off the set. If we are going to do this show, we are going to do it like two civilized adults, not like the trainer and the monkey." Elliott felt that she threatened Peters. After all, she was stealing the spotlight despite touring to promote his book. She found Peters to be chauvinistic and self-obsessed. "Everything he did was like the owner of the plantation, and he had no idea what he was doing [to other people]."[22]

Muriel Peters—who had her own problems handling her husband's narcissism, which factored into their eventual divorce—had this to say about Elliott: "She felt she was being used by him, and she was. I'm sorry to say it, actually. Nevertheless, it did her a lot of good to have the film *[The Eye of the Storm]* made, but that's another story."[23]

"I realized I was dealing with someone whose ego was bigger than the idea," Elliott said of Peters decades later. Despite Peters' objective to advance his career, Elliott eventually acknowledged that his bold decision to produce a documentary from her and those sixteen students did much good for everyone. "He did my dyslexic third graders who had been called the 'dummy group,' [. . .] He gave those kids a stature that their former teachers denied them daily. He gave them a self-image that they couldn't have gotten any other way." With a glimmer of pride in her eye, she maintained, "And those 16 kids are being used [to teach against discrimination] all over the world."[24]

* * *

Although *A Class Divided* expanded the Discrimination Day lesson plan outwards from the Midwest, a group in Iowa expressed admiration for Jane Elliott's work as a socially conscious pedagogue. Around the same time Doubleday placed Peters' book in bookstores, Scott, Foresman, and Company published the Eighth edition of Philip G. Zimbardo and Floyd L. Ruch's *Psychology & Life* with a section titled "Prejudice and Racism." The chapter maintained that Elliott's lesson on bias reveals how discriminatory treatment stunts the positive emotional and intellectual development of young children.[25] The passage featuring Elliott includes a single photo taken by Charlotte Button showing her huddled with *The Eye of the Storm* third-grade cohort, delighted that the exercise has ended. The publisher also incorporated a sampling of three before-and-after self-portraits the students sketched during the exercise.

A smaller publication, *Northwestern Bell Magazine*, also published a human-interest story on Jane Elliott in its Summer 1971 edition, "Education: We've come a long way. Now, where do we go?" Composed by freelance contributor Olivia Hansen, the cover story, "Brown eyes and blue eyes," offered nothing to answer how far education had evolved. Instead, he recounted everything seen in *The Eye of the Storm*. Hansen did include one student's crayon sketch of a scowling Elliott with devil's horns. The caption asked, "Devil or angel?" Hansen wrote that Elliott was neither nor gave her subject the final word. "This is a rough way to teach children that discrimination is wrong," she said. "And it's rotten to have to put kids through such an ordeal. I just hope they remember it."[26]

On Friday, October 13, 1972, Luther College bestowed another accolade on Elliott when she received its Distinguished Service Award. The award usually went to alumni during its homecoming festivities. Occasionally, Luther presented the annual honor to friends of the college. Distinguished Service Award recipients were nominated by alumni, faculty, and friends of the college and then selected by a committee of Luther faculty. Three criteria were used to determine winners: meritorious service to society, Christian conviction in a nominee's profession, and responsibility to the church.[27] Elliott accepted the token of recognition from Luther College with humility. Soon after the event, she never mentioned it to anyone ever again. She suspected that the headlines in the state and local press carried new pressure to be perfect at her job. People watched her every move, trying to catch her in a mishap. She wondered whether there was more she could do to prove to the people in her hometown that she was not a villain.

CHAPTER 15

EVIL EYE

"If children are so manipulatable, why don't we use what we know about child psychology to remove prejudice?"

—JANE ELLIOTT, UNIONTOWN, PENNSYLVANIA, MARCH 18, 1975

Jane Elliott assumed a leadership role in Riceville's bicentennial events when the nation was six years into commemorative planning to observe critical historical moments that led to the American Revolution. When first conceived on July 4, 1966, the American Revolution Bicentennial Commission undertook a singular ten-year campaign to celebrate the two-hundredth birthday of the United States. The commission had planned to hold an exposition in either Philadelphia or Boston. By 1972, however, organizational infighting coupled with ambitious townspeople across the country wishing to honor the United States resulted in the commission giving local communities the power to sponsor their bicentennial events. As a result, the 63rd General Assembly in Iowa passed a house bill establishing the Iowa American Revolution Bicentennial Commission.

The state-wide commission designed a three-fold approach to honor America's landmark anniversary built on the theme of "Heritage '76, Festival, USA, and Horizons '76." Those three distinct parts aimed to get Iowans involved in re-examining "the origins, values and the meaning of America"; to create special activities or events that bring attention to freedom while celebrating Iowa's cultural landmarks; and engage in projects that demonstrate "concern for future human welfare, enjoyment, and freedom, and to bring people together in a Bicentennial project of a lasting nature."[1] According to the Iowa Commission's final report, the state would claim 2,800 projects, events, and activities between 1972 and 1976. An estimated 225,000 Iowans participated in those projects, and the state boasted of having "led the nation in Bicentennial projects."[2] Of those quarter of a million Iowans, few in the grassroots could argue they were more eager to participate in such an endeavor than the woman who had made a career out of busying students in experiential learning. Elliott had an unparalleled passion for education and allegiance to her hometown. Then again, in 1972, her teaching style had been called "hogwash," and national figures characterized her as "shades of Adolf [Hitler]."[3]

For Elliott, mounting stress brought on by the desire to please her community—despite being in the national spotlight over the eye color exercise—motivated her to find ways to perform better as the teacher of Room 10 students at RCS Elementary. Acting as such, Elliott became the chair of the Howard County Bicentennial Commission. In that position, her master plan included an effort to build a public park in Riceville commemorating the country's bicentennial.[4] In 1972, the federal commission set aside a $1.2 billion fund to construct 100 to 500-acre state parks in Iowa honoring America's birthday. Whether or not she could attain any of that funding, Elliott thought a small bicentennial park built by her students would fit into the bicentennial's Horizon '76 theme.[5] Adjacent to the Jennison Inn and next to Fouts Standard Service was an acre of green grass primed to become the site for the project. On April 5, she and her Room 10 students planted the first tree of what would become Riceville's American Revolution bicentennial mini park named "The Village Green." It was an oak cherry tree. Elliott purchased the tree with funds raised through the class's sale of hand-made Christmas tags and holiday cookies. In writing about Elliott's new class project, the *Riceville Recorder* wrote: "[T]he Village Green will symbolize the qualities of determination, creativity, and independence which have helped to make this country and this community the 'land of the free.'"[6]

A year later, on March 29, 1973, Elliott's third-grade students added to the plot when they planted a seedling on the Village Green in the presence of Riceville Mayor Walter Gabelmann. The seedling came from Maryland's famous four-hundred-year-old Wye Oak, the largest white oak tree in the United States. Maryland's director of Forest Service, Adna R. Bond, had recently certified the sale of seedlings from the historic tree, which dated twice the age of the United States with a trunk measuring fifty-eight feet in circumference, a branch spread of 160 feet, totaling 102 feet tall. Elliott was one of the first in the country to place a mail order for a one-year-old seedling, six to eight inches in height, at the cost of $2, plus shipping and handling.[7] Room 10 had greater goals for the park. They envisioned a park bench, a welcome sign, and a cabin to decorate the site. Over the next three years, Room 10 students would raise additional funds for the park by collecting recyclable cans.

To mark the two-hundredth anniversary of the Boston Tea Party, Elliott's students "dramatized" the 1773 storming of the ship *Eleanor* in Boston by throwing over their desks—manufactured chests of tea. Her nephew, Tim Yager, son of her sister, Mary, portrayed one of the patriots "arrested and thrown into jail during the dramatization," recalled Elliott.[8]

Of course, Elliott's effort to use her classroom to answer the call of the bicentennial commission could not overshadow acclaim or controversy with the eye color exercise. In May, she appeared on Minneapolis television's *What Did You Do in School Today?* to talk about the classroom simulation on discrimination. Then, on August 17, the Riceville Public Library honored its hometown celebrity, two other local authors, and a local artist at an event marking its fiftieth anniversary.[9] Elliott was invited to design a presentation for William Peters's book about the discrimination day lesson, *A Class Divided*. Situated adjacent to her display was an art exhibit by Riceville High graduate, class of '70, and the University of Iowa rising senior, Michael Blake. With the permission of the library's director, Margaret Duncomb, Blake displayed five nude charcoal sketches. Elliott reportedly covered the sex organs with tape and drew a large "X" across one of his portraits. Blake and Elliott got into a shouting match over her actions. "There was a huge confrontation in front of the whole town," recalled Blake in an interview decades later. "Everyone was there," he added. "Jane's whole thing was she didn't want kids to learn about sex this way."[10] Blake, an Iowa Merit Scholarship recipient and University of Iowa Dean's list student, described himself as "the talk of the town" after confronting the blue-eyed, brown-eyed woman.[11] Elliott, meanwhile, brushed off the incident as just another encounter with her Riceville critics.

* * *

Elliott's discrimination exercise has an auspicious undertone despite taking place in the middle of a social studies course. The discrimination experience reveals the inability to see other people as valued beings of humanity that Elliott admittedly struggled with throughout her childhood and young adult life. As much as her lesson is intellectualized and debated amongst pundits, it had concrete manifestations in classrooms across the United States. For instance, a student-teacher at Midland Park High School in Hackensack, New Jersey, named Rosemary Balenger, attempted a rendition of Elliott's exercise with a group of seniors.

A senior at Ramapo College just a few years older than her students, Balenger learned of Jane Elliott and the eye color lesson years earlier when her Girl Scout troop watched *The Eye of the Storm*. When planning a unit about the Roaring Twenties, Balenger thought the exercise would help her students understand the political and social ostracism faced by Catholics, Eastern Europeans, and African Americans in different periods of American history. The unit also touched upon the re-emergence of the Ku Klux Klan and the treatment of Native Americans. Balenger's explanation for the exercise alludes to experiential learning practices. "I think the kids are concerned with the wrongs done to minority groups, but they have no directions," she explained to a reporter about why the role-play was beneficial for her all-white students at Midland Park High. On the first day of Balenger's two-day exercise, she placed the blue eyes atop her hierarchy, reflecting how the RCS third graders were divided in *The Eye of the Storm*. There were a few deviations: Ballenger's exercise was voluntary, and instead of armbands or collars, students pinned to their shirts orange paper cutouts called the "Evil Eyes." At the start of the lesson, Balenger instructed blue-eyed students to treat their brown-eyed peers as second-class. "Don't eat with them, date them, or socialize with them, in or out of school," said the teacher to a group of cynical seniors. Balenger said that by the end of day one, the brown eyes were "teased [. . .] Their friends would say, 'This or that is typical of you dumb brown-eyed people," Balenger told a local reporter. Roles were reversed on day two, though the brown eyes took no joy in devaluing their peers. As a result, Balenger's lesson steered off course.

Like the exercise was designed to do, Balenger's attempt made enough of a point to get students to think differently about how the history course's content could teach something about prejudice. Yet, this moment was fleeting for a student-teacher who was, in her words, a "comparative stranger" with very little rapport among those she tried getting to see the world from a new perspective. Newspaper reports of Balenger's "experiment" do not indicate parental complaints. However, the aspiring teacher suggested that it was a "simulation game" and that her senior students "didn't take it seriously."[12]

It is worthwhile to see reproductions of Jane Elliott's eye color lesson on discrimination in the context of its time. This example is demonstrative of a younger generation of well-intended educators hoping to contribute to efforts that fix virulent racism; to bridge gaps in American racial misunderstandings, racist myths that seemingly still undergirded white supremacist culture, and colorblind curricular and instructional practices twenty years after the *Brown v. Board of Education* decision outlawing racial segregation in public schools. That was Elliott's precise point the day six years earlier when she first taught the lesson at Riceville Elementary.

While the principled preservice teacher from Midland Park offered novel modifications to Elliott's exercise, two high school instructors from the Chicago area presented another case study on how educators adapted the lesson plan. Russell Watson was a twenty-six-year-old psychology and sociology teacher at DuPage County's predominantly white, suburban Wheaton-Warrenville High School. His colleague, Dale Berman, age thirty, was a history teacher at predominantly student of color Martin Luther King Jr. High School, located in Chicago's South Side. The two idealists created a student exchange in 1973, allowing students from both schools to "see the differences in lifestyles." Watson told a reporter from the *Chicago Tribune*, "[. . .] seeing the differences, they also see the similarities. If there are similarities, it is easier to form friendships" across cultural borders.[13] Watson, who taught a course called "Urban Community" and had reason to integrate the student swap program into his curriculum, would bus Wheaton-Warrenville students to King, where they would spend a day. Later in the semester, Berman (who taught United States history) visited Wheaton-Warrenville with his King High students. This cycle repeated every semester or twice a year for almost two decades.

Watson and Berman were more than idealistic schoolteachers; they were invested in seeing a change in American race relations. Watson had marched against housing discrimination with Martin Luther King in 1966 at Chicago's Marquette Park. During the event, he witnessed King "drop to a knee" after being hit on the head by a rock thrown by whites rallying against the demonstration. Other violence occurred that day, forcing the police to call in about 1,200 officers to protect King and 600 marchers from a mob estimated at 7,000 persons. A knife intended for King wounded a white marcher when thrown in the direction of the civil rights leader. In another instance, shots were fired after cars carrying Black passengers were pulled over by police officers. Crowds chanted "white power" and "Roses are red, violets are black, King would look good with a dagger in his back." People held signs that read "Martin Luther Coon" and hounded marchers. White allies like Watson were called "[N-word] lovers." The experience was so awful that King would later say he "had never seen such hate."[14]

A lifelong Chicagoan, Berman possessed a more storied involvement in the civil rights crusade and the Chicago Freedom movement. A Congress of Racial Equality member arrested at least three times for protesting redlining practices and other forms of housing discrimination, Berman marched at the August 1963 March for Jobs and Freedom in the nation's capital, where King delivered the "I Have a Dream" speech.[15] Berman also attended the Marquette Park march, though unbeknownst to Watson, and at CORE's rally to broaden housing opportunities at Cicero.

Watson and Berman first met when the former visited King High School during the summer of 1973 on a National Council for Christians and Jews field trip into Chicago. Watson had Jane Elliott in mind when pitching returning to King with his students at the school year's beginning. He had previously used *The Eye of the Storm* in his sociology and psychology classes. Despite students' requests to incorporate the Discrimination Day lesson into his lesson planning, Watson realized the experience would not have the same impact in a fifty-minute class compared to Elliott's full day with her elementary students. Alternatively, the Wheaton-Warrenville school teacher, who later became a finalist for the teacher-in-space Challenger space shuttle mission, found as much value in having his students spend a day at the inner-city school.[16] Berman, meanwhile, insisted that his students also visit Watson's suburban school. A singular approach granting Wheaton-Warrenville students the privilege of touring the city school would make the King High students feel like "fish in a fishbowl," Berman protested. They would be exhibits for white students to study. Acting accordingly, the two educators created a program enabling the two sets of students to change places for a day, tour each building, sit in on classes, and eat lunch together before participating in a debrief called "rap sessions."

The program almost never got started. While the principal at King High wanted to see the exchange occur, administrators at Wheaton-Warrenville maintained doubts. The excuse Watson received from the superintendent was that school district bus drivers refused to drive into the city. Additionally, the district code maintained that a district employee had to be responsible for busing students during school hours. Not to be deterred, Watson obtained a Charter Bus Endorsement or Class C driver's license required by the state of Illinois to chauffeur students to and from school-sponsored activities.[17] With no more excuses, the program began in 1973 with Watson first driving Wheaton-Warrenville students to King. Later in the school year, Watson rose early to pick up Berman's King High students, then transported them the twenty-five miles back to his suburban school.

Under the collaborative efforts of Watson and Berman, the exchange occurred twice a year under their supervision until 1986. When Watson moved on to teach preservice educators at the university level at the College of DuPage, a younger teacher continued the program until 1992. To Watson's estimation, about 4,500 students participated in the exchange during its nineteen-year run. Students involved in the inner-city exchange were given "buddies" from the partner school.[18] The buddies exchanged home addresses and phone numbers and would remain in constant contact each year of high school and beyond. As more and more teachers attempted to duplicate Elliott's eye color exercise in the coming years, Watson and Berman offered an innovative alternative, though lacking in program sustainability, to expose students to cultural diversity.

The magnum opus for Elliott during this time was not that schoolteachers saw her as inspiring. Her delight that year was an honor bestowed on her by the National Association for Mental Health. Since the release of *A Class Divided* several years prior, Elliott had been tenaciously digging in her heels on dyslexia. She recently joined the board of directors of the Upper Midwest branch of the Orton Dyslexia Society. As a director, she was involved in the programming and implementing policies to help children affected by the learning difference.[19] Her primary cause was to establish professional learning workshops to train educators in Orton-Gillingham phonics so they could better teach dyslexic children to read. "We need to train more teachers to teach dyslexic children," she told a group of educators in Lebanon, Pennsylvania. "These children are required to be in school, but no teacher is required to teach them correctly. With the right instruction, it is so easy for the child to be successful in school."[20]

* * *

In the spring of 1975, the Uniontown Area School District, located forty-five miles south of Pittsburgh, contracted Elliott to perform the eye color exercise on teachers and the community. Home to approximately 16,000 people, the city's school district at the time was sheathed in an ugly civil rights lawsuit.[21] Two years earlier, the Pennsylvania Human Relations Commission (PHRC), an organization born out of the Fair Employees Practices Commission to handle discrimination claims over housing, had flagged the Uniontown School District for maintaining a pattern of racial segregation.[22] In a commonwealth supreme court case decided on December 4, 1973, Uniontown's East End Elementary School was cited as the only school in the district maintaining a racially imbalanced student population. The school enrolled 124 Black students, or 55 percent of enrollment, to 100 white students. While district officials posited that East End was not segregated, the PHRC held firm to its definition that schools must maintain 50 percent Black and 50 percent white pupils. Anything contrary violated Pennsylvania's desegregation laws. According to PHRC, the solution was to bus Black children to schools outside the East End neighborhood. Uniontown school board directors countered with evidence that busing students out of neighborhood zones would increase property taxes up to 3 percent for mileage. It argued further that busing would frustrate Black families because their children would commute to schools outside their neighborhood.[23]

Still, the PHRC definition of desegregated schools left the school district with no choice but to comply with the state supreme court's order to submit a busing plan by March 11 and a September deadline to implement said plan. When the March 11 deadline arrived, the school board voted 6-3 to close the East End Elementary School and redistribute the students into the district's five other elementary schools to end the racial imbalance at the school.[24]

Upset that their children had to bear the burden of a problem they did not create, Uniontown's Black parents working under the name "Concerned Parents of East End" debated whether to protest the school district's actions. Many community leaders and parents voiced frustration to the local press. They sought a way to obtain a just resolution to the desegregation order by announcing a boycott come the first day of the fall semester.

When the school year commenced during the first week of September, most East End parents kept their children out of elementary, middle, and high schools. The group put extra pressure on the district with peaceful demonstrations outside Uniontown High School and the district administration building.[25] With the support of the Fayette County People for Progress, the Brownsville-Uniontown branch of the NAACP, and the East End Parent-Teacher Association, the Concerned Parents of East End declared they would only return their children to school and accept the closing of East End if the school board capitulated to a series of conditions presented in a position paper over Labor Day weekend. The parents demanded that a Black assistant superintendent be hired, along with Black teachers and paraprofessionals in every district school. They also requested professional development training to teach faculty and staff culturally responsive practices. The parents argued that the closing of their school conveyed a feeling of inferiority. The students maintained the impression that they were losing their school because they were "poor and Black." Acting accordingly, the parents insisted that the school board close a second school. If another school building were closed, it would "make a difference psychologically to those parents who feel their children have been 'singled out.'"[26]

Sustained inaction by the board enhanced activism by the Concerned Parents. After the first week of school, East End parents commenced a boycott of Uniontown businesses. After warning the Uniontown Chamber of Commerce of its intention, Rev. Howard E. Dantzler told the local daily *Evening Standard* that the boycott would continue to grow until "[there is] some positive action by the school board and officials." The Concerned Parents group arranged carpools from the Mount Rose Baptist Church to help boycotters shop outside the city.[27]

The local business protest served as a proving ground for the objectives of the East End parents. Almost two weeks into the school year, on September 11, the school board and the Concerned Parents of East End reached a mediated agreement with the board solicitor. Uniontown SD agreed to ask the PHRC for a one-year moratorium "without stipulations," which would allow East End Elementary to reopen for the 1974-1975 school year. The board submitted a revised desegregation plan to the PHRC detailing the closing of East End and one other city elementary school at the start of the 1975-76 school year. An African American man or woman would be hired into a position in central administration, but no guarantees were made that it would be the role of assistant superintendent. Black community members could serve on hiring committees, though the superintendent will still determine who receives jobs in the district. Community representatives were allowed to ride on school buses to supervise busing affairs. The board also agreed to create a "Desegregation Inservice Advisory Committee" and welcome the school district superintendent, Larry Sayre, as an ex-officio member. Other committee members included community residents, school board directors, faculty, and a Pittsburgh Human Relations Commission representative. The committee provided diversity training to the faculty and staff.[28]

A PHRC committee of seven eventually accepted the moratorium request with six affirmative votes and one abstention.[29] When East End Elementary reopened on Monday, October 14, the building's student demographic consisted of 128 students, ninety-three Black and thirty-five white—the largest disparity since the desegregation episode began.[30] In November, the district hired Dr. Francis A. Farmer Jr. as its first Black administrator and new supervisor of pupil personnel services and federal programs. Hailing from an administrative position at Slippery Rock State College, Farmer arrived in Uniontown, holding a doctorate from the University of Pittsburgh with expertise in curriculum.[31]

One of Farmer's first jobs was working alongside Superintendent Sayre to approve professional development training suggested by the in-service committee. During the spring semester, he and Sayre offered Jane Elliott an honorarium to facilitate the Discrimination Day lesson with Uniontown Area School District faculty, staff, and community.

On March 18, 1975, Elliott put teachers, students, and parents through the eye color exercise. For many program participants, the training was one of the most infuriating experiences of their professional careers. She felt the same by the end of her visit to Uniontown. An hour into the session, a blue-eyed male participant charged toward her: "This is garbage, just like everything that's gone on in this district," and then stormed off. There is a photograph in the *Evening Standard* of Elliott standing next to a seated Superintendent Larry Sayre, dressed in all black, with short, wedged hair and vintage spectacles. The picture, which shows the two in jovial moods, had to have been taken before the training with the educators and community members.

Their joyful expressions unraveled by lunchtime.

While local media reports acclaimed the training session, Elliott's recollection of the Uniontown experience was dark. During her closing remarks, years later, she recalled that a blue-eyed woman approached her with a piece of paper with cookie crumbs, crumpled napkins, and scraps of lint. She slammed it on the table near where Elliott was standing. "That's what this morning was. Garbage!" the woman exclaimed.[32]

Regarding all the blue-eyed participants, Elliott said, "Their brown-eyed peers got to see them behave in a way that brown-eyed and brown-skinned students were treated in that town at that time." As a visitor, Elliott heard horror stories about racial abuses in Uniontown's history from Farmer, the man responsible for chauffeuring her around town. Those stories prepped Elliott for the mob-like mentality during her session. Sadly, she readied herself; angry reactions from blue-eyed people were the norm. "These were only words," she added. "There were no threats of loss of jobs. There were no threats of being arrested. There were no physical threats in that situation. And they were all adults with degrees. And what they did and the way they responded to that; if a Black student would have responded that way in the classroom, they would have been kicked out of school. And the teachers of color recognized that." In her final analysis, Elliott felt the brown-eyed adults had exhibited behaviors that they would never have tolerated by Black students in their classrooms. "I think that brown-eyed black people that day learned more about their white peers than their white peers wanted them to know."[33]

During the lunch hour, Superintendent Sayre received an anonymous phone call with a threat against Elliott's life: "You'd better get that bitch out of town, or I'm gonna shoot her."[34] Several locals also took Elliott to Farmer's house after an afternoon session with students, keeping her unaware of the threat. Black men and women created a corridor from the front door to the sidewalk to shield the 5'2" visiting speaker from potential shooters as she ran into the house. Sentinels stood at the windows until sundown when a caravan of vehicles arrived later that night to sneak Elliott out of town.

The next day, Elliott attended the Tri-County Mental Health Association of Pennsylvania's eighteenth annual conference in Carlisle, west of Harrisburg. In the evening, she gave a speech at a dinner held in her honor inside Embers Restaurant, an establishment often hosting political headliners and banquets.[35] Since "Prejudice" was the conference's theme, her remarks began with the screening of the half-hour film *The Eye of the Storm*. She followed with remarks about her relationship with Room 10 students by drawing a line between reading literacy and color-conscious literacy. "Those 16 kids in *The Eye of the Storm* are all supposedly disabled readers and were never able to learn to read or to graduate from high school. People thought they couldn't learn [. . .] the fault was being placed on the students. Students weren't being paid to learn how to read. Their parents were paying teachers to teach the students how to read. But the teachers didn't know how to do it. And I did." She plugged the Rome Remedial Center's Orton-Gillingham certification program in Minnesota, emphasizing, "If teachers would take that course, which is available, and if colleges of education would force teachers to take a course in Orton Gillingham phonics, then every trainee, and every future educator, would know how to teach every child how to read."[36] She suggested if teachers could express that skin color had nothing to do with one's intelligence and that learning differences did not predetermine whether a child could read on grade level—then the problems of racism and reading literacy could be resolved. Thanks to Elliott's vitae that combined her classroom lesson on prejudice reduction with her role as a forum member at the White House Conference on Children, she was situated as well as one could serve as a traveling spokesperson of causes related to intellectual disabilities, dyslexia, and to promote good mental health.

Leaving the two-story motel the following day, Elliott felt uneasy. "I was alone and totally defenseless," she said in an interview forty-five years after the trip to Pennsylvania. The final morning in Carlisle, as Elliott packed her luggage before checking out and catching a taxicab to the airport, Elliott wondered if the person who issued the death threat was waiting for her to leave the room.

She stiffened her shoulders, opened the door, and marched quickly to the receptionist to check out. On the flight home, Elliott decided never to feel frightened again. "They may threaten me, they may destroy me, but they'll never frighten me again," she resolved.

> I was damned sure no number of adults in a workshop was going to scare me again [. . .] What I realized was that that same thing, in a smaller way, was happening to my kids in school. To junior and senior high school people and their teachers, who were treating my older son and eldest daughter that way. It was not the happiest moment of my life, but it was the best thing that ever happened to me because I was no longer afraid of what might happen to me.[37]

* * *

Shortly after the scare in Pennsylvania, Elliott and her Room 10 students returned to their celebrations of the American Revolution Bicentennial. On April 18, 1975, Room 10 students reenacted Paul Revere's midnight ride to Lexington, Massachusetts, by having student Todd Koenigs run through the halls bearing leaflets and knocking on random classroom doors, yelling, "To arms! To arms! The British are coming!" Koenigs did more than disrupt the teaching in other parts of the building; he obstructed a school board meeting by storming into the superintendent's office and tossing paper leaflets around the room before returning to Room 10.[38]

In May 1975, Elliott's students added eight feet by ten feet log cabin from telephone poles to the Village Green bicentennial park adjacent to the Jennison Inn. After learning from her brother-in-law, Keith Yager—an employee at the Farmers Mutual Telephone Company—that obsolete telephone poles were at the company's dump, Jane and Darald used their station wagon to transport dozens of discarded telephone poles from the boneyard to Village Green.[39] When completed, the cabin was furnished with an old pot-bellied stove and a small porch. Toiling at the park was a therapeutic escape from the pressures brought by her anti-racism work. Her obsession with giving Riceville a tangible gift generated a different kind of attention. That spring, a camera crew from the U.S. Information Agency on Bicentennial Projects visited Riceville to produce a short film and museum exhibit about Village Green. The exhibit would go in Chicago's Museum of Science and Industry. The documentary called Village Green Park a "model for the rest of the state."[40]

The short film about the park engendered greater interest in Elliott's pedagogy. That summer, after the *Riceville Recorder* nominated Room 10's bicentennial park for the Winnebago Industries of Forest City NAID Park Improvement award, judges from Iowa State University awarded Village Green a second-place prize of $300 and a plaque.[41] The judges said, "[A]lthough small, it is unique among entries. For the past two years, the third-grade class of Mrs. Jane Elliott have been developing a small park in the town, with access by foot. The park, although constructed by third graders, is used much by the local citizens. The money for developing the park has thus far come from the third graders recycling cans, bottles, and paper. The 'muscle' has been the children, plus their parents, working together. As all park administrators can attest, a major problem in parks is vandalism—but which child would destroy a park they themselves have built? A little math reveals that in only seven years, the first third-grade class involved in Village Green will be Seniors in High School." Of Elliott, the judges said, "It might be hard to find a better example of creative teaching and excellent community involvement—and the park is worth an award on its own merits. It is simple, well-placed, and well-suited for its intended use."[42] The town of Grafton's "Kindernook" facility and playground, translated from German, meaning "children," received the competition's top prize.[43]

After celebrating the second-place regional recognition for building Riceville a community-friendly park with her students, Elliott used the prize money to pay off the debt for the wooden shingles to roof the cabin. The Village Green, she recollected years later, gave her third graders "a feeling of their responsibility in the present to make something that would be there in the future." Her objective was to help students leave their signatures in their community. The fact that they created Village Green Park during America's bicentennial presented everyone who entered Room 10 with a chance "to do something real," she said, in a way that made "people in the future look at what they had done in a positive way [simply] because of something that happened in the past."[44]

Elliott tried to balance her day job with advocacy for dyslexia awareness and anti-racism. Before year's end, she again lectured about the eye color exercise. This time, Elliott spoke alongside Gerridee Wheeler, national president of the Mental Health Association, and Percy Knauth, groundbreaking author of *A Season in Hell*, a memoir about mental depression, at the annual North Dakota Mental Health Association conference in Dickinson, North Dakota on October 14-15, 1975. As she had in Pennsylvania earlier that year, she gave a film presentation of *The Eye of the Storm*. She facilitated a large group discussion on the psychological impact of labeling children with inferior physical and mental traits.[45]

Since her life remained relatively quiet over the next year, Elliott attempted to cast herself as the bicentennial woman. It was almost as if she was trying to transform herself into the town's educational do-it-all that she knew was impossible to achieve but worth the venture. This process reached a pinnacle on July 4, 1976, when Elliott chaired two of Riceville's Bicentennial program events. At half-past eleven in the morning, she facilitated reunions of the Round Grove School and her Room 10 students and their parents, who contributed to the construction of Village Green Park since the project's conception in 1972. The reunions took place in the shaded area of Village Green, east of the Jennison Inn. Later in the day, the community gathered again at the Jennison to consume a 250-pound Bicentennial Cake topped with 200 candles and containing Bicentennial fifty-cent pieces.[46]

In October, Elliott's parents, Lloyd and Gie, sold the lot which Village Green occupied to the City of Riceville for $1 if the Village Green "always remain[ed] a park."[47]

The inn's restaurant never recovered after Elliott's eye exercise incensed the community. Moreover, the inn never generated a profit without Jane and Darald's original marketing initiatives once employed as establishment owners. Before the end of 1977, Elliott's parents accepted that the Jennison Inn would never become a profit-making venture. Lloyd and Gie spent the remainder of their lives inhabiting the inn, which became a source of entertainment for the grandkids. After Lloyd died in 1990 and Gie's passing in 2008, new owners gave the inn its original name: The Burke Hotel. During that time and after, the lot east of the hotel, Elliott's Bicentennial Village Green Park, would remain in use, existing as the family's legacy to the town's center. For many succeeding years, the park has been used for children's book events and summer craft programs organized by the Riceville Community Schools and Riceville Public Library.[48]

One of the children's authors Elliott introduced to the students at their park was Roald Dahl. Already famous for *Charlie and the Chocolate Factory*, Dahl's newest book, *Danny, the Champion of the World*, is a tale about the pastime adventures of a widowed father and his only son while living in a caravan. Around the midpoint in the school year, Elliott and her Room 10 students wrote to Dahl at his home in Great Missenden, Buckinghamshire, England. They inquired about many of the book's most poignant moments, plus a request for the recipe to make Toad in the Hole, a sausage and batter dish the father and son share at the end of the story. Dahl replied to "lovely Jane Elliott and everyone in Room 10" on February 1, 1977.[49] Included in the correspondence was an authentic recipe given to him by his secretary, Marlene, whom he described as "a great cook." Upon receiving the letter, her Room 10 students were eager to run over to the Jennison Inn to put the recipe to use for their next classroom project. Sadly, it was one of her last memories working with Riceville's third-grade children.

At the end of the 1976-1977 school year, there was an opening at Riceville's junior high school. Elliott expressed interest in obtaining a transfer into the position mainly because students in the school were becoming unruly. In her memoir, Elliott described the middle schoolers as "big, tough, tyrannical kids."[50] Journalist Stephen Bloom, who invested decades tracking her career, attested to the degree of dysfunction described by Elliott in *A Collar in My Pocket*. "With or without her," he writes in his book about the eye color exercise, "Riceville Junior High in 1977 was a school beset with problems."[51] After a conversation with the outgoing RCS superintendent, Dean Weaver, Elliott agreed to leave her elementary position to teach seventh graders and help five other teachers and the new junior high principal, Steven Harnack, bring order to the school.[52]

CHAPTER 16

BULL'S EYE

"We don't know if these children will remember what they learned. But it's not likely that they will forget their courageous and creative teacher who made their lives retched for one day. And at the same time gave them the priceless understanding of human psychology."

—BILL BUETEL, 1970

"Next to the elimination of racism and sexism in the schools, my main interest lies in the identification and education of the dyslexic."

— JANE ELLIOTT, LEBANON COUNTY EDUCATIONAL HONORS SOCIETY, PENNSYLVANIA, 1978

No other political scandal defines the 1970s like Watergate. Since June 17, 1971, five burglars had been arrested in the Democratic offices at the Watergate apartment-business complex. Careers were ruined, men were imprisoned, and one political party became entrenched in corruption unmatched by a few events in American electoral history. During the early stages of the Watergate investigation, the 1972 Democratic nominee for president, George McGovern, spent the campaign's final weeks labeling the Nixon administration the most corrupt in American history. "At no time have we witnessed official corruption as wide or as deep as the mess in Washington right now," McGovern said. He added that a mix of Nixon's deceit tied to nearly three decades of Republican fearmongering led to the "steady corruption of our own precious values as a country."[1]

During a drawn-out series of events that made up the Watergate affair, the incumbent's abuse of power revelations seemed endless. President Nixon was forced to yield secretly recorded White House tapes contradicting previously released and edited White House transcripts. In an unrelated investigation that fell during the same timeframe, administration officials in the Nixon "plumbers" unit were identified for theft of psychiatric documents of Pentagon Papers defendant Daniel Ellsberg. The Watergate Committee discovered Nixon falsified income tax returns over four years and owed almost half a million dollars in back taxes.[2] The committee voted to recommend Nixon's impeachment for refusing to comply with its subpoenas for the White House tapes. In an unprecedented choice, the President of the United States resigned from office in August 1974. A month later, President Gerald Ford surprisingly issued an absolute pardon to free the former president "for all offenses [. . .] committed or may have committed or taken part in" during Nixon's time in the Oval Office.[3]

Continued disclosure of the Nixon administration corruption during the two succeeding years after his resignation generated more questions about "a new sense of moral and ethical grounding" in schools, as opinionist Roy Larson put it in a May 1976 *Associated Press* column.[4] Once again, the school system appeared at the center of the conversation. It seemed like issues of a bygone era; religion over science, Red-ucators brainwashing students with Soviet propaganda, the comic book plague increasing rates of juvenile delinquency, and ethnic studies curricula following the 1960s' social movements. These trends stirring in education made moral education imperative. School leaders from Chicago to Florida called for academic programming, children's literature, and humanities texts to teach students an understanding of moral perspectives across cultures and introduce critical thinking skills to make well-informed decisions.

A Gallup poll that year found that 79 percent of the population "favored moral instruction in schools." Supporters of moral education called for adding an "M" (morality) to the inexact epithet "3Rs" (reading, writing, arithmetic). By August, national surveys indicated that curriculum on moral education took over "almost half" of the schools in the United States.[5] In some school districts, curriculum writers designed general education courses and electives centered on moral learning. In most places, however, lessons on morality were organically integrated into traditionally taught curricula. In other words, a skill called "value-sorting" occurred when liberal arts teachers asked students to discuss the moral convictions of characters appearing in literature, film, history, and artwork. The framework for moral learning focused on two pillars: respecting authority figures and cultivating good manners. The discussion model supposedly helped students develop their values.

Naturally, proponents of moral education were met with fierce opposition. Critics of the newest trend in education considered teacher-led value-sorting as a pedagogy that indoctrinated students. Parents and community groups naturally contended that teachers would influence children during class discussions through body language, tone of voice, and expressions of favoritism toward specific students.[6] For teenage and adult learners, it was believed that any variation of moral education—defining values, sorting values, comparing values across cultures—would be ineffective in changing students' behavior in high school and college.

In this prism of educational narratives, Jane Elliott's eye color exercise, known for subjecting children to first-hand experiences in devalued stereotypes based on physical characteristics, became an instructional approach under intense scrutiny.[7] Long before anyone used the phrase "moral education," Elliott's Discrimination Day lesson forced her students and adult trainees to think about cultural racism, behavioral racism, biological racism, institutional inequity, and bias. The question of what the three Rs and an M should look like was a matter of public debate. Journalists and educators alike asked whether Jane Elliott's approach was ethical.

Instructors in schools of education offered alternatives to Elliott's pedagogy. At the University of Massachusetts, Sidney B. Simon published "values clarification kits" to help public school teachers avoid personal bias and indoctrinating practices. Simon's technique allowed students to write lists of personal preferences based on prompts about simple things ranging from hobbies and leisure activities to more complex topics such as race and religion. For instance, one exercise in the Simon curriculum asked students to list twenty hobbies. Then, students were asked to prioritize the five hobbies they preferred most. They were to check the items they loved to do alone and place an "X" on hobbies they loved to do with friends. While all responses were considered correct, students were expected to explain themselves. Simon's values clarification exercises "protect" teachers from valuing one set of beliefs and personal behaviors while devaluing those of another group. Students, meanwhile, learn what they value most.[8] Simon seemed to find the most support from religious leaders.

For Elliott, this was superficial learning. While she certainly thought it could engage students in storytelling, nothing experiential occurred in the Simon values kits. Since nothing was experiential, Elliott questioned how much learning about value diversity, empathy, and decision-making took place in that curriculum. Just as her methods were questioned, a few educational experts in attendance at the DePaul University conference "Moral Education: An Imperative in Today's Schools?" endorsed a "learn-by-doing" approach to inclusive excellence and value-sorting curriculum, citing Elliott's work.[9]

Dramatic debates over diversity and inclusion in schools across the public education system were serendipitous for the Palo Alto Unified School District during the summer and fall of 1976. Nine years earlier, the Palo Alto school district managed to bottle up news of a classroom experiment conducted by a Cubberley High School history teacher Ron Jones, who created a five-day lesson that turned a faction of students into fascists. Jones used his World History class to train students in the totalitarian ways of the Nazis. For a week, Jones and his students simulated the Third Reich. He built a classroom culture of fear that silenced the class's top academic students while emboldening lower-achieving students to take ownership of the learning environment. He introduced a new set of rules, which included sitting with perfect posture, standing at attention, and giving answers that were no more than three words. No one could laugh, and no one was permitted to challenge the new rules.

Monday through Thursday, Jones introduced creative slogans emphasizing Nazi themes. Monday featured the simulation's first mantra, "Strength Through Discipline." Jones also gave the movement a name: "The Third Wave."[10] Tuesday's mantra: "Strength Through Community," was enhanced by the party's official greeting, a raised cupped hand salute. On Wednesday, Jones issued membership cards and preached "Strength Through Action." He assigned students with commissions. Some created Third Wave banners to hang throughout the school corridors. He told others to stand guard at his classroom door to prevent "any student who is not a Third Wave member from entering this room." Several students became recruiters. It was a job carrying the mission to "convince twenty students in the adjacent elementary school" to adopt Third Wave ideology. Others received Gestapo-like assignments with instructions to inform Jones of counter-movements against the Third Wave. Thursday's "Strength Through Pride" mantra entrapped the student body into making the Third Wave the center of their lives.[11]

After just four days, the experiment got out of hand. First, Jones's "three brightest students" were "manhandled" by their peers for refusing to abide by Third Wave regulations. He indefinitely removed dissenters from his classroom. After about 200 students from other classes joined the Third Wave, administrators lost control of the student body. Banners and flags with Third Wave insignia hung from Cubberley High's walls. Dozens of students wearing Third Wave armbands skipped class to attend Jones' history lessons. Third Wave members started intimidating resisters. A few fights erupted. When faculty members put down the scuffles, Third Wavers flashed the cup-fisted salute as teachers hauled them off to the principal's office. Even Jones admitted that the experience of having the student body look at him as their "Fuehrer" transformed his behavior. Word spread to the other schools in the Palo Alto School District, where Third Wave branches emerged as vocal forces in the greater Santa Clara area.

On Friday, Jones finally ended the movement at an assembly where the students believed they would meet the Third Wave's national youth leader. Jones placed two television sets in front of the students and said, "Here is your leader." The students sat there for almost ten minutes. No leader appeared on the screens. The students realized they had been "manipulated," Jones recalled in his memoir.[12] A sixteen-year-old Third Waver, Steve Coniglio, remembered, "My most vivid image of the Holocaust was imagining people led into cement block rooms, the doors slamming shut, and then the gas coming in. Well, we waited two minutes, then five minutes, and no new leader appeared on the screen. Then I got hit with the same feeling and screamed, 'I'm getting out of here.'"[13] ABC has since turned Ron Jones's lesson on fascism into a hit movie titled *The Wave*, winner of Peabody and Emmy awards, and a 2010 documentary, *Lesson Plan: The Story of the Third Wave*.

While Palo Alto successfully kept one of its history teachers' experiential lessons out of the news in 1967, the publication of Jones' memoir, *No Substitute for Madness: A Teacher, His Kids, and the Lesson of Real Life* in 1976, generated a media firestorm at a time when educators and school communities sustained irreconcilable differences over the best method to teach children interpersonal skill and independent, critical thinking competencies. Palo Alto leaders eventually fired Jones not long after the Third Wave lesson (for a separate matter). Teachers like Jones often find themselves caught in community rage when they boldly test the public school system, especially if it clashes with the school community's values. Jane Elliott, like Jones, practiced a pedagogy that honed independent thinkers. Less than a decade had passed since her first eye color lesson plan, and unlike Jones, she still stood firm in the Riceville Community School system.

What could one do when national organizations still honored Jane Elliott for her bold commitment to disrupting prejudice in her schoolchildren? For Elliott, the explanation was simple enough. As a homegrown Ricevillean, she was protected in her job essentially because she was the only one willing and able to teach dyslexic children. Still, the accolades helped. In 1978, the

National Mental Health Association awarded her the "National Mental Health Association Award for Excellence in Education." As the recipient, she would spend the year on the road representing the Mental Health Association. She intended to speak on behalf of experiential learning, dyslexia, anti-racism, and, more explicitly, how those three concepts intersect. In a lecture tour along the East Coast marking the tenth anniversary of the Discrimination Day lesson, Elliott proclaimed the most pressing issue in education was "the identification and education of the dyslexic."[14] She said dyslexic children "must have phonics to learn to read." To that end, teachers must learn how to teach dyslexic students.

Elliott loved to tell people that her struggling readers "gained up to four years of vocabulary" after one year in her classroom.[15] This emphasis on making gains and boosting children's confidence with reading differences appealed to her audiences. Elliott commonly spoke with classroom teachers, school counselors, veterans' administrations, and student groups at various schools. There was genuine intrigue over how she connected dyslexia education with her exercise in early childhood anti-racism. Elliott drew a line from ignorance about race to ignorance about teaching students with disabilities. She drew a distinction between teachers that assume infallible authority by which struggling students get excluded from many aspects of teaching and their victims responding to the exclusion by misbehaving against so-called classroom norms. The traditional teacher's impatience to meet students at their skill level was reprehensible. The educator trained in anti-racism and Orton-Gillingham phonics she viewed as leading students out of cultural ignorance. Racism, she held firm, "is a mental problem."

Moreover, when talking to educators about dyslexia, Elliott found that most felt a child's inability to read was caused by a mental problem. "No, it isn't," she said. "It's a problem that is a result of that child having a different learning style and a different need."[16]

> So, when you have a child of color—when you have a melanacious or melanotic child in your classroom—if you don't understand that that child not only has the problem of being the wrong color in that classroom [. . .] that problem is exacerbated if that child is dyslexic.

> Teachers of all kinds [teaching] students of all kinds have to know that 20 to 30 percent of their students have a problem that you can fix. You can't keep them from being dyslexic, but you can teach them in such a way that they will learn how to deal with the printed language and numbers in a way that a

dyslexic can be successful. Albert Einstein was dyslexic. He was quite successful. Henry Ford was dyslexic. He was quite successful.

So, if teachers would just look at everyone of those kids who are having problems reading and say to himself or herself or themselves, "This kid could be the next Henry Ford," or "This person could be the next person who invents a cure for polio." 'Cause that's what you'd have in every classroom—you'd have kids who [succeed] in the future, but they won't do it if forced to lived down to their teacher's expectations of them because of a teacher's ignorance about race—which doesn't exist—[and ignorance] about skin color, and about learning problems, particularly dyslexia.[17]

For a moment, Elliott's advocacy for speaking out against labeling and stereotyping grabbed the consenting attention of columnists in the Deep South. Carolyn Decell, owner of *The Deer Creek Pilot* and author of the column "Trimmed in Lace," found similarities between Elliott's eye color exercise and the legend of a schoolteacher who mistook her students as superior academics. This unnamed new teacher obtained a job in a low-achieving school. On her first day, the principal handed her a class roster with numbers from 120 to 140 next to the picture of each student. The teacher assumed the numbers were intelligence ratings. The teacher interacted with her students all semester long like they were geniuses. Test score results at the end of the term showed significant improvement in the grades and behaviors of the students. At the summative evaluation meeting, the principal praised the teacher for her job with the students. The teacher responded: "But it's only to be expected from such superior students. Why you yourself gave me the list of intelligence ratings."

"They aren't intelligence ratings," the principal said. "They're the students' locker numbers."

Both stories show the power that a teacher has over student performance. "Not all of us are, or could be, teachers," wrote Decell. "But the lesson could be applied to all those whom our lives influence—even more perhaps than we ever know."[18]

Jane Elliott had become the premier advocate for a faltering education campaign against racial prejudice. Speaking to students at Fresno State University, activist Cyrus Keller argued, "We need to re-create a part of what existed in the Sixties but in different ways."[19] Civil rights activists like Keller believed that while Elliott was the leading voice sustaining the movement in the field of education, she was working largely in isolation. Her message, at the time, was hardly threatening to the populace still living in areas of racial and cultural isolation. If teachers label students as inferior, they will behave as such. "It's vital to look at them, children in particular, as very capable. Then they will be capable," Elliott said.[20] At that time, the context was that schools across the country still had trouble desegregating. Problems of academic achievement, behavior, and graduation rates were exacerbated at predominately white schools that employed very few teachers of color.

* * *

Like many well-meaning educators searching for creative ways to engage students in lessons about cultural diversity, teachers at C.T. Plunkett Intermediate School in Adams, Massachusetts, created a customized version of Jane Elliott's eye color simulation. To honor the birthday of Dr. Martin Luther King, Jr., Plunkett Intermediate Principal Richard Love approved a two-day discrimination role-play designed by Special Education instructor Alan Catrina and physical education teacher Terry Goodrich. It was scheduled for Friday, January 11, and Monday, January 14, 1980. Catrina and Goodrich made the exercise voluntary for students and teachers. For those participating, the volunteers were divided into privileged and underprivileged groups based on armband color. Black armband wearers were supposed to "submit to rules equated to those blacks had to endure," reported the North Adams *Transcript*, which included seats in the back of classrooms and restrictions to enter segregated restrooms and use segregated water fountains. The disadvantaged were also compelled to wait at the back of lunch lines. Those with white armbands would receive privileges on the first day of the exercise. If parents had not stopped the program, roles would have switched on day two.

The Thursday before the program commenced, the school's superintendent, Rolland G. Duval, told the *Transcript* "a barrage of irate parents" convinced authorities to pull the plug. Parental complaints primarily concentrated on teaching students "a past concept [about racism] that should be forgotten," according to reports, rather than about the ethics of the simulation's logistics. The armband exercise, wrote Catrina in a letter to the editor of the *Transcript*, "was in no way abusive to the children." He said, "Instead of us teaching the children a lesson in prejudice, the parents taught one to us."[21]

The Adams-Cheshire Regional School Committee, accountable for the governance of Plunkett Intermediate, is responsible for the official cancellation of the program. Committee chairperson, Donald J. Merlini, claimed his order to cancel the Martin Luther King, Jr. commemoration kickoff was because neither his group nor Superintendent Duval was informed about the role-play activity. Duval suggested, "Many parents thought the program was not voluntary."[22]

While Jane Elliott may have assumed teachers across the United States attempted the eye color exercise, stories of the good and the bad never returned to her in Riceville. Being considered America's anti-racist educator did not interfere with Elliott's commitment to her family or obligations at RCS Junior High. In October 1980, Elliott celebrated the marriage of her youngest daughter, Mary, to Riceville native Chris Jensen, a foreman at Wallace Business Forms. One of the soloists at Mary's wedding was Jensen's good friend, Raymond Hansen, the brown-eyed student featured in *The Eye of the Storm* who had unequivocally bought into his teacher's hierarchy when the blue eyes had superiority.[23] At the time of her wedding, Osage High School class of 1977 and early graduate of the University of Northern Iowa, Mary was an assistant manager at Darald's new privately owned store, Elliott's warehouse Mark-It in Osage.

Familial celebrations aside, her day job proved challenging. The decision to teach at Riceville Junior High demonstrates Elliott's commitment to building a better Riceville community. There are varying accounts of her motivation to switch grade levels. Journalist Stephen Bloom writes that she wanted to test out her eye color "experiment" with older, "hormonally turbocharged teenagers." He also suggests–and many statements made by Elliott throughout her life about her rapport with colleagues–the RCS Elementary staff were happy to see her go. "I'm damn glad she's gone," recalled junior high principal Steven Harnack. "She's your headache now!"

Meanwhile, Harnack, a Northeast Missouri State College graduate, admitted to Bloom that, as an outsider to Riceville, he underestimated the debate over the eye color exercise when he accepted the principal position at RCS Junior High. "If I had known what Jane had been doing," he said, "I would have stopped it." He called Elliott a "queen;" she indoctrinated her students, he expressed. "The kids buy into [the exercise] wholeheartedly when they're that age. What she did wasn't right."[24] His remarks to Bloom were given roughly forty years after he supervised Elliott's work. Time, contemporary political influences, and the realization that his words would appear in Bloom's book likely induced his statement about Jane Elliott. The fact is, Elliott conducted the exercise without infringement under his watch for seven years.

Meanwhile, Elliott says her primary motivation for moving to the junior high level was to restore order to the building. The Discrimination Day lesson, in her estimation, could help Harnack get control over the unmanageable students. "Some of the eighth-grade boys in that group were into grabbing, pushing, and shoving the girls," she wrote in her memoir. Remembrances of her middle school teaching experience center most around trying to defeat sexist and homophobic behavior. Bloom's research about the school culture discloses stories of drunken teachers, extramarital affairs, sexual assault, and hazing.[25]

What is clear is that Elliott tried more than others to connect with her troubled students. One such strategy was a motivational classroom mantra she called "KIDS!" which meant "Kids Interested in Doing Something!" KIDS! was her self-funded reading initiative yielding in a classroom library centered on cultural diversity. After a few years at the secondary level, Elliott channeled her artistic roots and accepted a role as co-director of Riceville High's 1981 spring musical *Carnival*, a story about an orphan girl who seeks to find her deceased father's friend at a European carnival.

Despite her commitment to her students and the school district, Elliott went to work feeling like her colleagues saw her as a pariah. The banter in the teachers' lounge at the junior high was no different from what she experienced at RCS Elementary. The N-word was commonly thrown around to mock Elliott's commitment to anti-racism. This was one thing Harnack conceded in his interview with Bloom. Harnack told stories about one RCS Junior High teacher who regularly asked Elliott, "How are the 'colored people' doing today, Jane?" Except the teacher would say the N-word. Harnack never batted an eye at the use of such language.[26]

Elliott often said she turned her classroom into a "microcosm of society" when conducting the eye color exercise. At Riceville Junior High, however, the culture of intolerance preceded her arrival. "It is difficult to raise non-sexist [and anti-racist] young men if they are constantly being conditioned by their elders and some of their adult role models" to ideas of racism and sexism. The battle to clean up the behavior of some of her colleagues and students reflected national discourse over the role of schools in moral education during the years succeeding the Watergate scandal. While she won over the media, the National Mental Health Association, and the National Education Association, she started questioning her ability to reach the people in her community. Riceville always presented the biggest challenge. In 1984, however, several former students from *The Eye of the Storm* documentary telephoned Elliott to say they would be in town to celebrate their class reunion and would like to arrange a get-together as a Room 10 group.[27] The idea was brilliant. She became, once again, hopeful that their voices could help break through to her beloved community.

* * *

In Riceville, it was typical to hold class reunions during the summer when the northern Iowa weather cooperated and at a time when most alumni were guaranteed to be off work. The Riceville High class of 1979 scheduled its five-year reunion for Saturday, August 11, 1984. Eyeing an opportunity to plug the lasting impact of the eye color exercise, Elliott telephoned Bill Peters to suggest a Room 10 reunion documentary. Elliott reached out to her former partner only after being encouraged to do so by her former students, now twenty-two and twenty-three-year-old adults. At the time, Peters worked as director of Yale Films, a production company associated with Yale University.[28]

Peters asked with excitement, "When will they be there?"

"August eleventh," Elliott replied.

"We'll be there with a film crew."[29]

There was more planning, however, that went into producing a show reuniting Elliott with her former third-grade students. Peters' storyboard contained notes featuring a sociology course taught to inmates at the Green Haven Correctional Facility. The maximum-security prison in Stormville, New York, used *The Eye of the Storm* documentary to talk with inmates about prejudice and discrimination for ten years. Prison officials and the course's instructor, Duane W. Smith of Duchess Community College, agreed to allow Peters to bring a film crew to document the inmates' discussion on the exercise. Elliott listened to Peters' idea about the New York prison and raised him another opportunity. She thought putting law enforcement officers, detectives, parole officers, prison guards, and other correctional personnel through the eye color exercise would be a good idea. Peters agreed. It would take some time, but Elliott eventually led training at the Iowa Department of Corrections in Coralville, scheduled a few weeks after the reunion with her former Room 10 students.[30] All and all, Elliott believed that if the public could see adults going through the exercise, this new film could be quite persuasive after they engaged in an open and honest debrief about the discomfort and trauma felt during the experience. Indeed, what Peters would ultimately produce, with Elliott as the film's lead, was a documentary that showed participants opening up about the transformative nature of the experience in post-training dialogues. What better way to show the world that the eye color exercise had a generational impact on bias disruption?

As a storyteller, Peters wanted to "follow up on these children as adults, to see what effects their early lessons from Mrs. Elliott had on their attitudes and behavior later in life."[31] This was his sales pitch. After rejections from ABC, CBS, and NBC, Peters convinced PBS to film the reunion for its educational program titled *Frontline*. Civil rights trailblazer and PBS correspondent Charlie Cobb signed on to narrate the film. Cobb later endorsed Elliott's work as "a fascinating study of both the effects and the dynamics of discrimination." In a promotional statement for the documentary, he said further, "We all think discrimination is damaging. But [. . .] the trauma experienced even in a classroom atmosphere is remarkable."[32]

On the morning of the class of 1979's five-year reunion, eleven of the sixteen *The Eye of the Storm* alumni and their families met Elliott, Peters, and the PBS film crew at the RCS community school building, which housed both the elementary and secondary schools. Two of the five who did not show up were the boys who succumbed to fisticuffs on the playground during the first day of the 1970 exercise. Russell Ring, who became a Riceville High football and wrestling star, died on May 8, 1979, just weeks before graduating from high school. Ring had sustained severe head injuries falling from the back of a pickup truck.[33] The other, John Benttine, owner of a motor repair shop, became a paraplegic after surviving an automobile accident.[34]

Elliott was pleased to see that Susan Ginder, now Susan Rolland, mother of three, was part of a military family. Her husband, Gregg, was stationed in the Air Force in Fayetteville, North Carolina. Rex Kozak was a high school history and government teacher in Amana, Iowa. Raymond Hansen remained in touch with Elliott and her children and worked as a paralegal in Chicago. She offered a motherly laugh when Roy Wilson told her he had slept in his pickup truck outside the school after driving overnight from Missouri to arrive in time for the gathering. Also, at the meeting that morning, Sheila Schaefer, Sandy Dohlman, Donna Reddell, Julie Smith, Vera Buls, Milton Wolthoff, and the former third grader who stole the limelight in the original documentary, Brian Saltou.[35]

Peters led everyone to a classroom in the high school wing of the building for a viewing of *The Eye of the Storm*—the first time as a group—on a sixteen-millimeter sound projector and screen. Elliott remembered having watched the documentary twice during that sitting. The second viewing was so the former students could get past seeing themselves as eight and nine-year-olds on screen and take in their transformations from the exercise. When the film ended, the group arranged chairs into a circle, and Elliott facilitated a discussion on the impact and ethics of the lesson on discrimination. "Prejudice has to be worked out young, or it will be with you all your life," said Susan Ginder Rolland in a comment that didn't make the film's final cut but was documented by an *Associated Press* journalist observing the screenings debrief.[36]

Raymond Hansen took a similar tone when it was his turn to speak. "I think every school ought to implement something like this program in their early stages of education."

Elliott asked, "Is the learning worth the agony?" A chorus of "Yeah" rang out.

Rex Kozak told the group that he wished he had one of those green collars that the inferior group would wear during the lesson "in my pocket" so he could "take it out and wave it at people when they made racist remarks."[37] Elliott later turned Kozak's comment into souvenir keychains she awarded to those who survived the exercise. She eventually made the phrase the title of her 2016 memoir. For the time, she levied another query:

"Should every child have the exercise or every teacher?"

"Everybody," exclaimed the group.[38] Kozak, who would eventually become a high school principal in LeGrand, Iowa, said off camera that he teaches a modified version of the exercise in his history and government classes when he observes prejudiced behavior by his students. Years later, for a story about the fortieth anniversary of the eye color exercise, Kozak told a reporter that as a principal, the exercise "factors into a lot of the decision-making that I go through on a day-to-day basis." He explained that the feeling and meaning of the lesson are "hard to shake."[39]

After the morning screening and debrief, the PBS camera crew followed the students to the class reunion picnic at Lake Kendrick. The alumni hosting the reunion grew resentful over the attention given to Elliott's students and told the crew to leave. As a result, the documentary Peters produced for *Frontline* features less of the students and more of Elliott leading a session of the eye color exercise with fifty employees from the Iowa Department of Corrections.

Elliott's performance in front of law enforcement officials was that of a seasoned veteran. Michael Whye of *The Des Moines Register* said Elliott played the role of a bigot "so convincingly that it is hard to believe she is actually fervently against discrimination." Since the 1970 session at the White House Conference on Children, Elliott routinely forced all blue-eyed participants to wait outside the seminar room while the brown eyes could sit, enjoy coffee, smoke, and chat with one another before commencing the session. During the longer-than-expected registration, the blue eyes received green collars and were forced to wait in a holding room. Unbeknownst to them, Elliott prepared the brown eyes on how to behave during the training. One man in the waiting room suggested they wait no longer and storm into the seminar room to "see what kind of reaction we'd get." Just as the blue eyes started mocking the concept of diversity training with threats of singing "We Shall Overcome," one of Elliott's assistants admonished the group: "We need to have you keep it down! I don't know how many times I need to give you that instruction."

If seeing Elliott's vintage placards proclaiming blue-eyed inferiority was not antagonistic enough, when the blue eyes entered the room, they were told to shove their belongings into a back corner. Then they were chided with comments like: "It would be to your advantage, people, if you could get to meetings on time." The seminar room was segregated into the upper-class brown and second-class blue sections. Elliott told the group to sit in the back, where seats were scarce. When one blue-eyed employee tried to sit in an empty chair in the brown section, she snapped: "You can't sit here! Only browns are allowed up here because they want to learn. Blues are to stay in the rear of the room. Sit. Stand. Do what you want. But be quiet."

Elliott especially lit into a man standing in the back of the room named "Roger" about listening skills, note-taking, and his blue eyes. "Blues are disruptive and argumentative," she announced to the room when Roger provided an excuse for every allegation she levied at him. "They have no desire to learn."[40] Elliott reinforced that blue-eyed people had little motivation to learn when she administered a written intelligence test skewed toward the brown-eyed group.[41]

Later during the debrief, Roger admitted that it took just a few minutes to feel "powerless against discrimination." He said, "I felt hopelessness" and "I saw how all-consuming bigotry can be." Roger revealed something to Elliott that she hoped to hear from someone in law enforcement: "I found myself thinking about my clients and perhaps seeing myself treating some in a certain way because of their record, the way they look, talk and other things as irrelevant as having brown or blue eyes."[42]

Peters's new documentary for PBS *Frontline*, "A Class Divided"—titled after the name of his 1971 book, *A Class Divided*—aired on various days and times across the country during the last week of March in 1985. This was seven months after the Room 10 reunion and Elliott's exercise with the Iowa law enforcement officials. The film began with an homage to Martin Luther King Jr. After the title sequence, Elliott was shown greeting her former students as they entered the Riceville school for the reunion. Peters then spliced into the documentary glimpses of the students reliving the Discrimination Day experience as they watched themselves as third graders in *The Eye of the Storm*. For those who had seen the original documentary, the last two-thirds of "A Class Divided" offered a novel look at those children as grown men and women and the exercise's profound impact on working in the criminal justice field.

Writing about the "Class Divided" reunion many years later, Elliot—who had her former third graders on her mind when she put pen to paper—said the documentary should have revealed to the world how valuable the exercise is for disrupting generational bias and discriminatory behavior. "If I had written the script," she explained, "[. . .] I couldn't have composed anything more gratifying to me or anything more supportive of the exercise than what [the former students] expressed [. . .]"[43] Professionals in careers where success depends on performance can gain insight from "A Class Divided." The exchange of views among inmates at the New York penitentiary and by those of the Iowa Correctional Department offers a revelatory glimpse into how the eye color exercise could convince adults to respect and protect the diverse nature of society, resulting in greater freedom for all.

* * *

Bill Peters produced the "A Class Divided" documentary in the fall, winter, and spring of 1984 and 1985. He was an opportunistic storyteller with a perpetual aura of altruism, and like the first go-round, Peters would cash in on this second film about Elliott and her exercise. Like *The Eye of the Storm*, Peters turned PBS *Frontline's* "A Class Divided" into another major publication. Peters received a book contract from Yale University Press to add five chapters to his 1971 Doubleday publication, *A Class Divided*. This new edition features a retelling of the Room 10 reunion and Elliott's eye color training with employees of the Iowa Correctional Department. When published in December 1987 under a revised title, *A Class Divided: Then and Now, Expanded Edition*, critics razzed Peters as a "pedestrian" writer who shared a "topical" story about how the blue eyes, brown eyes exercise on discrimination exposes adult learners to a form of "prejudice [that] has become more invisible [and] perpetuated by subtle psychological pressures rather than by signs on the restaurant door."[44] In this late stage of the Reagan administration, rising racial tensions in the United States and worldwide showed that integration was still not realized. If any resources could lead the world into post-racism, maybe it could be those provided by Peters and Jane Elliott.

PBS paid Elliott $300 for her lead role in the documentary. She eventually donated the money to the school district's library.[45] Like Peters, this latest film helped Elliott emerge again as a leading figure in the newest civil rights struggle. This time, she will be seen as more than an elementary school teacher.

PART THREE

RESULTS

CHAPTER 17

AN EYE ON JUSTICE

"I think the necessity for this exercise is a crime."

—JANE ELLIOTT, 1985

On the seventeenth anniversary of Martin Luther King, Jr.'s assassination, April 4, 1985, Elliott told more than 100 people from her alma mater, known then as the University of Northern Iowa, "I see us taking gigantic steps backward." It was a line echoing the concern of those in the anti-racism movement. "You're not responsible for slavery. You are responsible for what you're allowing to happen now," she explained. "You have the ability to change yourself and your attitude. You have the ability. You have the responsibility."[1]

Invitations to speak on college campuses about race and racism had become regular. However, the broadcast of "A Class Divided" made Elliott a person of interest within the corporate sector. After watching Elliott reign fury down on much bigger adult men and women working in the Iowa Department of Corrections, Linda Guillory, head of the human relations department at Denver-based Mountain Bell Telephone Company, a corporation servicing states in the Frontier West and Southwest regions of the United States, offered Elliott a temporary contract to join her department. Later renamed U.S. West, the company was known most as the publisher of the Yellow Pages and Mountain Bell White Pages directories. In the 1980s, its workforce had diversified significantly along the lines of sex, country of origin, language, and physical ability. To help manage cultural diversity in the company, Guillory's office was responsible for creating a program that would facilitate training on cultural "pluralism," the word used in the 1980s to describe societal and work-force diversity. Programming was intended to explore the benefits of a diverse workforce and to preclude any potential legal problems linked to allegations of racism, sexism, and disability discrimination.

Guillory was designing a three-day workshop, later retitled "The Pluralism Experiential Workshop: Valuing Differences." She wanted Elliott's help. The task was to send every current and future Mountain Bell employee through the multi-day training. She estimated that if forty workers could attend, it would take fifteen sessions to run everyone in the company through the training. Guillory said the training would begin in October, and Elliott would only be needed one day per workshop.

Guillory's work at Mountain Bell was part of a corporate trend in the 1980s to sponsor racial and ethnic-based affinity groups, direct mentoring to aid in job advancement for employees of color, and to provide a white, English-speaking, and Christian-dominant workforce education on how's and why's of turning the company into a multi-cultural institution. When watching "A Class Divided," Guillory saw something better than presenting information to a wary audience about why dominant views shouldn't be imposed upon historically marginalized people. Using a word like pluralism in 1985 fit well with "moral education," a curricular imperative espoused in the school system after the Watergate affair ten years earlier. For adult professionals, corporate pluralism training sustained school-age efforts to sort through diverse cultural values—to expose homogeneous workers to ideas and resources that otherwise would have remained out of one's consciousness. Elliott understood the importance of do-ing such work. A few years later, Elliott explained to a documentary crew from Germany the differences in how she viewed cultural and structural pluralism much differently from her siblings. She said her profession (educating children) forced her to read books that exposed her to different cultures and varied life experiences.

On the contrary, her brothers worked in professions that needed no such knowledge of the world and were thus more closed-minded over situational eth-ics and cultural respect.[2] With Elliott's exercise, Guillory could give Mountain Bell employees a jarring experience, whether they liked it or not.[3] She accord-ingly asked Elliott to facilitate the exercise on the second day of the three-day training.

Elliott agreed to do the contracting work for Mountain Bell. The contract stated she would work fifteen days every Wednesday from October 1985 to January 1986. The job meant Elliot would have to fly to Denver Tuesday nights, facilitate the three-hour eye color exercise Wednesday mornings, and return to Riceville later in the evening. She eventually asked her boss for an unpaid leave of absence for fifteen days during the four months. "I told [the principal] that I'd do all the preparation and planning for my substitute," she explained, which included tutoring her substitute how to teach Orton-Gillingham phonics "at no extra cost to the school district."[4] But rather than receiving the unpaid time off that she desired, Elliott resigned from her teaching position in the Riceville Community School District when the teacher's union, the Riceville Education Association, said she could not take off work without pay. Elliott was set to take in a $20,209.50 salary that school year, which placed her in the middle-to-upper tier of the RCS pay scale. She officially resigned at the monthly school board meeting, held on September 16, effective at the end of the month. The board voted unanimously to accept the resignation at its October 14 meeting. The board then voted affirmatively to pay Elliott $500 to train her replacement, Judy Tangey, from Dows, located ninety miles south of Riceville, during the last two weeks on the job.[5]

Elliott sat on the committee that hired Tangey. She remembered the young teacher as "absolutely brilliant in describing seventh graders and how she would teach them to read."[6] For two weeks, she worked furiously to teach her replacement how to use the Orton-Gillingham phonics resources. She insisted that Tangey observe her teaching approach in her classroom. After school, the two discussed the evidence Tangey collected during the audit. When she walked away from the classroom, Elliott felt confident her replacement would be an effective teacher of students with learning differences.

Elliott took a risk when she quit her teaching job after twenty years in the Riceville district. At the time of the decision, nothing was guaranteed except revenue earned from leading the fifteen workshop sessions. When explaining the decision later that fall, she said, "You can listen to lectures on racism, you can learn a whole lot about it in books, but when you experience it, it makes a difference—a considerable difference." She understood that her work on undoing discrimination with the exercise was at a historic crossroads. Cross-cultural sensitivity training stemmed from three stimuli: an outgrowth of the civil rights movement, including affirmative action initiatives; the forecasted changing American workforce; and the need to compete in the global market. If she could make the most of the opportunity, 1985 could be the year the eye color exercise tackled a two-headed monster: the American education system and the corporate arena. She said, "I can't think of anything more meaningful to be identified with."[7]

* * *

When hired to train employees at Mountain Bell in the fall of 1985, Elliott came up with the idea of giving a souvenir to those who underwent the eye color exercise. The mint green collars that the blue eyes were forced to wear hardly existed as a thing people wanted to keep as a memento. In fact, Elliott often found herself fetching the pieces of cloth from the trash so she could clean and iron them before the next workshop. An idea came to her during a Thanksgiving conversation with her daughters, Sarah and Mary. Sarah suggested she pass out a keyring that would remind people about the lessons from the workshop. Building on that idea, Elliott placed a tiny collar inside an acrylic. The acrylic piece would become the decorative end of a keychain.

The keychain, which Elliott called "a collar in my pocket," represented "the key to ending racism."[8] The acrylic itself is shaped like an eye. The green collar inside the acrylic becomes the eye's iris. A clear center exists as its pupil. She asked participants to carry the keyring to reinforce the feeling of the exercise. After all, they had survived the journey. "The exercise is the answer to solving the problem of racism," she said. Further, Elliott added a quote from Robert Burns. "'If some great power the gift could give us to see ourselves as others see us.' And this exercise," she closed, "is proof that you've had that opportunity to see yourself as others see you. How do you like it? And if you don't like it, change your behavior. Don't ask them to change their perception of you. Change your behaviors toward them."[9]

* * *

For Jane Elliott, leading a few diversity sensitivity sessions at Mountain West threatened her well-being more than giving up a salaried teaching position back in Riceville. As she admitted in her autobiography, the new job would likely generate physical threats from her adult learners. "If somebody shoots me, they'll make an instant martyr of me," she told her husband, Darald, when deliberating over the career change. Elliott went on to explain that she had trouble believing anyone was "dumb enough to risk having to celebrate Jane Elliott Day" after she was killed. "Just give me three years. If I can do this for three years, we can put away enough to buy a small business near Mary in San Diego and be reasonably comfortable without my teaching."[10]

Sure enough, when Elliott and her new partner, Linda Guillory, conducted the first eye color workshop with Mountain Bell employees, several of the men in the audience created one of the ugliest scenes in her experience as a diversity trainer. Several blue-eyed human resource personnel made a gallant effort to disrupt Elliott and Guillory's session. The HR staff, Elliott noted, had previously conducted orientation workshops for the company. So, it didn't help that they resented Elliott's presence as much as the discrimination role play turned them off. They "were not about to allow themselves to be manipulated by one small insignificant white female and one large angry black one," Elliott said. They were led by Herb Hackenberg, a Mountain Bell resource officer who wrote a company history that would be published a few months later as *Muttering Machines to Laser Beams.* Hackenberg and the disruptive blue-eyed contingent refused to comply with any of Elliott's instructions as soon as they were told to put on the collar. One member pinned the collar to the back of his pants and galloped around the meeting room like a donkey. When two others jumped onto a table and danced in a way perceived as "black dance," Guillory lost her patience and told Elliott she was taking the brown-eyed group and well-behaved blue eyes into another room. "There was no way the bad boys could win in this situation, and they finally realized it when we refused them entry into the workshop's new location," Elliott recalled years later.[11]

No matter how many people underwent the eye color exercise, Elliott kept adjusting the simulation until she found the best possible game plan for putting adults through the exercise. No more conference tables or pitchers of water. No more pencils and notepads. She decided she would shame any blue-eyed person who showed up without something to write. The blue eyes would be placed on "uncomfortable folding chairs in the center of the room." Elliott would provide only enough chairs for half of the blue-eyed group. She put the brown eyes in better chairs to look down on the blue-eyed group "so that we could keep the Blues under constant supervision." Rather than simply hanging offensive placards around the seminar room, she now regularly forced blue-eyed trainees to stand and read the signs. At the first moment of "stuttering" or "stammering," the participants were ridiculed for their reading struggles, she said, "blaming their illiteracy on eye color instead of the way they're being treated."[12]

Something she incorporated into the eye color exercise when working with the Iowa correction officers in 1984 was an intelligence test modeled after the Dove Counterbalance General Intelligence Test. This Black street culture survey included twenty-seven multiple choice questions (later reduced to fourteen) about vernacular slang, Bo Diddley, chitlins, and JET magazine. The intelligence test was something "the Blueys can't possibly pass," Elliott noted. The brown-eyed group would grade the papers, then read the scores aloud. Elliott then blamed the low scores on their eye color.

Before the break in the workshop, Elliott habitually instructed participants to write a paragraph describing how they thought the people in the opposite eye color group felt about them during the morning exercise. After recess, when Elliott rearranged the room into a discussion circle, the responses were used to engage the entire training class in a debrief. For all practical purposes, giving participants a chance to open up about feelings during the discussion was the moment of transformation. Elliott's manipulations during the simulation provided practical experiences used to get participants to the point of transcendence. Once among the original "delinquents" at Elliott's first workshop, Hackenberg was one of the individuals transformed by the experience. Hackenberg would later become a Blue Eyes/Brown Eyes Exercise facilitator.[13]

Before her fifteen workshop sessions ended, Elliott had survived a physical assault and several death threats. All the while, she showed up daily, flaunting her reflexive abrasive attitude. For that, Mountain Bell President Bob Blanz offered her a contract to continue working at the company through December 1988.[14] Blanz also utilized his connections with sister companies in the telecommunications and utilities industries. In 1986, Elliott received multi-year contracts from U.S. West Direct and the Public Service Company of Colorado. Through 1988, Elliott spent three days a week in Colorado. On Tuesdays, she led the eye color exercise during day two of Linda Giullory's three-day workshop for employees at Mountain Bell. On Wednesdays, she put U.S. West Direct employees through the workshop. The Public Service Company of Colorado workers received the same training on Thursdays.[15]

So, as she hoped, the fifty-three-year-old Elliott parlayed a short consulting contract into a new career, which meant she was free to hit the road. She traveled to Meriden and Connecticut to speak at the 75th Annual Connecticut Social Welfare Conference, to Cornell College (later University) to deliver a speech titled "Changing Our Views About Others," and Sewanhaka, New York, among other cities. The tour positioned Elliott as the voice at the "forefront of [racism] issue," as one reporter put it.[16] At a professional development workshop for educators at Long Island's Sewanhaka School District in November 1986, she put roughly fifty people through the eye color exercise. Three of the district's five high schools were more than 90 percent white in the town. Nearly all of the district's Black, Hispanic, and Asian students were enrolled in the other two high schools. The district employed 420 full-time teachers; five were Black, and four were Hispanic. The community also endured sporadic violence, as the homes of two Black families had been firebombed during the school district's attempts to desegregate its schools.[17] Administrative leadership took proactive measures by calling in Elliott to prepare its teaching staff with skills to disrupt biases.

According to Long Island press reports, Elliott put the staff through an agonizing two-hour simulation that led to two employee walkouts. She picked on a blue-eyed social studies teacher who claimed Christopher Columbus discovered America. "You can't discover a continent on which people are already living," she pugnaciously said. After explaining how brown-eyed people discovered America "thousands of years before Columbus was a gleam in his father's eye," Elliott accused the blue eyes of habitual lying. She said, "They lie today; they've been lying throughout history." Like the tradition in her workshops, Elliott stacked the program in favor of the brown eyes. She ensured brown-eyed educators could do no wrong and that the dysfunction in the Sewanhaka school system was due to blue-eyed privilege: "Children have been taught blue-eyed history by blue-eyed teachers to enhance the credibility of blue-eyed people," she explained. "Stop it!"

It was fitting to see Elliott's treatment of the blue eyes influence the behavior of the brown eyes in the room. When she refused to allow a blue-eyed teacher to grab a danish, a brown-eyed female staffer, described as a "young, black social worker," said, "That's the way it is, that's life."

Soon after that exchange, Elliott administered the "counterbalance" intelligence test. At least one teacher in training was so distressed that she couldn't complete the test. Most blue eyes failed. As tests were graded aloud, the social studies teacher contested the validity of such an examination. "I don't know the answers to these silly questions. [. . .] What you're saying doesn't mean anything to me. Let's be serious. I can't find one question that pertains to civil rights or the black experience." Elliott responded, "It doesn't matter to you because whites don't have to know about minority culture, but blacks have to know about white history just to get through grade school."

The fact that blue-eyed achievement on the exercise's performance measure was substandard did not go unnoticed by anyone in training, especially Elliott, who had seen these results by the discriminated group since she first started doing the exercise in 1968. This made for a richer debrief at the end of the workshop. When it was over, several educators sang praises about the training. One of the district's school psychologists called it "the most moving experience" she had ever had. A blue-eyed history teacher said, "It was a wonderful thing to be able to take off that collar, [. . .] but then I thought about the number of people who can never take off the collar."[18]

* * *

Another way to measure the impact of the eye color exercise is to document how many social archetypes and celebrities used their platform to get Elliott's message out to a larger audience. Oprah Winfrey was among the first to welcome Jane Elliott onto her show during this era of global perspective-taking and diversity education.

In the mid-1980s, Oprah wasn't yet a national pop sensation. Instead, she was a television personality still chasing Phil Donahue and Joan Rivers. Oprah first worked as a co-host for five years with Richard Sher on WJZ-TV's *People Are Talking*, airing out of Baltimore. In January 1985, she earned her show, *AM Chicago*, which aired locally on Chicago's ABC affiliate, WLS-TV Channel 7, from nine to ten o'clock in the morning. The Windy City carried the third largest television market in the country. Oprah flourished. An Oscar nomination for her role starring alongside Danny Glover and Whoopie Goldberg in the 1985 film, *The Color Purple* brought added attention to her show. Oscar buzz piqued the interests of a larger public wishing now to see Oprah's "bouncy, boisterous and brassy" demeanor on a national stage, wrote one reviewer.[19] Oprah selected Elliott as one of her last guests on her local talk show. Her authenticity drove her popularity as the sole host of a daytime show. In March 1986, Oprah announced that her show would soon be syndicated to a national audience, beginning in September.[20]

As the host of the newly renamed *The Oprah Winfrey Show*, Oprah featured Elliott's eye color exercise during sweeps rating week in the spring of 1986. For Elliott, who had never heard of Oprah before this moment, the call inquiring whether she would be a guest on the show was uninspiring. "I'd done several television news and talk shows by then," Elliott explained. "I wasn't nervous about being in front of cameras. And, since I'd done the exercise with numerous groups of adults by then, I wasn't nervous about my ability to deal with the participants and their reactions to the exercise." She knew better than to think an appearance on live television was guaranteed to run smoothly. Past experiences leading adults through the exercise presented concerns for Elliott. No one could edit the film if something went awry or if the audience grew overly angry or violent. On the contrary, Oprah and the show's producers could turn an audience eruption into a public relations bonanza just in time for the national broadcast later that fall. While Elliott didn't much appreciate the limited time she had to squeeze in both the discrimination exercise and its debrief, she ultimately agreed because, as she put it, "it was only a local show."[21]

She proved herself to be a cool customer, not as an authority, but as a pro who assumed a role of an eye-color bigot to demonstrate the absurdity of individual racist beliefs. Elliott's live exercise made for good entertainment too. According to Oprah, local viewers called her Chicago-based studio for weeks responding to Jane Elliott's exercise. "For weeks, people called in trying to explain to us, our staff, that their children who went to Yale and went to Harvard [despite being] blue-eyed," the talk show host said.[22] Taking that into account, Oprah decided to keep Elliott around.

Tangling with *Oprah* audiences seemingly became a defining aspect of Elliott's anti-racism advocacy during the ascent of daytime television talk shows in the 1980s. For a time, Winfrey considered her new small-town champion for marginalized populations to be someone she could groom into becoming a talk show host of some sort (like she would do for Dr. Phil, another regular on *The Oprah Winfrey Show*). Acting accordingly, Oprah invited Elliott back to the show one more time in 1986—a winter episode just after being syndicated nationally but before Oprah became the queen of daytime talk show television.

The December 1986 visit to *Oprah* marked the second time Elliott attempted the eye color exercise live on national television. During the opening monologue, as blue-eyed audience members sat with green felt collars wrapped around their necks in the center of the small studio and surrounded by a large group of brown eyes, Oprah promoted the forthcoming episode as a "unique learning exercise on prejudice." The talk show host explained that day's show aimed to help viewers understand how "prejudice unfolds."[23] Before going live, Oprah's team hung Elliott's discriminatory signs around the studio. They forced those with blue eyes into a holding room while Elliott prepped the brown eyes on how to master the dove counterbalance test and the listening skills. Although she encouraged the brown eyes to humiliate the blue eyes, many were reluctant to chime in on live television. Because viewers at home had been invited to phone in, Oprah relied on faceless callers to vouch for many of Elliott's insults and discriminatory statements, intending to fire up the audience.

Elliott later recalled this second visit to *Oprah* with disillusionment. She remembered thinking about fifteen minutes into the show when a self-ascribed blue-eyed blond called in to criticize how people of color play the system by accepting social welfare. At this moment, Elliott thought Oprah staged the entire program, that the show's producers recruited people with prepared questions and statements to rile up the audience for ratings. The cameras panned to the brown-eyed people of color anticipating an explosion, which, aside from a few points of correction on colorblind race policies and outlooks on society, came close to happening when a blue-eyed woman who admitted she judges Black people for their behavior asked Elliott for a solution to get Black people to "go back to Africa." Elliott had no option but to play along. She remained intense from start to finish, spurning "history written by, for, and about blue-eyed people to make blue-eyed people look good."[24]

The show, which concluded with a poignant message on racial sensitivity, would be remembered as a success because of the buzz that followed. Jane closed the program by saying, "What we did this morning is irrational; it is an 'experience' on racism. [. . .] We set out to prove to you people that we can make you act in ways that you would never act ordinarily. [. . .] You can pick out a group of people; you can accuse them of having certain characteristics. You can treat them as though your accusations, your judgments of them are absolutely true. You can make them take menial jobs. You can put them in the slow learners' group. You can call them [. . .] stupid. You can make them behave the way you expect them to, and then when they live down to your expectations of them, you can say, 'See, I told you so. You're just as dumb as I told you.' [. . .] You can change people from what they really are into what you want them to be, and you can do that in fifteen minutes."[25]

By the end of the next quarter, *The Oprah Winfrey Show* was seen on almost 150 television markets, representing 95 percent of the homes in the United States, making her a ratings superstar, "dwarfing" Phil Donahue for the "daytime talk-show throne," the *Associated Press* reported.[26] Elliott had something to do with getting the show off the ground. As it were, Elliott would appear on *The Oprah Winfrey Show* five times between 1986 and 1994. However, the idiosyncratic relationship between these women—one from Chicago and the other from Riceville—was just beginning.

* * *

Before year's end, Elliott started writing her memoir. The memoir included a chronicle of the eye color exercise and a letter to her four children. In the letter, she explained the details of the experience, including the fury from Riceville community members and exercise participants. Additionally, the memoir could exist as a tell-all through which the public could better understand why she was so determined to undo discrimination and expose the myth of racial categories. The book would not be an autobiography; instead, it would become a straightforward window into why she chose a life's work that challenged peoples' prejudices and behaviors toward others despite how her family had been impacted since first doing the exercise in 1968. Above all, Elliott started writing in 1986 because she had, by then, survived death threats numerous times. She wanted dearly for her children, Sarah, Mark, Mary, and Brian, who were now between the ages of twenty-five and thirty, to know the real reason behind the exercise—to lead people out of ignorance—and the contempt she absorbed that "could very easily cost me my life," she said, as a result of her anti-racism advocacy.[27]

"For several years, I've been trying to think of a way to leave a record for you," she wrote in the preface, claiming that previously produced books and documentaries by William Peters had omitted everything surrounding the resentment and jealousy generated by the exercise. "[. . .] I want you to know what happened as I experienced it."[28] When challenged to ponder the motivation for writing the memoir at eighty-eight, Elliott still felt a degree of trepidation over her life. "I wrote it for my children because I had become convinced that I wasn't going to be around to explain the whole thing to them." Admittedly an insipid writer, Elliott held concerns over who would be the one telling her story if she were killed by someone she angered during the exercise. "I wanted my words to have a greater impact on my offspring than the words of my critics had then," she articulated in 2022.[29]

Always cynical that her story would be of no interest to prying eyes, she eventually composed an unfiltered exposé into her most vulnerable moments as an educator whose every decision impacted those closest to her. She described her encounters with adversaries in Riceville, Osage, the District of Columbia, and Uniontown, among others that had not already been related to anyone following her career. She offered unkind opinions about troublesome learners and former colleagues, whether adolescents or adults. Sometimes the subjects of her brickbats were named; she mostly preserved anonymity.

The earliest chapters did more than recite well-known moments—what she was doing upon learning of Martin Luther King Jr.'s assassination and the particulars behind the documentaries produced by the Canadian Broadcast Company and ABC. Her description of those well-known events in Jane Elliott's lore gave readers insight into her deepest emotions and how she weighed and measured the potential implications of her actions. She described her emotional satisfaction after watching all her elementary students join in hugs after each exercise. Incredibly satisfying was writing what her students—who were repeatedly labeled "the dummy group" by her colleagues—achieved while in her class and later in life. There are other stories captured in her memoir that reflect the agony of seeing both her third-grade students and her four offspring face bullying that, in her estimation, were precipitated by her actions. The latter chapters offer details about her career as a diversity trainer in Colorado, Pennsylvania, and Iowa.

The book, however, leaves many moments of Elliott's life and the eye color experience unexplored. The exercise caused a severe breach in her family. Readers of the memoir will not learn of this harrowing aspect of Elliott's life. In her view, Elliott's mother, Gie, resented her for bringing shame to the family, which led to the failure of the family-owned Jennison Inn. Once her father, Lloyd, passed away on July 5, 1990, at age eighty-one, an already sizable rift between mother and daughter widened further.[30] The two rarely spoke earnestly to one another for another eighteen years before Gie's death.[31] Lloyd was the glue that held together the Jennison clan. Not only did Gie stop talking to Elliott, but with time, half of her siblings appeared to sever most communications.

In recent years, Elliott regretted not keeping better notes about the various eye color workshops she conducted with adults from 1968 through the new millennium.[32] She ceased working on the memoir full stop shortly after the project's initial start. By 1987, Elliott's children "had made lives for themselves," she said. Elliott also stopped worrying about how her family would survive without her. An email correspondence in 2022 provides a poignant insight into how Elliott considered the meaning of her life: she was destined to lead as many people as possible of ignorance:

> [I]f some[one] was ignorant enough to kill me, my husband and children would survive very nicely on what I had accomplished philosophically, in trying to educate the ignorant, and financially, on what I had put aside, where money was concerned.[33]

* * *

By the spring of 1987, it was clear that Jane Elliott was the most sought-after diversity trainer. Beginning that April and running through the next five years, Elliott would balance three days a week in Colorado with a heavy speaking tour across the United States. Profitability was never part of the equation when she first conducted the exercise. Indeed, it cost Elliott and her family money in those first years. Agreements with Mountain Bell, then U.S. West Direct, then Public Service of Colorado, and one contract at a school district or corporation after another, she earned more money after leaving the Riceville classroom than any Jennison, Benson, or Elliott ever imagined. This farmer's daughter turned schoolteacher, turned diversity trainer, eventually attained an entertainment lawyer, Susan Golenbock, to manage her speaking engagements and negotiate lecture fees and honoraria at a rate of 30 percent of the contract.[34]

In hindsight, it is easy to attribute Elliott's fame to a commitment to altruism—to explain her life as a series of bold decisions that exposed her five-feet frame to bodily harm to turn schools, workplaces, and communities into pockets of justice. Retracing her footprints through time and geography is so compelling that it is difficult not to acquire compassion for what happened to her: Jane Jennison was once considered a gem in Riceville. As for Jane Elliott, it appears her hometown made little effort to understand what she was doing, casting aside one of its own even as she continued to give back. Naturally, Jane Elliott possessed little reservations about making a career out of the eye color exercise after this moment. "I felt no qualms about charging for my work, in view of the fact that I had become a pariah in my own land," she noted.[35] How could one not embrace the passage paraphrased from the New Testament: *a man is a prophet, save in his own land*?

CHAPTER 18

EYE OF THE BEHOLDER

"It was not meant to be an 'experience.' It was an exercise—an inocula-tion against the disease of racism—and it works."

—Jane Elliott, 1999

After her two 1986 appearances on *Oprah*, Elliott traveled to a furnished Miami television studio, WPLG/TV Channel 10, to put a consortium of adults through the eye color exercise. She agreed to allow the station's camera crew to record the workshop for a city-wide initiative called "A World of Difference." The event was sponsored by the Anti-Defamation League (ADL) of B'nai B'rith and endorsed by the Dade County School Board as a "prejudice reduction and multicultural awareness" initiative. The "A World of Difference" program regularly used television, radio, and classrooms to speak to South Floridians about the area's richly diversifying population; to take head-on the ethnic, religious, and other cultural "misunderstanding[s] and divisiveness" facing the region.[1] This year-long, $1 million weekly program produced study materials, hosted forums, and produced vignettes and media specials designed to help local students and adults confront "everyday situations involving discrimination and stereotyping."[2] After considering the popularity of the PBS *Frontline* production of "A Class Divided," ADL and Miami's public television station sought Elliott's services to offer a version of the eye experience responsive to the citizenry of South Florida. The film would star, both as the discriminated and discriminators, Dade County educators, law enforcement officers, entrepreneurs, and business executives. The public would see and ultimately scrutinize the behavior of about sixty "unwitting participants," stated one review.[3] Elliott, who thought this parochial approach was righteous, duly agreed.

Producers at WPLG/TV eventually cut the three-hour exercise into a sixty-minute evening special titled *Eye of the Beholder*. The documentary, which won a Florida Emmy award and was eventually broadcasted nationally and internationally, aired six months later, on April 20, 1987, pre-empting *MacGyver* at eight o'clock in the evening on Miami's Channel 10. At the 30th Annual International Film and TV Festival of New York, held on November 13, Elliott's Miami-based documentary won a gold medal for best public affairs program. At the same ceremony, *Eye of the Beholder* picked up another gold for the best show in the news category, beating out entries from over twenty countries.[4]

The popularity of the *Eye of the Beholder* helped boost participation in the ADL B'nai B'rith "A World of Difference" campaign. Shortly after the documentary aired, schools in Broward and Monroe counties joined Dade in utilizing public and private resources to train hundreds of teachers and students in cultural diversity.[5] For some time, the educators that participated in *Eye of the Beholder* were expected to return to their respective schools with the lessons learned from Elliott's role-play. They were asked to put their colleagues and school board members through the exercise. It appears, however, that they were reluctant to do so, as they received no formal training in facilitating the workshop nor possessed the unfettered disposition so vital for a successful anti-discrimination simulation. Sandra Graham, a special education science teacher at Fort Lauderdale's Rogers Middle School and a blue-eyed *Eye of the Beholder* participant, advised that returning the training to their school would misstep any work to advance cultural competence within its teaching staff. "[F]eelings are very intense, and we have to work with these people afterward," she said, "so I don't know if it's a good idea" that anyone goes through the eye color exercise unless it is facilitated by Elliott.[6]

Eye of the Beholder generated new considerations over the ethics of what Elliott will soon rebrand as the Blue Eyes/Brown Eyes Exercise. In 1987, Deborah A. Byrnes and Gary Kiger, professors and researchers in the Departments of Elementary Education and Sociology, respectively, at Utah State University, commenced a one-year study that measured the eye color exercise's outcomes in prejudice reduction, behavior changes, and emotional stress. It wasn't just the *Eye of the Beholder* film that motivated Byrnes and Kiger to conduct the experiment. They felt preservice educators were not properly schooled in knowledge and skills to teach in a diversifying school system more than two decades after court-ordered desegregation and the implementation of school busing further to integrate schools in the South and the North. With a workforce still over-whelmingly white, Christian, and English-speaking, the scholars proposed revamping teacher preparation curricula "to address prejudice and discrimina-tion" in schools and society.[7] "Simulations can serve pedagogical purposes as part of the ongoing instruction in a course," they conclude in their final report.[8]

The only academic study dealing with Jane Elliott's eye color exercise had occurred fourteen years earlier. The 1973 experiment—conducted by Michael Jay Weiner and Frances E. Wright of the University of North Carolina, Greensboro—evaluated the behavior of thirty-one third graders divided into two groups and forced to endure a two-day simulation design in a way very similar to Jane Elliott's blue eyes, brown eyes program. The Weiner and Wright report deduced that the eye color exercise mitigates discriminatory behavior in elementary students; however, research results that evaluated whether oppres-sive environments have a bearing on academic performance were inconclusive.

On the other hand, Byrnes and Kiger studied 164 Utah State University students over a year. Of that number, fifty-seven white students were placed into an experimental group and forced to undergo a version of Elliott's discrimi-nation exercise. The remaining 107 students, mostly white, became the control group. This meant they would not endure Elliott's simulation.[9] However, both groups received education on multiculturalism as part of the regular curricu-lum. In other words, their professors made lectures and readings on cultural awareness integral to the education course. The film "A Class Divided" was part of the curriculum, about the discrimination experience with her third-grade students and the adults at the Iowa Correctional Department. Each Utah State student was required to take pre-tests and post-tests to assess growth in social scenarios that examined one's willingness to condone, ignore, or confront discrimination. Additionally, the tests helped Byrnes and Kiger evaluate the students' changes in social attitude regarding feelings of comfort when seeing a Black person occupy certain spaces, such as a college roommate, physician, governor, or dance partner.

As mentioned, only the experimental group underwent the three-hour eye color exercise: complete with collars, a waiting room, bigoted signs, segregated seating, segregated restrooms, and drinking fountains, Elliott's pop quiz on listening skills, the culturally biased intelligence test, praise toward the brown eyes, condemnation toward the blue eyes, and the feelings and perspectives essay followed by an hour-long debrief to conclude the simulation.[10] Byrnes and Kiger recorded participant comments during the debrief. They also col-lected additional feedback about the simulation in an anonymous post-exercise evaluation survey that asked participants to rate the "worthwhileness of the workshop." Responses suggest that the Blue Eyes/Brown Eyes Exercise has value. Regardless of eye color, participants collectively rated the workshop's worthiness a 9.3 out of 10.

Conclusions vary concerning attitude, social comfort, and lasting effects. To rate the eye color exercise's long-term effectiveness, Byrnes and Kiger waited a year before sending all participants a request to donate to Utah State University's Martin Luther King, Jr. fellowship fund. The results of this part of the study were inconclusive. Of the 164 participants, just three from the control group donated to the fund.[11] The results of the experiment's scenario attitude pre- and post-tests show changes to the attitude of students in the experimental group to be "statistically significantly higher" than those in the control group. Conversely, the experiment's social pre- and post-tests did not indicate changes to the participants' social comfort when near Black people.[12]

To the question over ethics, Byrnes and Kiger—whose work concentrates on adult learners, as opposed to pre-teens and adolescents—conclude that the Blue Eyes/Brown Eyes Exercise is a principled simulation as long as Jane Elliott, or any other facilitator, administers the workshop with an evaluative intention. As long as she conducts an assessment to measure the growth of her participants, the simulation should be considered a practice where the ends (learning about and reducing prejudice) justify the means (inducing stress to mitigate discriminatory behavior).[13] The researchers note that Elliott's exercise places participants into "short-term emotional discomfort." The temporary trauma experienced by participants is "worth the possible long-range benefit," Byrnes and Kiger state. Moreover, the researchers imply that education generally induces stress through high-stakes assessments, in-class presentations, and requirements to meet deadlines. Granted, they say, the psychological discomfort might be minor; however, anxiety is not an "unusual feature of the educational enterprise." From a right-to-know perspective, Byrnes and Kiger suggest that all eye color simulations be voluntary. They also offer a solution: the simulation's facilitator should provide general information to participants before the training. In other words, they conclude that the benefit of learning about prejudice, discrimination, and stereotyping in Jane Elliott's eye color exercise outweighs the ninety minutes to three hours spent in an emotionally intense situation as long as the simulation meets three standards: voluntary participation, disclosure of general information about cultural diversity, and an end of workshop debrief.

* * *

No research study—and more will be conducted over the next thirty years—will convince everyone that Jane Elliott's method of putting blue-eyed people on the receiving end of her abrasive teaching style is a principled instructional method. Protests against the exercise have rarely ever focused on whether learning takes place. Indeed, when pressed on the exercise alone, Elliott's harshest critics admit that learning occurs in each simulation. The question, quite frankly, is whether her determination to bully blue-eyed white people out of complacency is ethical. While the Utah State University study made its rounds in academia, the public remained oblivious to the discourse playing out at conferences and in ivory tower classrooms over Jane Elliott's work. As history indicates, local leaders across the United States remained fascinated by the discrimination classroom exercise for its potential to transform social relations.

In April 1987, Elliott traveled to Phoenix to lead several dozen people through an exercise one blue-eyed participant called a "game." The Phoenix-based Anytown America, a non-profit organization known for educating high school students on diversity affairs, offered Elliott the invitation to administer the simulation to a group of professionals. The core pillars of the aid agency, a national brotherhood model operating in Arizona since 1957, with auxiliaries in six states, concentrated on human relations, citizenship, and leadership skills through hard conversations about multiculturalism, prejudice, and discrimination.[14] Blue-eyed Ginger Hutton, an *Arizona Republic* opinion columnist, recalled facing "putdowns" during registration. "When Elliott signed me in," she wrote in her column a day after surviving the training, "I smiled and said something friendly. [Elliott] didn't respond." An uncouth Elliott made Hutton and her blue-eyed peers "objects of ridicule and scorn," she wrote, the moment collars were pinned around the necks of the workshop's downtrodden and told to wait in a holding room, where they stood or sat on the floor for almost an hour. The training almost turned physical when one of the workshop's registration helpers confiscated a cup of coffee from a blue-eyed woman who could access the refreshment table reserved for the brown eyes.

Hutton understood the importance of the training to achieve a greater understanding and respect for how those labeled as inferior persevere in a society where their voices are often silenced, and their experiences are commonly dismissed. Having lived the Blue Eyes/Brown Eyes Exercise from start to finish as one of its discriminated participants, Hutton's revelations explain how Elliott's simulation still garners a profound transformation among participants who know in advance what they are getting themselves into.

Every answer we gave was wrong, every move we made was wrong, everything we did was misinterpreted. [. . .] Although we knew it was just an exercise, it was interesting to note how we were affected. By the time the exercise was over, I was feeling a lot of anger and pain. I felt demoralized. When we were asked to give answers on a test, I was certain that I would not do well on it, that I couldn't think clearly. Part of the time I tried to escape by withdrawing into daydreams, but that was dangerous. A brown eye might ask me something, and I wouldn't know. When the exercise was over, and we blue eyes regained equal status with the brown eyes, Elliott asked us to write what we had learned. I found I was still afraid I wasn't doing it right. Other blue eyes expressed similar feelings and told of their pain and anger and how they couldn't wait for the "game" to be over. A black man said that, yes, he could see in our faces and body language that we couldn't wait for it to be over. And I thought, "I wish that I could do that. I wish I could walk out of here, and the game would be over." He said, "But I live that game every day."[15]

The Anytown America training left a lasting impression on school-centered approaches to increasing self-esteem in Black and Hispanic students at desegregated schools in Arizona. Hutton's column spoke for the cohort of city leaders that endured Elliott's agitation. Also pinning faith on Elliott's strategies were the unmistakable signs of progress among Phoenix educators, and the idea, as Elliott often put it, that racist children could be changed by their teachers.

* * *

In the winter of 1988, one teacher in a small Eastern Pennsylvania city utilized the eye color exercise in the educational space to shatter racism and bigotry. Pennsylvania declared Martin Luther King Jr.'s birthday a statewide holiday nine years earlier. Then in 1983, it became a federal holiday in the United States. Despite the state order and federal law, many schools refused to give students and staff off for the day. Most school districts in the Commonwealth implemented programming and assemblies to combat bigotry to mark the occasion. One of the schools that gave students the vacation day was Mosser Elementary School in Allentown. Fourth-grade teacher Cheryl Sandt devised her rendering of the Blue Eyes/Brown Eyes Exercise to teach her students why they'd receive a day off. Her eye color simulation was part of a push among Lehigh and Northampton County schools to focus on African American history lessons.

With the support of her principal, Harley Stewart, Sandt conducted a one-day simulation where she placed the blue-eyed students at the top of the classroom hierarchy. She forced "worthless" students with brown eyes to sit in the back of the classroom with their backs to the teacher.[16] The brown eyes were prohibited from talking to their non-brown-eyed peers for the day. Placed in the back of the transition lines, they were always last to class and last to receive lunch. At one point, Sandt, who had brown eyes, arranged for Principal Stewart to storm into her classroom with a directive to the brown eyes to stay late after school. They staged an argument over an afterschool appointment that Sandt had to schedule. Two students were in tears. By the end of the day, Sandt told her fourth graders the exercise's objective was to give them an idea of "what most blacks had to endure in restaurants, buses, hotels, and schools in the United States," reported the Allentown *Morning Call*. King, she explained, sacrificed his life to end the legal separation of the races; that is why a holiday exists to mark King's birthday.

Sandt did not anticipate the torrent of criticism that erupted once the *Morning Call* ran a story about her Martin Luther King Jr. Day lesson on January 18. A few days later, that paper's editorial board printed a column criticizing her with accusations of traumatizing the students. A local radio disc jockey dedicated a segment of his show to lambasting Sandts, calling for her termination. However, encouragement for Sandts arrived on January 28 when the School Board of the Allentown School District approved a resolution commending her and Principal Stewart for bravery in "instructing their students on the harmful effects of bigotry and discrimination."[17]

In later interviews, Jane Elliott spoke with pride but also misgivings that well-meaning educators like Cheryl Sandt attempted her exercise. At the time, however, she was unaware of most copycat instances. She carried a work schedule that kept her traveling the country speaking and training adults with the exercise.

In mid-October 1988, Elliott returned to her second "A World of Difference" conference in Miami. As the keynote speaker, she told 185 Dade County educators—most elementary teachers—that they could "increase or decrease the amount of racism in the lives of children." An event sponsored by South Beach organizations already familiar to Elliott, the Anti-Defamation League of B'nai B'rith, and WPLB-TV Channel 10, she insisted teachers try harder to end racism. "Racism is not something that is innate to human beings," she pronounced before the large crowd. If educators could undo the message that whites are better than racialized color groups, that men are superior to women, and that Christians are better than other religious groups, all Americans could envision a country of heterogeneous solidarity and pride. When Elliott exhorted that racism "did not exist until the 1500s [that] White people invented racism to give them justification for the things they were doing to people of color," the remark could be interpreted in two ways: as an homage to the democratic promise proffered in the Declaration of Independence, and, later, the Fourteenth Amendment; or as an assault on those who willfully perpetuate racial discrimination an entire generation after the civil rights movement.[18]

Back at her consulting job in Colorado with US West (formerly Mountain Bell), her contract was scheduled to expire after 1988. Some employees were excited to see her go. Although knowing they would never see Elliott again after their corporate-mandated pluralism training session, some considered her methods "self-righteous and cruel," as former US West employee Julie Pasicznyk told journalist Stephen Bloom in 2018. While not in disagreement with Elliott's anti-prejudice message, Pasicznyk was much happier knowing that Jane Elliott and her "evil" exercise were nowhere near the company. Pasicznyk considered the diminutive in size diversity trainer to be mad. "You can't be that good and that effective at cruelty without having something wrong with you," she said. "She's one of the two or three worst people I've ever met in my life."[19]

Others, like Sandy Juettner, found the workshop "embarrassing and humiliating and simplistic." Juettner expressed disappointment in the US West for keeping up its end of the contract. "I felt like a pawn," she said. "I felt used and ashamed. [. . .] I felt trapped. She manipulated us. It was an unbelievable breach of trust."[20]

Possibly for complaints over her method or because she had trained an army of facilitators at US West who could do the work at bottom dollar when her three-year contract expired at the end of 1988, Elliott's services were not retained. Despite those who loathed her, enough documents indicate she went out on a high note. "You have helped us build a reputation as a leader in combating the issues of racism and sexism," wrote US West pluralism training steering committee members Jan M. Fincher and R. Ann Welter. Because of Elliott, the women indicated enough employees volunteered to act as diversity trainers that sixty-three three-day workshops and 450 one-day workshops were planned for the following year. Fincher, the director of strategic performance, and Welter, manager of pluralism education, told Elliott that they now could facilitate the training "internally. [. . .] we would not be dependent on consultants." The new corporate objective, it appears, was to make the workshops "less costly," they told Elliott, and "expedite the process of getting everyone trained."[21]

Countless members of US West Communication expressed well-wishes and gratitude to Elliott in December 1988. An employee named Rocky proclaimed that Elliott helped him develop a healthy ethnic identity. "How can I say good-bye to you when you changed my whole perspective about how I feel about myself? [. . .] I have gone from being ashamed of my heritage and culture to being proud of who I am [. . .]"[22] Others expressed that the best part of having Elliott in the Mountain Bell/US West family came when they got to know her personally after the training. David Kohler called Elliott "a most intelligent" woman after having her at his place for dinner. "I experienced, for a brief time, what the ugly monster of discrimination can do to a person. [. . .] [Elliott] has been successful in helping people prevent the destruction of other people."[23] Employee Wanda Schick said her "personal commitment to improve the condition of all people is now part of my lifestyle [sic]."[24] A blue-eyed participant sent Elliott out with an affirming message. "I am blue-eyed," wrote Andrew Horner on December 2, 1988. "I recognize that in thousands of moments like this [workshop] with hundreds of US West employees, you have not just told us what it feels like to be on the receiving end of prejudice, but you have helped us to feel what it feels like. It has made a difference to me, and many others have told me it has made a difference to them. I am sorry to see you go. I will miss you."[25]

When Elliott said her final goodbyes to her first long-term consulting job in Colorado, the twelve-part television miniseries *War and Remembrance*, about the United States' involvement in World War II, aired on ABC primetime television. The program's retelling of the war spanned the week after the Japanese attack at Pearl Harbor to the day after the atomic bomb fell on Hiroshima. While not overly popular, the miniseries sparked discussion over whether students needed to be taught how to think empathetically. A harrowing part of the program shows Jewish prisoners in dehumanizing conditions inside a Nazi concentration camp, and it was among the first times the public saw such grotesque scenes of Nazi crimes against humanity. The program also captures Americans celebrating the deaths of Japanese soldiers drowning at sea. The dropping of the atomic bomb on Hiroshima, which resulted in an estimated death of 70,000 citizens within seconds of the explosion, left an unsettling question about how people become preoccupied with the self, resulting in the desensitization of harm done unto others.

Social psychologists wrote books on the topic of empathy. Preachers and teachers certainly tried to raise awareness of compassion in human relationships. Then again, if there was a practical learning experience that put people into a controlled environment designed to confront hostile circumstances head-on to teach empathy, Jane Elliott's eye color exercise had become the multicultural best teaching paragon by the end of the 1980s. No detractor at US West or elsewhere could deny that. As leading voice at the American Psychoanalytic Association Roy M. Whitman noted after watching *War and Remembrance*, there was a need to teach each other what it was like to face interpersonal and institutional discrimination. He said Elliott's inoculation "is essential if we are to lead an integrated, honorable life."[26]

* * *

National interest in Elliott's blue and brown eyes role-play picked up steam at the decade's end—when the forced busing of white students across city wards and county lines generated racial balance, and student enrollment still plagued many cities across the United States. During the last year of the Reagan administration, school officials who shunned forced busing found magnet schools to be an appropriate answer to segregation lawsuits emanating from civil rights organizations. An idea once used to generate student interest in learning, magnet schools became a practical "desegregation tool," wrote Linda Peterson of the *Tampa Tribune* in an article about the emerging popularity of magnet schools in Dade County. Magnet schools, which operated as specialized schools within any public school district, allowed parents to choose between enrolling their child in a district school and a magnet with a more diverse student population and a special academic focus. The concept allowed school officials to achieve integration, but only in isolation. Magnets necessitated an application process. Proponents of the school reform movement considered magnets "selective" and elitist. Studies of magnet schools in New York, Kansas City, Little Rock, San Jose, St. Louis, and Chicago in 1988 showed that students of color regularly ended up in the least requested magnet schools. Still, it took a "more complicated" busing plan to transport children across county lines to get to a magnet school with a racial balance. Other problems surfaced as local leaders evaluated the effectiveness of magnet schools. For one, magnets could only enroll 10 to 20 percent of any given school district's population, reported one NAACP lawyer investigating the issue in the South. Desegregation problems were still ubiquitous. While some magnets achieved racial balance, many school buildings in the home district found that their student demographic rates became more segregated.[27]

Elliott weighed in on the school busing issue by focusing on the demographics of the teaching staff at each level of education. "Most teachers are white, their college professors are white, the child psychology they study is about white children," she said, claiming that aspiring teachers sent out into the workforce were being taught that, as instructors of curriculum, they must manage their students as if everyone were white. "If all [teachers] know is how white children are supposed to behave, they're going to have problems with kids who act any other way." This is problematic, she reiterated to one reporter just after the 1988 Christmas holiday. "When black children are told that the constitution guarantees freedom and equality to all but are rewarded when they act like their white classmates, they get cynical" about the school system. To this degree, she also thought that white children were taught to believe that message.[28]

Elliott fired this ammunition at preservice teachers and general audiences along the East Coast when speaking at Lehigh University in Pennsylvania and New Jersey's Ridgewood Christ Episcopal Church, among many other engagements during the years that straddled the turn of the decade.[29] But it was the passing of her father, Lloyd, very early in the morning, on July 5, 1990, when she grew indignant at how much those ascribed as white resisted her message about the origin of prejudice and the root cause of discriminatory behavior. "My father died totally isolated," she told a documentary crew several years later. His unexpected passing occurred in his favorite room at the Jennison Inn while watching television after celebrating Independence Day with his grandkids in Riceville.[30] A few days later, Elliott helped pen a tribute to her father. It read:

Who loves the rain and loves his home?
And looks on life with quiet eyes.
Him will I follow through the storm.
And at his hearth fire keep me warm.
Nor hell nor heaven can that soul surprise.
Who loves the rain and loves his home?
And looks on life with quiet eyes.[31]

Every indication suggests Lloyd loved his home. It was a place his great-grandfather helped to settle. By the end, however, his hometown didn't love him back. Why? Elliott said it was "because he raised the town's "[n-word] lover."[32] When she thought about how her father lost the inn and his friends because members of the town couldn't stomach her eye color exercise and what her four children endured, Elliott's resolve to fight for freedom and fair treatment of all people hardened.

* * *

In September 1990, the people back in Riceville still heard about Jane Elliott and her discrimination lesson five years after leaving the community school district.

Elliott put forty-three Minnesotans through her exercise at a television studio in Minneapolis. The city's KSTP-TV Channel 5 hired Elliott to train Minnesota professionals in the eye color workshop as part of the city's new programming on racial prejudice. The special, which aired in the same broadcast range that served northern Iowa, was called "Eye to Eye." Like *Eye of the Beholder*, the program filmed for Miami public television in 1987, KSTP-TV debuted its one-hour special on September 24, before the Buffalo Bills faced off against the New York Jets on Monday Night Football. The format of Elliott's exercise followed her traditional three-hour blueprint, though the television producers edited the footage into a sixty-minute program, including commercial breaks.

The Minneapolis *Star Tribune* said Elliott "lays bare the ignorance and irrationality that underlie racial prejudice."[33] As was customary, confrontations with aggrieved participants commenced as early as registration when a man walked out "in a huff." For the forty-two who stayed, Elliott gave a "crash course in racial discrimination," wrote the local paper. For anyone who watched "Eye to Eye," the *Star Tribune's* reconstruction of the exercise was accurate. Viewers saw respected men and women from the community "shrink in size" and "lose their confidence" under the iron fist of Elliott's abusive deportment. "Eye to Eye" knit in scenes of Elliott's former third graders transforming into little bigots from *The Eye of the Storm*. What one account suggested, viewers were shocked to see "adults placed in similar circumstances behaved essentially the same as the children did." When pressed by Elliott to recount the four listening skills, most blue-eyed professionals failed to give correct answers. The last segment of the program shows moments of the exercise's debrief and follow-up interviews. The newspaper endorsed the exercise: "If 'Eye to Eye' doesn't open one's eyes, it's unlikely anything will."

Six months later, on March 3, 1991, one Los Angeles motorist of color came face to face with four white Los Angeles police officers in Lake View Terrace. Almost ninety seconds after their encounter, they incontrovertibly opened the eyes of the nation to not just the beating of Rodney King but to whether the Los Angeles Police Department (LAPD) and law enforcement, in general, possessed a pattern of discriminatory treatment toward racialized minorities. The debate that played out the following year did not find the nation seeing anything eye to eye, as the *Star Tribune* suggested. In the center of national discourse, Jane Elliott was assumed to be both an appraiser of American race relations and its fixer.

* * *

Jane Elliott's reputation as an authority on race relations reached new heights following the March 1991 beating of Rodney King and the April 1992 turmoil that gripped Los Angeles in the wake of the acquittal of four police officers accused of using excessive force during the traffic stop in question. As the nation watched coverage of the looting and bloody violence in South Central LA, several media outlets, both nationally and locally, called upon Elliott to provide insight into the racial reckoning across the country.

That month, Peter Jennings sent a camera crew to her home in Osage and the school Riceville to produce a four-minute feature spotlighting her as ABC's "Person of the Week." The segment aired Friday, April 24, on ABC News *Tonight* for the show's fifteen million daily viewers. The following day, she appeared in New York City at the ABC News Headquarters studio alongside Jennings for a ninety-minute live studio audience and a call-in program called "Prejudice: Answering Children's Questions." Considering television's "most under-served audience," Jennings designed his special program for children and set it to air at half-past eleven o'clock in the morning Eastern Standard Time, following the regular Saturday morning line-up of *Land of the Lost, Darkwing Duck, Beetlejuice, Slimer! And the Real Ghostbusters, Pirates of the Dark Water,* and *Bugs Bunny and Tweety*. He trusted parents would be there sitting beside the kids. The show, the journalist said, would "teach some children, learn from some children and teach some adults."[34] In particular, he believed the special would provide the appropriate messaging for parents who wanted to talk with their children about the racially charged disturbances on the West Coast. Jennings said parents "are often too embarrassed" to discuss with their children. This show, he believed, would make uncomfortable parents "quite gratified" to receive answers from him and his expert guests.[35] Jennings parroted a common Jane Elliott talking point when promoting the Saturday morning news special. With a human skeleton hanging behind him, Jennings explained, "We talk about racism all the time. What we should talk about is skin-ism." He used the skeleton to show children "that underneath their skin, human beings are pretty much alike."[36]

Jennings' performance hardly moved Jane. She later recalled the popular host's responses to viewer questions as "glib," certainly less than ideal.

> At one point, a young melanemic girl asked a question indicating that
> ugliness happens to people all the time, so why are we so upset about what
> happens to children of color occasionally. Jennings was sympathetic in his
> response to her, and I raced from my seat across the studio from him during

the commercial and demanded that he had just allowed that girl to minimize what happens to black kids on a daily basis. After the commercial, he admitted that he hadn't made the situation better.[37]

Elliott's efforts in assisting the ABC Network to provide programming that tackled racism in the wake of the Los Angeles uprising raised eyebrows. Among the first on television to jump at the chance to have her as a guest following ABC's "Prejudice: Answering Children's Questions" was Oprah Winfrey. During the late spring and summer of 1992, the newly christened queen of daytime television reached out to her reliable companion from Iowa for a set of episodes designed to vet America's racial divides. The plan began on May 1, when Oprah took the talk show on the road to Los Angeles. There, an enraged audience went back and forth, expressing grievances over colorblindness and racial self-reliance, the riots' morality, and the verdict's rightfulness. With Louis Gosset, Jr. by her side at times and a canvas of the Los Angeles skyline as the backdrop, Oprah did a fair job tempering emotions and allowing everyone time to speak. The studio audience in the episode "Aftermath of Los Angeles Riots" effected no change to the situation in Los Angeles or elsewhere. It was a microcosm of how society debated the aftermath of the Rodney King beating and subsequent carnage, as Oprah's show later described.[38] Less than two weeks later, she felt compelled to bring Elliott onto the show.

During a trip to Harpo Studios on May 13, Elliott appeared as a panelist alongside a group of parents with children in biracial relationships. Last, to be introduced to the audience, she came out swinging. Dressed in a black jacket and dark green blouse and wearing her signature glasses, Elliott wasted no time directing her antagonism toward a gentleman sitting directly to her left whom Oprah called "Ron." Ron was on the show because he disapproved of his daughter's Hispanic boyfriend. Elliott used Ron to offer the characteristic critiques of the "racist school system" and how "racism is a learned response [and] you have to be taught to be a racist." But she incited the audience into a frenzy when she called racism a "mental problem" and challenged viewers to reject common colorblind affirmations like, "I don't see color" and "I don't care if you're black, or brown, or green with purple stripes." She called these "very serious statements" that "lump people of color with [foreigners]," which suggests that those with darker shades of brown skin "are not citizens of this country."[39] Then, live on national television, she found an opportunity to run a play from her Mountain Bell pluralism training playbook, which also became a scripted aspect of her public addresses. Elliott grabbed a much taller and younger Black man from the panel. She told him to stand beside her, then asked the audience to highlight the differences.

She asked, "Do you people see any differences between us?"

"Height," the audience roared. They then said, "Sex." Elliott pointed out that sex and gender make a big difference in how the two are treated.

"Age," shouted the people in the crowd.

Everyone avoided their color difference, even after spending the show's first half discussing racism. "See!" she pronounced. "Nobody wants to say the c-word, color." She chaffed those who say, "When I see you, I don't see you as black." With rapt silence from everyone in the studio, including Winfrey, Elliott stressed the "importance" and "positive" of physical, emotional, and cultural differences. "Differences need not be seen as negative. They are positive; they are valuable. [. . .] It ought to be all right to be different."[40] This point was necessary to counter colorblindness. Any attempt to force people of color into a single dominant culture cripples all efforts to "cure racism."

Attacking Ron during the show's first segment was just a warm-up act. Elliott had more to say on undoing racism, and Oprah Winfrey was willing to stand by and let a schoolteacher-turned diversity trainer steal the spotlight. Elliott spent ten minutes during the bottom half of the show recycling another Mountain West talking point—substantiated by evidence, of course— about how the school system indoctrinates children with prejudiced ideas. She brought onto the stage a large projection map of the world.

The Mercator map, at the time, was commonly used as a teaching tool and bulletin board decor in classrooms across the United States. It presents a grossly distorted view of the world's land masses. For instance, the European continent appears larger than South America, though the southern portion of the Western Hemisphere is twice as large as Europe. Additionally, Greenland looks larger than South America, the Arabian Peninsula, and Africa. The Mercator map wrongly positions the Global North at the earth's center, which places the equator through the American Midwest, Europe, and East Asia. In other words, since the band is supposed to divide the earth into two equal parts does the opposite; Mercator's projection of the globe misleads all of those who study it. "All the white [dominant] countries are larger than they should be. And all the countries of people of color are smaller than they should be," she demonstrated. "This is a visual image that teaches children a lie."[41] Jane Elliott's instinct for speaking to people colloquially about such a weighty topic is why she brought the visual.

This pedagogical war over the world was brought to Elliott's attention by her sister, Mary, who first read about the debate in the *Des Moines Register*. When researching new material to incorporate into the pluralism training with employees at Mountain Bell, US West Direct, and the Public Service Company of Colorado, she formulated a way to use the map to articulate a message about social cognitive bias. The Mercator map presents a "northerner's view of the world," as geography scholar Marvin Gordon of George Washington University argued. That worldview, as presented in the classroom map, carries "ethnic implications," said Ward Kaiser, former director of Friendship Press Company, publisher of the Peters world map designed to counter the Mercator representation of the world. The Peters projection map—created by German cartographer Arno Peters—looks at the continents much closer to accurate size and position on the globe. While often criticized for distorting the actual shape of the continents, the Peters map, said Audrey Miller, who replaced Kaiser as director of Friendship Press in 1987, teaches students that "Third-World peoples are the Two-Thirds-World People."[42] Elliott synthesized their arguments into a thesis on why the Mercator map's white/European bias damages social relations by teaching children with ideas that countries inhabited by people of European descent are superior and that people who are ascribed as white maintain a global popular majority. "Teaching aides," like this "is what makes you and I racist," she said to Oprah.[43]

Though not as a guest on *Oprah*, albeit later, Elliott commonly distributed small postcards or legends of the Peters map to college students or corporate trainees to be affixed to classroom Mercator maps. It challenged them to reckon with the myth of white supremacy.[44]

On July 14, Elliott returned to *Oprah* to lead an unsuspecting studio audience through the Blue Eyes/Brown Eyes Exercise in an episode titled "An Exercise in Prejudice." For any of Oprah's followers who hadn't remembered, let alone heard of Jane Elliott by the summer of 1992, this episode has become one of Winfrey's most memorable, able to surpass the "Aftermath of Los Angeles Riots" in the *Oprah* cache. In fact, in 2017, when narrating a program for the Oprah Winfrey Network titled "Where Are They Now," Winfrey picked "An Exercise in Prejudice" as one of her former talk show's most popular episodes.

Conversely, Elliott doesn't possess the same delight for the episode as Oprah. The show, in her estimation, was rushed. She was flown back to Chicago just a few weeks after appearing on the interracial marriage panel. Although the blue-eyed audience members wore the collars and waited in isolation for an unreasonable amount of time while the brown eyes were served refreshments and informed about how the exercise would be conducted, Elliott admitted that she never felt comfortable with this appearance in front of *Oprah's* audience. One brown-eyed woman who refused to follow the simulation stormed out of the room when Elliott explained how the blue eyes would be treated during the exercise. Elliott sent an *Oprah* staffer after her to ensure she wouldn't "contaminate" the blue-eyed group.[45] She taped hand-drawn signs onto bathroom doors preventing blue-eyed use of certain commodes, and her traditional segregation placards weren't hung on the studio's walls. Still, Elliott removed several seats, which forced blue-eyed people to sit on the floor in front of the stage beneath the gazing eyes of the brown-eyed group. Time was limited. She had less than sixty minutes, including commercial breaks, to give the studio audience a sense of discrimination. That made it impossible to do much of anything but insult the blue eyes and heap praise upon the brown eyes. She could not facilitate the listening skills tests, lecture on discriminatory behavior, administer the culturally biased written exam, or lead the group through an in-depth debrief. She had to allow Oprah to work in the room with the microphone while she sat on stage like a bigot, heaping slurs at the blue eyes in the audience.

In the middle of the exercise, after a few blue-eyed people walked out of the studio during one of the commercial breaks, Elliott sensed that the producers had coached some in the audience. Although the exercise seemed to be going over well enough for the viewers at home whom Oprah said that Elliott "Teaches race relations" and a chyron often appeared on television screens declaring, "This is an exercise in racism," she fought the urge to call out the deception of Oprah's production.

Elliott would say that Oprah never went far enough to combat racism. "With her kind of following," she ranted years later when questioned about her experience with the talk show host, "if she decided to change the level of racism in this country, she could do it in one year. [. . .] She might have lost some viewers, but she would have made a positive difference. And I think she has wasted her chance to make a positive difference."[46]

Elliott later claimed that she was, and would always be, "the oddity of the moment," destined to fade once the newest issue pulls the media's attention elsewhere. "Fair enough," she recognized. "I don't pay anyone to give me the opportunity to educate people, and the networks don't pay me for the educating." To Elliott, the only important thing has always been to get the message out. "Give me a moment and a microphone, and I'll make people stop and think in ways they may never have thought before. That, I consider, a good thing, and I'll do it whenever I can."[47]

CHAPTER 19

THE PUBLIC EYE

"Perfectly lovely, logical, intelligent people get in this exercise, and they go all to hell because they have no power."

—JANE ELLIOTT 1996

It must have been pleasing for Jane Elliott to wake up a few days after her most recent visit to *The Oprah Winfrey Show* and see her former student, Rex Kozak, with a byline in a major Iowa newspaper. On August 3, 1992, Kozak appeared as a special columnist in the opinion section of the Cedar Rapids *Gazette*. Kozak, a middle school teacher in the Belmond-Klemme School District, who appeared as one of the students in the 1970 film *The Eye of the Storm*, wrote a piece that made sense of Elliott's discrimination lesson plan. His former teacher and her plan had made all kinds of waves around the country after she appeared on several television programs following the violence of the Los Angeles uprising.

Kozak's article, "Lesson for Life: Bigotry's Pain," however, presented two arguments. First, by offering a glimpse into the two-day eye color exercise through his perspective, Kozak contended that even children as young as eight were not permanently traumatized by Elliott's treatment during the simulation. He wrote that the efforts of his former teacher to educate each child about the anatomy of prejudice proved she genuinely cared about the student's well-being and success. That compassion precluded lingering animosity or trauma that her critics argued resulted from the simulation. Second, he said that although more than two decades had passed, he thought more often about the day he spent as the discriminator in Room 10. "I learned that discrimination happens very easily," he wrote. To disrupt racist tendencies, "You have to work at it every day." That is why he posited that Jane Elliott's simulation is integral to the gradual development of youngsters, helping shed light on how to manage personal emotions and relationships with others. "Although I could leave the blue-collar behind, I couldn't leave the sayings and gestures behind; they are still present today."[1]

Unsurprisingly, the exercise filtered down to educators nationwide who tried to emulate Elliott's pedagogy. Some pirated the Blue Eyes/Brown Eyes Exercise for benevolent purposes; many self-interested teachers were ineffective. Others found success. In Waterloo, Iowa, Hoover Intermediate School eighth-grade social studies teacher Dennis McCabe facilitated a string of exercises that students, colleagues, and parents came to appreciate. Unlike most Jane Elliott imitators who subjected students to poorly executed eye color role plays, McCabe sought Elliott's approval and mentorship long before designing his exercise. In 1991, he encountered Elliott at a lecture given to preservice teachers in Iowa. After conversing, he convinced Elliott to share her P.O. Box address and telephone number. The pair brainstormed ideas and, in the end, McCabe pleased her with assurances that, as he wrote in one letter to his new mentor, "I take this exercise very seriously, and that I am quite aware of the responsibility I assume when I conduct it."[2] According to his recollection, Elliott's only suggestion was to model his exercise after her adult workshops. That meant he would conduct the activity only one day with his students since he taught several students of color. Additionally, he would only subject the blue-eyed students to discriminatory treatment. Elliott stated that he needed to refrain from subjecting his "melanacious" students to discriminatory treatment.[3]

McCabe was known for showing his students *The Eye of the Storm* since he began teaching roughly ten years earlier. He said his students asked each year if he would put them through the simulation. Considering his newfound relationship with Elliott, he decided it was time. Starting in 1992, McCabe put his 130 eighth graders through the exercise. He gave them little knowledge and only en passant warning. He told the students the day before that they "would be participating in a special activity" but offered no hint as to the design of the lesson. Students entered the classroom the following day surrounded by offensive placards: "Would you let your sister marry a blue eye?" and a large blue eye graphic enveloped by the circle-slash. He found every way possible to subject his blue-eyed students to discriminatory treatment during his fifty-minute class periods. The debrief came on day two when students wrote and discussed what it felt like to be brown-eyed or blue-eyed. "What I tried to do yesterday," he explained during the discussion, while paraphrasing Elliott's inoculation ratio-nale, "was make you just a little bit sick. I wanted to cure you of a disease. [. . .] What I tried to do yesterday was inject you with a little bit of racism. [. . .] I tried to make you brown-eyed people racist bigots. I tried to make you blue-eyed people victims of those racists." According to one report in the Waterloo *Courier*, the students felt the exercise was "valuable."[4]

McCabe went on to turn his exercise into the kickoff lesson for a sixteen-day unit he called "Eracism." The content and timing of the unit "varied from year to year," he once explained, disclosing that there were times when he relied more on offering his pupils historical context about the enslavement of Africans. For twenty years, when it came time to conduct the simulation, his ability to segregate his classroom into privileged and underprivileged populations was executed with minimal controversy. "I taught in an era where I was granted a lot of autonomy," he admitted years later.[5] McCabe estimated that about 2,000 students survived the eye color exercise during his career.

McCabe taught in a school with a student population more diverse than what Elliott encountered two decades earlier. Future Pulitzer prize-winning journalist Nikole Hannah-Jones once attended Hoover Intermediate. Like McCabe, many across the country looked to utilize the Blue Eyes/Brown Eyes Exercise to prepare all-white groups for the time when workforce diversity would change, as indicated by all projections. National crises over race relations in the early 1990s placed a heavy burden on educators to help their pupils understand the nature of prejudice. McCabe was just one example of several teachers carrying that burden. Others, however, weren't as fortunate to come out of the discrimination role-play unscathed.

On January 20, 1993, three teachers at Park View School in Glen Ellyn, Illinois, west of Chicago, facilitated a Discrimination Day simulation on their fourth-grade students to mark the Martin Luther King Jr. holiday. They didn't come with the same support enjoyed by McCabe in Waterloo. Teachers Heidi Fitch, Carolyn Kouwe, and Suzi Kiker divided their students by birth months. They said any child born during the summer months, which amounted to twenty students out of seventy-four fourth graders, were "slower" and "not as bright" as those born any other time during the year.[6] The story that captured the community's attention was hearing that the June, July, and August birth-days had reduced time at recess, and they were forced to stand during an as-sembly while the other fourth graders were seated. The teachers also did not get the parents' consent before the exercise. According to a report in the *Chicago Tribune*, a repentant letter went home to parents at the end of the day.

A local psychologist, Thomas W. Phelan, wrote a letter to the school board on behalf of parents condemning the lesson as causing "moderate to severe emotional distress." Park View principal, Glenn W. Rogers, apologized to the public for "inconvenience or distress" and promised, "This type of incident will never happen again." He also expressed support for his staff, who found themselves "walking around on eggshells."[7] He feared the community uproar would "stifle creativity" with more than four months remaining in the school year.

* * *

Though Jane Elliott had been asked before by corporations and government agencies to lead adults through the eye color exercise, this racial unrest in the early 1990s generated greater interest in Elliott as a public speaker. Near the end of 1993, Elliott said that she had administered the Blue Eyes/Brown Eyes Exercise to approximately 101,000 people, most of whom were educators. She told students at the University of Wisconsin-La Crosse that, by proxy, about ten million students were impacted by her simulations.[8] Her records show that she facilitated about eighty training sessions annually between 1985 and 1993. At present, public schools and universities looked to Elliott not solely to lead the eye color exercise but to explain why racism so vehemently bedeviled society. She acted accordingly and arranged an intensive lecture circuit schedule with bookings at middle and high schools and universities in the Midwest and Pacific Northwest. Elliott gave the discrimination simulation, "A Collar in My Pocket," or a lecture about intersectional discrimination called "The Anatomy of Prejudice." The lecture would last sixty minutes to three hours, depending on the request.

Despite speaking in front of audiences at Millikin, Notre Dame, Willamette, and Iowa State, Elliott was most in her zone when visiting Margarita Middle School in Temecula, California, where her granddaughter, Rachel Jensen (Mary's daughter), attended as a sixth grader. Rachel's teacher, Mrs. Skumawitz, asked if she would visit her class to discuss the "Eye Color Exercise in Human Relations." Instead, she created an impromptu eye color experience once one student asked her to "Tell us about the 'brown eyes, blue eyes.'"

"All right," Elliott began, "what color are your eyes?"

"Uh, hazel," said the student.

Elliott retorted: "Okay, hazel is mostly blue. For this exercise, you are with the blue group. Go on to the back of the room."

That was when everyone in the room—including the teacher, Mrs. Skumawitz, and a local freelance reporter, Shari Crall, who was present to document Elliott's visit—realized they would get the experience of a lifetime. She launched into a hybrid exercise: part "A Collar in My Pocket" role-play, part "Anatomy of Prejudice" storytelling. She first moved all the non-brown-eyed students to the back of the classroom. When one blue-eyed girl squinted so Elliott couldn't tell, another blue-eyed student ratted her out. "Everyone knows blue-eyed people don't know how to behave. They are the only ones who cause problems," Elliott explained as she sent the tattle-teller to sit in timeout on the floor at a corner of the room. "They just don't seem to know any better."

While relating to the class that people in her hometown ostracized her family after first conducting the eye color exercise, she kept an eye on all the blue-eyed students in the back. If they adjusted in their seats, she would pass them a glare. She reminded them about their listening skills if they yawned or rested their head on their hands. She constantly degraded the behavior of blue-eyed people in general. About twenty minutes into her presentation, the blue-eyed boy, still sitting on the floor in timeout, asked a question. She complimented him for the question and then asked the class if he should be allowed back in a chair and join the general population of students. The students said no. Shocked, Elliott asked, "How many think he should stay on the floor?" Three students raised their hands. "How many don't care?" she also asked. All the other hands went up.

Eyeing an opportunity to challenge these middle schoolers on complacency over prejudice and witnessing discriminatory behavior, she proclaimed: "And that's why racism exists in America."[9]

* * *

A few weeks later, between Christmas and New Year's 1993, Elliott tested that theory in the Middle East. Following an eventful year, she and Darald visited their eldest daughter, Sarah, in Dhahran, Saudi Arabia. Eight years earlier, Sarah had married Abdulwahab 'Wahab' Mohammed Salamah. Sarah first met Wahab in Texas, where she lived with her brother, Brian, a heavy equipment operator contracted to build a dam near Crowell. Wahab was studying business at Texas Christian University in Fort Worth. After a long courtship, which included months apart as Wahab traveled to and from Saudi Arabia, and Sarah's conversion to Islam, the two were married at the Islamic Center of Cedar Rapids on January 11, 1985.[10]

This was Elliott's second trip to the kingdom; her first was in May of 1989, shortly after Sarah and Wahab gave birth to their first daughter, Sophia. During that visit, she spoke to about seventy-five students and teachers from the Dhahran Hills Residential Camp and the Dhahran Hills Junior High School.[11]

However, on this visit to the Arabian Peninsula in 1993, Elliott spoke to Wahab's colleagues at the Saudi Arabian Oil Company Aramco (Saudi Aramco) about racism in the United States.

Elliott's presentation to Saudi Aramco employees encouraged the company to critique ugly episodes of racial upheaval in the United States to think about varying forms of bigotry in their own country. She used the opportunity to talk about her "half-Saudi, half-American" granddaughters.[12] Elliott argued that bigotry is the same whether in the United States, Saudi Arabia, or elsewhere. "You can take a [person] who doesn't appreciate others who are different from himself and help turn him into a fully responsible and appreciative adult," Elliott explained. "That ought to be what education is all about."[13]

In Elliott's recollection, the Saudi Aramco presentation did not go over as well as she had hoped; however, it taught her a little about Saudi culture. Her in-laws told her that Saudi women wore abayas, niqabs, or burqas, not because Islam said so, but "to protect their women from the eyes of the men who wander through the desert." The comment brought Elliott to her feet, asking Wahab's father, Muhammed, to clarify whether that edict was an order from the Quran or a secular practice. It was a secular practice. She was nonplussed but failed to get full clarification when Darald suffered a heart attack. The family had spent much time hiking around the national park in Abha and playing with the grandkids. When grocery shopping with Wahab, Darald turned "as white as a sheet," Wahab later described, and nearly dropped two-year-old Miriam when his chest tightened.[14] Wahab rushed Darald to Aramco Services Hospital. Once stabilized, Jane and Darald returned home.

* * *

In the United States, the movement to teach about racial prejudice and discrimination in creative ways was reflected by schoolteachers who continued to customize Elliott's eye color exercise for practical reasons. In January 1994, a fifth-grade teacher at Sanders Park Elementary School in Pompano Beach, Florida, facilitated a modified version of Elliott's exercise that based discrimination on t-shirt color. "I felt so mad," said Arron Adams, a Black eleven-year-old blue shirt-wearer. "I didn't even want to look at the color red." Adams was one of thirty-one students who participated in the three-day simulation designed by his white teacher, April Fanaken.[15]

Ahead of the Martin Luther King Jr. holiday, Fanaken divided her students into three groups based on the color of the t-shirts she circulated to her students on Monday, January 10. Fanaken distributed a red, yellow, or blue shirt to each student. Those with red shirts were placed at the top of her hierarchy. Yellow-shirted students received varying degrees of privileges. Those wearing blue shirts received unfettered discriminatory treatment. "I wanted them to see how ridiculous [t-shirt color segregation] was," said Fanaken. "I just wanted them to relate that to intolerance."[16] Fanaken planned to run the exercise for the full week. After two days, however, she brought it to an abrupt end. On Wednesday, her students wrote about their feelings, and she led them in a debrief. "This was just shirts," said one of her fifth graders before adding, "Back then, it was [skin] color."

The exercise and subsequent debrief were seemingly impactful. A few days later, one of Fanaken's fifth graders nominated her for a teacher spotlight in the *South Florida Sun-Sentinel*: "Hi! My name is Crystal McKenzie! And I'd like to donate my teacher, Ms. April Fanaken, for a Teacher Profile! She's a great teacher, so I'd like to donate to her!"[17]

Fanaken was hardly the only teacher concerned about exposing her young students to cultural and racial inclusion content. Schools across the United States reported an uptick in racist and anti-Semitic material distributed at schools. Groups like the American Front in Oregon; Aryan Nations based in Hayden Lake, Idaho; the National Sozialistische Deutsche Arbeiter Partei-Auslands Organisation in Lincoln, Nebraska; and the numerous factions and sub-factions of the Ku Klux Klan and skinheads represented infamous white supremacists causing a spike in hate crimes in 1994. The Anti-Defamation League of B'nai B'rith and the Southern Poverty Law Center's Klanwatch were considered experts on the rise of white nationalism in America. The two organizations cautioned that "ignoring an 'infection' of racism is no solution" to the problem of white supremacist groups influencing school-age children, members of the military, and the police force.[18]

The spike in hate propaganda preserved Jane Elliott as the pre-eminent voice on race-conscious practices. In early 1994, she made her fifth and final appearance on *Oprah*. CBS marketed the episode by describing Elliott as "a controversial race expert" who had received more "love and hate mail than any other Oprah guest."[19] Again, she proved in front of a live audience that she could couple a no-nonsense attitude with dramatic talent that took her in and out of the character of a bigot to deliver a message that made people feel both uncomfortable and responsible for rising hate crimes. Racism, she said, was more prevalent because teachers lacked the knowledge, comfort, and language to talk with students about multi-racial history and culture. As a result, students have no mechanisms to disrupt the perpetuation of stereotypes.

In 1994, Elliott's top billing expanded into Canada, where she accepted a contract to conduct anti-discrimination training across the provinces for the Royal Bank of Canada.[20] During the spring, she spoke to corporate audiences in the Yukon. In April, Elliott challenged middle managers in Calgary and Whitehorse to hire more women and people of color. Her message resonated with the Workplace 2000 projection report showing that about 80 percent of those entering the workforce would come from those two diversity categories by the turn of the decade.[21] The following month, she conducted the Blue Eyes/ Brown Eyes Exercise for bankers in Edmonton. Fill Fraser, a Black columnist and broadcaster covering the region, said Elliott took him "as close as I have been to understanding the deep roots of racism."[22]

Before the trip's end, Elliott, traveling the Klondike Highway with Darald in a rental vehicle, stopped at Dawson City, a site described in her favorite poem, "The Cremation of Sam McGee" by the British Canadian poet Robert Service, the "Bard of the Yukon." The couple toured the Robert Service Cabin in the Klondike National Historical Park. When finished, Elliott panned for gold in Beer Creek, the Yukon's gold rush site.[23] The only travel experience topping this, she claimed later in life, was a safari across Australia at the end of the decade.

Upon returning to the United States, Elliott received a phone call from the Office of the Under Secretary of Defense with an offer to work as a diversity consultant for the Department of Defense (DOD). In May of that year, the DOD established "Human Goals," its mission statement for rooting out sexual harassment, sexism, anti-Semitism, racism, and extremism in the U.S. military. Facilitated by the DOD's Defense Equal Opportunity Management Institute at Cocoa Beach, Florida, the military faced scandalous accusations after opening positions across branches to women in the early 1990s. The Human Goals mission intensified after news broke that Air Force Chief of Staff Merill McPeak told the Senate Armed Services Committee that he would choose a male pilot over a better-performing female pilot.[24] Concerns also mounted when investigative journalists exposed cases of sexual assault on military encampments and violent hate crimes committed by current and former military members. The DOD looked to Elliott for leadership on better changing the culture of inclusion inside the U.S. military.

The DOD asked Elliott to fulfill two job requirements. She was first asked to become integral to the institute's diversity training "boot camp."[25] The boot camp was remarkably comprehensive. Structured as a fifteen-week course, topics included studies on racism, sexual harassment, power, and discrimination.

Class meetings featured an hour lecture followed by small group assignments. Her partner in the program was Colonel Ronald M. Joe, or "Colonel Joe," a DOD and U.S. State Department representative with a distinguished military career dating back to the war in Vietnam.[26] Elliott and Colonel Joe took the work seriously, as did the DOD, which informed all participants that "every move and word" was "monitored by the instructors." It was estimated that about 17,000 military personnel trained for assignments as equal opportunity advisers took the course.[27] As an added feature to the boot camp experience, Elliott put members of each military branch through the eye color exercise. Elliott's second duty was to help organize and serve as a symposium leader at the institute's annual conferences about culturally biased codes of conduct within the military. This meant she would moderate panel discussions about diversity issues. Modeled after her experience as a delegate at the White House Conference on Children in 1970, the institute's symposiums were contrived as solution-oriented colloquiums.

The results of Elliott's work are uncertain; however, a GAO survey taken just before her work with the DOD commenced shows it wouldn't have taken much to change the culture inside the military. At the start of 1994, between 93 and 97 percent of female students enrolled at American military academies reported "some form of sexual harassment," mostly from personal slights and sexist jokes.[28] After the passage of enough time to evaluate the institute's work, Colonel W. Darryl Goldman of the U.S. Army asked whether the diversity boot camp was the right approach for character development in the military. Writing for the *Military Review*, Goldman felt that while the DOD's Human Goals program was "admirable" and "worthy," its mission lacked "a sense of common target." He called the entire culture change initiative meek. Goldman never mentioned Jane Elliott, but the subtext of his article suggests the program was not sustainable without "institutionaliz[ing] aggressive programs."[29]

* * *

In the interim, Elliott made a living speaking about the anatomy of prejudice at public schools and universities across the United States. She delivered a lecture for the Students to Eliminate Prejudice Conference at Sergeant Bluff-Luton High School in West Iowa. During the winter and spring, Elliott addressed crowds at Indiana University and other Midwest and Southern schools at universities like Texas El-Paso and Salisbury State. Elliott was on fire, despite the uncertainty that her talks resulted in personal and institutional changes at the public schools, colleges, and universities where she spoke. One woman who underwent diversity sensitivity training modeled after the Blue Eyes/Brown Eyes Exercise, Diane Nelson, called for more of that type of experiential learning. Nelson, an opinion columnist for the *Modesto Bee*, conceded that any teacher who tried to emulate Elliott's anti-discrimination simulation at that moment of the mid-1990s would "get sued so quickly her head would spin." However, she insisted that educators and parents make "room for confronting issues head-on." Reflecting a sentiment felt by so many who go through the training with Jane Elliott, she proclaimed, "We need to lock ourselves in a room, if necessary, and once and for all, scale the wall that divides [us]."[30]

That summer, after speaking at UNC-Charlotte, Elliott received an out-of-the-blue long-distance phone call from German documentarian Bertram Verhaag. A former economics analyst, Verhaag had grown frustrated that the Munich parliamentary government ignored his findings and recommendations for policy change. Wanting to make a difference in the world, he entered the Munich College of Television and Film to learn how to make films for cinema and television that would lead to "serious [. . .] change in this world," he explained years later.[31] In 1976, he launched Denkmal Film, a European film company that would soon be known for its documentaries about individual struggles. Working closely at first with partner Claus Strigel, one of Verhaag's earliest films was the 1980 *Der Mensch an sich [. . .] / There is No Consideration [. . .]*, which chronicled the lives of senior citizens who could not prevent their homes from being destroyed to make way for the construction of luxury bungalows. In 1987, Verhaag and Strigel produced a film about the environmental destruction caused by nuclear power in the rural areas in and around Wackersdorf, near the Czechoslovakian border. For many years, nuclear physicists regularly cited the documentary, *Spaltprozesse/Nuclear Split* in discussions about nuclear energy politics. Their 1989 documentary *Restrisiko/Residual Risk* offers commentary on the recklessness of science denial. Verhaag sought Jane Elliott and her famed workshops on prejudice in the United States for his next project.[32]

Verhaag was intrigued by the Blue Eyes/Brown Eyes Exercise after catching glimpses of journalists discussing Elliott's workshop on international media. At this time, Germany was experiencing an uptick in neo-Nazi hate crimes following the unification of the East and West in 1990. White supremacists attracted young followers who scapegoated job shortages and lawlessness on foreigners, resulting in arson and mob violence against Asian, African, and other Eastern European refugees and migrant workers. The violence began en masse in September 1991 at asylum shelters in Hoyerswerda, a major refugee center in Saxony. It reached heights unseen since Nazi rule when Verhaag learned of the name Jane Elliott. The so-called "Hoyerswerda riots" escalated after right-wingers attacked leftist demonstrators protesting for refugee rights. In early 1992, another wave of neo-Nazi violence plagued Rostock, where hundreds of Germans rioted against Vietnamese refugees. A mob set fire to a hostel during the fracas. Since unification, German authorities have reported over 2,000 hate crimes against foreigners and Jews. Reports also revealed increased hate propaganda and signage like swastikas and Hitler salutes.[33] During this inflection point in German race relations, Verhaag discovered the Blue Eyes/Brown Eyes Exercise.

He called Elliott, asking if she would participate in a documentary about the "experiment." Elliott vacillated, then expounded: "I don't do an experiment. I do an exercise." She remained uncommitted to the project until Verhaag flew to Iowa and convinced her that he believed the exercise to be the answer to getting people to accept one another for who they are. Verhaag also ensured that the film would characterize the simulation as an exercise that puts participants through an active learning "experience." An experiment, she has since gone on to explain time and again, places subjects into a study where researchers take measurements. To her, an experiment putting nescient participants through a discrimination test would be unprincipled. If what she did was an experiment, she maintained, "then what we've been doing with black and brown and yellow and red people in this country has been an experiment." That, she said, "is illegal; it's unethical."[34]

In 1995, Verhaag and his small team, including three camera operators and two sound technicians, reported to Osage, Iowa intending to follow Elliott on her lecture circuit. The tour included "The Anatomy of Prejudice" lectures at Weber State, St. Cloud State, Southern Methodist, and Eastern Florida State (then-Brevard Community College) universities. Additionally, Jane delivered a three-hour "A Collar in My Pocket" eye-color workshop at the Des Moines Human Rights Commission's Tenth Annual Human Rights Symposium. It was two visits in the middle of the year. However, that became the most memorable part of Verhaag's experience documenting Elliott's anti-racism work.

The title sequence of Verhaag's film, named *Blue Eyed*, when released to the public the following year, shows Elliott speaking in front of an audience of nearly four hundred students, faculty, and the community at Chapman University in Orange, California. In the scene, Elliott asks the audience's white members, virtually every person in the lecture hall, to stand if they want to be treated the way customs and policies in the United States treat people of color. It is a mic-drop moment that has echoed through antiracist circles. The forty-five-second segment has remained a viral sensation on social media for decades, commonly used by public speakers to cut to the chase about racial imbalances in various institutions, ranging from school inequities, media representation, policing practices, voter suppression, and housing, among other concerns.[35] The idea first came to Elliott when speaking at the University of Minnesota earlier that spring. Her standard message proclaiming "all of us white folks" are responsible for maintaining racism had stirred discomfort from the Minnesota crowd. Never one to waiver, she antagonized her listeners by asking a simple question. She adjured, "If you, as a white person, would like to be treated as we treat our people of color, please raise your hand." Not one hand went up. After the event, Elliott told reporters, including the documentary crew from Denkmal Film, that the crowd's idle response to her query was like hitting them in the "solar plexus." She declared, "There's no denying that they know [discriminatory behavior] has to be going on."[36]

In part for a dramatic effect that played to the forthcoming documentary about her exercise but also to belabor the point that whites largely remain indolent when confronted with stories about how people from racialized color groups are treated, Elliott took the call-and-response to another level. At Chapman University, located near the home of Elliott's daughter, Mary, she beseeched the audience. "If you, as a white person, would be happy to receive the same treatment that our black citizens do in our society, please stand."

She glared into the risers, dressed in all black, waiting to see if anyone would stand. Everyone sat spellbound. Some looked dumbfounded, others agitated. "You didn't understand the directions," she told the audience. "If you white folks want to be treated the way blacks are in this society, stand." Yet again, no one stood. She pointed out the obvious conundrum. "No one is standing." She closed. "That says very plainly that you know what's happening, and you know you don't want it for you. I want to know why you are so willing to accept it or to allow it to happen to others."[37]

In addition to her college tour, Elliott spent much time in 1995 with a group of non-partisan civic leaders in Kansas City, where racial inequality besieged employment, education, and housing for years. Six years prior, the city's Republican Mayor Richard Berkley and Democratic Mayor pro-tem Emanuel Cleaver, who would be elected Mayor in 1990 and sworn in the following year, formed a collaborative called Kansas City Harmony. Comprised of local business owners, government officials, educators, and ministers, Kansas City Harmony carried a mission to "improve race relations, reduce prejudice and celebrate diversity" in the Kansas City metropolitan area. The region covered fifteen counties and two different cities, both named Kansas City, adjacently located along the border of Missouri and Kansas.[38]

Kansas City had been known for generations as "one of the most segregated cities in the country," according to the twenty-four-member interracial Kansas City Consensus Race Relations Task Force. In 1988, the task force released a ninety-page report detailing the local economy, which uncovered a long history of municipal neglect towards minority-owned businesses. The report also disclosed a wealth gap, with white households averaging twelve times that of the average Black household. "Wealth reflects assets accumulated over a lifetime and is a reminder that past discrimination has a major impact on current economic well-being," the authors wrote. While acknowledging that some readers will claim the report "unfairly" blames the white community for the socioeconomic condition of Black locals, they added, "prejudice has erected barriers to minority businesspersons that their white counterparts do not face," and "Black and Hispanic Kansas Citians are disproportionately likely to be employed as laborers or service workers rather than administrators."[39] In response to the report, the community group outlined an eighteen-month initiative to teach the citizens of the metropolitan area cultural tolerance. By 1990, Harmony established itself as an ongoing project with a mission to offer up to twenty programs annually that, according to records, "encourage dialogue about diversity and cultural issues" while challenging metropolitan leaders to assess policies and practices harming historically marginalized groups.[40]

In October 1995, Harmony asked Elliott to speak at its recognition luncheon celebrating locals that championed diversity-related projects, especially those working in schools to bridge cultural misunderstanding among students and between students and educators. With 350 people in attendance, and despite the celebratory nature of the evening, she admonished Kansas Citians for largely ignoring the work of Black civic leaders and educators. Elliott rationalized that her success as a race relations and cultural diversity consultant was largely because since she is white, her white counterparts more commonly listened to her than more experienced people of color. "I'm going to say things that people of color have been saying for 400 years," she said. Her "Anatomy of Prejudice" presentation came with a test. Harkening back to her years as a teacher, Elliott initiated a learning strategy to prime her listeners to commit themselves to learning something new. She challenged commonly used colorblind phrases: "I'm not prejudiced. Some of my best friends are black." "We're all the same inside. Let's concentrate on our similarities." "I don't see race when I look at black people." She then asked Black people in the room if they felt

those who ascribe to the statements mentioned above are free of holding prejudiced beliefs and discriminatory behavior. A chorus of "no" rang out.

Despite the short exercise, the audience largely maintained a deep silence
about color when she called on two city leaders, a white man and a Black woman,
up to the small stage where she spoke. She asked the audience to describe the differences between the two. Some in the crowd mentioned their gender difference.
Others commented that the man was taller than the woman. No one said the
color of either person's skin. Elliott suggested this was because white people are
"uncomfortable," even mentioning race. Since most leaders in Kansas City were
white, it is unfortunate that decisions had been made without understanding the
impact on the Black community. Those in the audience included school district
leaders, members of the Chamber of Commerce, elected officials, non-profit
chairpersons, and the clergy. She used the presentation to get every one of them
to use color-conscious approaches to fixing disparities in their respective professions while leading the community to think differently about racial presumptions. The message, she felt, struck the heart of Harmony's purpose.

"What they are really saying is, 'In order for me to feel comfortable with
you, I have to pretend you're not black,'" she said.[41] Since the city-wide policy
is made this way, she alleged that problems in the metropolitan area that could
be mitigated with a race-conscious lens continue to prevail. "There is no gene
for racism, sexism, ageism or homophobia," she posited. Hate can be unlearned
through an appreciation of difference: "People's color is an important difference. Instead of denying it or denigrating it, you'd better start appreciating it
and valuing it."[42]

This activity aims to illuminate how elites influence ordinary people into
behaviors that sustain social positioning, especially within the realms of social,
economic, and political inequalities. Said differently, it's a lesson on power.
There is a part of the call and response where Elliott digresses: "Racism, according to the dictionary, is a belief that race is the primary determinant of human
traits and capacities and that those racial differences produce an inherent superiority of a particular race. In other words, racism is regarding people positively
or negatively based on their race, i.e., the color of their skin and what is left
out of the definition, is having the power to institutionalize the belief."[43] Elliott
uses the moment to assert a point she makes every time she is allowed to speak:
that the public has been conditioned to that belief. "Eye color doesn't make you
a more- or less-worthwhile people, but if I treat you differently on the basis of
your eye color[,] I can make you react and behave in a different way, and that
will make others see you differently," she said.[44]

The lecture went quite well. Harmony subsequently asked Elliott to become part of the group's long-term programming. On February 17, 1996, organizers of the Kansas City, Kansas African American History Month Celebration asked Elliott to speak at its African American History banquet sponsored by the city's Human Resources Department. Her keynote address served as the capstone for a week-long program facilitated by police officers and firefighters of the African American Public Safety Officers Association. Activities in Kansas City, Kansas (KCK) included a career shadowing program for high school students, prayer meetings, gospel concerts, and an affirmative action forum.[45]

Elliott's keynote was not her only job in the metropolitan area during the week. She had been asked to facilitate the eye color exercise with city officials, the police department, and the Firefighters' Union Local 64. Six years earlier, nine Black KCK police officers filed a lawsuit against the city alleging hiring and promotion discrimination. Their suit was classified for class-action in the U.S. District Court after a group of Black firefighters in KCK sued their union for the same reasons.[46] As part of a settlement out of court, the KCK police department and firefighters in Local 64 were forced to undergo ongoing racial sensitivity training.

The Blue Eyes/Brown Eyes Exercise became part of the training upon Kansas City Harmony's recommendation. Harmony agreed to sponsor the work with Elliott, who brought with her two former colleagues from her time with US West Direct, Cookie Serenpa, and Colin Sprisebach.[47] While Harmony lacked funds to pay Elliott's typical remuneration, she agreed to conduct two exercises at a discounted price because the KCK police and fire chiefs permitted her to bring the Denkmal Film documentary crew to take footage of the workshops.[48] Elliott said one group was "nearly totally resistant and resentful."[49] Verhaag vouched for her assessment. Years later, the documentarian admitted to cutting out one KC Harmony group entirely from *Blue Eyed,* apart from a few clips of childish behavior inside the holding room before the workshop. When Verhaag finally completed the film, he spliced together scenes from one KC Harmony group and a group of educators and community volunteers at a workshop she facilitated in Minneapolis, Minnesota. Viewers of the final cut of *Blue Eyed* are typically so enamored by the exercise that they miss this major editing detail.

With great energy behind Elliott's work in Kansas City—though before the release of Verhaag's documentary—more and more public intellectuals invoked Elliott's message of white responsibility to combat racism. "As long as you enjoy the benefits of living in this racist society," she commonly told audiences, including those in Kansas City, "it is your responsibility to change what needs to be changed. Some of you may think you may never face the problem of racism. You will always be white and always be male. But I tell you, if you are lucky, you will get old, and perhaps for the first time, you will receive treatment based on physical characteristics over which you have no control. If you want to make changes, you must do it now."

Astrid Kersten, professor of administration and management at La Roche College, who arrived in the United States through the Netherlands, traveled to a few colleges to deliver lectures titled "The Concept of Everyday Racism."[50] At the University of Connecticut, associate professor of sociology, Noel Cazenave, created a course titled "White Racism" to expose "the existence of a color- and race-based system of group privilege."[51] Robert Jensen, a professor of journalism at the University of Texas at Austin, declared on the pages of the *Baltimore Sun* that his goal was "to talk openly and honestly" about the complex social phenomenon known as "white privilege," not by explaining how others benefit from skin color privilege, but how it has affected him.[52] The name Jane Elliott, and her message, perfectly captured the zeitgeist of the times.

* * *

Elliott's influence stretched across the Atlantic and hit close to the hearts of a team of anti-racism activists in Amsterdam. Founded in 1992 by journalist Suzette Bronkhorst, daughter of a Holocaust survivor, and Ronald Eissens, a political organizer, Stichting Magenta, also known as the Magenta Foundation, was fixated on Elliott's experiential learning anti-racism pedagogy. Bronkhorst and Eissen launched Magenta in response to the surge in xenophobic rhetoric and anti-Semitic and racist hate crimes amid a growing populist movement in Germany and other German-speaking countries during the earliest years of the decade. Very few documents exist about the foundation's origins, but its two founders were committed to countering hate speech with more speech.[53]

After seeing her on *The Oprah Winfrey Show*, Magenta's steering committee first became aware of Elliott's educational model. Lacking funds and the bandwidth to do much more than operate solely in the political arena and to track hate speech on the Internet, the organization pooled funds with Eindhoven-based human rights advocacy group Centrum Buitenlanders Oost-Brabant (later known as Stichting Palet) to contract Elliott to train the staff in the eye color simulation. From March 18 to 27, she trained eleven people from both organizations in a workshop titled "Oog in Oog" (Eye to Eye). Elliott went so hard on the trainees during the first two days that not all eleven would graduate from the program. In fact, during the heated simulation of the eye color exercise, Elliott made the blue-eyed event organizer—the chief executive from Centrum Buitenlanders Oost-Brabant who footed Elliott's travel and lodging bills—quit the training after he tried to "start a revolution" recalled trainee and future eye color trainer, Şeydâ Buurman-Kutsal. It was an experience Şeydâ called both "wonderful" and essential for "other people to feel [. . .] the position as a marginalized person."[54] Trainees spent the remaining days of the workshop "practicing over and over again" the eye color exercise, with Elliott observing with a critical eye. Şeydâ recalled that Elliott made every participant practice the trainer role until they proved to have the deportment to facilitate the program as intended.[55]

Elliott surprised the Magenta trainees during the training with a private screening of Verhaag's forthcoming documentary *Blue Eyed*. Verhaag and his longtime partner Claus Strigel had spent months editing up to seventy hours of speeches, workshop sessions, and interviews with Elliott, her daughter, Mary, and three of her former third-grade students to produce a ninety-three-minute documentary. They tried but failed to sell the film to ABC and HBO. Since no channel in the United States was willing to purchase air rights for the film, Verhaag was happy to gauge the effectiveness of the production by the reaction of Magenta employees. He accordingly sent a VHS copy to Elliott so she could use it in the Oog in Oog train-the-trainer program.[56]

After Elliott's departure, Magenta found a creative way to customize the eye color exercise for high school students in German-speaking countries. As an alternative for bringing students to a classroom and following Elliott's formula to precision, Şeydâ helped devise a three-hour eye color experience titled "School Zonder Racisme" (Schools Without Racism) that would take place onboard a boat. Magenta rented a longship and arranged for a five-week tour along the rivers and canals of the Netherlands, stopping at various cities in North Holland, Flevoland, Utrecht, and South Holland, allowing schools to experience the Blue Eyes/Brown Eyes Exercise Dutch-style. Once in the morning and again in the afternoon, cohorts of students arrived at the boat as if on a field trip. There, Şeydâ and the Magenta staff divided students into brown-eyed and non-brown-eyed groups. Inside the boat were six stations. Each station featured a multicultural learning experience, including an exhibit on South African history and culture, a display of racist comic characters, and music. As they rotated among the stations, students received different privileges based on the color of their eyes.[57] Students spent ninety minutes looking through the exhibits as they enjoyed preferential treatment or endured virulent discriminatory treatment. Another ninety minutes were spent "in an intensive debrief," Şeydâ said.[58]

Never the overbearing micromanager, Elliott had no idea that the Magenta Foundation altered the exercise to impose the discrimination role-play on teenagers, garnering a softer reaction from parents and watchdog groups. A deeply driven Jane Elliott soldiered on in 1996. The next to come calling was one of the United States' leading journalists.

* * *

Two months after her trip to Holland, Ted Koppel, Emmy award-winning host of ABC News *Nightline*, asked Elliott to participate as a guest on his evening news show during its special series *America in Black and White*, which ran during primetime hours from May 20 through May 24, 1996. One story featured during the special series focused on the hardships of Bridget Ward, a Black nurse's aide who chose to move out of Bridesburg, an all-white neighborhood in North Philadelphia, just five weeks after purchasing a home in the city's "whitest neighborhood," wrote Lea Sitton of the *Philadelphia Inquirer*. A single mother, Ward became reasonably concerned for the safety of her children after they received death threats and once people scrawled racial epithets on the steps leading up to her front door.[59] In the two-part feature, Koppel first interviewed Ward about her experiences in Bridesburg. The next night, he moderated a town hall meeting on white privilege with Ward's white neighbors. Koppel also examined the death of a seventeen-year-old Buffalo native who died as she crossed seven lanes of traffic to get to her job at the town shopping mall.[60] Local law did not permit buses to run from her neighborhood to stop at the mall.

Koppel's original plan for the Jane Elliott episode was not to use live interviews. He wanted an ABC crew to film Elliott delivering an "Anatomy of Prejudice" lecture at Northern Arizona University, splice in scenes from *The Eye of the Storm,* and interview two of her former students, Raymond Hansen and Donna (Reddell) May. Two things changed the original storyboard during the episode's production, scheduled to air on Thursday, May 23. First, Koppel was unhappy with the footage of the Northern Arizona lecture. He felt it was too inflammatory to keep his largely conservative television audience tuned in.

Moreover, the episodes aired earlier in the week on Buffalo's racist busing laws and white privilege in suburban Philadelphia turned away his "Pat Buchanan followers," as stated by an ABC News *Nightline* producer. Koppel reconfigured the feature on Elliott and her exercise. ABC then purchased rights from Denkmal Film to use some of Verhaag's yet-to-be-published footage of Kansas City fire and police personnel going through the Blue Eyes/Brown Eyes Exercise. Koppel subsequently boarded a plane for Iowa to conduct a face-to-face interview with Elliott. When the show aired, a live discussion with conservative pundit Robert Woodson slamming Elliott's work became the episode's feature. "The whole thing was a sham," Elliott said afterward, "it was so obvious an attempt to pander to the Pat Buchanan types that I actually laughed."[61]

Though disappointed in how ABC News *Nightline* used his footage with Koppel's voiceover without credit, Verhaag got the finished product, *Blue Eyed*, to premiere at The Interfilm Jury at the International Festival of Munich later that summer. With the momentum gained from positive reviews, namely a statement from the Interfilm Jury president, Eckart Bruchner, Verhaag ended up selling his documentary to television companies in South Africa, Brazil, Australia, and twenty-seven other countries.[62] The documentarian directed a film portraying the eye color exercise and an exposé describing how Elliott believed people get sucked into racist behavior. Chillingly, she compared the experiences of people ascribed as Black in the United States to how Jews felt in Europe before the Nazi "Final Solution." For European viewers, it was a weighty experience listening to Elliott describe an exchange with a Holocaust survivor and learn how that conversation inspired her to work harder. "Your students are very fortunate," Elliott recalls the Jewish woman saying to her in paraphrased form, "[. . .] the atmosphere you created for your students in your classroom with your Blue Eyed/Brown Eyed Exercise reminded me of the atmosphere, the environment, that the Nazis created for the Jews in Germany."

During the exchange, Elliott highlighted the impact that her exercise had on people of color, particularly Black individuals. They have told her that the experience depicted in the film is similar to how they live their lives every day. This sobering contrast for her European viewers emphasized the need for continued efforts to address issues of discrimination.[63]

The decision to release *Blue Eyed* as an educational program on public television across Europe, South Africa, and Australia was a hit with a cross-section of viewers. In Australia, Special Broadcasting Service, the nation's public programming station, received sixteen pages of positive comments, calling the program "nothing short of perfection" and "the most brilliant thing I have ever seen." An Aussie man identifying as a gay Aboriginal suggested: "Someone at one of the commercial stations could be smart enough to show this during prime time hours."[64] The *Stuttgarter Zeitung* couldn't get enough of Elliott. "It won't help much to be prepared to face Jane Elliott," declared an editorial in the newspaper, adding: "This elderly woman will tear down any shield." The daily, which printed out of Stuttgart, Baden-Württemberg, warned viewers that Elliott will come across as "the meanest, the lowest, the most detestful [*sic*]" and "the most hypocritical human being hell has ever spit back on earth." But the review closed with a concession that her exercise works, "she should be an example for all of us."[65]

The allure surrounding Jane Elliott with the release of *Blue Eyed* was symptomatic across Europe. When the documentary first aired over the winter season in late 1996, Marc Ruckebier, a high school senior from Dusseldorf, was among the many people enamored with Elliott's truth-telling, experiential learning pedagogy. A gay man forced to remain in the closet for fear of social ostracism or worse, Ruckebier thought, "I wish I had that superpower [to maintain an aggressive yet educative demeanor] that she has." He was captivated by how the eye color exercise exposed power dynamics, placing Elliott in a position where she could never be wrong. There were times he said, "I wanted to be as mean as she was [. . .] because I felt so inferior all of the time."[66] The exercise showed how quickly the rules could be changed, and he desired to become a rule-maker. Upon further introspection, the documentary made Ruckebier think deeper about a larger system that influences bigotry-motivated behavior: that there are invisible forces—a system, per se—that teach children intolerance.

Ruckebier's encounter with *Blue Eyed* occurred by happenstance. On vacation to a family home in Spain, Ruckebier's mother, Annemarie, a schoolteacher and witness to Germany's post-Nazi recovery, happened upon the program when clicking through television channels. Thinking that it would help her formulate teaching strategies to pull the full potential out of her students that hailed from marginalized communities of Dusseldorf, she called Marc in from another room to watch. Annemarie later purchased the film from Verhaag's company. Marc, after that, "watched it over and over," he admitted. He eventually became one of Elliott's European eye color exercise facilitators.

Meanwhile, Marc's mother, who was most concerned with how slow the school system adapted to the growing diversity of Jewish and Turkish Muslim students, became a professional development trainer at her school. She was intrigued by the educational aspect of Elliott's exercise—the debrief—and wanted to put her students and colleagues through something similar. Annemarie often shared her copy of *Blue Eyed* with her teaching colleagues in her role directing professional learning. These actions were part of a growing diversity training movement in Germany modeled after the Blue Eyes/Brown Eyes Exercise.

In January 1997, the film debuted in the United States at the Nortel Palm Springs International Film Festival. Unlike those in Europe who did not know Jane Elliott's work before the release of *Blue Eyed*, the audience in the United States found something new in Verhaag's documentary. On the one hand, all previous films or television specials about the eye color exercise focused on student reactions during the experience. On the other hand, when wrapping up the final production, Verhaag captured Elliott's inner thinking. Films like the Canadian Broadcasting Company's *The Way It Is* (1968), ABC's *The Eye of the Storm* (1970), PBS's "A Class Divided" (1985), and Miami's Channel 4 public television *Eye of the Beholder* (1987) focused mainly on the fluctuating behavior of exercise participants. Sure, Elliott was at the center of those films. That fact notwithstanding, the producers of those features—Stephen Banker (CBC), William and Muriel Peters (ABC and PBS), and station officers at Channel 4 in Miami—aimed to show transformation through Elliott's bullying tactics. In other words, the public fixated on the execution and outcome of the exercise.

In contrast, Verhaag's production offered two new perspectives. First, he aimed to document his subject's life beyond the exercise. Critics might say *Blue Eyed* (1996) should have included more perspectives, as Elliott is the only one interviewed in the film. Discussions with her daughters, at least one granddaughter, and several students from *The Eye of the Storm* ended up on the cutting room floor. Pundits may argue that Verhaag's interviews with Elliott provide a limited scope of the exercise's impact on her life. Jane Elliott-ill-wishers could claim that Verhaag portrayed her as a victim of a town gone mad. Despite disparagement, *Blue Eyed*, winner of six awards in the United States and Europe, including the prestigious German Media Civis Award that carried a $7,500 prize, uncovers the value of Elliott's exercise by allowing her to speak her logic. "I'm only doing this as an exercise [and] every child knows it's an exercise. And every child knows it's going to end at the end of the day," she explains in the film.[67] For over ninety minutes, Verhaag weaves in and out of unguarded discussions with Elliott and her facilitation of the eye color exercise on members of the police and fire departments in the Kansas City metropolitan area.

Elliott's voice in isolation highlights the second approach Verhaag wanted to convey in the film. Initially, he wanted to juxtapose previous documentaries by producing a film without narration. "I wanted to tell the story of the exercise without any commentary," Verhaag recalled when asked about the film in 2022. Elliott's voice would be it. "The interviews with her and the speech [at Chapman University]" plus the eye color workshop "became that commentary."[68] Much of *Blue Eyed* captures Elliott in her most vulnerable state. She chokes up when discussing the pervasiveness of discriminatory behavior, brooding when discussing on film how her parents lost almost all of their patrons at the Jennison Inn. "Their business was killed because of what I do." She divulges stories about how her children were treated because of the exercise. "Someone said good deeds don't go unpunished [. . .] It wouldn't have bothered me as much if I had been the only one exposed to that kind of behavior, but no one ever confronted me, in all those years, to this day. [. . .] but they got at me through my children. And I find that very, very difficult to forgive."[69]

Critics in the United States offered Verhaag the same degree of praise as the pundits had in Europe. Reviewers, attendees, and the organizers at the Nortel Palm Springs International Film Festival in January 1997 were enamored by *Blue Eyed*. In the Palm Springs Daily, *The Desert Sun*, one reviewer called it "a journey through an emotional maze." Approbation for Verhaag includes acclaim for the film's transcendence: "Few films can claim that they have the power to change somebody's life. Guaranteed, this one will."[70] Another critic, Fielding Buck, wrote that Verhaag "throws in a few arresting images" and that his film's subject "brings clarity to a complex subject."[71]

During the weekend leading up to the national Martin Luther King Jr. holiday, Verhaag appeared during one showing at the Courtyard Theater to take questions from the audience.[72] The tape snapped just a few minutes into the screening. As the people waited for theater employees to fix the film, Verhaag entertained the audience with a question-and-answer. On the way out of the theater after the event, a group of Black audience members serenaded Verhaag with a chorus of "We Shall Overcome."

Eventually, California Newsreel, a San Francisco-based nonprofit that has distributed educational films with themes related to justice since 1968, acquired the rights to distribute *Blue Eyed*. The corporation, which called the film "The most challenging and candid diversity video ever made," created a shorter version, lasting just over fifty minutes, and composed a companion guide for classroom instructors, human resource officers, and diversity trainers.[73] For $295 plus shipping, this shortened edition emphasizes the debrief session Elliott facilitates after the exercise. The debrief, it is believed, holds added value for teachers and trainers. In any exercise, it has commonly been the forgotten piece of the Blue Eyes/Brown Eyes Exercise. It is, nonetheless, the part that synthesizes experiences in a way that leaves a lasting emotional impact.

* * *

It is difficult to evaluate the impact televised documentaries have on the public because ratings only show the number of homes using a television. There is no emotional barometer collecting data on how viewers respond to the film. Moreover, people use television as an escape, a source of entertainment that late-British filmmaker Jerome Kuehl described as a "mechanical companion."[74]

Films about Jane Elliott's exercise, however, stand as the anomaly for a genre of filmmaking that measures success by the ability to "Make people think," according to Canadian filmmaker Donald Brittain. For *Blue Eyed*, and other films about the Blue Eyes/Brown Eyes Exercise that came before and after, Jane Elliott is a subject that frankly changes minds.

To Elliott's surprise, it wasn't just documentarians interested in her life's work. Two prominent A-list actresses were taken to Elliott and the eye color exercise. Less than a week after the ABC News *Nightline* debacle, Hollywood was abuzz over the prospect that a movie might be made about the Blue Eyes/Brown Eyes Exercise. Actress Julia Roberts, fresh from her role as Julianne Potter opposite Patrick Dempsey in *My Best Friend's Wedding*, announced that her new production company, Shoelace Productions, Inc., would produce a film about Elliott's discrimination lesson. It was believed that the film would address the exercise's impact on the Riceville community.[75] Shoelace Productions President Pliny Porter and aide Brian Cowden would collaborate on the screenplay. The Disney Corporation entertained the role of handling distribution. Susan Sarandon, star of *Bull Durham*, *Thelma & Louise*, and, most recently, *Dead Man Walking*, agreed to play the role of Elliott in the film, tentatively titled *A Class Divided: A True Story*.

It was Sarandon's doing that generated media speculation over the movie. In a May 1996 interview with *Body, Mind, & Spirit* magazine, the actress, who was promoting her role as the voice of Miss Spider in the forthcoming Disney animated live-action feature *James and the Giant Peach*, said she was reading a book. It was likely Bill Peters' *A Class Divided*, for she remarked that it was "about a woman who is a teacher. After the assassination of Martin Luther King, she divided her third-grade class into brown- and blue-eyed children to explain discrimination to them." She revealed, "I'm working on that" with Julia Roberts's film company; she teased, "but we don't know when we'll get the script in shape."[76]

Though Elliott never met Julia Roberts, she had the memorable experience discussing the movie over tea with Porter, Sarandon, and the latter's husband, Tim Robbins, in New York City. She said Sarandon was among the most impressive people she had met up to that point. She described the Oscar winner as a "barbed wire with an electrical charge." She added:

> I had thought she was tall and broad-shouldered. After all, hadn't she bested Tommy Lee Jones in *The Client*? Not tall. Not broad-shouldered. Average height, slim, energetic, not perky (I hate perky), businesslike, friendly, and

preoccupied. Not disinterested, but busy-minded. Thinking of many issues and details while listening to me describe what I do and how and why I do it. Practical, pragmatic, precise, and professional. No nonsense and no schmoozing! I'm impressed.[77]

Only relatively awestruck, Elliott unflinchingly challenged Porter, Sarandon, and Robbins over how she wanted the film to focus on the exercise and not become a "some silly" love story between her and Darald. The media didn't know what to make of the potential movie. Was it going to end up being a made-for-tv film? Who was going to play Darald? A combination of factors—lack of funding, Elliott's control over the script, and inability to build a cast—resulted in a dropped project. There was a time when Pliny Porter sent Elliott approximately forty pages that offered the hook to prove the movie could be a bankable project. Then, in early October 1997, Cowden completed a full screenplay draft and asked Elliott to comb through the manuscript, which is now housed inside the Jane Elliott papers at the University of Iowa Library.

While pleased by Porter's prose and Cowden's storytelling, she wasn't happy with its accuracy.[78] By the end of the year, references to a movie about the Blue Eyes/Brown Eyes Exercise, disappeared from Elliott's media coverage. Sarandon and Roberts, meanwhile, moved on to another project. In 1998, they co-produced and co-starred in Shoelace Productions' most successful film, *Stepmom*. Sarandon received a Golden Globe nomination for Best Actress in a Motion Picture Drama for her tear-jerking performance as Jackie Harrison, a divorcee whose storyline concentrates on a troubled relationship with her daughter while silently battling terminal cancer.

When asked how she felt that an A-list actress would play her in a movie, in a fitting fashion, Elliott tied the response to her anti-racism work: "Don't I look like Susan Sarandon?" She laughed at her question, then added, "Yeah. Well, if you don't see differences in people, she and I look alike, right?"[79]

CHAPTER 20

EYES OF THE WORLD

"If I had it my way, Jane Elliott's ingenious exercise would be repeated in every third-grade class. What it showed [sic] is that we all will grasp at any excuse—eye color, skin color, gender or religion—to believe that we are better than someone else."

—DAVID CROWDER, EDITOR, EL PASO TIMES, 1992

The Blue Eyes/Brown Eyes Exercise changes people, said Bertram Verhaag. Experientially, it makes people "more aware," he said, of how naturally controllable circumstances divide people in endless ways. On account of new attention brought to the eye color exercise through *Blue Eyed* and rising racial tensions in pockets of the United States, one school district in Palm Springs hoped Verhaag's statement could have a transformative impact on its student population. Knowing that Jane Elliott was in town to field audience questions at one of the last screenings of *Blue Eyed* at the Marquis Crowne Plaza Resort & Suites, the principal at Palm Springs High School reached out to Elliott for consulting help. Racial tensions had bubbled over during the winter months of the school year. Since 1993, the school had offered multicultural programming, requiring students to pass a conflict resolution course to graduate. Those attempts failed to mitigate problems as student fights became uncontrollable during the 1996-1997 school year. The principal, Richard Williams, expressed deep concern over a "series of brawls" between Black and Hispanic groups. He hoped Elliott could explain how her exercise if executed properly, would generate a uniting tenor in the Palm Springs Unified School District. By separating people by the color of their eyes, she explained that her workshops customarily create a feeling of "We've got to get together." Racially minoritized groups, she said, "already own a disproportionately small share of the pie." However, when they fight among themselves, "they do nothing to increase their overall share."[1]

Her overture to the students of Coachella Valley, where Palm Springs High School is situated, had to be weighed against the more prominent national drama. For starters, by the end of the 1990s, few had expected the rate of immigrants into the United States, who were mainly coming from Spanish-speaking countries of Latin America, to exceed the pace at which Eastern Europeans entered during the nineteenth and early twentieth centuries. As traditionally Black and Jewish neighborhoods became overpopulated with new Hispanic arrivals, friction surfaced between Black and Hispanic neighbors. Adults competed for jobs in already impoverished communities. For instance, social and economic tensions in South Central Los Angeles and a faltering school system led to gang warfare. The conflicts included control over neighborhood zones, healthcare, and jobs. Hospitals that once treated Black patients were now filled with Hispanics that consumed attention and medical services. In 1997, the unemployment rate for Black males were as high as 25 percent in some parts of the country.[2] Those more significant societal problems easily permeated classrooms.

Modern racism, which is defined by a relatively new term "colorblind society," had replaced old-fashioned racism, such as Jim Crowism. One 1997 study out of the University of Kentucky gathered empirical data on this shift. While old-fashioned racism posited that Americans with African ancestry were biologically inferior to European Americans and that segregation was (as a result) an accepted social practice, modern racists of the post-civil rights era cloaked racist beliefs with declarations that white supremacy is immoral and racial discrimination in any form no longer exists. Modern racism, the researchers claimed, is a form of cultural racism fueled by "perceptions that African Americans, in general, aren't willing to work hard and often violate the tenets of the Protestant work ethic." The researchers analyzed essays written by almost 500 white undergraduates at the university. Essays described attitudes toward African Americans as positive or negative using a Likert-style measure called the Modern Racism Scale. The study shows nearly 40 percent of those surveyed claimed African Americans get more than they deserve. Additionally, the survey indicates that almost half believe Black people are prejudiced toward whites and that there is a difference between "good blacks" and "bad blacks."[3] The Kentucky academics hypothesized that the percentage showing racial presumptions would have been greater if the experimental group were older.

Scientifically based or not, Elliott remained the most effective white race relations spokesperson shedding light on the anatomy of racist sentiments. She spent most of 1997 touring schools and attending conferences. She delivered Martin Luther King, Jr. Holiday addresses at Detroit's Madonna University and SUNY Cortland. In March and April, she told audiences at Winthrop University, Bloomfield College, Baltimore's Carroll Community College, and the "Pluralism: Blueprint for the 21st Century" Conference in Houston, "We could destroy racism if we choose to."[4] Opinion columnists invoked Elliott's name in stories about professional golfer Fuzzy Zoeller, who called twenty-one-year-old Masters Tournament champion Tiger Woods "that little boy." Zoeller suggested the clubhouse "not to serve fried chicken next year. Got it. Or collard greens or whatever the hell they serve." Writers also referenced her work in stories about police departments undergoing anti-bias training to improve relations between law enforcement officers and communities of color.[5] After the summer break, Elliott was back on campuses telling audiences that everyone possesses bigoted beliefs and that overcoming racism is hard but possible. "It's going to take me the rest of my life to overcome it," she regularly said.[6] Crowds at St. Joseph, Missouri Western State College, Texas Union, Luzerne County (PA) Community College, and Southern Utah University were especially receptive to her message.

On September 28, Elliott conducted the Blue Eyes/Brown Eyes Exercise on young professionals and high school and college students in Milford, Nebraska. Instead of collars, she used green stickers to identify everyone with blue eyes. As usual, she forced the blue eyes into an isolation room at the Milford campus of Southeast Community College, about twenty miles west of Lincoln, where they sat starving for forty-five minutes. Meanwhile, the brown eyes enjoyed a meal with Elliott as they learned how she would operate the exercise. Elliott ensured the blue-eyed participants could see the brown eyes walking into the meeting room with trays full of food. When released from isolation, the blue eyes could pick up food but were forced to eat in "humiliation" on the floor while the brown eyes sat around the perimeter. Two blue-eyed participants with physical problems received chairs, but Elliott found ways to discriminate against them during the training. One report described the brown eyes as "laughed and wise-cracked," just as Elliott wanted. After eating, Elliott's helpers instructed the blue eyes to carry everyone's trays to the kitchen and clean off the tables where the brown eyes had previously dined.

Elliott looked at one of the blue eyes and said, "Boy, do you want to leave the group and join the brown eyes?"

"No," he replied. "I have blue eyes, and I'm proud."

"This is real dumb," Elliott scolded. She then required the male participant and a few other blue eyes to recite her "listening rules." They struggled. Their penmanship was atrocious, according to Elliott, who criticized their spelling and lack of punctuation. Whatever they did, wrote Bill Reeves of the *Lincoln Journal Star*, was wrong. It was apparent she had dented their cognitive abilities. "You're going to learn something black kids learn very early," she said. "You smile like a skunk eating bumblebees whether you want to or not." Her antics were aided by the well-coached brown eyes, who called the blue eyes "ignorant, disorganized, and lazy."[7]

Elliott only forced participants to endure her nastiness for an hour. She then spent two hours facilitating the debrief, where participants wrote essays and spoke about what they had experienced. "The exercise hurts," reported Reeves, "but [it] helps change people's attitudes in a way no straightforward 'lecture' about the evils of racism could do."[8]

"It is sad that in 1997 people are still hiring me to come in and do this god-awful exercise—because of the amount of racism in this country today." A taxed Elliott said on her way out. However, in places around the country, there was evidence that she had impacted those that survived the "Collar in My Pocket" workshop. In Minnesota, a minister challenged a coffee shop owner to take down a sign that read, "If your wife can't cook, keep her for a pet and eat here." After experiencing Elliott's exercise, he said he "could not continue to come there unless the owner took the sign down."[9]

It wasn't just in Minnesota that people challenged others to be better humans. At least three documentaries about Jane Elliott's eye color exercise—*The Eye of the Storm*, "A Class Divided," and *Blue Eyed*—made rounds throughout South Africa, where Nelson Mandela was in his third year as president of a country trying to resolve a dreadful history of apartheid. During a tour through the United States in 1997, white South African dissident Margaret Legum used speaking events to talk about the value of the eye color discrimination exercise. "I couldn't believe it," she said, speaking of Elliott's third-grade students she had seen in either *The Eye of the Storm* or "A Class Divided." "It's not so much that the kids in the group who got disparate treatment misbehaved; they couldn't think. They couldn't do the assignment. The ill-treatment they were getting had that much of an effect on them. Incredible."[10] Though invited on several occasions, Elliott never "had the time or the courage" to journey to the republic, she said.[11] Even without Elliott's presence, the eye color exercise was a popular reference point by South African officials striving to heal that nation. The content of Jane Elliott's videos became proclamations about state violence. While it was common to see underrepresented non-dominant groups in other countries made up of the poor, less educated, and disenfranchised, the non-dominant group in South Africa had usurped power through violence and the implementation of a legal state that caused the dominant group to grow sick, die sooner, and live in perpetual poverty. The system, in other words, was manufactured by people. Because of Elliott's eye color exercise, there is proof that people can undo those systems.

Farther away in Australia, Elliott's anti-racism doctrine was heard loud and clear that same autumn.

* * *

When it comes to exposing racism, wrote Tony Squire, entertainment columnist for the *Sydney Morning Herald* in New South Wales, Australia, look no further than those who "do nothing to prevent racism." That was the lesson Squire extracted after watching *Blue Eyed*. On September 23, 1997, Australia's public service channel, Special Broadcasting Service (SBS), aired the documentary *I'm Not a Racist, But* [. . .] as part of its weeklong commitment to anti-racism programming. It came after a nationwide debate over the subtle, or closeted, racial animosity against Aboriginal Australians. Years earlier, in 1992, the High Court of Australia ruled in a case known as the *Mabo* decision that Aboriginal and Torres Strait Islander people had indigenous rights to the land on which their ancestors had lived for several generations.

Named after Edward Koiki Mabo, the Aboriginal Australian land rights activist from the Torres Strait Islands, the case nullified a doctrine known as "terra nullius." Claiming that Australia was "nobody's land," terra nullius had once made it easy for European settlers to seize much of Australia.[12] While the holding in *Mabo* was a watershed moment for Aboriginal land claims and reconciliation efforts to discuss and fix past problems, political ambiguities triggered resistance among many in the white Australian community. The scene grew more complicated during election season in 1996 when Australian Liberal Party leader, Pauline Hanson, said "mainstream Australians"—and by that, she meant white Australians—had become victims of reverse racism "by those who promote political correctness" and an immigration policy that resulted in Australia being "swamped by Asians. [. . .] [with] their own culture and religion [who] form ghettos and do not assimilate." Hanson's comments, defended by first-year Australian Prime Minister John Howard as free speech, caused a fracture in the country's efforts to unify and build closer ties with Asian people.

When a tabloid journalist from the Melbourne *Sun Herald* questioned Hanson's comments, Hanson proclaimed, "I am not a racist. I know in my heart I'm not a racist. [. . .] I take people on who they are."[13] SBS programming ran with Hanson's phrase, "I am not a racist."

The qualifier, "I am not a racist, but [. . .]" was considered by socially conscious thinkers to be "the most dangerous threat to race relations at the time."[14] In the United States, where the passage of civil rights legislation in the mid-to-late 1960s expunged most *de jure* forms of discrimination, still existent across the country was the preconceived notion that racism was no longer a problem. It was argued that whites were the current victims of discriminatory treatment caused by affirmative action. It was a play by conservative leaders to trumpet reverse discrimination. In Australia, the *Mabo* case and government-cosigned reconciliation also seemingly cured the nation of racism. To this degree, the "I'm not a racist, but [. . .]" crowd still controlled many of the institutions in both countries. All the same, "I'm not a racist, but [. . .]" was typically followed by something divisive, if not altogether racist. It's an apology given ahead of an offensive comment.[15] When *Blue Eyed* aired for the first time that fall, many across Australia couldn't talk civilly about the nation's systemic issues, such as astonishingly poor rates of healthcare, imprisonment, literacy, and poor housing plaguing Australians of color. That is how SBS boldly positioned its weeklong series *I'm Not a Racist, But [. . .]*

Within forty-eight hours of its premiere of *Blue Eyed*, SBS received "a staggering" 2,500 phone calls. The station revealed that "no other program in SBS's seventeen-year history has caused such reaction."[16] Reviews called the film a "stunning piece that reveals the slime of racism." The *Sydney Morning Herald* described it as "blindingly illuminating and perfectly timed, given the debate haunting this country."[17]

Elliott was oblivious to the reaction in the Land Down Under until she received a phone call from *The Sun Herald* asking for quotes for a profile piece it would run. Then the SBS announced it was going to recast the documentary in October. To promote the rerun, producers at SBS offered Elliott an all-expense-paid trip for her and Darald to fly to Sydney and appear as a guest on its prime-time show *Insight*.[18] This would be her first trip to Australia and only her second trip out of the Western Hemisphere since traveling to the Netherlands in 1996 to conduct the Blue Eyes/Brown Eyes Exercise in Eindhoven.

Elliott still carried a demanding lecture and diversity training schedule in the United States. This meant she would not arrive in Oz until November.[19] In the meantime, the station primed its viewers with a screening of *Blue Eyed* in October. *The Age* reported it was the "most watched" program in SBS history.[20] As one reporter suggested, Jane Elliott had become a "household name" in Australia.[21]

When Elliott set foot in Australia, the media rolled out the red carpet. They gave her a welcoming platform to speak her mind. She pulled no punches. Elliott had studied up on the issues. Pauline Hanson, she said, was a racist. Elliott warned them not to give her too much leash lest she became prime minister. She said the United States existed as a case study: in her estimation, Ronald Reagan was like Hanson. This populist politician went to the top by scapegoating America's problems on people of color and leftists. "The whole thing is that it's ridiculous, irrational, and unrealistic to treat people unfairly on the basis of a physical trait that they have no control over. But as well as crushing other people's talents, it ruins your own humanness. You are limiting yourself, your experiences, your education. It really cripples everyone. Racism is a handicap. It keeps you from being what you could be."[22]

Before the year's end, the Sydney press issued the Golden Armchair Award to *Blue Eyed* for Best Imported Documentary. Verhaag's film was selected over *The Story of Maya Lin*, a profile on the architect who designed the Vietnam Memorial in the District of Columbia, and others titled *The West*, *Painted Babies*, and *The People's Century*. One voter criticized *Blue Eyed* as "didactic and overlong." Most voters, however, valued the film's message about facing Australia's dividing forces head-on. Elliott's "ruthless umpiring of her own game," said Doug Anderson, one of the award show's judges, "and her tenacious, confrontationist approach made it irresistible." The film, he added, "was scarifying in its exposure of deep-seated—even subliminal—racist mindsets."[23]

Just days away from turning sixty-four, Elliott left Down Under feeling like she impacted the country during her quick visit. Alison Stewart of the *Sydney Morning Herald* supported that suspicion with an endorsement claiming Elliott is a "remarkable woman." Stewart conceded there was no way not to see Elliott as a "bully," but she posited that the diversity trainer is "rabid about injustice." Furthermore, she positioned Elliott as an educator with "shatteringly simple" methods. Indeed, Stewart intimated, "To achieve her ends, people are often left upset, angry, and hurt. But Elliott is concerned about the big picture—that people leave her workshops never again to sit by and accept discrimination."

Therein lies Jane Elliott's motivation—the ends justify her means. Hardly an inkling of care for what others thought of her, Elliott went to Australia just as she once had with KC Harmony, or before that at Mountain Bell, and even earlier when at the White House Conference on Children in Washington D.C.

Her singular purpose was to challenge people into action. "If there were more Jane Elliotts and fewer Pauline Hansons, the world would surely be a fairer place," wrote Stewart.[24]

Another conflict over land rights surfaced in Australia between Aboriginals known as the Wik and Thayorre people and the pastoral leaseholders in northeastern Australia that fall and winter. After the High Court sided with the Wik and Thayorre people—claiming that native title rights could co-exist—Prime Minister Howard issued a ten-point plan just days after Elliott departed from Australia, stating the "pendulum" had swung "too far in the Aboriginal direction." Howard's plan would "return the pendulum to the centre." The Australian House of Representatives and Senate would debate the prime minister's policy proposal for the next ten months. At the moment, however, proponents for Aboriginal rights cited Elliott's work to advance their cause. On Elliott's birthday, November 30, Prime Minister Howard gave the nation another primetime Sunday night address, further explaining his Wik policy. As soon as he finished, SBS aired Elliott's *Blue Eyed* film again. Warradale resident, Greg Bowyer, wrote to the *Sydney Morning Herald*, "Is Jane Elliott still in Australia?" He suggested she "deliver her confronting workshop on prejudice and racism for both houses of the Federal Parliament—as a matter of urgency."[25] A few days later, SBS aired another Jane Elliott classic, "A Class Divided."[26]

* * *

After zigzagging across the United States during the winter and spring of 1998, Elliott rested before returning to Australia to embark on a lecture tour of the island. Sponsored by SBS, and dubbed "The Anatomy of Prejudice, The Jane Elliott Tour," Elliott set out to speak at multiple venues from May 14 to 29 at the Darling Harbour Convention Centre and Sydney universities. To promote her tour, SBS rescreened "A Class Divided" on April 30 and again on May 6. The station showed *The Eye of the Storm* for the first time on May 4 and broadcast *Blue Eyed* again on May 11.[27] SBS advertised the first two films as paramount to help children "coping [with] all the beastliness" of racism. The latter, station executives said, "takes a broader line with adults."[28] The publicity generated enough excitement for what many Australians considered a visit from one of the most consequential figures walking the planet. Elliott and her exercise were "mesmerizing," wrote Antony Lawes, entertainment columnist in Sydney. Elliott's exercise "does something that a truckload of textbooks and learned lecturers can never do: show how discrimination begins and how it is perpetuated."[29]

On returning to Australia, Elliott found a curious enough audience to spread her message that "there's no such thing as race." She explained that Christian evangelicals constructed the "four or five different races" five hundred years earlier to establish superiority among various inferior cultural groups measured by skin color and religion. "Human beings come in different sizes, shapes, colors, and genders, but we're all members of the same race," she said. "When we stop teaching children to see color as a negative, we will do away with racism."[30]

Those words were just the idealism that her Australian sponsors hoped she would convey. Favorable media coverage of the tour indicates that what Australians liked even more was Elliott's frankness: "We don't need to be talking about racism, anyway. There is just one race—it's the human race. And the physical differences are a result of adaptation to the natural environment. They are not because God decided we are going to be different colors." Elliott's speeches show her addressing audiences calmly but with passion. At this time, she was referring to the problem of racism as actually "skinism," her term for what most call in the present-era colorism. In one speech, she says, "When you start referring to the problem as the problem of skinism, all of a sudden, it's ridiculous instead of making sense. It is ridiculous to judge people on the amount of melanin in their skin."[31]

There is very little evidence that she encountered direct resistance anywhere on the continent. Elliott spent two weeks traveling around Australia with Aboriginals, including a three-day stay in Melbourne from May 27 to 29, delivering her One Race message. She succeeded at this by talking about "hope for the future." She made similar tones that would align with her right-of-center critics. "Eventually, we are going to start teaching that there's no such thing as race," Elliott said. Obsessed with telling others, "We are all members of the same race," she aimed to convince skeptics that change was good for Australia and humanity. "Many people are desperately afraid of change. But you can't have growth without it."[32]

After returning to the States, her life was flooded with several weighty trials and tribulations. After purchasing a summer home in Sun City, California, closer to her daughter, Mary, and grandchildren, her eldest sibling, Charles, age seventy, died of a heart attack at the Mitchell County Regional Health Center.[33] He was the first of Elliott's siblings to pass away since the death of three-year-old Anne in 1945 and the first to follow their father, Lloyd, who died eight years earlier. Elliott's year ended with lectures at Bucknell College, Owensboro (Kentucky), Hawkeye Community College, Lehigh University,

Florida Atlantic University, College of St. Benedict, South Dakota School of Mines & Technology, Franklin College, and the universities of Wisconsin-Oshkosh and Western Michigan. On December 29, however, her sister, Jean, died of acute asthma in her Decorah home, leaving behind a husband, a son, three daughters, and seven grandchildren.[34]

A week after her sister's funeral, Elliott refocused her mind with an appearance on the Australian weekly, one-hour indigenous arts radio show *Awaye!* The show was known for blending live and recorded music with interviews and documentary news. *Awaye!* was the country's only national indigenous arts and culture program hosted by Aboriginal broadcasters.[35] It also worked to celebrate Aboriginals living throughout the world. Her call into the show included two other justice warriors, Lillian Holt and Andrew Jakobowicz.[36]

* * *

Four years earlier, one teacher at Germantown Middle School in Memphis had launched "discrimination week," a five-day Black History Month program designed to raise consciousness about the historical treatment of racial minorities. At the Memphis school, students traditionally read Mildred Taylor's *Roll of Thunder, Hear My Cry,* during the school week, about a Black family facing discrimination in Great Depression-era Mississippi. In 1999, however, besides reading the Newbery Medal-winning novel, students were put through a discrimination role play based on Jane Elliott's eye color exercise. At this school, the teacher used school uniforms to enforce segregation rather than creating a caste based on the color of the student's eyes. The day before the exercise, students drew cards from a deck to determine what color suit they would have to wear to school. Those drawing diamonds were assigned to the discriminated group on the first day of the exercise, and those who drew clubs faced discrimination on the second day. The disadvantages were plenty; students were last in line for lunch and stood in the hall facing the lockers while the privileged students used the restroom. While in class, their seats were moved to the back of the room, and they were told to put their backs to the teacher. They were ignored when they raised their hands. They could not talk to their friends who wore the opposite color suit. They were forced to clean up the cafeteria and classroom, often to catcalls and slander from dominant group members. On one occasion, two students got into a fight. Several were bullied. Name-calling was commonplace.[37]

Information about the exercise was sent home to parents seeking approval ahead of the program. One newspaper report claimed that while "a small number of parents questioned the exercise," once the school administration explained its purpose, the "parents agreed to allow their children to participate." A few students opted out without penalty. A week later, for the school's capstone event, Germantown middle school students received a visit from Holocaust survivor Eleanor Ehrlich.[38]

Stories about educators across the United States and worldwide attempting variations of the Blue Eyes/Brown Eyes Exercise commonly made the press. To Elliott's dismay, however, in the winter of 1999, there was one particularly troubling headline. Minneapolis's *Star Tribune* ran a story titled "A Hard Lesson" with a picture of a former student, Dona Jo Keller standing in front of Riceville Community Elementary School. The reporter, Susan Hogan-Albach, suggested that Elliott's exercise "forever changed" Riceville into an embittered community that grew to despise one of its daughters. Hogan-Albach said, "Instead of taking pride in Elliott's accomplishments," residents fumed. She wrote: "Teachers resented the attention she received. Some locals complained that blacks might be drawn to their town. Her children were taunted and beaten by other kids." She quoted a new Methodist pastor to Riceville, Rev. Edythe Hill, perhaps out of context, as claiming the hostility toward Jane Elliott still pervaded the community. She also quoted an anonymous minister from town as having said, "I was trying to collect money recently for a school in Africa, and a number of older people said to me, 'Aren't we just throwing money down the drain?'" Do any whites go there?"[39]

Before the exposé, Elliott had been on record describing how her children and parents were treated after first doing the exercise. Not just in public speeches, but in *Blue Eyed,* she revealed that her father died in 1990, mainly in isolation despite spending a lifetime serving the Riceville community. While the coverage of her advocacy often yielded positive results, Ricevilleans seemingly blocked it all out. Hogan-Albach suggested the town's annual Johnson & Johnson-sponsored war on mosquito shootout was more popular among town residents than was Jane Elliott and her war on racism.[40] This is why when a newspaper in a neighboring state, though circulated in northern Iowa, quoted Elliott's "hard feelings," the anger resurfaced. Many in Riceville felt a line had been crossed. There is no telling whether Hogan-Albach used Elliott's quotes out of context: "These small communities are going to be kicking and screaming into the twenty-first century whether they like it or not," Elliott said, "but they're still preaching and teaching the rightness of whiteness." She added, "Teachers destroy children on the basis of skin color every day. They should be the ones going through the exercise."[41]

On February 11, locals filled two pages of the *Riceville Recorder* with letters slamming Hogan-Albach's characterization of Riceville as a "hick town" with a culture preventing Black Americans from moving into the area. The newspaper's editor, M.E. Messersmith, claimed Hogan-Albach's piece included at least one fake source. He also came to Elliott's defense. "I have had the pleasure of knowing Jane Elliott for many years," he said, "and it's hard for me to believe that she gave some of the quotes printed in the article."[42]

There were plenty who disagreed with Messersmith's defense of Elliott. One of her former students, a seventh grader who had gone through the eye color exercise during one of Elliott's last years working in Riceville schools and asked that her name be withheld, said she "greatly lamented" Elliott's comments about Riceville. According to the editorial, Elliott twisted the truth about what happened to her family after the 1968 Discrimination Day exercise.

> [. . .] her assertion that her children were mistreated because of her experiment is just plain wrong. She had moved away by the time I was around, but her sister's family lived right next door. Whenever Ms. Elliott's children would visit their cousins next door, I would be sure to head for home because they were just plain mean. I imagine, though, that other children dealt with their violence with a little bit of their own violence. [. . .] she might consider other possibilities before indicting the whole town.

This writer conceded that the eye color exercise positively influenced her life. "My class voluntarily chose to participate," she explained, adding that "it proved to be an experience I shall not soon forget."[43]

Elliott's brother, Sam, was another who responded to Hogan-Albach with an editorial in the *Riceville Recorder*. He did not mention that Elliott was his sister; Sam, who lived in Burlington then and considered himself an outsider, offered remarks defending the "extreme friendliness, respect, and consideration" Riceville had to offer visitors. "Do not get overly concerned by the rantings of a staff reporter from the *Star Tribune*," he steadied. "Keep smiling—keep up the good work."[44]

For researchers trying to reconstruct her life, at no time was the rift between Elliott and her hometown more apparent than in 1999. Almost a decade later, one Riceville resident said the town possessed a "love-hate madness" toward Elliott. She had certainly removed the filter if there ever was one. At this time, she was beset by the deaths of her siblings.[45] Her work also intensified with the brutal murder and trial of James Byrd, a Black man tied to the back of a pickup truck by neo-Nazi Aryan Brotherhood members and dragged for nearly three miles in Jasper, Texas. At an event in Tallahassee, Elliott lambasted Ward Connerly, a Black consulting millionaire championing the end of affirmative action at California universities, which he called "a diversity charade."[46] She told a crowd at the Tallahassee Race Relations Conference that winter, "Resist. We've had affirmative action in this country for white males for 400 years, and there was no problem with it. It only became a problem when women and people of color began to be treated more fairly than they had been treated in the past."

Admittedly, Elliott accepted the moniker "infamous." Despite a burgeoning reputation as a firebrand who ruffled audiences, organizers of socially conscious public events kept contracting her services. Tallahassee's equal opportunity director, Sharon Ofuani, said she wanted Elliott to speak to her community because she talks "straight about race."[47] The assessment was spot on. "I make people uncomfortable. I'm fully aware of that," Elliott admitted. "They know that I'm opposed to racism, and they've been raised in a racist society. And they also know that I'm going to be in their face."[48]

Her ability to make people feel uncomfortable was no accident. It was indeed the real Jane Elliott. She found the perfect target at the most inopportune time. Elliott had been paid $7,500 to deliver a speech at the Clinton Administration's March 8, 2000, Education Department seminar on the state of education. At the White House, Elliott's remarks focused on her niche—to discuss how prejudice materializes in young children and how those feelings manifest into discriminatory behavior. According to Erica Lepping, spokeswoman for Education Secretary Richard Riley, Elliott's talk took an unexpected turn. During her remarks, Elliott called Republican presidential candidate Texas Governor George W. Bush and his brother, Florida Governor Jeb Bush, racists. While sounding off on the upcoming presidential election, she plugged a down-ticket vote for the Democratic Party. The comment was "spontaneous and unanticipated," said Lepping, who knew this news would generate a torrent of criticism from Republican lawmakers. "We certainly don't endorse the comments, and they don't reflect our views."[49]

Elliott's attacks on Republicans, ranging from former President Ronald Reagan to future President Bush, angered the very people diversity trainers, in general, hoped to reach through their workshops. Writing for Pennsylvania Conservatives on Mother's Day 2000, Muriel Crabbs mocked Elliott's work as "head games" and "Mean-spirited, man-hating, gender feminism, victim-based race indoctrination."[50] The growing movement of diversity training on college campuses followed the steady diversification of predominantly white institutions, compounded by many ugly episodes of hate crime violence at the end of the 1990s. From 1997 to 1998, the Clinton Administration launched a community and campus-wide race initiative called "Dialogue on Race," which Conservatives attacked as a maneuver to defend affirmative action. Social justice advocates, like Jane Elliott, described the program as "lackluster" and "rudderless," a failed initiative of "timid talk when bold action was needed."[51] Indeed, the action was needed after the racially incentivized 1998 murder of Byrd in Texas. The murder of Matthew Shepard—a gay student attending the University of Wyoming—that same year was equally disturbing. To do its part, colleges at the turn of the millennium implemented orientation strategies hoping to fend off instances of hate crimes and sexual assault. For instance, at Wake Forest, the *Blue Eyed* film was mandatory viewing for freshmen at new student orientation. In the wake of this growing movement, Crabbs called the entire approach for social consciousness on college campuses liberal "reprogramming."

"Now wait a minute," Elliott would say about attacks on trying to educate the populace about racism, homophobia, sexism, and religious intolerance. No child is too young. No person is too old "to know what's going on." She defended anti-racism work as "leading people out of ignorance." Children, she argued, "see and hear what's being said, and you owe it to them to tell them why you, and the rest of the country, are upset [. . .], so that, when it happens later on, they will recognize it and fight back. If my father hadn't been vocal in his condemnation of Adolf Hitler and his minions, I wouldn't be as aware as I am."[52]

All signs of patience dropped from the sixty-seven-year-old, who had seen enough madness in the world since introducing the eye color exercise more than three decades earlier. Growing more impatient with progress, Elliott traipsed the lecture halls of college campuses, hotel conference rooms, and convention centers of large and small cities in the United States, Canada, and Australia once again as if trying to expedite the path to racial harmony.

She was, by the aughts, quite simply, angry.

CHAPTER 21

ANGRY EYE

"Your racism is your problem. Don't make it someone else's problem."
—JANE ELLIOTT, OREGON STATE UNIVERSITY, 2003

In the winter of 2001, George W. Bush was sworn in as President of the United States. Elliott had been a loud critic speaking adamantly against his candidacy during campaign season. When the Supreme Court ruled the election victory belonged to Bush, Elliott had about enough of a country she saw as sickened with racial discrimination. Thousands of Black voters in Florida were, as she believed, deliberately disenfranchised by the court's decision. Bush had taken the oath of office despite losing the popular vote by half a million votes. During his inaugural address, the newly sworn-in president reached out to voters of color with a "solemn pledge," as he called it, to "work to build a single nation of justice and opportunity."[1] It wasn't enough to prevent Elliott from becoming intensely bitter about the next four years.

Divisions also existed between Elliott and her family, whom she described as "conservative Republicans" wondering "what the hell my problem was." While speaking at the Canadian Association of Statutory Human Rights Agencies conference in Whitehorse, Yukon, she told an audience that she had become alienated by her siblings and mother for her criticism of Bush. She then projected that the Bush administration would set the work of racial justice advocacy "back eons."[2]

Such speaking events brought out angry emotions and unfettered criticisms of people interfering with the work of undoing racism. Elliott had once hoped the new millennium would usher in the beginning of the end of racially incentivized behavior and colorblind policymaking. "We were on our way up until the 1980s," when Ronald Reagan held two terms in office. "It got a little better with Clinton," she said, "but Bush," with his proposed tax cuts to the wealthy and No Child Left Behind education policy, which threatened to reduce funding for low-achieving schools. She argued that the implications of Bush's new education reforms would cause already low-achieving students to feel jaded by the system. The pressure to boost state standardized scores would be placed on poor and urban school districts predominated by students of color. Bush's new high-stakes testing policy "brings these ethnocentric attitudes back again," she said. Speaking specifically about No Child Left Behind, she asked, "Who do you think this [education] policy is going to serve? It definitely isn't going to be the poor or colored kids."[3] Pointing journalists in the direction of including more voices from communities of color in news reports, Elliott explained, "They'll say their situation is much better in some ways than it was in 1950, but vastly worse in many ways than it was in 1980."[4]

A few months later, she delivered the keynote at the University of Calgary's Diversity Summer Institute. Her message that societal and school curricula brainwashed all people into holding racist beliefs was poignant. In her standard prickly way, she proclaimed that despite everyone being educated to possess ideas about inferiority and superiority, no one had to behave in such ways, causing, as per usual, discomfort among those in the crowd. After the event, Elliott expressed concern about her ability to impact the general public in an interview. She suggested that despite having invested thirty-three years of her life into facilitating the eye color exercise and speaking to audiences about prejudice reduction worldwide, she moved to think that her work required a boost of adrenaline. "I'm really tired," she said. "I'm real tired of working on this project, but I'm not going to stop as long as there's lots of problems out there."[5]

It helped that several audience members found her words to be mind-blowing. "She makes you think that maybe everything you know and believe is not based on true fact and maybe everything you know is a fallacy," said attendee Shalini Gupta.[6] One had to consider Gupta's comments when, on August 3, the Palm Springs International Festival of Short Films aired the world premiere of Elliott's newest documentary *Angry Eye*. Produced by Elliott's entertainment lawyer, Susan A. Golenbock, and an experienced co-producer and director, William Talmadge, *Angry Eye* shows her facilitation of the Blue Eyes/Brown Eyes Exercise with about twenty-five psychology students from Bard College.[7] Although she had conducted the exercise dozens of times with college students, this was the first film to show her with a group of coeds. The students had little idea what they were getting into even as they registered at the crack of dawn—a time Elliott selected to get the teenagers and early twenty-somethings irritated before arrival. According to Elliott's recollection, they only knew they could receive a one-hour psychology credit for participating in the exercise.[8]

Elliott, who now had more than thirty years of experience conducting the exercise, was unvarnished in her treatment of the blue-eyed coeds. By the end of the workshop, she had made two women cry, and several others fought to hold back tears. Her formula was simple: after jarring the blue eyes with scorn during registration and the unpredictable lockdown in the holding room, Elliott's workshop consisted of efforts to humiliate victims when they entered the seminar room. In her training handbook, *A Collar in My Pocket*, she works from an itinerary; however, she proved pragmatic by jumping on any blue-eyed slip-up to berate the underprivileged cohort. *Angry Eye* shows Elliott pillorying the students as they look for a spot to sit in the segregated blue-eyed section. When she grew tired of lambasting students about their indecisiveness over where to sit, she forced a few blue-eyed participants to read the signs of subjugation on the walls. She vocally pummeled those who struggled to read each word with proper pronunciation and then transitioned to the "listening skills" portion of the workshop. Elliott was able to subdue a young woman, who broke into tears after first struggling to say the listening skills in the way Elliott wanted. She also did not have paper and a pencil. Additionally, she failed to remember passages from a tongue-twisting memory test.

The memory test included reciting the following: "One hen; two ducks; three squawking geese; four limerick oysters; five corpulent porpoises; six pairs of Don Alverzo's tweezers; seven thousand Macedonians in full battle array; eight brass monkeys from the ancient sacred crypts of Egypt; nine apathetic, sympathetic, older diabetic men on roller skates, with a marked propensity towards procrastination and sloth; ten lyrical, spherical, diabolical denizens of the deep whom all stall around the corner of the quo of the quay of the quivery, all at the same time."

After struggling, the student walked out of the workshop in tears.

Elliott's relentlessness was vexing. It enabled her to draw back and forth from what the blue-eyed coeds were experiencing regarding Elliott's prejudiced behavior against them with anti-Black racism and homophobia: she drew on themes of perception, freedom, power, and defense mechanisms. She even invoked the memories of James Byrd, Matthew Shepherd, and Emmett Till when explaining that students in her exercise have the choice to escape discriminatory treatment.

She said those three individuals did not, nor do people of color on any day in America. During that exchange, *Angry Eye* participants realized the point of the exercise. While it isn't clear whether she administered the culturally biased Dove counterbalance test during the session, participants realize the malleability of gender identity, class, and religion. Skin color, however, cannot change. That was a key point of discussion once students were asked to write three adjectives describing how they felt people of the opposite eye color looked during the exercise and three adjectives explaining how they felt during the simulation. At one point, a white-passing man of indigenous lineage and an LGBTQIA+ woman named Claire challenged Elliott over separate degrees of pain experienced by different marginalized groups. "All of my previous experiences with judgments and prejudice, etcetera, were being invalidated," Claire contended.

The debate over the issue was not resolved until a month later. The formal debrief was not held that day. Elliott and her team decided the exercise would have a greater impact if students stepped away for a few weeks to process the experience. When Elliott returned to Bard, it took the voices of Black coeds to get Claire and her classmates to see it from Elliott's view. She drilled that to understand the power dynamics of racism in interpersonal relations, we must juxtapose the abolition of laws that once maintained a social order with the rise of colorblind frameworks that only widened racial disparities across social, educational, economic, and political institutions. To accomplish this, she called to the front of the room Claire and a straight Black male several inches over six feet tall named Rasul to participate as visuals for a discussion on polite, colorblind etiquette that became an established practice among baby boomers and Generation X. The group was comfortable pointing out gender differences on cue but lacked the courage to discuss color differences. Elliott impressed: "You don't have the right to say to a person, 'I do not see you as you are. I want to see you as I would be more comfortable seeing you.' [. . .] People," she authoritatively said, "don't deny differences."

Angry Eye shows Claire changing her view in real-time, which is how Elliott saw it. "It was simply remarkable to watch Claire's reaction to the large melancious male who stood beside me as we talked about differences. His responses, as he answered my questions, caused Claire to turn her head so that the camera could not see her tearful reactions to his words."[9] Claire, Elliott said twenty years later, "was so determined, at the beginning, to see herself as the only one who had experienced any discrimination in the group."

When the exercise was done and the students returned for the formal debrief, Claire presented a warm endorsement of the eye color exercise. "Every experience you have is an opportunity to see yourself in a new way, and if you close your mind to that if you didn't learn anything from this experience, then I say, 'It sucks to be you.'"[10]

"I'm tearful and fearful and rededicated to the idea that we do learn by doing," said Elliott in 2022 after watching *Angry Eye* for the first time in years. If "every person who has power in any position" watched "what these young people went through, for a couple of hours, and what they learned as a result of the experience," she said, drastic changes could be made to disrupt discriminatory behavior.[11]

Filmmakers produced the five previous documentary films about Elliott's discrimination simulation with one eye on social justice and another looking to profit from the public's fascination with the eye color exercise. Where films like *The Eye of the Storm* and "A Class Divided" were produced for a nationally televised audience, *Blue Eyed* gave her attorney-agent, Susan Golenbock, an idea. Elliott's Blue Eyes/Brown Eyes Exercise could be turned into training videos and sold to human resources departments, the military, civic organizations, and universities for training purposes. *Angry Eye* was Golenbock's first independent adventure. Golenbock went on to launch a movie and television production and distribution company, Admire Productions, Inc., based in Pound Ridge, New York, to produce training videos and sell other resources centered around Elliott's work. Golenbock possessed more than two decades working in entertainment law, including a tenure at the Cannon Group, work in litigation at Bernstein and Obstfeld, and as a partner at Weisenfreund and Golenbock.[12] The business move ensured most royalties would stay with Golenbock and her team. Intimating in an interview years later, Elliott remained oblivious to the business aspect of her lawyer's work. Elliott received just a small portion of *Angry Eye* proceeds. Golenbock's company would eventually purchase rights to sell *The Eye of the Storm*, "A Class Divided," and *Blue Eyed* from ABC, PBS, and Denkmal Films, respectively, for several hundred dollars apiece. At a time before YouTube, the opportunity to sell training and orientation videos of Elliott's exercise seemed lucrative. In Elliott's estimation, she made pennies from the enterprise.[13] Golenbock worked to build a Jane Elliott Empire, including a web-based organization, Diversity Delivers, that warehoused most of the films about the eye color exercise, including multi-disc combination packs to better serve the diversity training needs of any organization.

As it turned out, *Angry Eye* was a salable resource for college instructors, social psychologists, and civic leaders. Purdue University became one of the first colleges that hosted public screenings of *Angry Eye*. Elliott's old friends at Kansas City Harmony held community discussions on the film. She even joined the group once for an event titled "A Dinner with Jane Elliott." The television program coincidentally titled *The Passionate Eye* in Canada and Australia, known for showcasing international documentary films, including *Blue Eyed* in the late 1990s, regularly aired *Angry Eye*.[14] It was a hit at the American Film Institute's Film Festival in Los Angeles and later picked up six awards: Audience Winner at Palm Springs International Film Festival; the CINE Golden Eagle Award; the Chris Award at the Columbus Film and Video Festival; the New York Festival's Gold World Medal; the Bronze and Silver Axiem Awards; and a Silver Telly Award.

Now Golenbock's team had some momentum for another Jane Elliott training video. The next film, produced under Angry Eye Productions, LLC., was *The Stolen Eye*. It shows Elliott as the "blue-eyed bitch for the day," as she put it, in Australia, where she previously spent a significant amount of time in 1997 and 1998. The Australians proclaimed to have a "unique form of racism." Elliott challenged that notion. "Racism is racism," she said, stating off-camera that the history of settler colonialism draws striking comparisons to the treatment of indigenous persons in North America. "I'm not here to criticize Australia. I am here to do an exercise in discrimination based on eye color so that people will understand more about the racism that is in their society."[15]

All adults this time, the *Stolen Eye* cohort had an inkling of what they were getting into when signing up for the experience. Many were insinuated to have witnessed Elliott's celebrity a few years earlier. The name of the film, *Stolen Eye*, is a deeply rooted reference to the practice of stealing Aboriginal children from their families. Authorities had estimated that the government took about 100,000 children nationwide between 1943 and 1972. Those children were given to welfare workers and missionaries. The children were then placed into the homes of white parents. Australia's child separation program aimed to Christianize and Westernize the Aboriginals, eventually discouraging girls from marrying Aboriginal men.[16]

One brown-eyed female participant in *Stolen Eye* was a child survivor once taken from her parents. About halfway into the film, the woman reveals she was thirty when she finally discovered her biological mother. "I am a stolen generation, and I work with stolen generations trying to get an apology from this nation for what happened to us," she said. It was a moving moment that had many blue-eyed participants in tears. *Stolen Eye* juxtaposes her testimony with the voluntary departure of two white, blue-eyed men who couldn't endure Elliott's browbeating. Their choice to leave the workshop enabled Elliott to discuss the three separate and distinct personalities that surface every time she does the exercise. Drawing on the work of psychologists Robert Davidson and Alvyn Freed, Elliott describes the child ego-state, adult ego-state, and parent ego-state. She said the exercise results in the intersection of all three personalities, exposing transactional exchanges of emotions resulting from a failure to understand how contrasting views of the world generate conflict. Elliott explained that those who behave the ugliest in her workshops sink right into the child's ego state, a personality distorted and suppressed by the actions of the parental figure. In the workshop, Elliott exists as the parent. The child's ego surfaces when Elliott forces the blue eyes to give up more freedom than anticipated.[17]

By design, the exercise positions the brown eyes into the adult ego state, responsible for providing reasons for why Elliott is treating the blue eyes in a discriminatory way. As previously stated, Elliott, the workshop leader, reflects the parent ego state. Her sole duty is to force the blue eyes into fear, anger, and doubt. As the parent in the room, Elliott realizes she must remain steadfast in telling the blue eyes how to act through constant needling, or as psychologists generally call them, put-downs or "discounts" in the form of jokes and sarcasm. Elliott takes it a step further, however. Every exercise, she immediately gets to work scolding and discounting the blue eyes during registration, followed by the discomfort and uncertainty of the holding room and then the onslaught of derisive comments the moment they enter the seminar room. The blue-eyed victims slip into a suppression state when segregated into a non-brown section. "You put them in such a situation where they can't be in their parent ego state," Elliott explains to those who had to be eye color exercise facilitators.[18] Victims of this simulation adjust their behavior to Elliott's antics.

The exercise opens the door for discourse on how the three ego states intersect with ongoing discriminatory behavior. In the debrief, Elliott argues that children repeat their parents' behavior. It is common, she argues, to see recreations of the same pattern of behavior across generations that harms people from historically marginalized groups.

While valuable for its lessons, *Stolen Eye* received less media attention generated by every other training video. Once completed, SBS chose not to nominate *Stolen Eye* for national or international awards.

Australia was a country like no other for Elliott. Indeed, it was among the few locations she chose to tour after fulfilling her contractual obligations.

* * *

After returning to Iowa, Elliott searched for that homely feeling she once enjoyed over thirty years ago. There were moments when people across the

Hawkeye State found her anti-racism work paramount for race relations. On August 25, the Iowa Commission on the Status of Women awarded Elliott the Christine Wilson Medal for Equality and Justice. The medal, named for the commission's first chair, has been given annually since 1982 to an individual serving the cause of equality and justice.[19] Not taking the distinction lightly, she realized irony came with the honor. Many years later, she spoke profoundly about that irony:

> Every Black woman in Iowa knows more than I do about racism. And every Black woman in Iowa has received worse treatment for a lifetime that I have received, like [nasty editorials from critics]. I can throw them in the trash or wrap up my garbage in them. But when you are a Black woman, and you have been saying these things quietly for 50 years, and all you get from it is you lose your job, or your son loses his life, or you are shown the worst kinds of places to live in if you want to move, or if the laws are written against you and your very presence in this country, and books are written about how awful it is that "we" have to "deal" with you—to call me "one of Iowa's amazing women" is to discount all of the really amazing women in Iowa who are no melanemic. And I appreciate them saying, Yes, she's an amazing woman."
> But, if it's amazing to discuss racism in a way that says it's wrong, that should not be amazing. That should be what we are all doing. That should simply be an everyday experience for melanic women in Iowa [. . .] to say, "Let's get rid of racism."

When pressed on her enduring anti-racism work that generated a torrent of criticism as something that should be acknowledged, she retorted, "But I can walk away from that. [. . .] I can choose to be or not to be exposed to that nonsense. But no woman of color in the state of Iowa can choose to be or not to be exposed to that. It is part of her life. [. . .] so to call me an amazing woman is totally ridiculous."[20]

* * *

As was the norm since *The Eye of the Storm* quite literally took the world by storm in 1970, well-meaning teachers at every level of education hoping to utilize the discrimination role-play exploited Elliott's relentless drive. The Martin Luther King Jr. Day holiday in 2004 was especially peppered with media coverage exposing teacher attempts to copy the Blue Eyes/Brown Eyes Exercise. Some attempts found parental praise. Others received ridicule. Each story highly questioned teacher ethics.

The first story broke at Welby Elementary School in South Jordan, Utah, on January 22. A veteran teacher, Colleen Shewell, deliberately tailored her classroom discrimination exercise by dividing her second-grade pupils by hair color the day after the King Holiday. Unlike hair-color exercises that seemingly placed blondes at the bottom of the hierarchy, Shewell, a twenty-six-year teacher who identified as half-Japanese, granted privileges to those with blond hair, whom she labeled "white kids," and students with non-blond hair as "black kids." Most Welby parents with children in the class described the experience as "brilliant," reported Mike Cronin of the *Salt Lake Tribune*. Though absent of African Americans, Hispanic students were in Shewell's classroom. "I thought it was great," said Thomissa Nielsen, a parent of five children, one of whom was a black-haired boy in Shewell's class. "My son came home, and he was extremely passionate. He fully grasped the concept. It was a conversation topic the entire night." Shewell also received praise and support from her superiors, including Assistant Principal Brent Shaw and Executive Director of the Jordan School District's west-central area, Kerrie Naylor.[21]

Not everyone in South Jordan felt the same about the simulation. Community leaders cautioned Shewell and the school district's administrative team. Richard Gomez, the educational equity coordinator for the state's education department, said, "You have to first get the permission of the school and parents and then have enough time to do debriefing." To provide experienced advice, Jeanetta Williams, president of the Salt Lake City chapter of the NAACP and a Jane Elliott Blue Eyes/Brown Eyes trainee, offered a bit dated tip for Jane Elliott's standards. Williams warned that practitioners of the exercise had to "show the point" of discrimination "by doing it both ways, so each group experiences the negative feelings felt."[22] Elliott, by 2004, was advising practitioners to put blue-eyed persons at the bottom of the caste, thus ensuring that only white people experience discrimination. She also suggested that the exercise be done in one sitting with a thorough debrief to end the simulation.

Indeed, a thorough debrief was the prime focus at Pittsville Elementary School in Wisconsin that winter. To mark its Martin Luther King Day commemorative lessons, second-grade teacher Jeannie Pavlik, known for ingenuity and participatory pedagogy, divided her seven and eight-year-old students by gender and hair color. It was a method that created a confusing hierarchy of privileges. Pavlik said it resembled the systemic nature of colorism and sexism in the United States. The teacher awarded the boys individual attention. Blondes of any gender, meanwhile, were barred from using the classroom water fountain and were restricted to the hallway restroom. Non-blondes could use the classroom facility. "I want prejudice to not make sense," said Pavlik. Her lesson was well-received by at least the editorial board for the local *Marshfield News-Herald*. "If prejudice, bias, and discrimination don't add up to third graders," the board wrote, "then why are they so prevalent today in central Wisconsin and across America? [. . .] The purveyors of hateful words and thoughts—intentional and unintended—are everywhere. And those are just the people who put it in print." The board offered a final complimentary remark: "A lot of people ought to be spending a day in Jeannie Pavlik's class at Pittsville Elementary School because they sure missed something important the last time around."[23]

Things grew unpleasant at the opposite end of the country. Kindergarten, first, and second-grade teachers at Pine View Elementary School in Land O'Lakes, Florida's Pasco County School District, customized their version of the discrimination role-play. The teachers divided students by the color of a dot they planned to distribute at the start of the school day. The exercise, however, never occurred once a parent of a kindergartener complained to Pine View's principal, Monica Joiner, that the lesson was "teaching children separation and racism." While Principal Joiner suspended the activity before it materialized, she defended her staff as believing "they could help the children understand in the smallest way the unfair times people had lived in."[24]

Just ten of the 601 students at Pine View were African American. According to the teachers, the dot exercise was an idea of a student seeking a teaching degree from the University of South Florida. Some Pine View staff cosigning the lesson also experienced the exercise a year earlier when attending one of Jane Elliott's Blue Eyes/Brown Eyes Exercise workshops at Saint Leo University, a private liberal arts college located a few miles north of Land O'Lakes.[25]

Halfway across the country, an English teacher at Peak-to-Peak Charter School in Lafayette, Colorado, tried incorporating a Discrimination Day exercise into a ninth-grade English literature class's study of *Othello* by making students wear blue cards on a string as a badge of disgrace. One Peak-to-Peak parent said her son "was required to smile ingratiatingly, bow his head and beg people to tie his shoes for him."[26] The superior group wore yellow cards. With help from a school counselor, that teacher told the discriminated group they would receive Fs for their work and have failing grades placed on their final transcript. There was no debrief at the end of class.

Such examples show that there is no mastery without apprenticeship. Though inclinations to help create a harmonious future were understood by most onlookers, cases like Pine View and Peak-to-Peak demonstrate the need for professional learning on integrating lessons on empathy into the curriculum.

The execution was bad, and Jane Elliott became the scapegoat for denouncing all lessons that included themes of diversity and inclusion in the school system. After the uproar at Peak-to-Peak Charter, Linda Seebach, an opinion columnist for the *Rocky Mountain News* in Denver, called Elliott's training "cruel to kids" in a nationally syndicated column. She said Elliott was a "disgrace" and suggested that all forms of diversity training should abruptly stop.[27]

Elliott, who had no clue that educators she had never spoken with conducted poorly administered simulations, would have something to say to the likes of Seebach and other pundits. Her work was primarily with adult learners—corporate and community leaders—whom she hoped would speak to young children about cultural differences as something to be valued. People of color "can't opt out of discrimination," she said to a group of students and teachers at Winchester Thurston School. The community at the independent, coeducational preparatory school, located in Pittsburgh, Pennsylvania, hosted Elliott to learn more about the impact of intersectional discrimination. The school's administrators shared concerned over controversial headlines surfacing about a small number of schools across the country over misinformed, though well-meaning educational practitioners doing more harm than good with its diversity programming. Bluntly, Elliott said discrimination is "what we teach in America. The whiter you are, the brighter you are. If you're black, get back."[28] Her parting advice: first, educators should incorporate the voices and stories of people of color in coursework. Second, teachers must receive proper training to establish the right degree of rapport with students and parents to design and execute lesson plans that provide students with a color-conscious lens that values diversity and works toward inclusion worldwide. She added that no person, teacher, or C-Suite leader should administer any version of the discrimination exercise without becoming appropriately certified.

* * *

Jane Elliott was back on the circuit conducting the eye color exercise at Exxon, AT&T, and the U.S. military; she also gave speeches across the United States when accolades came intermittently.[29] In the fall of 2005, the McGraw-Hill Foundation announced its thirty most consequential educators. Having spent almost four decades as a prominent voice on anti-racism and student services for people with dyslexia, the publishing house named Elliott one of its most important figures who influenced education. The list includes not just Elliott's hero, John Dewey, but also Benjamin Bloom, Jean Piaget, Kenneth Clark, Ivan Illich, Horace Mann, Mary McLeod Bethune, W.E.B. Du Bois, Booker

T. Washington, Plato, Aristotle, Confucius, and Paulo Freire.[30] That same year, University of Iowa journalism professor Stephen Bloom, who first met Elliott in 2003 for a potential book, composed an online exposé for *Smithsonian Magazine* titled "Lesson of a Lifetime." A year later, at seventy-two, the *Des Moines Register* honored Elliott as a "voice against racial discrimination" during Women's History Month.[31] In 2007, media pundits began referencing the "godmother of diversity training." Indeed, diversity consultants, including the District of Columbia-based National MultiCultural Institute and the Business Training Media, Inc. in Encino, California, looked to Elliott's training videos as a vital resource for proposing services to potential clients.

Several right-wing pundits remained unconvinced that Elliott's type of diversity training was ethical. They even doubted diversity training works at all, typically besmirching facilitators as grifters preying on an intersection of converging topics: global competitiveness, generation gaps, and cultural inclusion in schools, federal departments, the military, and the corporate world. As Elliott's popularity rose in these arenas in the mid-2000s, she became the punching bag for all diversity training-related initiatives. Her lectures on college campuses, training videos, and direct work with a multitude of adult professionals, coupled with an online presence was something not imagined when she left the classroom to start a career as a diversity trainer in 1985. Despite the changes in technology and Elliott's increasing popularity as a diversity trainer, the criticism against her grew more intense. Writing for *Front Page Magazine*, policy analyst Carl Horowitz called Elliott the country's "long-reigning Dominatrix of Diversity" and a "white Louis Farrakhan." He posited that the eye color exercise creates "divisions [and] resentment." Perhaps more damning, he said her approach causes the "increase in judgments based on race."[32] Other intellectuals, like University of Pennsylvania professor of history Alan Charles Kors, writing in *Reason*, an online publication serving academics, called Elliott "the Torquemada of thought reform."[33] The jab referenced Tomás de Torquemada, the first grand inquisitor of the Spanish Inquisition. These disparagers labeled Jane Elliott and her disciples instruments of an extreme left-wing indoctrination enterprise resembling Mao Zedong's cultural revolution.

A few months later, it was 2008. After Black History Month lectures at Spokane Community College, Gonzaga University, and other venues closer to her Sun City home along the West Coast, Elliott returned to Iowa in late March, a week ahead of the fortieth anniversary of the very first Discrimination Day exercise. On the evening of March 27, she addressed a crowd at Iowa State University in Ames. Her three-hour session included a screening of *The Eye of the*

Storm. After an interactive presentation that seemingly pleased event organizers, it was apparent that not everyone was happy to have her in town. The local reporter working on the story about the landmark commemoration, Lisa Rossi, admitted difficulty finding people willing to talk about Elliott or the exercise. She wrote, "Not everybody welcomes her back to Iowa [and] Many residents in her hometown hung up the phone this week at the mention of Elliott's name."[34] It was clear that diversity training detractors and Jane Elliott critics had taken a toll. In fact, at this moment, the *Washington Post* released a review of thirty-one years' worth of data from 830 midsized to large. U.S. workplaces showed that "mandatory" diversity training was followed by drops in the number of women and Black men in management positions by almost 8 percent and 12 percent, respectively. The mandatory diversity training reflected in the *Post* survey did not include Jane Elliott's model, but still, anything diversity training-related made her guilty by association.

Less than three months later, on June 15, Elliott's mother, Margaret "Gie" Jennison, died at age ninety-six while residing at the Riceville Family Care Facility. Her relationship with Gie was so strained that despite living a few miles away at her summertime home Osage, she was absent from her mother's side during those final days. She even refused to attend the memorial service at Riceville's Welcome Center and Immaculate Conception Catholic Church funeral.[35]

Elliott's resolve at this time was the presidential election of Barack Obama. While she did not campaign for the Illinois Senator, the election of the United States' first Black president was prescient. Like much of the country, Elliott felt Obama stood an excellent chance of defeating John McCain following the economic downturn at the end of the Bush administration. However, the reality that white supremacist groups saw a "dramatic" increase in interest among people on the far right was distressing. Moreover, reports that authorities in Tennessee arrested potential assassins unnerved campaign supporters. Once Obama was duly elected on November 4, Elliott expressed deep concern about obstructionists: "Whatever a black person does," she said of his election, "he has to do twice as good as a white person to be thought of as half as good." A month into his term, she commented, Obama "mustn't look angry because we have demonized Black men. He knows exactly how to get accepted. He's a bargainer [. . .] and that's okay if that's what it takes to get white people to listen."[36] He was riding a 64 percent approval rating at his inauguration.

The hope that Obama would unite the country was a fantasy by Elliott's estimation. A public opinion poll released after his first six months in office proved her correct. By the fall, the president's approval rating dropped below 50 percent. Republicans who once stood with Obama at a rate of 46 percent when sworn in now approve of his job at 16 percent.[37] Anti-Obama avidity reared its head on September 9, 2009, at a joint session of Congress just eight months into his presidency when Rep. Joe Wilson (R-SC) shouted, "You lie!" in the middle of remarks about healthcare. Days later, former President Jimmy Carter speculated that racial animus was behind Wilson's outburst: the South Carolina lawmaker was a member of the Sons of the Confederate Veterans and a proven advocate of keeping the Confederate battle flag at state capitol grounds in Charleston. Was it right for Carter, and by proxy, Jane Elliott, to label Representative Wilson a racist? The context of the moment explains such allegations. Studies conducted by political scientists during Obama's first term revealed "Obama" was a "prevalent [keyword] term in racially charged searches" and predicted that—owing to racial animus—the incumbent was guaranteed to lose "three to 5 percentage points of the popular vote" in the next presidential election.[38]

An undercurrent intensifying racial animus in Obama's job as President of the United States was the emerging birther movement pushed by reality tv star Donald Trump. Using questions over Obama's Hawaiian birth certificate, Trump eyed up a future presidential run. He buoyed allegations about Obama's real citizenship. When Republican leadership hesitated over whether to silence Trump's birther conspiracy, Elliott lost all patience.

At this instant, the demand for Elliott as a lecturer and diversity facilitator increased after instances of racist email messages about President Obama and First Lady Michelle drew national attention.[39] It was one thing if racist dog whistles emanated from the political arena since Elliott could only lambaste Trump and elected officials stoking racial antipathy. Still, for managers in the corporate world boxed into legal corners to avoid discrimination lawsuits, Elliott had the opportunity to reach the working class. While newly-formed diversity-related LLCs and management companies profited most during this time, Jane Elliott's name lingered as the one who provided a ground-breaking, experiential learning experience that well-intentioned corporate committee leaders could not find anywhere else.

CHAPTER 22

EYE ON THE PRIZE

"You can't cure stupid, but you can change ignorance."
—JANE ELLIOTT, CORWITH-WESLEY-LUVERNE HIGH SCHOOL, 2013

Just as Elliott toured the country speaking about growing racist and xenophobic rhetoric since Obama's election, Great Britain became engulfed in a political firestorm over the election of Nick Griffin, leader of the perceived anti-Semitic and racist British National Party. In October 2009, the BBC invited Griffin onto its political panelist show *Question Time*. While facing a torrent of opposition on the show, Griffin's appearance amounted to free widespread exposure for the British National Party. After the *Question Time* appearance, the Party proclaimed that it picked up 3,000 new members within a few days.[1] Griffin and his party's introduction into the mainstream warranted a response from Diane Abbott, the first Black woman elected to the British Parliament and then-Labour representative of more than 70,000 people in Hackney North and Stoke Newington. In *The Independent*, Abbott cautioned that Far-Right views buoyed by a worsening recession generated "classic conditions" for "the rise of a Fascist Party."[2] She said Griffin and the British National Party amounted to the second coming of the Nazis.

Abbott's warning sounded all too similar to the tone advanced across the American landscape by Jane Elliott. As a result, lawyer and apparent head of marketing Jane-Elliott, Susan Golenbock arranged for Elliott to tour through the United Kingdom and Ireland in 2009, conducting the Blue Eyes/Brown Eyes Exercise. The trip's capstone was the chance to put British citizens through the exercise inside a brick warehouse enclosed by a barbed-wire fence resembling a Nazi concentration camp in London for a British television special.

This new film, *The Event: How Racist Are You?* aired October 29, 2009, on Britain's Channel 4. All thirty participants were volunteers, but as the show's narrator revealed at the film's onset, they had no idea they were walking into a simulation of an apartheid state. Elliott's paradigm remained the same. Blue-eyed participants were mistreated while registering, especially one man with an eyebrow piercing who made the mistake of smirking at Elliott while calling her "so masterful." His remark antagonized Elliott to the point that she mouthed the F-bomb: "Keep your fucking mouth shut," she insisted. The man with the eyebrow-piercing and his blue-eyed colleagues then spent almost two hours in the holding room. When allowed to enter the seminar room, the first thing they saw were large banners proclaiming, "Go Home, Bluey!", "Only Brown Eyes Need Apply," and "Blue-Eyed People and Dogs, Keep Out!"

Elliott was in her forty-first year facilitating the discrimination simulation. Produced for a local audience, *How Racist Are You?* is the most challenging and perhaps cringe-worthy of her assignments captured on film. The program intermittently shows clips of Elliott at age thirty-four guiding her third-grade Riceville Elementary students through the experience. This juxtaposition exposed Elliott's transition—though questionably instigating children to turn on one another in the Riceville school, she appeared likable and winsome in *The Eye of the Storm.* Thinking back to that moment, even critics from ultra-conservative states had described Elliott as "touching and beautiful; [. . .] a teacher those kids in Riceville, Iowa, are lucky to have."[3] But after standing in fire for four long decades, she looked worn, a countenance caused by familial divides and media caviling. She was dug in, resentful of dealing with adults who thought more of themselves than of the wellbeing of other people.

To aid in the film's production, Elliott agreed to have two psychologists observe the exercise in real-time via livestream to offer viewers expert commentary about the blunt refusal of blue-eyed participants to acknowledge racism was still a problem in their society. The addition of psychologists was a new aspect of special televised programs of eye color simulation. For this program, it was needed. The blue eyes were quite rebellious to what she was trying to orchestrate. No matter the experiences shared by the brown-eyed people of color in the room, a few blue eyes refused to concede that they were part of the problem. One psychologist explained: "Blue-eyed people are defending the system," proclaiming that everyone has been a victim of discrimination.[4]

While Elliott walked away from the session disappointed in her ability to reach the blue eyes, pundits in Britain were complimentary of her efforts. "Maybe Elliott is right," wrote television critic Robert Epstein. After weighing race relations in the United Kingdom and beyond, Epstein conceded that not much has changed regarding interpersonal relationships. He said, "We do, as a society, need to be bullied out of our complacency—even if [Jane Elliott's] exercise does get up the noses of those of us who have moved beyond laughing at racist jokes."[5]

* * *

The tug-of-war between Conservatives and Progressives over the relevancy of teaching inclusion at schools and workplaces persisted into the 2010s. Between 2009 and 2010, several academic studies published by researchers at Yale University, the University of South Australia, and Columbia University, along with a report issued by sociologists studying more than 800 companies spanning thirty years, showed "mandatory" diversity training programs made "little difference" in interpersonal relations despite billions of dollars spent by the majority of the Fortune 500 companies.[6] The problem, Elliott contended, was in the way diversity trainers—and well-intentioned school teachers—operated in her wake. Training styles varied in content, duration, execution, strategy, curriculum, and philosophy.[7] Elliott hadn't envisioned that her foray into what was initially called pluralism training at Mountain Bell in 1985 would lead to a nationwide movement of multicultural diversity training. Her mistake, concededly, was that she was not involved in the national discourse on how facilitators should conduct training.

Be that as it may, Elliott had the stomach to fight her detractors while also fighting for the multicultural democracy promised to all citizens in the nation's founding documents. The next decade would be defined by her effort to both rewrite the language used to talk about racism and to tutor headstrong eye-color facilitators to carry on her role-play training. As it soon moved into its fiftieth year of performance, the exercise would be followed with Elliott's suggestions for how to institutionalize culturally inclusive practices and policy in schools and workplaces. The two ideas—anti-racist language and experiential antiracist simulations—were commensurate objectives.

There was no formal business plan other than building the One Race website at janeelliott.com. Simultaneously, her lawyer Susan Golenbock sold her training videos through Diversity Delivers/Admire Productions at diversitydelivers.org.[8] Elliott would also wait for universities, schools, corporations, or civic groups to call with a speaking request. Whenever the opportunity arrived, she followed an effective, time-honored formula by asking whites in the audience to stand if they would like to be treated the way Black people are treated today. Like clockwork, everyone always remained seated. Each time she'd say, "You just admitted you know racism is happening."[9] She'd use the moment to get people to think critically about social norms. "Anybody here who considers themselves a member of the white race, stand up." Several would stand. "Anybody here who considers themselves a member of the black race, stand up." More would stand. "Stand up if you consider yourself part of the brown race," she commanded. More stood. Elliott habitually went on. "Stand if you consider yourself part of the yellow race. Stand if you consider yourself part of the red race." Elliott would reach a point when everyone in the auditorium, classroom, or convention hall was standing. Then, after studying the room, she'd say: "Now, everyone who considers themselves part of the human race, sit down." In concert, the people would sit.[10]

She maintained that race is a construct that "came out of France in 1580" to assign citizenship rights and other privileges to skin-color categories. Where skin color is concerned, color categories as separate races are "a misnomer," Elliott regularly said.[11] "There are not four or five different races," she told audiences nationwide. "There is only one race on the face of the Earth, and we are all members of that race: the human race." She said, race "is a lie perpetuated so some of us can see ourselves as superior to others. You've got to stop believing it, and you have got to stop living it."[12]

Elliott has assumed a responsibility that many others see as an impossible task. Even so, she would argue that racialized language—Black, brown, red, yellow, and white—is at the core of sustained interpersonal racial divisions. Now able to reference DNA studies, everyone in the human race, she positioned, is a "shade of brown." Her advocacy can be relentless, overwrought with colloquialism, but she introduced a marvelously distinct vernacular for her following. "We have to stop using the words of the 13th and 14th centuries to deal with problems of the 21st century," she contended. Elliott spoke explicitly, in her view, about how destructive separating people by racial categories is for national unity. She has maintained for decades that people should be identified by one of the human body's most complex molecules: melanin. Melanin is the dark-colored pigment found in skin, hair, and the iris of the eye responsible for coloring those features.

Humans, she stated, are just varying shades of brown. She regularly asked audiences: why are people called white and Black? By 2010, her hair had turned white. She wore a white sweatshirt periodically with a quote she credited to Nathan Rutstein: "Prejudice is an emotional commitment to ignorance." Sometimes, she walked on stage wearing a white sweatshirt with the phrase, "God created one race: the human race. Human beings created racism," to which she credited herself. She would say, "My hair and sweatshirt are white. My skin is not."

Therefore, those people ascribed as "white," or those with pale or fine peach-colored skin, are "melanemic," she explained, for having bodies that lack enough melanin for protection from the damaging rays of the sun—"just as anemic describes those who don't have enough iron in their blood to keep them healthy."

According to her new vernacular, those with varying shades of brown skin, or whom society typically labels "brown," "red," "yellow," or "people of color," should be ascribed as "melanacious." Melanacious, she said, describes those with enough melanin in their skin for partial protection from the sun's rays. She said, "It makes sense just as a place that is greater than the average is referred to as 'spacious.'" She said that most people on earth are melanacious, whereas melanemic individuals comprise less than 20 percent of the world's population.

Additionally, Elliott claimed there are "melanotic" people. Melanotic describes those whose skin has a great deal of melanin and is "almost black."

Finally, she wanted anyone identifying as mixed-race to follow the descriptor "mosaic." Mosaic, she claimed, "is an art form that is new, unique, and made of many different elements. It, for me, describes those who are the result of a combination of several different colors and or cultural groups." For someone to call themselves mixed-race or someone else mixed-race, she said, "is to indicate either that the one using the term is ignorant or that the person you are describing is from another planet."

> Obviously, the terms "melanemic" and "melanacious" are not in the dictionary; I made them up in order to find words that are accurate rather than inaccurate when describing the colors of human skin. Are they harder to say and remember than "black" and "white"? Of course, they are. But there is no negative connotation in any of these [. . .] words unless you are still determined to use the words from the 14th and 15th centuries to describe people in the 21st century.[13]

This simple logic—that all people are more similar than they are different—meant she was willing to challenge not just her conservative critics but progressive allies and racially-proud intellectuals of color that aligned with her on causes of social justice. Speaking alongside Angela Davis at the University of Houston several years later provided her a large and public platform to explain her One Race creed: "That means that every one of us is a thirtieth to fiftieth cousin to every other person in this room."[14] This message seemingly struck a chord with the political activist sitting to her right. An advocate for prison reform and racial justice since before the first eye color exercise in 1968, Davis immediately liked Elliott. According to Elliott, Davis suggested the two go on tour together to address audiences on race and racism.[15]

The degree of criticism Jane Elliott has received only intensified over the five decades she facilitated the Blue Eyes/Brown Eyes Exercise. With its increasing number of social media outlets in the 2010s, the Internet made it easier for condemnation to reach the populace. This is despite the occasional letter to the editor supporting Elliott while cosigning the discrimination simulation like the one written by an Ogden, Iowa resident to the *Des Moines Register* in 2011 proclaiming the state's politicians were growing more culturally intolerant. "Perhaps [Elliott's] elementary students could teach some Iowans about discrimination and how no good comes from it," wrote Judy Paulson.[16]

Jane Elliott never ceased to debate this idea in her mind. Speaking in 2022 about a turn in American society to ban books focusing on race and sexuality, those of which were primarily written by melanacious and melanotic authors, she made a keen observation. "[A]s I return to those 'bad old days,' it seems to me that I am being berated for doing for two days, for a good reason, the things that [racists] are still doing," as she referenced the years conducting the exercise with her elementary and middle schoolers in the 1960s and 1970s. At eighty-eight years old, she called book bans and anti-critical race theory legislative maneuvers "disgusting." Comparing how she and her children were treated in Riceville five decades earlier to how the voices of people of color and their allies were silenced for trying to build an inclusive society in the early 2020s, Elliott said those lawmakers are dealing with their own "inadequacy." She said, "their determination to excoriate anyone who truly tries to lead students out of ignorance" is engaging in genuine efforts at "indoctrination instead of real education."[17]

As always, she looked back on her life to make sense of the current state of race relations. Even in the middle of Obama's two terms, the anatomy of prejudice remained the same. Elliott told a group of students and faculty at northern Iowa's Corwith-Wesley-LuVerne High School in May 2013 that the problem was not the differences between people of color and those identifying as white. The problem is society's small-minded, blinkered view reserved by self-interests that keep one another in a perpetual state of ignorance. Rather than honest education about the history and the racialized divisions American policymakers have maintained long into the twenty-first century, the school board approved curricula conditions students "of the racist variety. [. . .] 180 days of the year, eight hours a day."[18]

She surveyed the auditorium's surroundings. Several heads nodded in agreement, and others sneered in disapproval. Elliott thought about her monolithic upbringing in Riceville and understood where her life could have been if she hadn't opened windows into the lived experiences of others. She ruminated over how the very first Discrimination Day exercise impacted her students and felt encouraged that most of those children gave notice that racism develops casually and, after that, lingers primarily out of interpersonal seclusion. She wondered, however, if she was running out of time to inspire educators. Elliott pulled the microphone closer and stared intently at the teachers standing along the walls in ominous positions overtop the students.

"You can't cure stupid, but you can change ignorance."[19]

CONCLUSION

"IF YOU WANT TO BE LOVED, DON'T DO THIS."

"Racism is not the biggest problem in the U.S.; ignorance is, and while you were born ignorant, you were not born a racist. That is a learned response. Unlearn it."

—JANE ELLIOTT IN *MS. MAGAZINE*, OCTOBER 2021

Nothing could stop Jane Elliott from traveling the country and giving her "Anatomy of Prejudice" speech. While she seldom conducted the Blue Eyes/Brown Eyes Exercise at this moment of her career, Elliott took solace in having trained a few dozen facilitators in the skills to put adults through the simulation. There was a spirit of celebration in her Osage home in the spring of 2013. Though race relations were still lamentable, she was encouraged by many workplaces to invest in efforts to value diversity and inclusion through initiatives that attract and retain the best workers, no matter cultural differences, and to appeal to a diversifying consumer or client base. Elliott was sometimes too exhausted to respond to requests for her consulting services. Still, she was pleased corporate CEOs, and educators found value in the diversity training movement she started forty-five years earlier. One business school dean at the University of Maryland, Joyce E.A. Russell, credited Elliott for paving the way for workforce inclusionary practices. Many top companies were holding more than diversity workshops. Chief executives encouraged employee efforts to form affinity groups and task force teams to network and ensure every worker felt like a valued workforce member.[1]

Her work still prevailed abroad, especially in German-speaking countries where Şeydâ Buurman-Kutsal of Stichting Magenta had built a team of Blue

Eyes/Brown Eyes facilitators. Buurman-Kutsal had launched her own diversity training company that she conveniently named Şeydâ. Now on her team were Sabine Sommer and Jürgen Schlicher of Germany, and Marc Ruckebier, the formerly frightened eighteen-year-old German high school student who found purpose when first watching *Blue Eyed* seventeen years earlier. In 2013, Şeydâ and Marc traveled to Iowa to visit Elliott. Since then, Şeydâ's team has put more than 8,000 people through the exercise. They even brought Elliott back to Amsterdam to put police officers through the exercise. While in Europe, Elliott conducted a workshop in Berlin and hosted a Blue Eyes/Brown Eyes train-the-trainer program in Rotterdam.

Working alongside Elliott made Şeydâ a force in Europe. In 2017, a Netherlands documentary crew produced a film about the eye color exercise led by Şeydâ and her team inside a factory near Schiphol Airport. The film aired on Netherlands Public Broadcasting (BNN) and looked similar to Elliott's 2009 London-based BBC special *How Racist Are You?* The exercise occurred in an empty factory building where thirty unknowing people were divided by eye color. The blue eyes received green collars and were locked in a "dreary" holding room as Şeydâ coached the brown eyes on their superiority. Two psychologists sat in an inconspicuous location and made observations about participant behaviors. Inside the seminar room, Şeydâ strung offensive signs from the ceiling and arranged segregated seating. Like Elliott so often did, Şeydâ made a blue-eyed blond woman cry and quit the exercise before one of the staffers convinced her to return. The incident resurfaced during the post-exercise debrief, enabling the cohort to discuss group synchrony and interrogate societal power and privilege. The broadcast shows most participants walking away, claiming that Şeydâ's exercise had changed them.

Like Elliott, Şeydâ has had her experiences dealing with hardship due to her commitment to putting people through the exercise. Images of knives and death threats arrived via fax to her home from anonymous critics of her work. Şeydâ's husband didn't support her choice to facilitate the exercise, leading to a divorce. Despite moments of having to call in heavy security, she has continued to do the exercise because "I see no better way to explain how racism works, how exclusion works," she said. "It's something you never forget." The momentary trauma, she posits, is "a good thing."[2]

When visiting Osage in 2013, Elliott said something to Şeydâ that has always resonated, and it continues to steady her resolve: "If you want to be loved, don't do this."

* * *

Jane Elliott's life changed on September 24, 2013, when her husband, Darald, died inside their home in Osage. His death wasn't sudden; Darald had battled a rare neurodegenerative disorder known as multiple systems atrophy. Although she knew the time she had with her husband of fifty-eight years was limited, Elliott was devastated. The memoriam she wrote for the local newspaper spoke of private moments enjoyed by the couple. "He loved [. . .] slow dancing with his wife, sitting in 'dirty old airports' and watching the people go by," she revealed in the obituary. Darald had once gifted Elliott two hanging swing chairs that can be seen in *Blue Eyed*. He fashioned them on the side deck porch of their Osage home, where the two jointly made many important life decisions. "[S]winging on the porch, [. . .] watching his kids and grandkids come and grow and go" were among his most cherished pastimes, she wrote.[3]

Adjacent to the Elliott home north of Highway 9 on Primrose Avenue is a church building originally constructed in 1890 and once utilized as the Burr Oak Free Baptist Church until 1945. After World War II, Leo Township purchased the building and used it as a community center accommodating a rural school and grain bin. The community also used it as a caucus and voting center and for 4-H club events.[4] The Mitchell County Historical Society assumed ownership after community leader Ed Smolik purchased the church and the acre of land it rests on in the 1960s. Finally, in 2004, more than a decade before Darald passed, the Elliotts made the historical society an offer. Infested with woodchucks and condemned wooding, Jane and Darald hired a contractor to turn it into a guest house, fitted with a loft on the west end of the building and an enclosed porch on the opposite. Owing to their experience as owners of the Jennison Inn, where they held many marital ceremonies and receptions, the Elliotts added a kitchen, restroom, and balcony bridal suite with a large bi-fold door and a view to look down into the chapel area for weddings.[5] Shaded by trees and located along the relatively busy T48 thoroughfare of Osage, it was where Jane held Darald's funeral.

Darald's passing provided a purpose for Elliott to return to writing her autobiography. Titled *A Collar in My Pocket: Blue Eyes/Brown Eyes Exercise*, she dedicated the memoir to her late father, Lloyd Jennison, "who made me what I am," she wrote, and to Darald, which she explained, "who married me because of what I could become." She also devoted the book to her four children, Sarah, Brian, Mary, and Mark, "who love me in spite of it all." What started as a memoir in 1986, Elliott's decision to try once again to finish the project was a much-needed cathartic escape from an ailing heart.

The poignant moment of the introduction provides readers with an obvious sign of the times. Writing on December 11, 2015—the date she put the finishing touches on the manuscript—Elliott opened with the expression, "OMG!" an acronym for "Oh my God!" It became nearly ubiquitous in text messages, Internet chat rooms, and commonplace gossip circles, even though the saying had once been considered taboo in her earliest days as an educator and while growing up on the family farm. "I honestly thought that there would come a time, in my lifetime, when describing this exercise for other people to read would be unnecessary," she said in the final remarks of the memoir's introduction. "How wrong I was."[6] The passage is a peculiar insight into where Elliott's mind was at the time. While staying mainly out of the media headlines since the passing of her husband, she sometimes accepted speaking engagements at America's colleges and universities. Meanwhile, before controversy surfaced again, her trained facilitators traveled domestically and internationally to conduct the eye color exercise at corporations and schools. Elliott refused to accept royalties from anyone she taught to conduct the exercise—friendships only, she said.

At this moment in Elliott's life, she had established quite the following through the sales of her memoir, public speaking engagements, and viral social media videos. Unbeknownst to Elliott, Susan Golenbock, her entertainment attorney-agent, seemingly built a small empire out of the Blue Eyes/Brown Eyes Exercise. At the website Diversity Delivers, Golenbock sold Elliott's training videos for several hundred dollars a pop to any individual or corporation who made a request. The DVD collection included seven original commercial films (*The Eye of the Storm*, "A Class Divided," *Blue Eyed*, *The Angry Eye*, *The Stolen Eye*, *Eye Opener*, formerly *How Racist Are You?*, and *Indecently Exposed*). The Golenbock team added compilation videos: *Wide Eyed* and the *Wide Eyed Facilitator Guide*. Interested parties could also purchase packaged deals. The Government "Gold" Package included *The Eye of the Storm*, *Angry Eye*, *Blue Eyed*, and a facilitator guide. The Budget-Conscious Library Builder Silver Package came with *The Eye of the Storm*, *Wide Eyed* and the *Wide Eyed Facilitator Guide*, *Blue Eyed*, and *Angry Eye*. The Global Training Package included all three international films—*Stolen Eye*, *Indecently Exposed*, and *Eye Opener*.[7] According to Elliott, she received very little, if any, remittance from Golenbock's business adventure.

The wedge between Elliott and Golenbock expanded further when Mary Elliott, Jane's daughter, sold One Race apparel and *A Collar In My Pocket* books for the Elliott estate through the One Race website.[8] Profits generated through Elliott's website remained with Elliott, causing Diversity Delivers representatives to question why the Golenbock team wasn't receiving any of the profits. Control over Blue Eyes/Brown Eyes' marketability produced a volatile situation between Elliott and Golenbock that resulted in legal action left unresolved at the time of this book's publication.[9]

During the early stages of the 2016 Democratic presidential primary, former Secretary of State Hillary Clinton faced a torrent of criticism from the burgeoning campaign of Vermont Senator Bernie Sanders. At a Sanders rally held at Morehouse College in Atlanta, rapper Killer Mike (also known as Michael Render) invoked Jane Elliott when trying to discredit the secretary's cachet of presidential qualifications. Elliott remembers meeting Render for the first time when speaking at St. Louis in late 2015. Render had attended her "Anatomy of Prejudice" lecture in the city. He introduced himself after she finished. They remained in touch during the early stages of the presidential election since both held profound reservations about the growing popularity of reality television celebrity, real-estate mogul, and Obama birther conspiracy theorist Donald Trump. Elliott was adamantly opposed to Trump's candidacy "the minute I heard that he was running," she said. His earliest speeches were "reminiscent of the kinds of speeches that Adolf Hitler gave," she once proclaimed.[10] To that end, she believed Sanders was the best candidate to win the general election, not just because she felt many across the United States would refuse to vote for a woman, but because Clinton once worked in the Obama administration. It was apparent that Trump and the Republican Party were set on stoking fear and resentment toward the nation's first and only African American president to turn out the vote.

When speaking to a crowd of 4,800 people, Render said the former first lady would be "slow to move on issues of racial justice." He added, "When people tell us, 'Hold on, wait awhile.' And that's what the other Democrat is telling you. 'Hold on, Black Lives Matter. Just wait awhile.' 'Hold on, young people in this country, just wait awhile.' But I talked to Jane Elliott a few weeks ago, and Jane said, 'Michael, a uterus doesn't qualify you to be president of the United States. You have to be—you have to have policy that's reflective of social justice.'"[11]

While Render operated as one of the most outspoken Sanders supporters among those in the music industry, Elliott had not come out publicly to endorse any candidate in the election. She certainly didn't invite her rapper-friend to disclose the content of their conversation either, though she didn't much care that he did. The new friendship with the rapper aside, she found her name dragged through the mud by supporters of the Clinton campaign during the Democratic primary. She had been used as a wedge in an intra-party squabble over which candidate could better appeal to the needs of historically marginalized people.

Despite Sanders' eventual defeat to Clinton, Elliott and Render grew closer as friends during the election season. While in California for Coachella that spring, Render visited Elliott and her daughter Mary's family near her summer home, which had been relocated to Menifee. Elliott also saw him in Atlanta, where he owned several barbershops. She would eventually accept invitations to attend at least two of his concerts.[12]

Through Render, Elliott eventually befriended Grammy award-winning hip hop artist T.I., whose real name is Clifford Harris. She appeared on his popular podcast *Expeditiously* to try to unite diverse populations through her One Race message. In T.I.'s single "Warzone," released in September of 2016, just two months before the presidential election, Elliott's voice narrates the track's outro. "If you white folks want to be treated the way blacks are in this society, stand. Nobody is standing here. That says very plainly that you know what's happening. You know that you don't want it for you. I want to know why you're so willing to accept it or allow it to happen to others."[13] The soundbite is taken from Elliott's Chapman University speech featured so poignantly in Bertram Verhaag's film *Blue Eyed*. T.I. would go on to call her "a brilliant, amazing, kick-ass [sic] person" who provides "brutally honest, rational, logical, intellectual [sic] insight on racism [. . .]. She is a true gem. A real-life American hero!"[14]

The 2016 election results would become the most consequential of Elliott's long life. The general election that made Trump chief executive of the United States was marked by several issues. Firstly, the leak of a lewd video of Trump speaking with *Access Hollywood's* Billy Bush about groping women. Secondly, pundit debates over whether the Republican nominee was racist, willing to appeal to racist people, or neither. Thirdly, evidence surfaced that Donald Trump Jr. accepted help from Russia to dig up dirt on the Democratic nominee. Finally, despite Clinton's three million vote margin in the popular vote, Trump emerged victorious and became the forty-fifth President of the United States. Elliott was beside herself.

Trump's refusal to distance himself from Far-Right white nationalists during his term in office made those four years among the most taxing of Elliott's life.

* * *

Not long after the August 2017 white nationalists "Unite the Right" rally in Charlottesville, Virginia, Jane Elliott participated in a lecture tour of the country. The circuit began that September once schools opened for the new semester. She accepted requests to speak at events hosted by the NAACP and Iowa and Arizona State universities. She also keynoted events at the University of Michigan with journalist Roland Martin and at the University of Houston alongside famed racial justice activist Angela Davis. Before year's end, Elliott entertained opportunities to speak with reporters from Milwaukee PBS affiliate Black Nouveau and NBC News.

"There is nothing in this country that is not impacted by racism," Elliott claimed while touring the Southwest a few days before her eighty-fourth birthday. She told a doting crowd in Phoenix that prejudice is an attitude that "can't hurt anyone." On the other hand, she cautioned, "Discrimination is a behavior, and people get killed because of it every day."[15] In such moments of reflection, the latest victim of discriminatory behavior, Heather Heyer, was on Elliott's mind. After Heather was killed by a twenty-one-year-old white nationalist who drove a car into a crowd of anti-fascist protesters in Charlottesville, Elliott predicted life would only get more difficult for outspoken critics of racism. "We could destroy it," she told NBC News that fall. "People who are racist aren't stupid; they're ignorant. And the answer to ignorance is education."

Emboldening racist ignorance was the newly elected President of the United States, Donald Trump, in her estimation. Trump, who inspired the "Unite the Right" coalition of white supremacists, sat at the head of "the most Hitlerian administration I've ever seen," she told award-winning journalist Chandra Thomas Whitfield. In NBC News' feature story, titled "Educator Jane Elliott Talks Trump, Kaepernick, and Fixing Racism," Whitfield laments the Blue Eyes/Brown Eyes Exercise as "bold" and a solution to overcoming the "myth," as Elliott puts it, that "one group of humans is superior over another based on skin color."[16]

While the large media outlets presented affirming portrayals of Jane Elliott, local newspapers covering school events offered a less-tolerable take on the eye color exercise. In Kennesaw, Georgia, Big Shanty Elementary School students had been encouraged to dress in Civil War attire for its annual Civil War Day commemoration in 2017. Ahead of the event, school officials sent a note home to parents encouraging children to come to school wearing overalls (one parent believed represented attire worn by enslaved Africans) and other "Civil War clothing." The letter home included a picture of a man dressed in Confederate uniform, claiming, "Use your resources to ensure that your costume is as accurate as possible." The controversy surfaced when word broke that a fifth-grade student dressed as a plantation owner said to a Black classmate, "You are my slave." The parent of the Black student attracted almost 70,000 views on her Facebook post about the incident. After the *Associated Press* picked up the story, education professor Sandra Schmidt at Teachers College at Columbia University told journalist Jeff Martin that role-playing having anything to do with discrimination has been problematic since Elliott's Blue Eyes/Brown Eyes Exercise in 1968. Schmidt said Elliott's exercise is the "pitfall" of classroom simulations.[17]

Few ever questioned Elliott to her face about the ethics of the eye color exercise. Though never shy to defend the exercise, she was only ever asked to explain its origin and impact on the third-grade students at Riceville Elementary. "Why eye color? Eye color and skin color are caused by the same chemical: melanin," she defended late in her life. "There's no logic in judging people by the amount of a chemical in their skin. Pigmentation should have nothing to do with how you treat another person, but unfortunately, it does."[18] And, she professed, the eye color exercise shows how those prejudices turn into harmful actions.

* * *

When in Osage, Elliott would take her books onto her side patio and relax in the suspended rocking chair that Darald once bought her. Her home was mostly quiet without her husband, although her daughter, Sarah, had some years earlier returned to northern Iowa. Additionally, bizarre encounters with spiritual phenomena at her church house next door generated a form of amusement. A photograph taken around this time captures a ghostly figure walking behind Jane and Sarah in the building's kitchen. Then, acting on word that Civil War-era spirits inhabited the grounds around the church structure, grave hunter Neal Dushane told Elliott how to use divining rods to communicate with the apparitions. If used properly, the rods would indicate burial sites and paranormal activity around her property. Dushane then visited the property to see for himself. He found more than a dozen lost graves, plus the names and occupations of those buried around the church.[19]

Elliott also spent much time along the West Coast. Indeed, she owned a summer home in Sun City and later Menifee. In Snohomish, Washington, her sixty-year-old son, Brian, a licensed farrier, had fallen very sick. Elliott was very close to him when he passed away on July 11, 2018.[20] Elliott returned Brian's body to Iowa, where a memorial service was held at the Burr Oak Hall in Osage. The church building on Elliott's property was used for his celebration of life ceremony. Elliott admitted that she "suffered dearly" after Brian's death but that "he is in a better place." She had now lost her father, husband, and eldest son. Had Elliott lived any other lifestyle when Brian died, she might have kept her heartache private. With a large following expecting her to be a thought leader and ally to communities of color responsible for providing the language to help endure beyond dark moments at the end of the decade, she didn't have the choice to hide.

On December 15, Elliott's alma mater, the University of Northern Iowa (UNI), formerly the Iowa State Teachers College, awarded her an Honorary Doctorate of Humane Letters. Joining her in honor was novelist and poet Nancy Price, whose stories, which include the bestseller *Sleeping with the Enemy*, are set mostly in Cedar Falls and on the UNI campus. Elliott accepted the honorary doctorate knowing that her work had been "greeted with praise and criticism." The university touted her as "the consummate example" of what UNI can produce while also vindicating the Board of Regents' unanimous vote to bestow the degree to Elliott because she "has given of herself to the world."[21]

The University of California, Riverside, became the second institution of higher education to bestow an honorary doctoral degree to Jane Elliott. The University of America in Temecula, California, became the third in 2023. Although she refused to allow anyone to call her "Doctor," and even though she rarely, if ever, told anyone she received such tributes, she admitted that the degrees from UNI, Cal-Riverside, and America were deeply humbling.[22]

During the next two years, the public's wrangling over Jane Elliott's impact on society kept surfacing. On the one hand, in March 2019, for instance, amid the blackface controversy of Virginia Democratic Governor Ralph Northam, Elliott was a leading voice in explaining the root causes of discriminatory behavior. She pleaded for anyone listening to her to believe that honest and culturally inclusive education is the key to reducing the number of racist incidents. While columnists cited her exercise as proof educational programs can work, she spoke more about school investment in curricular tools that make students from historically marginalized groups feel "valued, recognized and appreciated."[23]

However, controversy surfaced whenever an untrained teacher attempted variations of her discrimination role-play. One slave auction simulation that forced Black students to line up against a wall wearing imaginary shackles and auctioned to their white classmates at Chapel School in Westchester County, New York, compelled an investigation by the state's Attorney General Letitia James. James concluded that reenactments separating children based on race "have no place in New York classrooms or classrooms throughout this country."[24] That same school year witnessed a fourth-grade classroom in North Carolina participating in a game titled "Escaping Slavery." The simulation involved a punch card that told students they would be "severely punished and sent back to the plantation to work as a slave" if their group got into trouble as they fled toward freedom. In Virginia, one school had its third, fourth, and fifth graders run through an obstacle course while pretending to be freedom seekers navigating safe houses along the Underground Railroad.

Elliott conceded that while irresponsible, there were well-meaning intentions behind those experiential lessons. She made sure to clarify, however, that they were not at all like her eye color simulation. She told the *Associated Press* that she stood by the Blue Eyes/Brown Eyes Exercise despite criticism and poor representations of reenactments gone astray because it boosted student performance and revealed to participants the determining factors leading to discriminatory behavior. Other, more meager attempts were just performative gestures. "Every student in my classroom who went through that exercise performed at a higher level academically than they had before because they found out the day they were on the top in that exercise how really smart they were."[25]

Michael Judge, grandson of the late Dinsmore Brandmill, former principal at Riceville Elementary School, argues in the *Wall Street Journal* that his grandfather wholly endorsed the exercise. When considering the context of time and place, Elliott is right to presume the world is a better place because of the Discrimination Day role-play. Judge writes of his grandfather that even having survived World War II, Elliott taught him the "dangers of scapegoating whole populations and the importance of reiterating, even when we fall short, that we are all equal in God's eyes." Since her work was committed to confronting the causes and symptoms of discrimination among the most impressionable age group, he always "had her back."[26]

* * *

Without knowing it, Jane Elliott has always been part of the sustained ongoing debate over what racism is, from where it is generated, and how central it is in driving day-to-day human interactions. She is not an academic that could be described as a critical race theorist. However, her argument—stretching back to her first lecture tour in the 1970s—was without counternarratives or diverse, representative voices, educational curriculum works to indoctrinate all Americans into a white racial frame of the world. It is a frame that values Euro-centric norms while devaluing all other racialized color groups and cultures. In other words, racist power and influence are firmly established natural determinants in how people experience American society. Her fifty-one-year-old argument was elevated with the August 2019 publication of the *New York Times* "The 1619 Project," a collection of long-form essays examining the role of slavery in establishing the United States of America. The publication's lead author, journalist Nikole Hannah-Jones, claimed that 1619, the year that enslaved Africans first arrived in the British colonies, should be considered the birth year of the nation. Jones' argument generated much consternation among historians who criticized the project's marginalization of the Spanish slave system in Florida and the enslavement of Native Americans. Also critical of "The 1619 Project" were conservative personalities calling the entire publication an anti-white mischaracterization of the American economic and religious enterprises that centuries before brought Europeans to the New World. Both in the moment and over the years since Elliott has endorsed "The 1619 Project" as a valid counternarrative account inclusive of much-needed voices of color to tell the American story.

In vintage fashion, Elliott conveyed the landmark anniversary and publication as a reminder of the slow-moving arc of racial progress. "Unfortunately for all of us, we have now forgotten what this country was founded on, and we have turned it over to someone who wants to turn it into an oligarchy," said Elliott, who spoke of the downslide of race relations after two years of Trump's presidency. "We're in danger right now of losing the democracy those men fought so hard to put together and what people for the last 400 years have fought to keep together."[27] It was more than the threat that the American democratic promise would fail. Elliott's unabashed bluntness exposed the conservative push to silence or otherwise cancel the voices of Black Americans that, in her view, worked harder than any other racialized group to build a more perfect union. Why censor The 1619 Project? Why ban race and sex education? Elliott reasoned it had everything to do with white Conservatives growing upset that Black writers were redefining the United States and giving a reason for the youth to question the myth of American exceptionalism.

Herein lies the last frontier in Elliott's anti-racism crusade.

* * *

On September 22, 2020, Donald Trump issued Executive Order 13950 prohibiting the United States Uniformed Services and federal government contractors from offering professional learning that "inculcates in its employees any form of race or sex stereotyping or any form of race or sex scapegoating."[28] The order was issued a month and a half before his failed presidential re-election bid and was officially called "Combating Race and Sex Stereotyping." It was aimed at silencing people like Jane Elliott, who "are pushing a different vision of America [. . .] grounded in hierarchies based on [. . .] identities rather than in the inherent and equal dignity of every person as an individual."[29] The language of the order is written as if Trump had Elliott in mind when he (or his policy writer) put pen to paper: the actual racists are the ones pushing a "pernicious and false belief that America is an irredeemably racist and sexist country; that some people, simply on account of their race or sex, are oppressors; [. . .]"[30]

The order abruptly halted anti-bias training in federal departments, including the Equal Employment Opportunity/Diversity Management office of the U.S. Justice Department. Other anti-bias programming, anti-racism, and gender studies programs in higher education funded by federal grants were blocked before November's election. Within a year, the attack on curricula conscious of race, and sexual identity reached a point many historians considered more disturbing than the McCarthy-era anti-Communist witch hunts of the 1950s.

The situation intensified further when the Conservative think tank, The Manhattan Institute for Policy Research, published "Woke Schooling: A Toolkit for Concerned Parents" in June 2021. The publication ginned up parents across the country with a new bogeyman with pronouncements that critical race theory (CRT) deemed white Americans "bigots and racists" and denounced critical pedagogy in general as not just "counterproductive and divisive" but "illegal" according to the Fourteenth Amendment. "Training and activities in public schools (and, potentially, private schools that have accepted federal funding) that divide students by race demean certain students as 'oppressors' or inherently evil, or they compel students to profess certain beliefs that may run afoul of their state and federal rights."[31] As Republican politicians moved to ban "The 1619 Project" and CRT from becoming part of school curricula, conservative parents turned out in droves at school board meetings across the United States that summer and fall. The Trump team's Presidential Advisory 1776 Commission buoyed the effort, which issued a treatise for "restoring patriotic education." By the fall of 2021, school boards in conservative districts terminated some teachers while pressuring others to leave the profession. A wave of red states passed or proposed CRT or "divisive concepts" bans. Regardless of the state, each divisive concept bill used the same language, indicating no real problem with educators being "divisive," teaching students that white people possessed an inherent gene making them racists, or advocating discrimination against white people to achieve equity.

While Donald Trump was out of office, Elliott couldn't escape the new conservative turn at using public and private schools to litigate culture wars. At the Central York School District in York County, Pennsylvania, the school board released a list of resources teachers and librarians were prohibited from bringing into the district's schools. Jane Elliott's training videos, as were the random YouTube clips featuring interviews with Elliott, were included on the list of banned texts.[32]

In the decade before Trump became President of the United States, it would have seemed incomprehensible that a movement to ban books and other resources carrying topics of race and sexual identity would have found itself so sweeping and efficacious. After all, public and private schools had long sought answers to increasing achievement and engagement amongst growing diversity in America's student bodies. Studies out of Stanford and San Francisco State show that interdisciplinary ethnic studies programs increase attendance, boost academic achievement, lower the number of disciplinary infractions, and lead to higher graduation rates among students from middle school to postsecondary education.[33] The new Conservative "Make America Great Again" movement, buttressed by Christian nationalism, found a common antagonist in the social justice canon—and Jane Elliott was part of the company. The book-banning Right, driven by what it claimed was reverse racism in pedagogical form, faced little political resistance from centrists or Left-of-center elected officials. School board members commonly acquiesced, and the Democratic Party offered little leadership in responding to the surge of attacks on educators.

Then, on Saturday, May 14, 2022, an eighteen-year-old from Conklin, New York, murdered ten Black people and wounded three others in a racially mo-tivated assault at a Buffalo supermarket out of fear of the "great-replacement." Not at all different from the Nativist credo "Jews will not replace us" once chanted at the "Unite the Right" rally in Charlottesville four-and-a-half years earlier. The "great replacement" theory contends that the drive for a more inclu-sive society, which includes changes to immigration laws, LGBTQIA+ rights, race-conscious legislation, access to voting, interracial marriage, and abortion, are designed to eliminate the white race. It was not lost on Elliott how much harder it is to restrict public access to body armor and AR-15-style rifles than to ban books and videos explaining how someone like the shooter becomes radi-calized into white supremacist domestic terrorism. Whether people like it or not, Jane Elliott's life work has been committed to educating others about how young white people get exposed to racist ideology. While drawing irony to the fact that those proclaiming the "great replacement" theory are representatives of a group that quite literally replaced the indigenous population through disease, war, assimilation boarding schools, and legislation, she argued a racially moti-vated aggressor is never truly an outlier. Ever since a racist terrorist murdered Martin Luther King Jr. on April 4, 1968, Elliott contended some children take discriminatory action because they are indoctrinated by almost every institution of American society into believing in some version of the replacement theory.

Such moments take Elliott back to the "Anatomy of Prejudice" lecture circuit of the 1980s and 1990s when she would challenge melanotic people in the audience to stand if they "want to be treated the way blacks are in this society." Routinely, none would stand. To Elliott, the "great replacement" theory indicates that its believers know and avail themselves of the fact that racialized minorities and people of other marginalized groups are treated differently by policy and practice throughout the United States. The ignorance that underpins this ideology is at the root of prejudice. That prejudice morphs into discriminatory actions when elevated and validated by authority figures.

One day before the Buffalo shooting, Elliott conceded that getting banned had become a "mixed blessing." Although she worked less and enjoyed more free time, she said, "The [one race] message isn't getting out there as much, and I think we need it more than ever."[34] The context of that statement concerned the politicization of the United States Supreme Court in the wake of reports that the six pro-life justices would overturn *Roe v. Wade,* pushing the nation closer to the end of church-state separation. Those words, nonetheless, foreshadowed the fatal shooting in Buffalo.

After enduring fifty-five years of attacks, she resolved to expand her One Race message with a three-pronged treatise.

Without Blacks, there would be no whites.

Without Jews, there would be no Christians or Muslims.

Without women, there would be no men.[35]

There have been few voices like Jane Elliott straddling the twentieth and twenty-first centuries. While she inspired social psychologists, educators, military leaders, and civic leaders, she also angered people in those groups. Despite any criticism, what is true is that her work and words will resonate for generations. Racism and other forms of intolerance agonizingly endure. Yet, the drive to "recognize, accept, and appreciate" the inherited and cultural differences of marginalized Others always remained Jane Elliott's steadfast resolution.[36] Her straightforward unifying message about One Race may forever permeate the world's interminable search for love in the face of an unending problem. Undeterred by mounting hate crime violence, book bans, attacks on voting rights, threats against women and the LGBTQIA+ community, and an increased tenor of authoritarianism driven partly by a pseudo-Christian nationalist movement, Jane Elliott proved that she would never quietly retreat.

She would always stand her ground, after all, because the single greatest uncontrollable trait we in humanity possess is that we are all simply different shades of brown.

JANE ELLIOTT CHRONOLOGY

August 25, 1927	Marriage of an unwed pregnant couple, eighteen-year-old apprenticing farmer Lloyd "Ginny" Jennison and Margaret "Gie" Rose Benson, the fifteen-year-old daughter of devout Catholics.
November 30, 1933	On Thanksgiving, Mable "Jane" Jennison is born in Riceville, Iowa, the fourth of Lloyd and Margaret's seven children.
July 30, 1934	Darald Dean Elliott is born in Boone, Iowa, the only child of Edwin, a twenty-five-year-old farmer, and seventeen-year-old housewife, Bertha Ellsberry.
September 21, 1944	Jane concludes her participation in her one-room schoolhouse's milkweed pod ration drive for World War II.
March 17, 1945	Jane witnesses her younger sister, Anne Irene, die of convulsions due to tonsillitis sepsis.
December 10, 1947	Jane and her two older sisters, Mary and Jean, form the troupe "The Three Jills" to sing for money.
February 26, 1948	James Samuel, "Jim," who later prefers "Sam," joins the troupe, which rebrands as "Three Jills and a Jim," and later "The Four Jennisons."
February 22, 1952	Jane enrolls in a nursing course sponsored by the Red Cross, intending to enter the medical field.
June 1952	After her father's insistence, Jane begins studying to become an elementary teacher at the Iowa State Teacher's College in Cedar Falls, Iowa.
February 1953	Jane student-teaches at Hawthorne Elementary School in Independence, Iowa, under the tutelage of innovative instructor Hazel Grant, a target of anti-Communist McCarthyites.

August 1953	Jane receives an emergency certification from the state of Iowa to begin teaching at the Randall School in Randall, Iowa.
September 1953	Jane starts dating Darald Elliott, a grocery store manager in Boone, Iowa.
July 1954	Jane receives a standard elementary teaching certification from Iowa State Teachers College.
January 30, 1955	Jane marries Darald in Boone. Real-estate lender and future Iowa Congressman Rev. Merwin Coad serving as the officiant.
September 1955	Jane teaches one semester at Napier, Iowa.
December 1955	Jane resigns from teaching to move with Darald to Waterloo, Iowa, and start a family.
August 16, 1956	Jane and Darald's first child, Sarah, is born.
September 10, 1957	Brian, the second of four children to Jane and Darald, is born.
February 11, 1959	Jane gives birth to her third child and second daughter, Mary.
April 13, 1961	Jane delivers the fourth and last child, Mark.
August 7, 1962	Darald receives a promotion to work as manager of Waterloo's National Tea Food Store in the city's Black neighborhood.
June 1963	Civil rights protesters picket Darald's grocery store for failing to hire Black employees.
September 5, 1963	Jane and Darald return to Riceville after purchasing the Burke Hotel, later, Jennison Inn from Jane's brother, Charles.
September 1964	Jane returns to teaching by accepting a Riceville Elementary Community School position.
December 1967	Jane turns ownership of the Jennison Inn over to her parents, Lloyd and Margaret.
April 4, 1968	Martin Luther King Jr. is assassinated in Memphis, Tennessee.
April 5 and 8, 1968	Jane conducts the first Blue Eyes/Brown Eyes Exercise, then called Discrimination Day.

May 31, 1968	Jane appears on the *Tonight Show* with Johnny Carson alongside actor James Garner and the band The Box Tops.
August 19, 1968	Jane conducts the Discrimination Day lesson with adult males in the Osage Rotary Club in Osage, Iowa. This is the first time she attempts the exercise with adults.
April 18, 1969	Jane earns her first publication with an article titled "Exercise in Discrimination" in Scholastic Magazine, Inc.'s *Scholastic Teacher.*
September 17-20, 1968	Journalist Stephen Banker and a film crew from the Canadian Broadcasting Corporation visit Riceville to film Jane's Discrimination Day lesson for a special titled "The Way It Is."
October 6, 1968	Banker's documentary—the first film of Jane's eye color exercise—appears on Canada's public affairs program "The Way It Is." The viewer response is split ideologically.
February 23–25, 1970	Filmmakers William and Muriel Peters bring a documentary crew to Jane's class to film *The Eye of the Storm* for the ABC special *NOW.*
May 11, 1970	*The Eye of the Storm* premiers on ABC. It brings newfound fame to Jane Elliott. It also generates a National Education Association copyright investigation into the origins of the eye color exercise.
July 24, 1970	Jane delivers her first eye-color workshop for educators at the University of Iowa's Urban Education Workshop. The session is titled, at the time, "An Experience with Discrimination."
September 29, 1970	Jane appears on the *Virginia Graham Show* and reveals to the nation that her children have been victims of physical and verbal abuse because of her anti-discrimination work.
December 1970	Jane joins the Children Without Prejudice panel at the White House Conference for Children and Youth, putting several hundred adults through the eye color exercise.
July 1971	ABC and Jane Elliott win the George Peabody Broadcasting Award from the Henry Grady School of Journalism at the University of Georgia.

August 1971	William Peters' book *A Class Divided*, about Jane's eye color exercise, is published by Doubleday.
August 5, 1971	Jane moves with her family to Osage after a colleague warns her that teachers and students are targeting her children.
August 6, 1971	Jane first appears on the *Today Show* with William Peters to help promote *A Class Divided*.
August 16, 1971	Jane and Peters are guests on the *Phil Donahue Show*. The episode airs on several live and delayed markets nationwide through October.
August 17, 1971	Jane and Peters appear on Howard Miller's *Chicago* to discuss the eye color exercise and *A Class Divided*.
January 20, 1972	Jane appears on the Christian weekly half-hour television talk show, *Christopher Closeup*.
May 1974	Jane completes the work toward her bachelor's degree at Iowa State Teachers College and begins working toward a master's in education administration at the same institution.
November 26, 1974	Jane receives the Mental Health Association Award for her activism in providing services for students with dyslexia.
March 18, 1975	Jane escapes a death threat after leading educators and community members through the Blue Eyes/Brown Eyes Exercise in Uniontown, Pennsylvania.
August 1977	Jane agrees to a transfer to Riceville Middle School, where she conducts the eye color exercise annually for the next seven years.
August 11, 1984	William Peters returns to Riceville to film an *Eye of the Storm* reunion documentary for PBS *Frontline*, this time called "A Class Divided."
March 1985	PBS *Frontline's* "A Class Divided" documentary premiers nationally.
September 16, 1985	Jane resigns from the Riceville Community School District to begin her diversity training consulting career at Mountain Bell.
December 1986	Jane first appears on *The Oprah Winfrey Show*.

April 1987	Jane allows a local television crew in Miami, Florida, to film her eye-color exercise for a special program titled *Eye of the Beholder*.
October 14, 1988	Jane serves as keynote speaker at the A World of Difference Conference for Dade County Elementary Educators.
July 5, 1990	Jane's father, Lloyd, dies at the age of eighty-one.
September 24, 1990	A Minneapolis public television channel gains permission to film Jane's Blue Eyes/Brown Eyes Exercise for a program called "Eye to Eye."
April 24-25, 1992	Jane is named ABC-TV "Person of the Week" for appearing alongside Peter Jennings on *World News Tonight* and a special titled "Prejudice: Answering Children's Questions" to engage with families about racism following the violence of the Rodney King verdict.
August 1992	Jane appears for a second time on *Oprah*.
February 24, 1994	Jane has her third appearance on *Oprah* and is advertised as someone who receives more "love and hate mail than any other *Oprah* guest."
April 25, 1994	Jane begins her international tour with the Blue Eyes/Brown Eyes Exercise when she accepts an offer to tour Canada during the spring of 1994.
December 1994	Jane begins working for the Department of Defense's Equal Opportunity Management Institute (DEOMI) in Florida.
October 26, 1995	Jane begins intensive work with a Kansas City metropolitan area group called "KC Harmony."
December 1995	Jane opens conversations with actress Susan Sarandon and Pliny Porter, president of Julia Roberts' production company, Shoelace Productions, for a movie starring Susan Sarandon as Jane.
March 19-27, 1996	Jane spends nine days in the Netherlands training eleven facilitators from Stichting Magenta on the Blue Eyes/Brown Eyes Exercise.
May 23, 1996	Jane appears on *Nightline* with Ted Koppel.
June 1996	The internationally acclaimed *Blue Eyed* documentary produced by the German company Denkmal Film makes its world premiere.

June 1996	Disney announces a movie, *A Class Divided*, about Jane Elliott starring Susan Sarandon and produced by Julia Roberts' production company Shoelace Productions.
November 1997	Jane visits Australia for the first time following the popularity of *Blue Eyed*.
May 1998	Once again, Jane tours Australia, delivering speeches across the country.
March 8, 2000	Jane delivers a presentation at the White House for the Department of Education where she calls Texas governor and presidential candidate George W. Bush and his brother, Jeb, racists.
December 2000	German *Vogue* profiles Jane.
Spring 2001	Jane returns to Australia for the third time to film a training video, *The Stolen Eye*, featuring her Blue Eyes/Brown Eyes Exercise.
August 25, 2001	Jane receives the Iowa Commission on the Status of Women Christine Wilson Medal for Equality and Justice Award for her contributions to equality and justice.
October 2001	Jane films *Angry Eye* with college students at Bard College.
ca. March 2005	The McGraw Hill Foundation announces Jane as one of thirty consequential teachers in the history of education.
May 20, 2007	William Peters, the documentarian who helped build Jane's acumen as a race relations expert filming *The Eye of the Storm* in 1970, dies.
June 15, 2008	Jane's mother, Margaret "Gie," dies at age ninety-six.
October 29, 2009	Jane's newest Blue Eyes/Brown Eyes Exercise training video, *How Racist Are You?* a film for Channel 4 in Britain, airs for the first time in Great Britain.
September 24, 2013	Jane's husband, Darald, dies of multiple systems atrophy inside their Osage home.
February 18, 2016	Jane is publicly criticized after rapper Michael Render, also known as "Killer Mike," proclaimed in front of 4,800 persons at Morehouse College that she said "a uterus doesn't qualify you to be president of the United States" when discussing Hillary Clinton at a Bernie Sanders rally during the 2016 Democratic primary.

July 11, 2018	Jane's son, Brian, dies at age sixty in his home in Snohomish, Washington.
December 15, 2018	Jane receives an honorary doctorate from her alma mater, the University of Northern Iowa, formerly Iowa State Teachers College, at its winter commencement ceremony.
March 15, 2019	References to Jane as a leading race relations expert resurface amid the blackface scandal of Virginia Governor Ralph Northam.
March 12, 2020	COVID-19 quarantine lockdowns begin.
March 29, 2020	The *Des Moines Register* names Jane one of seventeen Iowa women, including suffragist Carrie Chapman Catt and civil rights icon Edna Griffin, who changed the world.
May 25, 2020	The murder of African American George Floyd in Minnesota leads to national and international Black Lives Matter protests and Jane's return as a leading voice in discussions on race and racism.
June 1, 2020	Nearly fifty-two years to the day after she first appeared on *The Tonight Show Starring Johnny Carson*, Jane is a guest on *The Tonight Show Starring Jimmy Fallon*, to discuss her story and the fallout from the murder of George Floyd.
October 5, 2021	Journalism professor, Stephen Bloom, publishes a searing critique of Jane's Blue Eyes/Brown Eyes Exercise.
October 22, 2021	Jane begins writing as a contributor to *Ms. Magazine*.

NOTES

Introduction: The Anatomy of Jane Elliott

1. David Crowder, "If you say, 'I'm not prejudiced,' then that probably means you are," *El Paso Times* (El Paso, TX), July 26, 1992, 1G.

2. Rhoda Amon, "Lesson in bigotry through child's eyes," *Newsday* (Melville, NY), August 23, 1971, A13.

3. William Peters, "A Class Divided," PBS Frontline, Season 1985, Episode 9.

4. Jane Elliott, *A Collar in My Pocket: The Blue Eyes Brown Eyes Exercise*, (Osage, IA: CreateSpace Independent Publishing Platform, 2016), 15.

5. John Raymond, "Blue, Brown Eyes Learn Hard Lesson," *The Atlantic Constitution*, August 8, 1971.

6. The Rock Newman Show, "Jane Elliott on the Rock Newman Show," May 26, 2016, RockNewman-Show. Retrieved at https://www.youtube.com/watch?v=fF9s0as_d_4.

7. Jane Elliott, Letter to Marylin "Mickey" Alcorn, Riceville, IA, April 4, 1968, Jane Elliott Files. 1968 Correspondence, Iowa Women's Archives, University of Iowa Libraries.

8. Elliott. Letter to Alcorn. Ibid.

9. Roland Martin, Interview by author, Washington D.C., May 25, 2022.

10. Martin, Ibid

11. Max Rafferty, "Classroom's Not Soapbox for Teacher's Opinions," *Salt Lake Tribune* (Salt Lake City, UT), November 15, 1970.

12. Stephen G. Bloom, "Lesson of a Lifetime," *Smithsonian Magazine*, September 2005. Retrieved at https://www.smithsonianmag.com/science-nature/lesson-of-a-lifetime-72754306/

13. Stephen G. Bloom, *Blue Eyes, Brown Eyes: A Cautionary Tale of Race and Brutality*, (Berkeley, CA: University of California Press, 2021), xi and xvii.

14. *Sydney Morning Herald* (Sydney, New South Wales, Australia), "Test as clear as black and white," November 23, 1997; *The Charlotte Observer*, No title, October 17, 1994.

15. Jane Elliott, Interview by author, Iowa, September 4, 2021.

16. William Peters, *A Class Divided: Then and Now*, (New Haven and London: Yale University Press), 6; Christina Theophilos and Raju Ramanathan, *Preventing Bullying: A Manual for Teachers in Promoting Global Educational Harmony*, (Bloomington, IN: Balboa Press. 2020), 40.

17. Joy Stilley, "Teacher has a unique method to teach meaning of prejudice," *Brownwood Bulletin* (Brownwood, TX), October 3, 1971.

18. See books by Robert Wald Sussman, *The Myth of Race*, (Cambridge, MA: Harvard University Press, 2016) and Allan Chase, *The Legacy of Malthus: The Social Cost of the New Scientific Racism*, (New York, NY: Alfred A. Knopf. Inc. 1977).

19. UHGCSW, "A Conversation on Race and Privilege with Angela Davis and Jane Elliott," University of Houston, September 6, 2018, Retrieved at https://www.youtube.com/watch?v=S0jf8D5WHoo; Jane Elliott. Interview by author, Iowa, September 5, 2021.

20. U.S. Congress, Amendments To Christopher Columbus Quincentenary Jubilee Act: *Hearing before the Subcommittee on Census and Population of the Committee on Post Office and Civil Service House of Representatives One Hundredth Congress First Session on H.R. 2309 A Bill to Amend the Christopher Columbus Quincentenary Jubilee Act*, (Washington: U.S. Government Printing Office, 1987), July 7, 1987, 19.

21. Ivan Van Sertima, *They Came Before Columbus: The African Presence in Ancient America*, (New York: Random House Trade Paperbacks, 2003), x.

22. Jane Elliott, Interview by author, Iowa, July 9, 2021.

23. Unknown author, "White Expert Tells How Racism is Taught and Learned," *JET* Magazine, July 13, 1992, 12-14.

24. Jane Elliott, Interview by author, Iowa, September 4, 2021.

25. Jane Elliott, Interview by author, Iowa, May 5, 2021.

26. Jane Elliott, "K-5 Professional Learning," Nyack, New York. Nyack Area School District, K-5 Public School Teachers, May 10, 2021.

27. Roland Martin Unfiltered. "DeSantis signs FL election law; Jane Elliott talks race in America; Baby killed in police chase," Roland Martin Unfiltered, May 6, 2021. Retrieved at https://www.youtube.com/watch?v=7ADhkSGkiEo&t=2618s

Chapter 1: A Twinkle in One's Eye

1. *Riceville Recorder*, September 12, 1917.

2. Samuel Greene Jennison, Ancestry.com, *U.S., Find a Grave Index, 1600s-Current* [database online], Lehi, UT, USA: Ancestry.com Operations, Inc., 2012; Ann Elizabeth Jennison, Ancestry.com, *U.S., Find a Grave Index, 1600s-Current* [database online], Lehi, UT, USA: Ancestry.com Operations, Inc., 2012.

3. *Riceville Recorder*, "Mrs. Charles Jennison," February 21, 1917; Author unknown, "Oakdale Township. Plat book of Howard County, Iowa," (W.W. Hixson & Co. 1930), The University of Iowa Libraries Map Collection https://digital.lib.uiowa.edu/islandora/object/ui%3Ahixson_813; *Riceville Recorder*, "Guess Who," December 14, 1950,Author unknown, "Plat book of Howard County, Iowa, 1930," (W.W. Hixson & Co. 1930), 17. Plat book of Howard County, Iowa, 1930: Hixson Plat Map Atlases of Iowa (uiowa.edu)

4. *Riceville Recorder*, "Charles H. Jennison, 1834-1917," October 17, 1917.

5. *Riceville Recorder*, March 6, 1912.

6. *Riceville Recorder*, March 30, 1905.; *Riceville Recorder*, March 15, 1906; *Riceville Recorder*, November 22, 1906.

7. *Riceville Recorder*, "Some Achievements of the W.C.T.U. of Iowa," July 23, 1919.

8. *Riceville Recorder*, "W.C.T.U.," September 29, 1926; *Riceville Recorder*, "W.C.T.U. Meeting," March 28, 1923; *Riceville Recorder*, "W.C.T.U.," September 28, 1927; *Riceville Recorder*, "Friends in Council," November 9, 1927.

9. *Riceville Recorder*, "W.C.T.U. Notes," March 9, 1921; *Riceville Recorder*, "All-day Meeting at Little Cedar," May 18, 1921; *Riceville Recorder*, "W.C.T.U. Institute," January 25, 1922.

10. *The Riceville Recorder*, "Riceville H.S. 15 Luther Preps 6," October 28, 1925; *The Riceville Recorder*, "Riceville 7 Nora Springs," December 1, 1926; *Riceville Recorder*, "Another Victory for Riceville H.S.," October 15, 192; *Riceville Recorder*, "Waukon 14 Riceville 3," October 14, 1925.

11. Jane Elliott, Interview by author. Iowa, June 9, 2021; Karen Mason, "An Oral History Interview with Jane Elliott, 11/4/2009," Osage, Iowa. Copyright 2009, The University of Iowa. Iowa Women's Archives.

12. *Ottumwa Tri-Weekly Courier* (Ottumwa, IA), "Is a Great Event," June 26, 190; *Sioux City Journal* (Sioux City, IA), "Well Known Priest Dies," November 24, 1903.

13. *Riceville Recorder*, "High School Commencement.," June 5, 1918.

14. *Riceville Recorder*, "Students of Miss Ketchum Gave Recital," March 5, 1924; *Riceville Recorder*, January 31, 1923.

15. *Riceville Recorder*, "Riceville Music Club Has Meeting Monday," December 4, 1947; *Riceville Recorder*, "Music Association Elected Officers," September 29, 1949.

16. *Riceville Recorder*, "Margaret Jennison, 9," June 19, 2008.

17. Mason, "An Oral History Interview with Jane Elliott."

18. According to Jane Elliott, Lyde often told the family that she was related to boxer James Corbett. Jane Elliott. Zoom interview by author. Iowa, June 22, 2021.

19. Iowa State Board of Health. Certificate of Marriage for Lloyd Charles Jennison and Margaret Benson, August 25, 1927; *Riceville Recorder*, November 16, 1927; *Riceville Recorder*, "Riceville's Fine Public School System," August 18, 1926.

20. *Riceville Recorder*, April 24, 1918.

21. State Historical Society of Iowa, Des Moines, Iowa, "Iowa Birth Records, 1888-1904," State Historical Society of Iowa, Des Moines, Iowa, Ancestry.com, *Iowa, U.S., Birth Records, 1856-1944* [database on-line], Lehi, UT, USA: Ancestry.com. Operations, Inc., 2017; *Riceville Recorder*, "Thank You Dr. Walker," February 1, 1979; *Riceville Recorder*, "The Three Doctors Walker," July 4, 1946.

22. *Riceville Recorder*, March 21, 1928, 4.

23. Mason, "An Oral History Interview with Jane Elliott."

24. *Riceville Recorder*, "Many Farmers Lose Land," June 7, 1933; *Riceville Recorder*, "Farm Bureau Notes," March 15, 1933.

25. *Riceville Recorder*, "Clark Jennison Gored by Bull," September 13, 1933.

26. Jane Elliott, Interview by author, Iowa, June 9, 2021.

27. *Oelwein Daily Register* (Oelwein, IA), "Reno Predicts General Strike in the country," February 23, 1933; *Estherville Daily News* (Estherville, IA), February 28, 1933.

28. Loren Donelson, "600 Million Bushels of Corn," *The Terril Record* (Terril, IA), February 16, 1933.

29. Jeffrey T. Manuel, "Iowa's Original Ethanol Debate: The Power Alcohol Movement of 1933-1934," *The Annals of Iowa 77* (2018), 41-78.

30. *Oelwein Daily Register.*, "Henry A. Wallace Says He is One of the Team as He Talks of Relief," March 1, 1933.

31. Jane Elliott, Interview bu author. Iowa. June 9, 2021; Jane Elliott. Interview by author, Iowa, June 11, 2021;

32. *Riceville Recorder*, "The Three Doctors Walker," July 4, 1946.

33. Elliott, Interview by author, Iowa, June 9, 2021.

34. Ibid.

35. *Riceville Recorder*, "Young People Unite In Marriage," July 5, 1922.

36. Jane Elliott, Interview by author, Iowa, September 4, 2021; *Riceville Recorder*, "Young People United in Marriage," July 5, 1922.

37. Jane Elliott, Interview by author, Iowa, June 9, 2021.

Chapter 2: Dry Eyes

1. Jane Elliott. Personal interview with the author. Osage, IA. September 4, 2021. 8.

2. *Riceville Recorder*, November 22, 1944,

3. Jane Elliott Interview by author, Iowa, September 4, 2021

4. Jane Elliott, Interview by author, Iowa, September 22, 2021.

5. Ibid.

6. Newspapers misprint the school sitting on the Rasmussen family property, a farm situated adjacent to the Jennison Round Grove farm.

7. Jane Elliott, email message to author, September 26, 2021.

8. Jane Elliott, Interview by author, Iowa, September 22, 2021.

9. Jane Elliott, Interview by author, Iowa, June 8, 2021.

10. *Riceville Recorder*, "Rural Teachers Meet Here on Saturday," September 23, 1937; *Riceville Recorder*, June 8, 1939.

11. *Riceville Recorder*, January 7, 1943.

12. Gossard Corsets, "How to Select Your Corset," Ad, publisher unknown, 1916.

13. Mason, "An Oral History Interview with Jane Elliott,"16.

14. *Riceville Recorder*, "Riceville," March 19, 1941; *Riceville Recorder*, "Royal Home Workers," October 8, 1941.

15. *Lime Springs Herald* (Lime Springs, IA), "Rural Schools Opened Mon. For the New '49-'50 Year," September 8, 1949.

16. *Riceville Recorder*, March 26, 1947; *Riceville Recorder*, March 20, 1947.

17. *Riceville Recorder*, March 4, 1948.

18. Jane Elliott, Interview by author, Iowa, September 22, 2021.

19. Cassandra Leff, "Riceville schools a part of Iowa history," *Riceville Recorder*, July 16, 2009.

20. Jane Elliott, Interview by author, Iowa, September 23, 2021 *Howard County Times* (Cresco, IA), "Round Grove School House in Jamestown Destroyed by Fire," February 23, 1944.

21. *Riceville Recorder*, "Round Grove School," September 6, 1945.

22. *Riceville Recorder*, "War Talk," September 27, 1939.

23. Jane Elliott, Interview by author, Iowa, June 9, 2021.

24. *The Courier* (Waterloo, IA), "Riceville Farmer Loses 52 Hogs with Cholera," December 16, 1941.

25. Jane Elliott, Interview by author, September 22, 2021; *Globe-Gazette* (Mason City, IA), "Samuel Jennison, 80, Retired Farmer, Dies at Home in Riceville," December 15, 1941.

26. Jane Elliott, Interview by author, Iowa, September 22, 2021; National Archives at St. Louis, MO, *WWII Draft Registration Cards for Iowa, 10/16/1940-03/31/1947*, Record Group: Records of the Selective Service System, 1947, Box: 242; *Howard County Times* (Cresco, IA), "Read Estate Sales," March 31, 1943.

27. Jane Elliott, Interview by author, Iowa, June 9, 2021.

28. *Riceville Recorder*, "News From the Past," March 12, 1998; *Riceville Recorder*, "Need in Europe Told by Farmer at Banquet Here," December 10, 1947; *Riceville Recorder*, "'The Four Jennisons,'" February 26, 1948; *Riceville Recorder*, "McKinley Speaks at Legion Armistice Day Observance," November 13, 1947; *Riceville Recorder*, "Beef Cattle Banquet Held," March 24, 1949; Jane Elliott, email message to author, December 6, 2021.

29. Jane Elliott, Interview by author, Iowa, June 9, 2021.

30. *Elma New Era* (Elma, IA), "Naval Reserve Wants Men from 17 to 50 Years," December 11, 1941.

31. *Cresco Plain Dealer* (Cresco, IA), "Dedicate Memorial August 19," August 13, 1941; *Cresco Plain Dealer* (Cresco, IA), "Honor Roll Names Boys in Service," August 26, 1943; Jane Elliott, Interview by author, Iowa, June 11, 2021.

32. Jane Elliott, Interview by author, Iowa, September 22, 2021.

33. *Elma New Era* (Elma, IA), June 12, 1941; *Howard County Times* (Cresco, IA), "Riceville," December 9, 1942; *Riceville Recorder*, "Senior at Luther College," September 7, 1938.

34. Jane Elliott, Interview by author, Iowa, June 9, 2021; Keri Bugenhagen, "Veterans encouraged to record history," *Cresco Times Plain Dealer* (Cresco, IA), November 9, 2011; Jane Elliott, email message to author, September 27, 2021; *Elma New Era* (Elma, IA), "Letters from our soldiers," September 17, 1942, 1.

35. *Riceville Recorder*, "Mary Irene Benson Prosper Jeffries Marry." June 27, 1946. 1; National Archives at St. Louis; St. Louis, Missouri; *WWII Draft Registration Cards for Iowa, 10/16/1940-03/31-1947*; Record Group: *Records of the Selective Service System, 147*; Box 241.

36. *The Courier* (Waterloo, IA). "News of Northeast Iowans in Service of Their Country," December 3, 1944; *The Courier* (Waterloo, IA), "30 Osage Boys Get Farm Class Awards," March 13, 1936. 19; Jane Elliott, Interview by author, Iowa, June 9, 2021.

37. *Howard County Times* (Cresco, IA), "Get a Sugar Book!" May 6, 1942.

38. Jane Elliott, Interview by author, Iowa, June 11, 2021.

39. Stewart Asher, "Picking a Pod to Save a Life," *Philadelphia Inquirer*, May 14, 1944.

40. *Howard County Times* (Cresco, IA), "Harvest Big Crop of Milkweed Pods in Howard County," October 18, 1944; *Riceville Recorder*, "Jamestown," September 21, 1944; *Cresco Plain Dealer* (Cresco, IA), "Launch Campaign for Collection of Milkweed Pods," September 14, 1944; *Howard County Times* (Cresco, IA), "Complete Milkweed Pod Collection Here," January 3, 1945; Jane Elliott, Interview by author, Iowa, June 9, 2021; Jane Elliott, Interview by author, Iowa, September 22, 2021; Stewart Asher, "Picking a Pod to Save a Life," *Philadelphia Inquirer*, May 14, 1944; *Elma New Era* (Elma, IA), "1255 Bags of Milkweed Pods Collected by School Pupils," January 4, 1945.

41. *Riceville Recorder*, "The Three Doctors Walker," July 4, 1946.

42. Jane Elliott, Interview by author, Iowa, June 8, 2021; Jane Elliott, Interview by author, Iowa, September 4, 2021.

43. State Historical Society of Iowa, Des Moines, Iowa, "Anne Irene Jennison Passes Away Suddenly," *Iowa Death Records for Anne Irene Jennison*; *Riceville Recorder*, March 22, 1945.

44. *Riceville Recorder*, "Round Grove," February 27, 1947.

Chapter 3: Cast Eyes Down

1. Jane Elliott. Zoom interview with the author. Osage, IA. October 5, 2021.

2. *Riceville Recorder*, "Aunt Jemima at Saratoga Thursday, 18th" and "Pancake Day and 'Aunt Jemima,'" March 11, 1948; Jane Elliott, Interview by author, Iowa, October 5, 2021.

3. Jane Elliott, Interview by author, Iowa, October 5, 2021.

4. Ibid.

5. Ibid.

6. *Riceville Recorder*, "Roving Reporter," September 14, 1950; *Riceville Recorder*, "Wildcat Tales," May 24, 1951. 5; *Riceville Recorder*, "Roving Reporter," September 29, 1949.

7. *Lime Springs Herald* (Lime Springs, IA), "Rural Schools Opened Mon. for the New '49-'50 Years," September 8, 1949; *The Courier*, April 22, 1951.

8. Jane Elliott, email message to author, Iowa, October 2, 2021.; *Riceville Recorder*, "Riceville Ties Greene Hom'coming," October 18, 1951.

9. Alfred Larsen is a pseudonym.

10. Jane Elliott, Interview by author, Iowa, October 5, 2021.

11. Elliott. *A Collar in My Pocket*. 2.

12. Mason, "An Oral History Interview with Jane Elliott," 36.

13. *Riceville Recorder*, "Edward 'Burl' Armstrong, 79," May 10, 2012.

14. Jane Elliott, Interview by author, Iowa, October 5, 2021.

15. *Riceville Recorder*, "Jean Jennison Valedictorian of High School Graduating Class," May 31, 1951; *Riceville Recorder*, "To Attend College," August 16, 1951.

16. *Riceville Recorder*, "Quotation for Today," April 21, 1949.

17. Jane Elliott, Interview by author, Iowa, October 5, 2021.

18. David Hajdu, *The Ten-Cent Plague: The Great Comic-Book Scare and How It Changed America*, (New York, NY: Farrar, Straus and Giroux, 2008), 1-6.

19. Nick Lamberto, "Quiet Drive at Knoxville Promotes Better Reading," *Des Moines Register* (Des Moines, IA), February 27, 1955.

20. *Star Tribune* (Minneapolis, MN), "Majority Feels Most Comic Books 'Bad'; Censorship Favored," March 6, 1949.

21. *Riceville Recorder*, "Quotation for Today," April 21, 1949.

22. *Des Moines Register* (Des Moines, IA), "Lyda Jennison of Riceville Is Dead," October 5, 1951; Jane Elliott, Interview by author, Iowa, October 5, 2021.

23. *Riceville Recorder*, September 29, 1949; *Riceville Recorder*, "Wildcat Tales," December 14, 1950.

24. Jane Elliott, email message to author, September 14, 2021.

25. Jane Elliott. Interview by the author, Iowa, September 9, 2021; Mason, "An Oral History Interview with Jane Elliott," 14.

26. Bloom. *Blue Eyes, Brown Eyes, 23*.

27. *Riceville Recorder*, "Lights! Camera! Action!" November 23, 1950.

28. *Riceville Recorder*, "Riceville Music Club Organized," September 25, 1947; *Riceville Recorder*, "Music Association Elected Officers," September 29, 1949; *Riceville Recorder*, "Riceville Music Club has Meeting Monday," December 4, 1947.

29. Jane Elliott, email message to author, October 2, 2021,

30. *Riceville Recorder*, January 17, 1952; Jane Elliott, Interview by author, Iowa, October 10, 2021.

31. U.S. Census website, United States Census Bureau. U.S. Decennial Census and Iowa Data Center, Retrieved March 29, 2020.

32. *Howard County Times*, "Minstrel as Popular as a Good Circus," October 1918.

33. *Riceville Recorder*, March 13, 1935; *Howard County Times*, "Legion Minstrel is Next Big Attraction," October 19, 1927.

34. *Elma New Era*, "Public School will Present Minstrel Show," November 21, 1940; *Riceville Recorder*, "Minstrel Show By McIntire High School," March 6, 1947.

35. Jane Elliott, email message to author, October 2, 2021.

36. Jane Elliott, email message to author, October 2, 2021.

37. *The Montana Standard* (Butte, MT), "Red Cross Active in Many Fields," March 1, 1953.

38. Jane Elliott, Interview by author, Iowa, October 5, 2021; *Riceville Recorder*, "Red Cross Nursing Classes Start Thursday," February 28, 1952; *Riceville Recorder*, "56 Receive Red Cross Nursing Certificates," May 29, 1952; *Riceville Recorder*, "Home Nursing Class," May 8, 1952; *Globe-Gazette* (Mason City, IA), "Medals Earned by North Iowa Men," February 24, 1969; *Globe-Gazette* (Mason City, IA), "Here in Mason City," June 30, 1950; *The Courier* (Waterloo, IA), "Stays on Job With Texas Polio Victims," August 31, 1952; *Globe-Gazette* (Mason City, IA), "45 New Cases of Polio Daily at Ft. Worth," October 3, 1952.

39. *Times Plain Dealer*, "Cancer Society to Again Grant 50 Nursing Awards," December 2, 1953.

40. *Howard County Times*, October 27, 1948; *Howard County Times*, December 1, 1948.

41. *Riceville Recorder*, "Emergency Polio Drive Launched," September 22, 1949; *Riceville Recorder*, "Emergency Polio Drive Comes to an End," October 6, 1949; Jane Elliott, Interview by author, Iowa, October 5, 2021.

42. Jane Elliott, Interview by the author. Osage, IA. June 11, 2021; Jane Elliott, Interview by author, Iowa, October 5, 2021.

43. Jane Elliott, email message to author, April 5, 2022.

44. At the time, Aunt Blanche Hogan was teaching kindergarten at Dunkerton School, in Blackhawk County, Iowa.

45. *Carroll Daily Times Herald* (Carroll, IA), "Iowa Still Has One Trolley Car," March 9, 1951.

46. *Globe-Gazette* (Mason City, IA), "LeRoy Dunn in safety work at Michigan State," June 27, 1960; *Globe-Gazette* (Mason City, IA), "Doctor of philosophy degree is conferred on LeRoy Dunn," July 3, 1963; Jane Elliott, Interview by author, Iowa, July 5, 2021; UNI Athletics, "UNI Celebrates Black History Month: A Panther Timeline," Assessed October 13, 2021, Retrieved at https://unipanthers.com/news/2020/2/29/uni-celebrates-black-history-month-a-panther-timeline.aspx.

47. Jane Elliott, email message to author, Iowa, October 6, 2021.

48. Iowa State Teachers College, "1952 Old Gold," *UNI Yearbooks*, 15; *Mount Pleasant News* (Mount Pleasant, IA), "Maucker Named ISTC President," June 30, 1950.

49. Jane Elliott, Interview by author, Iowa, October 5, 2021.

Chapter 4: Apple of Her Eye

1. Hary Church Chappell and Katharyn Joella Allen Chappell, *History of Buchanan County, Iowa, and Its People, Volume 1*, (Buchanan County, IA: S.J. Clarke Publishing Company, 1914), 584-87.

2. Gertrude Stein, *Everybody's Autobiography*, (New York, NY: Random House. 1937), page unknown; Roy R. Behrens, "Gertrude Stein: An Author's Fondness for Her Iowa Friends," February 4, 2022, Iowa Source.com, retrieved at https://www.iowasource.com/2022/02/04/gertrude-stein/

3. George Yancy, *Educating for Critical Consciousness,* (New York and London: Routledge, 2019), 106-07.

4. *The News-Press* (Fort Myers, FL), "Hazel Grant. August 18, 2007," August 24, 2007; *The Bulletin-Journal* (Independence, IA), "Mrs. Grant is Named to Chapter Office," April 13, 1962.

5. Phyllis Fleming, "40 Years in School," *The Gazette* (Cedar Rapids, IA), May 9, 1965.

6. Jane Elliott, Interview by author, Iowa, October 19, 2021.

7. Ibid.

8. *The Courier* (Waterloo, IA), "Says Attacks on Schools Lessening," July 13, 1953; Larry Tye, *Demagogue: The Life and Long Shadow of Senator Joe McCarthy*, (Boston and New York: Houghton Mifflin Harcourt, 2020), 337-39.

9. Edward L. Fike, "The Human Scene," *Rocky Mount Telegram* (Rocky Mount, NC), March 8, 1953.

10. Tris Coffin, "Washington Daybook," *The News* (Frederick, MD), May 14, 1949.

11. *The Brooklyn Daily Eagle* (Brooklyn, NY), "Some Thoughts on the Red-ucators," October 18, 1950; Stuart J. Foster, "Red Alert!: The National Education Association Confronts the 'Red Scare' in American Public Schools, 1947-1954, *Education and Culture*, Fall 1997, 1-16.

12. Robert Morrill Sand, "Sandscript," *Ridgewood Herald-News* (Ridgewood, NJ), March 19, 1953.

13. *Miami Herald*, "Beware of Red-ucators, State DAR Parley Warned," April 1, 1952; *Palm Beach Post* (West Palm Beach, FL), "Noted Speaker Will Address GOP - Sponsored Park Meeting," March 31, 1952.

14. *Times-Herald*, "Big List of Red Fronts," December 8, 1947.

15. Landon R.Y. Storrs, *The Second Red Scare and the Unmaking of the New Deal Left*, (Princeton, NJ: Princeton University Press, 2013), 189-90.

16. *Fresno Bee* (Fresno, CA), "McCarthy, College Professor Clash During Hearing," June 19, 1953; *The Bee* (Danville, VA), "Harvard Paper Challenges Sen. McCarthy," November 7, 1953.

17. *Oshkosh Northwestern* (Oshkosh, WI), "Eyes of America on Wisconsin Primary," September 6, 1952.

18. *Daily Mail.* (Hagerstown, MD), "Defense Fund for Lattimore," January 12, 1953; M. Stanton, "Chapter 29: Owen Lattimore," *Blacklisted by History: The Untold Story of Senator Joe McCarthy and His Fight against America's Enemies*, (New York, NY: Crown Forum, 2007), 111-14; John Thomas Flynn, *The Lattimore Story*, (New York: Devin-Adair Publishing Company, 1953), 1-6.

19. Jane Elliott, Interview by author, Iowa, October 6, 2021.

20. Ibid.; Jane Elliott, Email message to author, October 7, 2021.

21. Jane Elliott, Interview by author, Iowa, October 6, 2021.

22. Ibid.

23. Jane Elliott, Email message to author, October 7, 2021.

24. Jane Elliott, Interview by author, Iowa, October 19, 2021.

25. *Ames Daily Tribune* (Ames, IA), "Randall School Spruced Up," August 29, 1953.

26. Jane Elliott, Interview by author, Iowa, October 19, 2021.

27. Ibid.

28. State Historical Society of Iowa, "Darald Dean Elliott," *Iowa Birth Records, 1856-1944*, Des Moines, Iowa.

29. Jane Elliott, Interview by author, Iowa, October 19, 2021.

30. Ibid.

31. Nadine Subotnik, "From Where We Sit," *The Gazette* (Cedar Rapids, IA), September 13, 1953; *Des Moines Tribune* (Des Moines, IA), "'Moon' Movie is Test Case for Public," August 14, 1953.

32. Jane Elliott, Email message to the author, October 14, 2021.

33. Jane Elliott, Interview by author, Iowa, June 18, 2021; Jane Elliott, Interview by author, Iowa, October 19, 2021.

34. *Ames Daily Tribune* (Ames, IA), November 19, 1954.

35. Jane Elliott, Email message to the author, April 5, 2022; Jane Elliott, Interview by author, Iowa, June 18, 2021; *Riceville Recorder*, "Jane Jennison and Donald Dean Were Married Jan. 30," February 10, 1955.

36. Walter Shotwell, "Pastor Coad Tells of Race for Congress," *The Des Moines Register* (Des Moines, IA), November 8, 1956; Daniel Pedersen, "Coad peddles real estate 'secrets,'" *Des Moines Register* (Des Moines, IA), March 29, 1981.

37. *Riceville Recorder*, "Jane Jennison and Donald Dean Were Married Jan. 30," February 10, 1955.

38. *Ames Daily Tribune* (Ames, IA), "Randall Teacher Gets Linen Gifts at Recent Shower," February 18, 1955.

39. Jane Elliott, Interview by author, Iowa, July 5, 2021; UNI Athletics, "UNI Celebrates Black History Month: A Panther Timeline," Assessed October 13, 2021, Retrieved at https://unipanthers.com/news/2020/2/29/uni-celebrates-black-history-month-a-panther-timeline.aspx; Bloom, *Blue Eyes, Brown Eyes*, (Berkeley: University of California Press, 2021), 25, 41.

40. Bloom. Ibid., 27.

41. Jane Elliott, Interview by author, Iowa, November 5, 2021.

Chapter 5: Eye Opening

1. *Globe-Gazette* (Mason City, IA), "Richer Tells of Support," March 19, 1956; *Muscatine Journal* (Muscatine, IA), "UWF Engages Regional Fieldman," December 4, 1961; *Globe-Gazette* (Mason City, IA), "Remember?" December 5, 1964.

2. *Globe-Gazette* (Mason City, IA), "'Sabrina Fair' Successful Comedy for Little Theater," January 25, 1956.

3. *Globe-Gazette* (Mason City, IA), "Richer Tells of Support," March 19, 1956.

4. *How the Great Religions Began* is a book by Joseph Gaer, published in 1930 by Robert N. McBride & Co. In one review by the *Los Angeles Evening Post*, Gaer is credited with succeeding to write an account of the origins of the major religions for middle and high school age children. SOURCE: *Los Angeles Evening Post*, "How the Great Religions Began," March 13, 1930.

5. Pageant Magazine, "Recall Unhappy Episode at Riceville Schools." *Des Moines Register* (Des Moines, IA), June 9, 1968.

6. *Riceville Recorder*, "Rev. William Bohi Accepts Ministerial Position in Havelock, IA", June 27, 1957.

7. *Times Plain Dealer* (Cresco, IA), "Riceville Teacher firing Draws Wide Publicity in State," March 21, 1956.

8. *Globe-Gazette* (Mason City, IA), "Richer Tells of Support," March 19, 1956.

9. *Riceville Recorder*, March 22, 1956; *Times Plain Dealer* (Cresco, IA), "Riceville Teacher firing Draws Wide Publicity in State," March 21, 1956.

10. *Riceville Recorder*, March 22, 1956.

11. Jane Elliott, Interview by author, California, November 26, 2021.

12. *Globe-Gazette* (Mason City, IA), March 27, 1956.

13. The Des Moines Register, March 27, 1956.

14. Globe-Gazette (Mason City, IA), "5 Riceville Pupils Back in Class," March 20, 1956.

15. The Courier (Waterloo, IA), "May Appeal Firing From Riceville Teaching Post," March 20, 1956.

16. Des Moines Register (Des Moines, IA), "Is Good Teaching a Crime?," March 20, 1956.

17. Iowa City Press-Citizen (Iowa City, IA), "Richer, Controversial Teacher, Is Drafted," June 4, 1956; Fred Lazell, "What Has Happened to Them?," Des Moines Tribune (Des Moines, IA), September 24,

1962; Globe-Gazette (Mason City, IA), "Church is Theater," October 20, 1966; Midge Verhein, "Teacher Quits Job to Start Delafield Theater," Waukesha Daily Freeman, July 21, 1966; Waukesha Daily Freeman (Waukesha, WI), "Church Conversion to Theater Begun," September 3, 1966.

18. Jane Elliott, Email message to the author, November 26, 2021.

19. Jane Elliott, Interview by author, Iowa, November 5, 2021.

20. Jane Elliott, Interview by author, Iowa, June 22, 2021.

21. Jane Elliott, Interview by author, Iowa, 5, 2021

22. Jane Elliott, Interview by author, Iowa, June 22, 2021.

23. Elliott, Interview, Iowa, June 22, 2021; Riceville Recorder, September 19, 1957.

24. Elliott. Ibid.

25. Jean H. Baker, Margaret Sanger: A Life of Passion, (New York: Hill and Wang, 2011), 115-16; Chicago Tribune (Chicago, IL), "FDR Approves Pill for Use in Birth Control," May 10, 1960; Interagency Coordination in Drug Research and Regulation, "Hearings before the subcommittee on reorganization and international organizations of the committee on government operations United States Senate, Eighty-Eighth Congress, First Session: Review of Cooperation on Drug Policies Among the Food and Drug Administration, National Institutes of Health, Veterans' Administration, and Other Agencies," March 21, 1963, (Washington: U.S. Government Printing Office, 1964), 1262.

26. The Messenger (Belleville, IL), "Birth Control Pills: Potentially Harmful," January 18, 1963; Globe-Gazette (Mason City, IA), "Can't tame a headache," December 19, 1964; Tennessean (Nashville, TN), "Doctors, Clerics differ here on use of Birth Control," February 5, 1961; Chillicothe Constitution-Tribune (Chillicothe, MO), "A Birth Control Pill Poses Moral and Social Questions," February 28, 1961; Los Angeles Times (Los Angeles, CA), "Three Drawbacks Seen in Birth-Control Pills," February 19, 1961; ,Baltimore Sun, "Birth control Pills Taken: Death Probed," August 5, 1962; Charlotte News (Charlotte, NC), "6 Deaths Probed for Link with Birth Control," August 4, 1962; El Paso Herald Post (El Paso, TX) "Doctors Question Safety of Birth Control Pills, July 12 1962; News Tribune (Tacoma, WA), "Woman who took Birth Control Pills Dies," August 10, 1962.

27. Chicago Tribune, "The Pill," March 4, 1962a.

28. Jane Elliott, Interview by author, Iowa, June 22, 2021.

29. Jane Elliott, Interview by author, Iowa, October 19, 2021.

30. Jane Elliott, Interview by author, Iowa, June 22, 2021.

31. Jane Elliott, Interview by author, Iowa, June 22, 2021.

32. Jane Elliott, Email message to the author, October 14, 2021.

33. Mason, "An Oral History Interview with Jane Elliott," 17-18.

Chapter 6: An Eye Color Test

1. Lena M. Hill and Michael D. Hill, Invisible Hawkeyes: African Americans at the University of Iowa during the Long Civil Rights Era, (Iowa City: University of Iowa Press, 2016), 103-04, 150-52.

2. Deborah Fink, Cutting Into the Meatpacking Line: Workers and Change in the Rural Midwest, (Chapel Hill: University of North Carolina Press, 1998), 131-32.

3. Marcia Walker-McWilliams, Reverend Addie Wyatt: Faith and the Fight for Labor, Gender, and Racial Equality, (Champaign, IL: University of Illinois Press, 2016), page unknown.

4. Pat Kinney, "Anna Mae Weems," The Courier (Waterloo, IA), June 19, 2015; Sunday Register (Des Moines), "Labor Acts to Assure Civil Rights," December 11, 1960.

5. The Courier, "33-Year-Old NAACP Plans Fete Monday," August 1, 1954.

6. The Courier, "Negro Leader Stabbed While Autographing Books," September 21, 1958.

7. African American Historical and Cultural Museum, "Anna Mae Weems interview with David Jackson III," African American Voices of the Cedar Valley (Map Tour), Updated 2011, Assessed October 22, 2021, Retrieved at https://aa-voices-musueum.uni.edu/video_anna.

8. The Courier, "Motorcade Planned for Dr. M.L. King," November 10, 1959.

9. The Courier, "Martin Luther King, Leader of Bus Boycott, to Speak Here," November 5, 1959.

10. The Courier, "Work for Humanity, Dr. King Advises," November 11, 1959.

11. The Courier, "No Incidents as Picketing of Woolworth's Here Carried Out," April 24, 1960; The Courier, "To: Consumers of Waterloo Area, April 22, 1960.

12. Jane Elliott, Interview by author, Iowa, June 22, 2021.

13. Mason, "An Oral History Interview with Jane Elliott,"18.

14. Jane Elliott, Interview by author, Iowa, June 27, 2022.

15. The Courier, "Store Pickets Withdraw as Negroes Hired," July 1, 1960; Jane Elliott, Interview by author, Iowa, June 22, 2021.

16. The Courier, "New National Tea to Open Tuesday," August 5, 1962.

17. Jane Elliott, Interview by author, Iowa, November 5, 2021.

18. Jane Elliott, Interview by author, Iowa, November 5, 2021.

19. Jane Elliott, Email message to the author, October 23, 2021.

20. Jane Elliott, Interview by author, Iowa, June 22, 2021; Jane Elliott, Interview by author, Iowa, October 19, 2021.

21. The Courier, "Council Bluff Man State NAACP Head," November 20, 1960.

22. Office of History and Preservation, Office of the Clerk, U.S. House of Representatives, Black Americans in Congress, 1870-2007, (Washington D.C.: U.S. Government Printing Office, 2008), 508; JET Magazine, "Till's Mother Marches," October 29, 1970. 33.

23. JET Magazine, "Words of the Week," April 7, 1960. 30.

Chapter 7: A Passionate Eye

1. Riceville Recorder, "Burks Big Opening," August 7, 1902; Riceville Recorder, "The Hotel Burke, Riceville, Iowa," November 20, 1902.

2. Marilyn Arvidson, "Retains Look of Days Gone By," The Courier, March 7, 1960.

3. Jane Elliott, Interview by author, Iowa, November 5, 2021; Riceville Recorder, "Burke Hotel is sold to Mr. and Mrs. Charles Jennison on June 1," June 6, 1963; Globe-Gazette (Mason City, IA), "Burke Hotel sold in Riceville," June 4, 1963; The Courier, "Burke Hotel at Riceville Sold," June 6, 1963; Jane Elliott, Interview by author, Iowa, November 5, 2021.

4. Charles's eldest son, Lloyd, named after his and Jane's father, coined the nickname "Ginny Gunfighter." According to Sarah Elliott, Jane's eldest daughter, the nickname originated from the elder Lloyd's love for Louis LaMore westerns. Those who called him Ginny Gunfighter were family men and close friends. Records indicate Lloyd was indifferent about the nickname. Sarah provides this account: "while I sat with him as [Lloyd] died, and insisted I use his term, 'Gramps', from that day forward." SOURCE: Sarah Elliott, Text message to the author, October 30, 2022; Jane Elliott, Interview by author, Iowa, November 5, 2021.

5. The Courier, "Hotel Management Change at Riceville," September 8, 1963.

6. Jane Elliott, Interview by author, Iowa, June 9, 2021; Bloom, Blue Eyes, Brown Eyes, 27.

7. William Peters, A Class Divided: Then and Now, (New Haven and London: Yale University Press, 1987), 18-19.

8. Fill Fraser, "Roots of racism revealed in teacher's blue-eyed, brown-eyed classroom test," Edmonton Journal (Edmonton, Alberta, Canada), May 13, 1994.

9. Jane Elliott, "Notes written by J.E., 1979," Undated manuscript, Iowa Women's Archives, University of Iowa Libraries, 5.

10. Jane Elliott, Interview by author, Iowa, November 5, 2021.

11. Ibid.

12. Ibid.

13. Riceville Recorder, "Quarterback Club holds meeting; discuss final payments on scoreboard," September 19, 1963; Riceville Recorder, "Football Special!!!," October 10, 1963; Riceville Recorder, "Notice," October 24, 1963.

14. Riceville Recorder, "We are Serving Meals, Morning, Noon, And Night," December 5, 1963; Riceville Recorder, "Collection of gifts and monies for Howard Co. Home being made," December 16, 1965; Times Plain Dealer, "Riceville Residents Give Gifts to Two County Homes," January 1, 1964; Jane Elliott, Interview by author, Iowa, November 5, 2021.

15. Riceville Recorder, "Wanted!," April 2, 1964.

16. Riceville Recorder, "Quarterback Club to hold Slave Auction Saturday," October 10, 1963.

17. Herald and Review (Decatur, IL), "Changed from June 24 to July 1," June 20, 1944; Adams County Free Press (Corning, IA), "Annual Slave Auction Mar. 26," March 24, 1977; Winona Daily News (Winona, MN), "Young People of Nazarene Church to Have 'Slave Auction,'" February 24, 1940.

18. Evening Vanguard (Venice, CA), "Slave Auction Sells War Stamps," December 3, 1943; Sharon L. Schmeling, Capital Times (Madison, WI), November 8, 1988; Chillicothe Constitution-Tribune (Chillicothe, MO), "Old South Banquet Theme," May 6, 1961.

19. The Bridgeport Post (Bridgeport, CT), "'Slave Auction' Said 'Degrading' By PTA Leader," October 12, 1974.

20. Riceville Recorder, "Saturday, November 22," November 20, 1969.

21. Jane Elliott, Interview by author, California December 22, 2021; Riceville Recorder, January 9, 1964.

22. Riceville Recorder, October 29, 1964; Riceville Recorder, August 1, 1963.

23. Mason, "An Oral History Interview with Jane Elliott," 17-18.

24. Riceville Recorder, August 26, 1965.

25. Jane Elliott, Interview by author, Iowa, November 5, 2021; Jane Elliott, Interview by author, Iowa, September 4, 2021.

Chapter 8: Eagle eye

1. Riceville Recorder, "PTA Executive board meets to formulate plans for coming events," June 18, 1964.

2. Iowa City Press-Citizen (Iowa City, IA), "Stanley, Ray Win GOP Contests," September 4, 1968; Muscatine Journal (Muscatine, IA), "David M. Stanley, E.R. Hicklin on Ike Committees," August 15, 1956; Riceville Recorder, "Announces candidacy," August 10, 1967.

3. Jane Elliott, Interview by author, Iowa, November 16, 2021.

4. Ibid.

5. Riceville Recorder, Title unknown, July 20, 1967.

6. Riceville Recorder, "Mrs. Paula Rome," January 26, 1967.

7. Jane Elliott, Interview by author, Iowa, November 16, 2021.

8. Ibid.

9. Riceville Recorder, "Completes course," July 20, 1967; Times Plain Dealer, "Elementary Staff Announced," August 12, 1970.

10. Riceville Recorder, Title unknown, July 20, 1967; Jane Elliott, Interview by author, Iowa, November 16, 2021.

11. The Kansas City Star (Kansas City, MO), "The Schools Are Involved in a War of Classical and Utilitarian Ideals," March 29, 1938.

12. John Dewey, Democracy and Education: An Introduction to the Philosophy of Education. (The MacMillan Company, 1922), 228-29, 266.

13. Jane Elliott, Interview by author, Iowa, August 13, 2021.

14. Jane Elliott, Interview by author, Iowa, December 22, 2021.

15. Jane Elliott, Interview by author, Iowa, November 16, 2021; Riceville Recorder. August 18, 1966.

16. Ced Kurtz, "Educating the Dyslexic Child," The Daily News (Lebanon, PA), May 8, 1978.

17. Jane Elliott, Interview by author, Iowa, November 5, 2021.

18. Jane Elliott, "Good Listeners have quiet hands, feet, and mouths," Notepad. Jane Elliott's Personal File, Osage, IA, Date Unknown.

19. Jane Elliott, Interview by author, Iowa, November 17, 2021

20. Ray Hansen, Interview by author, Minnesota, October 26, 2021.

21. Jane Elliott, Interview by author, Iowa, July 5, 2021.

22. Mason, "An Oral History Interview with Jane Elliott," 27; Jane Elliott, Interview by author, Iowa, July 5, 2021; Riceville Recorder, "Room 10 third graders observe Energy Awareness Week," December 13, 1973.

23. Mason, "An Oral History Interview with Jane Elliott," 27.

24. Ibid., 29.

25. Riceville Recorder, "Room 10 third graders observe Energy Awareness Week," December 13, 1973.

26. Jane Elliott, Interview by author, Iowa, July 5, 2021.

27. Jane Elliott, Email message to the author, December 8, 2021.

28. Bloom, Blue Eyes, Brown Eyes, 35-6.

29. Ibid. 34.

30. Bertram Verhaag, Unpublished footage, Blue Eyed, 1995, Orange, CA, Jane Elliott Personal File, Osage, IA.

31. Martin Luther King, Jr. and Clayborne Carson ed., The Autobiography of Martin Luther King Jr. (New York, NY: Warner Books, 1998), 325.

32. Harvard Sitkoff and Eric Foner, The Struggle for Black Equality, 1954-1992, (New York: Macmillan, 1993), 199.

33. Bob Wilcox, "'I Have Leaders' Support,'" Miami News (Miami, FL), December 25, 1967, 33.

34. Joel Stone and Thomas J. Sugrue, Detroit 1967: Origins, Impact, Legacies, (Detroit, MI: Wayne State University Press, 2017) i.

35. The Courier, "Rights Commission Report Says Facts Show Sallis Death Suicide," June 29, 1966; Globe-Gazette (Mason City, IA), "Waterloo man given five-year prison term," November 1, 1966.

36. Muscatine Journal and News-Tribune (Muscatine, IA), July 10, 1967.

37. Sioux City Journal (Sioux City, IA), "Waterloo Riot-Scarred Area Quiet," July 11, 1967.

38. Des Moines Register (Des Moines, IA), "Throw Fire Bombs, Loot in Waterloo," July 10, 1967.

39. Nick Lamberto, "Strife-Torn Waterloo in Uneasy Calm," July 11, 1967.

40. The Boston Globe, "King Reorganizes Agency for Drive on Poverty," December 13, 1967.

41. Martin Luther King, Jr., "On Equality" in The Atlanta Constitution (Atlanta, GA). "Dr. King Discusses Equality," January 1, 1968.

42. Dale Kueter, "Students find truth in a lie," The Gazette (Cedar Rapids, IA), August 3, 1992.

43. Jane Elliott, Unlabeled VHS Cassette, Date unknown, Jane Elliott Personal Files, Osage, IA, 1995

Chapter 9: Without Batting an Eye: A Daring Exercise

1. Jane Elliott, Email message to the author, November 17, 2021; Elliott, A Collar in My Pocket, 8-12

2. Jane Elliott, Email message to the author, November 17, 2021.

3. Elliott, A Collar in My Pocket, 4.

4. Jane Elliott, Interview with author, Iowa, July 1, 2021; Bruce Stewart, "Draft Proposal for Jane Elliot [sic] Documentary and Associated Product Development," Unpublished manuscript, Date Unknown, Jane Elliott File. Osage, IA.

5. Elliott, A Collar in My Pocket, 9.

6. Ibid., 5-6.

7. Ibid.

8. Ibid. 2.

9. Ibid., 6.

10. Jane Elliott, Interview with author, Iowa, July 5, 2021.

11. Jane Elliott's notes inscribed on Brian Cowden, "A Class Divided: A True Story Screenplay," Unpublished manuscript, October 8, 1997, Jane Elliott Files, Iowa Women's Archive, University of Iowa Libraries, 16.

12. Jane Elliott, Interview with author, Iowa, July 5, 2021; Elliott. A Collar in My Pocket, 12.

13. Peters, A Class Divided, 21.

14. Ibid., 23.

15. Elliott, A Collar in My Pocket, 9.

16. Ibid., 20.

17. Peters, A Class Divided, 23.

18. Jane Elliott, Interview with author, Iowa, July 5, 2021; In her book A Collar in My Pocket, Jane says the name of the blue-eyed student was Carol, daughter of a Lutheran minister. The RCS yearbook from that year does not list a Carol since she arrived at the school after the yearbook was sent to production.

19. Jane Elliott, Interview with author, Iowa, July 5, 2021.

20. Peters, A Class Divided, 24-5.

21. Elliott, A Collar in My Pocket, 25; Jane Elliott, Interview with author, Iowa, July 5, 2021.

22. Jane Elliott, Interview with author, Iowa, July 5, 2021

23. Jane Elliott, Interview with author, Iowa, July 9, 2021.

24. Author unknown, "In the Eyes of the Beholder Story Line," unpublished manuscript, Jane Elliot Personal Files, Osage, IA.

25. Jane Elliott, Interview with author, Iowa, July 5, 2021.

26. Peters, A Class Divided, 35.

27. Ibid., 38.

28. Riceville Recorder, "Mrs. Jane Elliott to appear on the Tonight Show in New York," May 30, 1968.

29. Author unknown, "In the Eyes of the Beholder Story Line," unpublished manuscript, Jane Elliot Personal Files, Osage, IA.

30. Jane Elliott, Interview with author, Iowa, July 5, 2021; Elliott, A Collar in My Pocket, 23.

31. Elliott, A Collar in My Pocket, 37-8.

32. Martin Luther King, Jr., Letter from Birmingham Jail. London, England: Penguin Classics, 2018.

33. Elliott, A Collar in My Pocket, 21.

Chapter 10: The Eyes Have It: The Biggest Little Town in Northease Iowa

1. Elliott, A Collar in My Pocket, 38; Jane Elliott, Interview with author, Iowa, July 9, 2021.

2. Riceville Recorder, "Mrs. Jane Elliott to Appear on Tonight Show in New York," May 30, 1968.

3. Riceville Recorder, "Mrs. Jane Elliott to appear on Tonight Show in New York," May 30, 1968.

4. Riceville Recorder, "This is how discrimination feels," April 18, 1968.

5. Total population of Riceville is stated in an article about the Iowa Press Association Convention awarding the Riceville Recorder with an award. SOURCE: Riceville Recorder, "Received Honorable Mention at Iowa Press Convention," April 25, 1968.

6. J. James Rathnam, Letter to Mrs. Donald J. Button, New York, NY, June 13, 1968, Jane Elliott Files, 1968 Correspondences, Iowa Women's Archives, University of Iowa Libraries.

7. The Tonight Show, "Martin Luther King Jr.: 'The Economic Problem is the Most Serious Problem'" YouTube. The Nation, February 23, 2017; Journal and Courier (Lafayette, IN), "Belafonte Subs," February 3, 1968.

8. Riceville Recorder, "The World of 4-H," October 5, 1967; Elaine Andrews, "4-H-Science from Practical Education," Community Connections for Science Education: History and Theory You Can Use, National Science Teachers Association Press, 2001, 49-50.

9. Riceville Recorder, "4-H photography group to meet Thursday, Feb. 17," February 10, 1966; Riceville Recorder, "Diane Feldt wins 'Best Fair' photo award," August 17, 1967; Riceville Recorder, "4-H depends on leaders," October 5, 1967.

10. Jane Elliott, Email message to the author, November 23, 2021; Sarah Elliott, Interview with author, Iowa, January 20, 2022; Riceville Recorder, "Memorial Service," November 23, 1972.

11. Riceville Recorder, "Mrs. Elliott to appear on Tonight Show in New York," May 30, 1968.

12. Elliott, A Collar in My Pocket, 39; Jane Elliott, Interview with author, Iowa, July 9, 2021.

13. Riceville Recorder, "Mrs. Elliott to appear on Tonight Show in New York," May 30, 1968.

14. Donald Button, "Red Alert—Red Alert—Red Alert," Date unknown, Riceville, IA, Jane Elliott Files, 1970 Correspondence, Iowa Women's Archives, University of Iowa Libraries.

15. Jane Elliott, Interview with author, Iowa, 27, 2022.

16. Jane Elliott, "Jane Elliott notes," 1970 correspondences, Jane Elliott File, Iowa Women's Archive, University of Iowa Libraries.

17. Elliott, A Collar in My Pocket, 39.

18. Jane Elliott, Interview with author, Iowa, July 9, 2021.

19. Holly George-Warren, A Man Called Destruction: The Life and Music of Alex Chilton from Box Tops to Big Star to Backdoor Man, (New York, NY: Penguin Books, 2014), 72-3.

20. Jane Elliott, Interview with author, Iowa, July 9, 2021.

21. Ibid.

22. Ibid.

23. Elliott, A Collar in My Pocket, 40.

24. Mrs. Loretta Ohrmann, Letter to Mrs. Darld [sic] Elliott, Baltimore, MD, July 13, 1968, Jane Elliott Files, 1968 Correspondence, Iowa Women's Archives, University of Iowa Libraries; Mrs. DRT, Letter to Mrs. Jane Phillips [sic], Montgomery, AL, Date unknown, Iowa Women's Archives, University of Iowa Libraries.

25. Des Moines Register, "Recalls Unhappy Episode at Riceville Schools," June 9, 1968.

26. Loretta Marion, Letter to Mrs. Jane Elliott, Riceville, IA, November 20, 1968, Jane Elliott Files, 1968 Correspondence, Iowa Women's Archives, University of Iowa Libraries.

27. Loretta Marion, Letter to Mrs. Jane Elliott, New York, NY, March 18, 1969, Jane Elliott Files, 1968 Correspondence, Iowa Women's Archives, University of Iowa Libraries.

28. Wes Birdsall, "Rotary Club Memo: Program for Tuesday, August 20, 1968," Osage, IA, Jane Elliott Files, 1968 Correspondence, Iowa Women's Archives, University of Iowa Libraries; Jane Elliott, Letter to Miss Gracie Adkins, Riceville, IA, August 26, 1968, Jane Elliott Files, 1968 Correspondence, Iowa Women's Archives, University of Iowa Libraries.

29. Elliott, A Collar in My Pocket, 43.

30. Jane Elliott, Interview with author, Iowa, November 16, 2021; Riceville Recorder, "Would you like to have a foreign student for Thanksgiving?," November 21, 1968; Globe-Gazette, "Foreign Students Visit," November 25, 1969.

31. Jane Elliott, Interview with author, Iowa, June 9, 2021; Mason, "An Oral History Interview with Jane Elliott." 55-6.

32. Douglas F. Sherwin, Letter to Mrs. Darald Elliott, Mason City, IA, November 23, 1968, Jane Elliott Files, 1968 Correspondence, Iowa Women's Archives, University of Iowa Libraries; Douglas F. Sherwin, Letter to Mr. John Smith, Mason City, IA, December 2, 1968, Jane Elliott Files, 1968 Correspondence, Iowa Women's Archives, University of Iowa Libraries.

33. Riceville Recorder, "Camermen [sic] to be in Riceville 3 days, September 17, 18, 19," September 5, 1968.

34. Elliott, A Collar in My Pocket, 46.

35. Ibid.; Michael Judge, "My Grandfather and the 'Blue eyes-Brown Eyes' Lesson," Wall Street Journal Opinion, September 17, 2019, Retrieved at https://www.wsj.com/articles/my-grandfather-and-the-blue-eyes-brown-eyes-lesson-1523052806

36. Elliott, A Collar in My Pocket, 47.

37. Judge, Ibid.

38. Jane wrote in her memoir A Collar in My Pocket that the exercise for CBC occurred in October 1969. She also mentioned that the uprising in Waterloo occurred in October. She had the dates wrong on both accounts.

39. Lexington Herald (Lexington, KY), "Youth Curfew Set in Town after Riots," September 15, 1968.

40. Des Moines Register, "Black History Course Set at Waterloo," September 14, 1968.

41. Jane Elliott, "The Way It Is," Documentary, VHS, Canadian Broadcasting Corporation, 1968, Jane Elliott's Personal Files, Osage, IA.

42. Windsor Star (Windsor, Ontario, Canada), "'[N-word] with parka - - portrait of Eskimo image," September 30, 1968; Elliott, A Collar in My Pocket, 47-48.

43. Jane Elliott, Letter to Dear Mr. Letts, Riceville, IA, Date unknown, Jane Elliott Files, 1968 Correspondence, Iowa Women's Archives, University of Iowa Libraries.

44. John Brant to Pliny Porter, May 27, 1996, Jane Elliott Files, 1968 Correspondence, Iowa Women's Archives, University of Iowa Libraries.

45. Mrs. Peter Dunlop, "Letter to CBC. The Way it is," October 6, 1968, Jane Elliott File, 1968, Jane Elliott Files, 1968 Correspondence, Iowa Women's Archives, University of Iowa Libraries.; Mrs. Anne Tylsesley, Letter to CBC, October 6, 1968, Jane Elliott Files, 1968 Correspondence, Iowa Women's Archives, University of Iowa Libraries.

46. G.M. Bodrufton, Letter to CBC, October 7, 1968, Jane Elliott File, 1968, Jane Elliott Files, 1968 Correspondence, Iowa Women's Archives, University of Iowa Libraries.

47. Todd Brandau, "Discrimination Day Reflection," September 20, 1968, Jane Elliott Files, 1968 Correspondence, Iowa Women's Archives, University of Iowa Libraries.

48. Sister Trudy Richardson, MA., "CBC's The Way It Is," Kamloops, BC, October 7, 1968. Jane Elliott Files, 1968 Correspondence, Iowa Women's Archives, University of Iowa Libraries.

49. Fred McFadden, "The Way It Is," Scarborough, Ontario, October 8, 1968, Jane Elliott Files, 1968 Correspondence, Iowa Women's Archives, University of Iowa Libraries.

50. Jane Elliott, Interview with author, Iowa, June 9, 2021; Mason, "An Oral History Interview with Jane Elliot," 65; Jane Elliott, Interviw with author, California, December 22, 2021.

51. Elliott, A Collar in My Pocket, 50-51.

52. Riceville Recorder, "Elections for extension council set in 4 townships," December 5, 1968.

53. Ellen Hoffman, "Blondes Having 'Less Fun,'" Courier-Journal (Louisville, KY), February 19, 1969.

54. Diane Bernard, "Social experiment targeting blond students is recalled," Santa Fe New Mexican (Santa Fe, NM), December 30, 2019.

55. Diane Bernard, "'No blondes allowed': 50 years after a junior high experiment, students say it had 'a big impact,'" Washington Post, December 29, 2019.

56. Janesville Daily Gazette (Janesville, WI), "Blondes Have Less Fun," February 27, 1969.

57. Chicago Tribune, "Discrimination Test at Niles North Sparks Discussion," February 8, 1970.

58. Elliott, A Collar in My Pocket, 53.

Chapter 11: Eye of the Storm

1. Elliott, A Collar in My Pocket, 54.

2. Riceville Recorder, March 5, 1970.

3. Martin Luther King, Jr., Letter to Bill Peters, Montgomery, AL, April 25, 1956, The Martin Luther King, Jr. Papers Project, Stanford University.

4. Jocelyn Y. Stewart, "William Peters, 85; writer examined U.S. race relations," Los Angeles Times, May 27, 2007.

5. Muriel "Mike" Peters, Email message to the author December 1, 2021.

6. St. Lucie News Tribune (Fort Pierce, FL), "William Peters, film producer," May 25, 2007.

7. Anniston Star, "Wm. Peters Misses Goal in 'Temper,'" April 26, 1959.

8. William Peters, "Mississippi and the Fifteenth Amendment," CBS Report. Season 4, Episode 2, Aired Sept. 26, 1962, Retrieved from C-SPAN, American History TV, February 13, 2021 at https://www.c-span.org/video/?c4497511/user-clip-mississippi-fifteenth-amendment

9. Muriel Peters, Interview with the author, New York, December 1, 2021.

10. Ibid.

11. Elliott, A Collar in My Pocket, 54-65.

12. Thomas H. Wolf, Letter to Jane Elliott, February 11, 1970, New York, NY, Jane Elliott Files, 1970 Correspondence, Iowa Women's Archives, University of Iowa Libraries.

13. Jane Elliott. Email correspondence with the author. Menifee, CA. December 8, 2021. 6:21 PM.

14. Elliott. A Collar in My Pocket. 59 and 74.

15. Riceville Recorder, March 5, 1970; Muriel Peters, Interview with author, New York, December 1, 2021.

16. Peters, Ibid.; Jane Elliott Email message to the author, December 8, 2021.

17. Jane Elliott, Interview with author, Iowa, July 22, 2021.

18. Jane Elliott, Interview with author, Iowa, June 27, 2022; Author unknown, Student Records, Jane Elliott Files, Blue Eyed, Brown Eyed Exercise, Iowa Women's Archives, University of Iowa Libraries.

19. Jane Elliott, Interview with author, Iowa, July 22, 2021.

20. Richard Nixon, "Statement About National Brotherhood Week, 1970," February 20, 1970, Retrieved at https://www.presidency.ucsb.edu/documents/statement-about-national-brotherhood-week-1970.

21. William Peters, "The Eye of the Storm," May 11, 1970, YouTube. The Realdude, "Eye of the Storm Jane Elliott 1970," April 23, 2017, Retrieved at https://youtu.be/6gi2T0ZdKVc.

22. When she conducted the eye color exercise at Riceville Elementary, Jane Elliott put blue-eyed students on top of the classroom hierarchy on day one. Why? Because there were no students of color It was only when Jane habitually conducted the exercise with adults, many cohorts containing men and women of color, that she placed the blue eyes on the bottom upon the commencement of the exercise. When asked, she could not recall why she changed her approach for the 1970 "The Eye of the Storm" recording; though, she suggested, it may have been because the blue-eyed students that year were greatly outnumbered by their brown-eyed peers. SOURCE: Jane Elliott, Interview with author, California, December 22, 2021.

23. Jane Elliott, Interview with author, Iowa, July 22, 2021.

24. Ray Hansen, Interview with author, Minnesota, October 26, 2021.

25. Elliott, A Collar in My Pocket, 76.

26. Mary Elliott, unpublished edition of Blue Eyed, VHS, Denkmal Films,1995.

27. Rex Kozak, "Lesson for life: bigotry's pain," The Gazette, August 3, 1992.

28. Ibid.

29. Peters, A Class Divided, 32.

30. Elliott, A Collar in My Pocket, 78; Jane Elliott, Email message to the author, December 8, 2021.

31. Bill Buetel, "The Eye of the Storm," ABC Now, May 11, 1970.

32. Muriel "Mike" Peters, Letter to Jane Elliott, New York, NY, March 2, 1970, Jane Elliott Files, 1970 Correspondence, Iowa Women's Archive, University of Iowa Libraries.

33. Muriel "Mike" Peters, Letter to Jane Elliott, New York, NY, March 13, 1970, Jane Elliott Files, 1970 Correspondence, Iowa Women's Archive, University of Iowa Libraries.

34. Ibid.

35. Muriel Peters, Interview with author, New York, December 1, 2021.

36. Jan Horgen, "How Far have we come?," Globe-Gazette, August 15, 1999, S1,S10.

37. Ray Hansen, Interview with author, Minnesota, October 26, 2021.

38. ABC News Business Office, Consent Form, Anatomy of Prejudice, March 3, 1970, American Broadcasting Company, New York, NY, Jane Elliott Files, 1970 Correspondence, Iowa Women's Archive, University of Iowa Libraries.

39. John Leonard, "Ghetto for blue-eyes in the classroom," Life, May 8, 1970.

40. Elliott, A Collar in My Pocket, 78.

41. Muriel Peters, Interview with author, New York, December 1, 2021.

42. Ray Bennett, "Television," Windsor Star (Windsor, Ontario), June 17, 1970.

43. Globe-Gazette, "Riceville teacher is on move promoting novel," August 7, 1971.

44. Jane Elliott, Interview with author, July 5, 2021.

45. John Brant, Letter to Pliny Porter, May 27, 1996, Jane Elliott Personal Files, Osage, IA, 29.

46. Muriel "Mike" Peters, Letter to Jane Elliott, May 12, 1970, New York, NY, Jane Elliott Files, 1970 Correspondence, Iowa Women's Archives, University of Iowa Libraries.

47. Globe-Gazette (Mason City, IA), "Riceville class to be on ABC," May 8, 1970.

48. Ray Bennett, "Television, Windsor Star (Windsor, Ontario), June 17, 1970; ABC Merchandising News, "ABC News NOW Series Special 'Eye of the Storm' Available to Educational, Industrial Groups," ABC, New York, NY, June 11, 1970, Jane Elliott Files, 1970 Correspondence, Iowa Women's Archives, University of Iowa Libraries; Susan T. Mitchell, Letter to Mrs. Elliot [sic], ABC Company Merchandising Inc., New York, NY, July 2, 1970, Jane Elliott Files, 1970 Correspondence. Iowa Women's Archives, University of Iowa Libraries.

49. Baltimore Sun, "'Maryland Weekend' Program To Feature Farm Museum," August 6, 1970.

50. Mason, "An Oral History Interview with Jane Elliott," 45.

Chapter 12: More Than Meets the Eye

1. Mary Carroll, Letter to Dear Mrs. Elliott, Colorado Springs, CO. May 14, 1970, Jane Elliott File, 1970 Correspondence, Iowa Women's Archives, University of Iowa Libraries.

2. Wilda Wood, Letter to Mrs. Jane Elliott, Colorado Springs, CO. May 14, 1970, Jane Elliott File, 1970 Correspondence, Iowa Women's Archives, University of Iowa Libraries.; Patricia McCormack, "Students Learn First Hand of Segregation Injustice," St. Joseph News Gazette, September 28, 1966; Austin American, "'Project Misery,'" December 8, 1966; Jim Bigney, " [. . .] Now They Know How Segregation Hurts," Boston Sunday Globe, December 3, 1967.

3. Carroll, Ibid.

4. Joyce Brothers, "What To Do When Tots Are Prejudiced," Herald Journal, February 21, 1967.

5. Wood, Ibid., May 14, 1970.

6. Donald H. Morrow, Letter to Roger L. Thorson, Washington D.C., May 28, 1970, Jane Elliott File, 1970 Correspondence, Iowa Women's Archives, University of Iowa Libraries.

7. Jane Elliott, Letter to Mrs. Wilda Wood, Riceville, IA, June 4, 1970, Jane Elliott File, 1970 Correspondence, Iowa Women's Archives, University of Iowa Libraries.

8. Jane Elliott, Letter to Marylin "Mickey" Alcorn, Riceville, IA, April 4, 1968, Jane Elliott Files, 1968 Correspondence, Iowa Women's Archives, University of Iowa Libraries.

9. Ken Caunce, "A lesson in hatred," Windsor Star, May 16, 1970; Ray Bennett, "Television," Windsor Star (Windsor, Ontario), June 17, 1970.

10. Caunce, Ibid., 3.

11. Ibid.,3.

12. Ibid., 3; Caunce, "Discrimination: Students react in varied ways," Windsor Star, May 16, 1970.

13. Ken Caunce, "A lesson in hatred," Windsor Star, May 16, 1970.

14. Max Rafferty, "Color 'game' hogwash," The Times (Munster, IN), November 15, 1970.

15. Ibid.

16. Don Walz Jr., Letter to Jane Elliott, Winona, MN., ca. November 1970, Jane Elliott File, 1970 Correspondence, Iowa Women's Archives, University of Iowa Libraries.

17. Jane Elliott, Letter to Don Walz Jr., Riceville, IA, November 30, 1970. Jane Elliott Files, Jane Elliott File, 1970 Correspondence, Iowa Women's Archives, University of Iowa Libraries.

18. Jane Elliott, Interview with author, Iowa, August 9, 2021.

19. Ibid.

20. Ibid.

21. Michael Jay Weiner and Frances E. Wright, "Effects of Underground Arbitrary Discrimination Upon Subsequent Attitudes Toward a Minority Group," Journal of Applied Social Psychology, March 1973, Volume 3, Issue 1, 96-7.

22. Weiner and Wright, Effects of Underground Arbitrary Discrimination Upon Subsequent Attitudes Toward a Minority Group, 97-100.

Chapter 13: A Black Eye: Anatomy of Prejudice

1. Philadelphia Inquirer, "President Would Preserve Home," January 26, 1909.

2. White House Conference on Children, "White House Conference on Children, Report to the President," Washington D.C., United States Government Printing Office, 1971, 2-4, 304.

3. Ted C. Taylor, Letter: Dear Mrs. Elliott, Overland Park, Kansas, October 9, 1970, Jane Elliott File, 1970 Correspondence, Iowa Women's Archives, University of Iowa Libraries.

4. Catherine Hinchey, Letter to Dear Mrs. Eliott [sic], Hazelwood, MO, October 9, 1970, Jane Elliott File, 1970 Correspondence (Folder 3). Iowa Women's Center. University of Iowa Libraries.

5. Elliott, A Collar in My Pocket, 85.

6. The Gazette, "Dissent-Ridden Conference on Children ends," December 21, 1970.

7. White House Conference on Children, "White House Conference on Children, Report to the President," Washington, D.C., United States Government Printing Office, 1971 in Bloom, Blue Eyes, Brown Eyes, 110.

8. Jane Elliott. Letter to Cynthia. Undated. Jane Elliott Papers, the Iowa women's Archives at the University of Iowa Libraries.

9. Handwritten notes, Undated, Jane Elliott Papers, The Iowa Women's Archives at the University of Iowa Libraries in Bloom, Blue Eyes, Brown Eyes, 116.

10. Elliott, A Collar in My Pocket, 87-8.

11. Ibid., 89.

12. Toni House, "Blue Eyes Get Picked On," Washington Star, December 16, 1970.

13. Handwritten notes, Undated, Jane Elliott Papers, The Iowa Women's Archives at the University of Iowa Libraries in Bloom, Blue Eyes, Brown Eyes, 116.

14. Toni House, "Blue Eyes Get Picked On," Washington Star, December 16, 1970.

15. Ibid.

16. Olivia Hansen, "Brown eyes and blue eyes," Northwestern Bell Magazine, Summer 1971, 16, Jane Elliott Personal Files, Osage, IA.

17. Jane Elliott, Interview with author, California, December 29, 2021.

18. Kenneth B. Clark, Prejudice and Your Child, (Boston, MA: Beacon Press, 1955) and Kenneth B. Clark, "American Education Today," Integrated Education 3, No. 6, (December 1965-January 1966), quote in White House Conference on Children, "White House Conference on Children, Report to the President," (Washington D.C.: United States Government Printing Office, 1971), 296-8.

19. White House Conference on Children, "White House Conference on Children, Report to the President," (Washington D.C.: United States Government Printing Office. 1971), 299.

20. The Gazette, "Dissent-Ridden Conference on Children Ends," December 21, 1970.

21. Jane Elliott, "Dear Mike and Bill," December 28, 1970, Jane Elliott Mostly family, 1966-1994 Correspondence, Iowa Women's Archives, University of Iowa Libraries.

22. Elliott, A Collar in My Pocket, 94-6.

23. Jan Horgen, "How Far have we come? Daughters lost friends after exercise," Globe-Gazette, August 15, 1999.

24. John Brant, Letter to Pliny Porter, May 27, 1996, Jane Elliott Personal Files. Osage, IA.

25. Bloom, Blue Eyes, Brown Eyes, 141.

26. Ibid., 139.

27. Ibid., 139-40.

28. Riceville Recorder, June 11, 1970.

29. Ruth Dupuis, "One-room school lives on as home," Globe-Gazette, July 5, 1999.

Chapter 14: Eye to Eye or a Class Divided?

1. Oakland Tribune (Oakland, CA), "Scientists Trying to Avoid Hot Race-IQ Capacity Issue," April 22, 1971.

2. Richard D. Lyons, "Scientists Shun Confrontation on Causes of Differences in I.Q.," The New York Times, May 3, 1970.

3. Joel N. Shurkin, Broken Genius: The Rise and Fall of William Shockley Creator of the Electronic Age, (New York and London: Macmillan, 2006), 216-7.

4. Shurkin, Broken Genius, 270.

5. Hutchinson News (Hutchinson, KS), "The Library Fair," September 11, 1971.

6. Hutchinson News (Hutchinson, KS), "Test Scores Show No Basic Racial Difference," September 4, 1971; Jane R. Mercer, "Pluralistic diagnosis in the evaluation of Black and Chicano children: A procedure for taking sociocultural variables into account in clinical assessment," in C.A. Hemandez, M.J. Haug, & N.N. Wagner (Eds.), Chicanos: Social and psychological perspectives, 1971, 19(1), 23-8; William Krasner, Labeling the Children, (Washington, D.C.: U.S. Department of Health, Education, and Welfare, August 1976), 11-2.

7. Winona Daily News (Winona, MN), "Winona man elected to PTA post," April 23, 1971.

8. Santa Maria Times (Santa Maria, CA), "'The Eye of the storm' Collects Peabody Award," June 19, 1971.

9. William Peters, Letter to Mrs. Darald Elliott, New York, NY. June 1, 1971, Jane Elliott Files, 1971 Correspondence, Iowa Women's Archives, University of Iowa Libraries.

10. Riceville Recorder, "Letter to the Editor," August 12, 1971; The Courier, "Award Given for Experiment in Discrimination," July 22, 1971.

11. Estherville Daily News (Estherville, IA), "U of I teacher workshop holds segregation test," June 23, 1971.

12. Len DeCarlo, "Program on Discrimination Held Here," Morning Herald (Uniontown, PA), March 20, 1975.

13. Globe-Gazette, "Riceville teacher takes 'eye game' to U of I," August 25, 1971; Riceville Recorder, "U of I experiments with bigotry in Iowa teaches workshop," August 26, 1971.

14. Muriel Peters Interview with author, New York, December 1, 2021.

15. William Peters, Letter to Jane Elliott, November 16, 1970, New York, NY. Jane Elliott Files. 1970 Correspondence, Iowa Women's Archives, University of Iowa Libraries.

16. Jane Elliott, Letter to Susan, Riceville, IA, July 6, 1970, Jane Elliott Files, 1970 Correspondence, Iowa Women's Archives, University of Iowa Libraries.

17. Peters, Letter to Jane Elliott, Ibid.

18. Beth Durchschlag, "Teacher Makes Pupils See the Realities of Racial Bias," Courier-Post (Camden, NJ), July 30, 1971.

19. Rod Riggs, "From My Point of View," Ames Daily Tribune (Ames, IA), July 24, 1971.

20. Jean Booth, Letter to Mrs. Elliott, New York, NY, July 19, 1971, Jane Elliott Papers, 1970 Correspondence, Iowa Women's Archives, University of Iowa Libraries.

21. Globe Gazette, "Riceville teacher is on move promoting new novel," August 7, 1971.

22. Jane Elliott, Interview with author, Iowa, August 13, 2021.

23. Muriel Peters, Interview with author, New York, December 1, 2021.

24. Jane Elliott, Interview with author, California, December 29, 2021.

25. Linda Kaitis, Letter to Mrs. Darald Elliott, January 25, 1971, Jane Elliott Files, Business Concerning Book, 1971, Blue-eyed, Brown-eyed Exercise, Iowa Women's Archive. University of Iowa Libraries.

26. Olivia Hansen, "Brown eyes and blue eyes," Northwestern Bell Magazine, Summer 1971, 14, Jane Elliott Personal Files, Osage, IA.

27. Riceville Recorder, "Distinguished Service Award," October 19, 1972; La Crosse Tribune (La Crosse, WI), "8 to Receive Award From Luther College," October 10, 1963.

Chapter 15: Evil Eye

1. Robert W. Dillon and Don N. Kersten, "Iowa and the U.S. Bicentennial, 1776-1976: Final Report," Iowa American Revolution Bicentennial Commission, December 1976, 2.

2. Ibid., 11.

3. Max Rafferty, "Classroom's Not Soapbox for Teacher's Opinions," Salt Lake Tribune (Salt Lake City, UT), November 15, 1970.

4. Dillon and Kersten, Ibid., 47.

5. Times Plain Dealer, "Park Project Gets Bicentennial Endorsement; Funds Awaited," November 29, 1972.

6. Riceville Recorder, "In hopes of establishing ARB mini-park, 'The Village Green' in Riceville," April 27, 1972.

7. Daily Times (Salisbury, MD), "Marylanders Can Grow Their Own 'Wye Oak,'" March 21, 1973.

8. Elliott, A Collar in My Pocket, 127.

9. Star Tribune (Minneapolis, MN), May 31, 1973; Riceville Recorder, August 16, 1973; Courier, "Riceville Authors Came Calling at Library's Jubilee," August 26, 1973.

10. Bloom, Blue Eyes, Brown Eyes, 150-1.

11. Times Plain Dealer, "Michael Black Gets Merit Scholarship," April 22, 1970; Riceville Recorder, "Named to Dean's list," July 12, 1973.

12. Record (Hackensack, NJ), "Brown vs. Blue – a Midland Park lesson in bigotry," February 28, 1974.

13. Chicago Tribune, "Suburb teens expect 'the worst,' find friends," November 7, 1978.

14. Russell Watson, Interview with author, Wisconsin, May 29, 2022; Newsday (Melville, NY), "Chicago Whites Hit King With Rock," August 6, 1966; Newsday, "Whites Feel Cops Clubs," August 6, 1966; Dale Berman, Interview with author, Illinois, June 1, 2022.

15. Russell Watson, Email message to the author, Berlin, WI. May 24, 2022.

16. Susan Skowron, "2 area teachers launch hopes for space mission," Daily Journal (Wheaton, IL), April 11, 1985; Marv Collison, "Wheaton teacher is finalist for Space Shuttle Mission," Wheaton Leader, March 27, 1985.

17. Watson, Ibid., May 29, 2022.

18. Watson, Email message to the author, Berlin, WI, May 24, 2022.

19. Courier, "Mrs. Jane Elliott cited by mental health group," November 26, 1974.

20. Ced Kurtz, "Educating the Dyslexic Child," Lebanon Daily News, May 8, 1978.

21. Morning Herald (Uniontown, PA), "Target Date Given," January 3.

22. Lancaster New Era (Lancaster, PA), "Gov. Lawrence Signs Pa. Fair Housing Bill," February 28, 1961.

23. The Pittsburgh Press (Pittsburgh, PA), "Rights Panel Pressing 3 More School Boards," January 6, 1974; Evening Standard (Uniontown, PA), "Desegregation Plans," January 4, 1974.

24. Evening Standard (Uniontown, PA), "School decision," March 29, 1974; Evening Standard (Uniontown, PA), "Black Boycott Grows," September 9, 1974.

25. Evening Standard (Uniontown, PA), "Protest Set in East End," September 3, 1974.

26. Evening Standard (Uniontown, PA), "East End Groups Still Oppose School Plan," August 29, 1974.

27. Daily Courier (Connellsville, PA), "Protest Spills Over to Boycott Uniontown Stores," September 7, 1974.

28. Daily Courier (Connellsville, PA), "Accord Reached in Early Hours at Uniontown," September 11, 1974.

29. Evening Standard (Uniontown, PA), "Moratorium Approved on School," October 1, 1974.

30. Daily Courier (Connellsville, PA), "Uniontown East End School Will House 128 Students," October 10, 1974.

31. Evening Standard (Uniontown, PA), "Uniontown Area Gets Black Administrator," November 19, 1974. 10; Evening Standard (Uniontown, PA), "In-Service Session," March 21, 1975.

32. Jane Elliott, Interview with author, California, April 24, 2022.

33. Jane Elliott, Interview with author, Iowa, August 9, 2021.

34. Jane Elliott, Interview with author, Iowa, August 9, 2021; Elliott, A Collar in My Pocket, 130.

35. Duncannon Record (Duncannon, PA), "Prejudice will be theme," March 6, 1975.

36. Jane Elliott, Interview with author, Iowa, August 9, 2021; Sentinel (Carlisle, PA), "Mental Health Conference Scheduled at Embers Tonight," March 5, 1975.

37. Jane Elliott, Interview with author, Iowa, August 9, 2021.

38. Elliott, A Collar in My Pocket, 127.

39. Jane Elliott, Interview with author, California, December 22, 2021.

40. Riceville Recorder, "Log Cabin constructed by third-grade class on Village Green," May 22, 1975.

41. Riceville Recorder, "'Village Green' entered in Park contest," June 19, 1975.

42. Riceville Recorder, "Village Green was chosen as second place winner," July 17, 1975.

43. Globe-Gazette, "Grafton's Kindernook wins award." July 8, 1975. 13; Riceville Recorder. August 14, 1975. 1.

44. Jane Elliott, Interview with author, California, December 22, 2021.

45. Bismarck Tribune, "Mental Health Unit to Meet," October 13, 1975; Bismarck Tribune, "Kiwanians to Hear Free-Lance Writer," October 13, 1975.

46. Riceville Recorder, "Riceville celebrates July 4th with a grand showing," July 8, 1976; Courier, "Festival set in Riceville," July 1, 1976.

47. Riceville Recorder, October 7, 1976; Riceville Recorder, October 14, 1976.

48. Courier, "Riceville hopes to bridge two eras," December 26, 1976.

49. Roald Dahl, Letter to Jane Elliott, Gipsy House, Great Missenden, Buckinghamshire, England, February 1, 1977, Jane Elliott Personal Files, Osage, IA.

50. Elliott, A Collar in My Pocket, 109.

51. Bloom, Blue Eyes, Brown Eyes, 141.

52. Superintendent Dean Weaver retired at the end of the 1977 spring term. The new superintendent, Norman Kolberg, entered the position the same year Jane Elliott started teaching in junior high.

Chapter 16: Bull's Eye

1. United Press International. "McGovern blasts Nixon administration corruption." The Oshkosh Northwestern (Oshkosh, WI). October 2, 1972.

2. Press-Telegram (Long Beach, CA), "Nixon tax lawyer to prison," December 19, 1974.

3. Gerald Ford, "President Gerald R. Ford's Proclamation 4311, Granting a Pardon to Richard Nixon," September 8, 1974, Retrieved from the Ford Library Museum at https://www.fordlibrarymuseum.gov/library/speeches/740061.asp.

4. Roy Larson, "Should Moral Education be Part of Today's Schooling?" Tampa Times, May 15, 1976.

5. Maureen Robb, "CC Publisher is a Leader in Moral Education," Contra Costa Times (Walnut Creek, CA). August 15, 1976.

6. Amitai Etzioni, "Education in morality poses an ethical dilemma in schools," Chicago Tribune, October 13, 1976.

7. Etzioni, Ibid., 1.

8. Ibid.

9. Roy Larson, "Should moral education be part of today's schooling?," Tampa Times, May 15, 1976.

10. Carol Pogash, "Teacher's Lesson: He turned his students into 'Nazis,'" San Francisco Examiner, July 11, 1976.

11. Ron Jones, No Substitute for Madness: A Teacher, His Kids, and the Lessons of Real Life, (Covelo, CA: Island Press, 1976), 11-16.

12. Ibid., 20.

13. St. Cloud Times, "Nazi test almost gets out of control," date unknown.

14. Daily News (Lebanon, PA), "Educator Society's Speaker," April 26, 1978.

15. Daily News, "Educating The Dyslexic Child," May 8, 1978; Daily News, "Celebrated Teacher is MHA Guest," April 29, 1978.

16. Jane Elliott, Interview with author, California, December 22, 2021.

17. Ibid.

18. Carolyn Decell, "The power of suggestion pretty strong," Sun Herald (Biloxi, MS), September 25, 1980.

19. Hanford Sentinel (Hanford, CA), "Anti-racism needs boost," November 1, 1980.

20. Carolyn Decell, "The power of suggestion pretty strong," Sun Herald (Biloxi, MS), September 25, 1980.

21. Alan Catrina, "Prejudice thwarted M.L. King program," North Adams Transcript (North Adams, MA), January 16, 1980.

22. North Adams Transcript (North Adams, MA), "Role playing program canceled by school board," January 15, 1980.

23. Riceville Recorder, "Mary Elliott and Chris Jensen exchange vows," November 20, 1980; Raymond Hansen, Interview with author, Minnesota, December 29, 2021.

24. Bloom, Blue Eyes, Brown Eyes, 147.

25. Ibid., 146-8.

26. Ibid., 151.

27. Jane Elliott, Interview with author, California, December 29, 2021; Hansen, Interview with author, Minnesota, December 29, 2021.

28. St. Lucie News Tribune (Fort Pierce, FL), "William Peters, film producer," May 25, 2007.

29. Elliott, A Collar in My Pocket, 114-5.

30. William Peters, A Class Divided: Then and Now, Expanded Edition, 141.

31. Town Talk (Alexandria, LA), "Exercise in Discrimination Teachers Students Tolerance." March 23, 1985.

32. Ibid.

33. Lime Springs Herald (Lime Springs, IA), "Athlete killed," May 10, 1979; Riceville Recorder, "Russell Ring funeral at Riceville school," May 16, 1979.

34. Des Moines Register, "Riceville 'Class Divided' is reunited," August 12, 1984; Riceville Recorder, "New faces in business," October 14, 1982

35. Elliott, A Collar in My Pocket, 115.

36. Daily Sentinel (Grand Junction, CO), "Eye-color exercise taught kids tolerance," August 28, 1984.

37. Jane Elliott, Email message to the author, December 28, 2021.

38. William Peters, "A Class Divided," PBS Frontline, Season 1985, Episode 9.

39. Mary Stegmeir, "Racism lesson turned world's eyes to Riceville." Courier, December 14, 2008.

40. Michael Whye, "'Blue eyes' learn about bigotry," Des Moines Register, March 24, 1985.

41. William Peters, "A Class Divided." PBS Frontline, Season 1985, Episode 9.

42. Michael Whye, "'Blue eyes' learn about bigotry," Des Moines Register, March 24, 1985.

43. Elliott, A Collar in My Pocket, 118; Daily Sentinel (Grand Junction, CO), "Eye-color exercise taught kids tolerance," August 28, 1984.

44. Los Angeles Times, "Now in Paperback," December 6, 1987.

45. Riceville Recorder, September 20, 1984.

Chapter 17: An Eye on Justice

1. Pat Kinney, "Innovative teacher keeping an eye on discrimination," The Courier, April 5, 1985.

2. Blue Eyed, directed by Bertram Verhaag (1996; Munich, Germany: Denkmal Film), DVD.

3. Jane Elliott, interview by author, California, December 29, 2021; Kevin R. Hopkins and William B. Johnston, Opportunity 2000: Creative Affirmative Action for a Changing Workforce, Prepared for Employment Standards Administration U.S. Department of Labor, (Indianapolis, IN: Diane Publishing Co., 1988), 92-4.

4. Elliott. A Collar in My Pocket. 121.

5. Kathleen Megan, "Lesson in Racism Catapults Teacher to Forefront of Issue," Hartford Courant, November 22, 1985; Riceville Recorder, "Annual Financial Statement," August 1, 1985; Riceville Recorder, "Increase of 30 students in RCS classes over 1984-85 enrollment," September 19, 1985; Riceville Recorder, "RCS board hires attorney to represent them in bargaining," October 17, 1985. 1.

6. Jane Elliott, interview by author, California, December 29, 2021.

7. Kathleen Megan, "Lesson in Racism Catapults Teacher to Forefront of Issue," Hartford Courant, November 22, 1985.

8. Jane Elliott, interview by author, California, December 29, 2021.

9. Jane Elliott, interview by author, California, September 29, 2021; Jane Elliott, Email message to the author, California, December 28, 2021.

10. Elliott, A Collar in My Pocket, 130-1.

11. Ibid., 132.

12. Ibid., 132-3.

13. Ibid., 132, 145-51.

14. Jane Elliott, interview by author, California, December 29, 2021.

15. Jane Elliott, interview by author, California, December 29, 2021.

16. Kathleen Megan, "Lesson in Racism Catapults Teacher to Forefront of Issue," Hartford Courant, November 22, 1985; The Gazette, "Cornell lecture," February 10, 1986; Michael H. Cottman, "Education." Newsday, November 12, 1986.

17. Michael H. Cottman, "Education," Newsday, November 12, 1986.

18. Michael H. Cottman, "Education," Newsday, November 12, 1986.

19. The Evening Times, "Oprah Winfrey Show to be Syndicated," March 13, 1986; Fred Rothenberg, "Debuts: 'Oprah Winfrey Show and David Brenner's 'Nightlife,'" The Index-Journal, September 10, 1986.

20. Baltimore Sun, "Everybody wants Oprah, but she's promised to stay where she is," February 3, 1985.

21. Elliott, A Collar in My Pocket, 165; Jane Elliott. Interview by author, California, July 29, 2021.

22. Oprah Winfrey, The Oprah Winfrey Show, VHS, 1986, Jane Elliott Personal Files, Osage, IA.

23. Oprah Winfrey, The Oprah Winfrey Show, VHS, 1986, Jane Elliott Personal Files, Osage, IA.

24. Ibid.

25. Jane Elliott, The Oprah Winfrey Show, VHS, 1986, Jane Elliott Personal Files, Osage, IA.

26. Austin American-Statesman, "Oprah Winfrey to hit Austin airways," March 6, 1987; Call-Leader, "Oprah beating Donahue in TV ratings," June 16, 1987.

27. Jane Elliott, email message to author, January 6, 2022.

28. Elliott, A Collar in My Pocket, vi-viii.

29. Jane Elliott, email message to author, January 6, 2022.

30. Riceville Recorder, "Services for Lloyd Jennison," July 12, 1990; Globe-Gazette, "Lloyd Jennison," July 6, 1990.

31. Globe-Gazette, "Margaret 'Gie' Jennison," June 17, 2008.

32. Jane Elliott, email message to author, January 6, 2022.

33. Jane Elliott, email message to author, January 6, 2022.

34. Jane Elliott, interview by author, California, March 7, 2022.

35. Jane Elliott, email message to author, January 6, 2022.

Chapter 18: Eye of the Beholder

1. Anti-Defamation League of B'nai B'rith and the Dade County Public Schools, "Pamphlet: A World of Difference: A Conference for Dade County Elementary Educators," Miami, Florida, October 14, 1988, Jane Elliott Personal File, Osage, IA.

2. Miami Herald, "A World of Difference," August 20, 1986.

3. A World of Difference, "Media Focus: 'Eye of the Beholder,'" Fall 1988, Jane Elliott Personal File, Osage, IA.

4. Miami Herald, "Florida Emmys," November 20, 1987.

5. Miami Herald, "A World of Difference is extended," October 7, 1987.

6. Miami Herald, "A harsh experiment," April 17, 1987.

7. Deborah A. Byrnes and Gary Kiger, "Prejudice-Reduction Simulations: Ethics, Evaluations, and Theory into Practice," Simulation & Gaming, Vol. 23, No. 4, December 1992, 457-8.

8. Byrnes and Kiger, "Prejudice-Reduction Simulations," 468.

9. Of the 164 study participants, 57% were freshmen, 20% sophomores, 16% juniors, 5% seniors, 2% graduate students. Deborah A. Byrnes and Gary Kiger, "Ethical and Pedagogical Issues in the Use of Simulation Activities in the Classroom: Evaluating the 'Blue Eyes-Brown Eyes' Prejudice Simulation," Utah State University–Logan, Department of Elementary Education, Department of Sociology, Paper presented at the Annual Meeting of the Northern Rocky Mountain Educational Research Association, Jackson, WY, October 1988. 7-8.

10. Byrnes and Kiger, "Ethical and Pedagogical Issues in the Use of Simulation Activities in the Classroom," 12-13.

11. Ibid., 18.

12. Ibid., 467-8.

13. Ibid., 22.

14. The Shreveport Journal, "Camp Anytown USA," January 30, 1987.

15. Ginger Hutton, "Game demonstrates pain of discrimination." Arizona Republic, April 26, 1987.

16. Susan Youngwood, "Students received lesson in prejudice," Morning Call, January 18, 1988.

17. Morning Call, "ASD names business manager," January 29, 1988.

18. Felicia R. Lee, "Teachers told they can end prejudice in their students," Miami Herald, October 15, 1988.

19. Bloom, Blue Eyes, Brown Eyes, 169.

20. Ibid., 170-1.

21. Jan M. Fincher and R. Ann Welter, Letter to Jane Elliott, Lakewood, Colorado. December 2, 1988, Jane Elliott personal collection, Osage, IA.

22. Rocky, Letter to Jane Elliott, December 5, 1988, Jane Elliott personal collection, Osage, IA.

23. David C. Kohler, Letter to Jane Elliott, December 5, 1988, Jane Elliott personal collection. Osage, IA.

24. Wanda Schick, Letter to Jane Elliott, December 6, 1988, Jane Elliott personal collection. Osage, IA.

25. Andrew "Andy" Horner, Letter to Jane Elliott, December 2, 1988, Jane Elliott personal collection. Osage, IA.

26. Roy M. Whitman, "How can we teach empathy?" Cincinnati Enquirer, February 18, 1989.

27. Lindsay Peterson, "Magnet school called racial solution," Tampa Tribune, December 27, 1988.

28. Lindsay Peterson, "Eye-color test reverberates for 20 years," Tampa Tribune, December 27, 1988.

29. Jennifer Ritenour, "Teacher explains roots of racism, famous experiment," Morning Call, October 20, 1988; Darren La Padula, "King's nonviolence theme of village essay contest," Sunday News, December 10, 1989.

30. Riceville Recorder, "Services for Lloyd Jennison," July 12, 1990; Sarah Elliott, Interview by author, Iowa, January 20, 2022.

31. Riceville Recorder, "Memorial to Lloyd Jennison," July 12, 1990; Globe-Gazette, "Lloyd Jennison," July 6, 1990.

32. Blue Eyed, directed by Bertram Verhaag (1996; Munich, Germany: Denkmal Film), DVD.

33. Star Tribune (Minneapolis, MN). "KSTP's 'Eye to Eye' eye-opening." September 24, 1990. 1E and 9E; Star Tribune. "Broadcast/Evening." September 24, 1990. 8E.

34. Peter Jennings quoted in Ben Kubasik. "Jennings host of specials on prejudice, rape." Lexington Herald-Leader (Lexington, KY). April 25, 1992. 17.

35. Des Moines Register. "Former Osage teacher will be on ABC program." April 19, 1992. 8; Elliott. A Collar in My Pocket. 185.

36. Kokomo Tribune (Kokomo, IN). "ABC's Jennings brings out his 'skeleton.'" April 25, 1992. 14.

37. Jane Elliott, email message to author, January 13, 2022.

38. OWN. "An Oprah Show Audience Weights in on the Rodney King Verdict." The Oprah Winfrey Show. May 13, 1992. Retrieved July 21, 2020.

39. Tarbaby Remus, "Jane Elliott en el Show de Oprah Winfrey. 1992. Ejercicio de los ojos azules/ojos café," YouTube, October 28, 2014, 16:36, video, https://www.youtube.com/watch?v=7W2hxcvB1yQ

40. Tarbaby Remus, "Jane Elliott en el Show de Oprah Winfrey. 1992. Ejercicio de los ojos azules/ojos café," YouTube, October 28, 2014, 16:36, video, https://www.youtube.com/watch?v=7W2hxcvB1yQ

41. Wa Mu, "Jane Elliott racism 101 How to know if you a racist," The Oprah Winfrey Show, YouTube, May 1992. 5:38, video, https://www.youtube.com/watch?v=Ja8AG4uLFK8&t=154s

42. Robert Cwiklik, "New view of world is on horizon," Chicago Tribune, September 25, 1987; Jane Elliott, Interview by author, Iowa, July 9, 2021.

43. Jane Elliott, interview by author, Iowa, July 29, 2021.

44. Jane Elliott, interview by author, Iowa, July 29, 2021.

45. Elliott, A Collar in My Pocket. 172.

46. Jane Elliott, interview by author, Iowa, July 29, 2021.

47. Jane Elliott, email message to author, January 13, 2022.

Chapter 19: The Public Eye

1. Rex Kozak, email message to author, January 5, 2022; Rex Kozak, "Lesson for life: Bigotry's pain," The Gazette, August 3, 1992.

2. Dennis McCabe, letter to Jane Elliott. November 20, 1991, Waterloo, IA, Dennis McCabe Personal File.

3. Dennis McCabe, interview by author, Iowa, July 9, 2021.

4. Jackie Young, "The eyes have it," The Courier, December 26, 1991.

5. Dennis McCabe, email message to author, July 10, 2021.

6. Don Babwin, "Lesson in prejudice backfires on 4th-grade teachers," Chicago Tribune, February 4, 1993.

7. Ibid.

8. La Crosse Tribune, November 7, 1993; La Crosse Tribune, November 11, 1993; Larry Fruhling, "Race bias in brown, blue," Des Moines Register, December 29, 1996.

9. Shari Crall, "Racism isn't a game," The Californian, December 2, 1993; Jane Elliott, email message to author, January 13, 2022.

10. Sarah Elliott, text message to the author, Osage, IA, March 9, 2022.

11. Arabian Sun, "Human Relations Expert Explains Historic Classroom Exercise," June 7, 1989.

12. Jane Elliott, interview by author, California, March 7, 2022; Elliott, A Collar in My Pocket, 177-9; Jane Elliott, Personal notebook "Wed. Dec. 29, 1993," Unpublished manuscript, Osage, IA, Sarah Elliott Personal Files.

13. Arabian Sun, "Human Relations Expert," June 7, 1989.

14. Sarah Elliott, interview by author, Iowa, March 8, 2022.

15. Deborah P. Work, "Light in the Blackboard Jungle," South Florida Sun Sentinel, December 14, 1995. E1.

16. Pradnya Joshi, "Teacher uses colorful shirts to give lesson in discrimination," South Florida Sun Sentinel, January 13, 1994.

17. South Florida Sun Sentinel, "Could this be tax deductible?" February 6, 1994.

18. Dan Eggen, "Ignoring an 'infection' of racism is no solution, experts contend." Des Moines Register (Des Moines, IA). February 27, 1994. 4B.

19. The Guardian, February 24, 1994. 54; The Guardian. February 19, 1994. 124.

20. Jane Elliott, interview by author, Iowa, June 28, 2022.

21. William B. Johnston and Arnold H. Packer's 1986 report Workforce 2000: Work and Workers for the 21st Century identified four key trends in the American workforce: The American economy should grow at a relatively healthy pace; manufacturing will be a much smaller share of the economy in the year 2000 than in 1987; the workforce will grow slowly, become older, more female, and more disadvantaged; and the new jobs in the service industries will demand much higher skill levels than in 1987. SOURCE: William B. Johnston and Arnold H. Packer, Workforce 2000: Work and Workers for the 21st Century, (New York, NY: Alliance of New York State Arts Organization, 1986), 5-8.

22. Carol Howes, "Middle managers fear losing power—expert." Edmonton Journal, April 26, 1994; Fill Fraser, "Roots of racism revealed in teacher's blue-eyed, brown-eyed classroom test," Edmonton Journal, May 13, 1994.

23. Jane Elliott, interview by author, Iowa, June 28, 2022.

24. Melita Marie Garza. "Military has 'boot camp' to stamp out harassment." South Florida Sun Sentinel, November 17, 1996.

25. Garza, Ibid. 1.

26. Department of Defense. "DoD WorldWide Equal Opportunity Conference: Ensuring Tomorrow's Readiness." Defense Equal Opportunity Management Institute Office of the Under Secretary of Defense. December 5-9, 1994. Cocoa Beach, FL. 14-15.

27. Garza, Ibid. 7.

28. NSIAD-94-6, "DOD Service Academies; More Action Needed to Eliminate Sexual Harassment." January 31, 1994. Retrieved at https://www.govinfo.gov/content/pkg/GAOREPORTS-NSIAD-94-6/html/GAOREPORTS-NSIAD-94-6.htm.

29. Colonel W. Darryl Goldman, US Army, "The Wrong Road to Character Development? Military Review. January-February 1998, No. 1.

30. Diane Nelson, "Flowers beneath the same big sun." Modesto Bee (Modesto, CA). September 17, 1995. B2.

31. Bertram Verhaag, interview by author, Germany, April 23, 2022.

32. Ian Aitken, Editor. Encyclopedia of Documentary Film. New York, London. Routledge, Taylor & Francis Group. 2006. 284.

33. Jack Lakey. "Hate groups said striking a chord with jobless youth." Edmonton Journal (Edmonton, Alberta). March 21, 1994. A3; San Angelo Standard-Times (San Angelo, TX). "Racism in Germany revives horrible past." December 2, 1992. 8A.

34. Martin Luther King, Jr. Center for Nonviolent Social Change, "The King Center's Beloved Community Talks: Racism and the Miseducation of America, A Conversation between Dr. Bernice A. King and Dr. Jane Elliott," August 11, 2020. YouTube. October 12, 2021, 49:17, video, https://www.youtube.com/live/ZjfreE9_WZE?feature=share; Jane Elliott, Interview by author, California, February 12, 2022.

35. The Late Show with Stephen Colbert, "Killer Mike's Homework for White Americans: Learn From Jane Elliot [sic]," June 2, 2020, YouTube, 4:18, video, https://www.youtube.com/watch?v=mYAXzTT9b1E

36. Mary Hill, "Former teacher plans workshop on racism," Des Moines Register, May 9, 1995.

37. Blue Eyed, directed by Bertram Verhaag (1996; Munich, Germany: Denkmal Film), DVD.

38. Kevin Murphy, "Misperceptions may kill race relations plan," Kansas City Star, August 12, 1988; Author unknown, "Harmony Focuses on Bridging the Divide," Date unknown, Retrieved January 27, 2022, from https://www.kcharmony.org/.

39. Gromer Jeffers Jr., "Minority economy report ready," Kansas City Times, December 8, 1988; Kansas City Star, "A Consensus report on race relations," December 16, 1988.

40. Tanyanika Samuels, "Harmony focuses on bridging the divide," Kansas City Star, January 10, 2005.

41. Mary Sanchez, "Speaker talks frankly about race, prejudice," Kansas City Star, October 27, 1995.

42. Glenn E. Rice, "Barriers still exist between blacks and whites," January 8, 1996.

43. Jane Elliott, "A Collar in My Pocket Training Manual," unpublished, Iowa, Jane Elliott Personal Files, Osage, IA, 30-33.

44. Ibid. 28.

45. Regina Akers, "Safety officers help bring history to life," Kansas City Star, February 15, 1996. 10; Kansas City Star, "Pioneer in race relations research to be speaker," February 15, 1996.

46. Kansas City Star, "Police, firemen set forum," April 17, 1990; Rick Alm, "black firefighters in KCK sue the city," The Kansas City Star, March 31, 1990.

47. Jane Elliott, interview by author, California, February 11, 2022.

48. Elliott, A Collar in My Pocket, 181.

49. Ibid.

50. Pittsburgh Post-Gazette, "Professor, others taking positive steps toward equality," January 14, 1996.

51. Noel A. Cazenave, "Why I will teach a course on white racism," Hartford Courant, February 18, 1996.

52. The Baltimore Sun, "White privilege shapes the U.S," July 19, 1998.

53. In the final days of 1992, a demonstration of about 100,000 people joined hands in a human chain in Nuremberg and a torchlight march of 4,000 occurred in Wuerzburg. Boston Globe, No titled, December 18, 1992, 17.

54. Şeydâ Buurman-Kutsal, interview by author, Netherlands, February 25, 2022.

55. Şeydâ Buurman-Kutsal, email message to author, March 10, 2022.

56. Bertram Verhaag, interview by author, Germany, April 23, 2022; Şeydâ Buurman-Kutsal, Interview by author, Netherlands, February 25, 2022.

57. Şeydâ Buurman-Kutsal, interview by author, Netherlands, February 25, 2022.

58. Ibid.

59. Lea Sitton, "Harassment forces resident out of white neighborhood," Pittsburgh Post-Gazette, May 5, 1996.

60. John Carmody, "'Nightline' takes look at race in America," Lansing State Journal, May 21, 1996.

61. Elliott, A Collar in My Pocket, 186.

62. Bertram Verhaag, Interview by author, Germany, April 23, 2022; Eckart Bruchner, "The Interfilm Jury at the International Festival of Munich 1996 Recommends Blue Eyed," Publisher unknown, 1996, Jane Elliott Files. Osage, IA.

63. Blue Eyed, directed by Bertram Verhaag (1996; Munich, Germany: Denkmal Film), DVD.

64. Lindsay, Letter to Jane Elliott, Date unknown, Sydney, Australia, 1997, Jane Elliott Personal Files, Osage, IA.

65. Stuttgarter Zeitung, January 16, 1997 cited in Elliott, A Collar in My Pocket, 183.

66. Marc Ruckebier, Interview by author, Spain, September 25, 2021.

67. Blue Eyed, directed by Bertram Verhaag (1996; Munich, Germany: Denkmal Film), DVD.

68. Bertram Verhaag, Interview by author, Germany, April 23, 2022; Marion Kramer, Letter to Dear Mrs. Elliott. Cologne, Germany, September 22, 1997, Jane Elliott Personal Files, Osage IA; Marion Kramer, Letter to Dear Mrs. Elliott, Cologne, Germany, October 1, 1997, Jane Elliott Personal Files. Osage IA.

69. Blue Eyed, directed by Bertram Verhaag (1996; Munich, Germany: Denkmal Film), DVD.

70. Desert Sun, "Blue Eyed," January 5, 1997.

71. Desert Sun, "blue eyed," January 23, 1997.

72. Palm Desert Post, "Film fest events slated in honor of King Holiday," January 16, 1997.

73. California Newsreel, "The 'Blue-Eyed/Brown-Eyed' Exercise: Learning from 30 years of diversity training," San Francisco, CA, 1997.

74. Fred Haeseker, "TV documentary impact 'impossible to measure'," Calgary Herald, August 30, 1979.

75. Atlanta Constitution, "Roberts, Sarandon team up," August 28, 1996.

76. Susan Sarandon interviewed by Body, Mind, Spirit, "Susan Sarandon: An Intimate Interview," May 1996, New York, NY, 48.

77. Elliott, A Collar in My Pocket, 190.

78. Brian Cowden, "A Class Divided: A True Story," Unpublished manuscript, Screenplay, October 8, 1997, Jane Elliott Papers, Iowa Women's Archives, University of Iowa Libraries.

79. Karen Merk, "American society feeds racism, speaker says," Courier-Journal, June 11, 1996.

Chapter 20: Eyes of the World

1. Douglas Haberman, "Teacher's lesson in prejudice is still an eye-opener," Desert Sun, January 26, 1997.

2. Ben Stocking, "Quietly, black and Latinos seek common ground," News and Observer, May 4, 1997.

3. Karen Merk, "Researchers link 'modern racism' with earlier type," The Courier-Journal, March 15, 1997.

4. Nicole Gustin, "'We could destroy racism if we choose to.' sociologist suggests to Winthrop audience." The Herald, March 2, 1997.

5. Gadlfy Productions, "Fuzzy Zoeller Racist Fried Chicken Joke to Tiger Woods @ 1997 Masters," YouTube, April 7, 2015; Lewis W. Diuguid, "Bigotry is in mind, not genes," Kansas City Star, April 26, 1997; Phil Milford, "Del. police seminar targets biases," News Journal, June 17, 1997.

6. Dianna Borsi, "You Are A Racist," St. Joseph News-Press, September 24, 1997.

7. Bob Reeves, "Blue-eyes lesson teaches empathy," Lincoln Journal Star, September 29, 1997.

8. Bob Reeves, "Blue-eyes lesson teaches empathy," Lincoln Journal Star, September 29, 1997.

9. Douglas Haberman, "Teacher's lesson in prejudice is still an eye-opener," Desert Sun, January 26, 1997.

10. Margaret Legum was a South African dissident living with her husband, Colin, in Great Britain after being banned from their homeland for opposing apartheid policies. SOURCE: James Patterson, "The effects of being preferred," The Indianapolis Star, October 18, 1997.

11. Jane Elliott, email message to author, February 13, 2021.

12. Peter H. Russell, Recognizing Aboriginal Title: The Mabo Case and Indigenous Resistance to English-Settler Colonialism, (Toronto, Buffalo, London: University of Toronto Press, 2005), 1-3.

13. Sydney Morning Herald, "Pauline Hanson in Asian eyes," December 14, 1996.

14. Chris Cox, "Target should be closet racists," Asheville Citizen-Times, October 16, 19997.

15. Ibid.

16. The Age, "Elliott eyes Australia," October 23, 1997.

17. Sydney Morning Herald, "Sunday Choice," November 29, 1997.

18. Sydney Morning Herald, "Test as clear as black and white," November 23, 1997.

19. Jane Elliott, email message to author, February 16, 2022; The Age, "Elliott eyes Australia," October 23, 1997.

20. The Age, "Blue Eyed tour," April 2, 1998.

21. Sydney Morning Herald, "About Us: A Class Divided," May 4, 1998.

22. Sue Williams, "Test as clear as black and white," Sydney Morning Herald, November 23, 1997.

23. Sydney Morning Herald, "Not the Logies," December 22, 1997.

24. Alison Stewart, "Watch and learn: Blue Eyed," Sydney Morning Herald, November 24, 1997.

25. Greg Bowyer, "Urgently," Sydney Morning Herald, December 2, 1997.

26. Sydney Morning Herald, "Eye of the beholder," December 3, 1997.

27. Sydney Morning Herald, "Without prejudice," April 13, 1998; The Age, April 30, 1998.

28. Sydney Morning Herald, "Thumbs," May 11, 1998.

29. Antony Laws, "About Us: A Class Divided," Sydney Morning Herald, May 4, 1998.

30. Sydney Morning Herald, "Test as clear as black and white," November 23, 1997.

31. Jane Elliott, speech delivered to police officers in Chicago, Illinois, 1995. n.d., Jane Elliott personal files.

32. Sue Williams, "Test as clear as black and white," Sydney Morning Herald, November 23, 1997.

33. Globe-Gazette, "Charles V. Jennison," August 8, 1998; Riceville Recorder, "Services held for Charles Jennison, 70," Times Plain Dealer, August 12, 1998.

34. The Courier, "Decorah—Jean Jenkins," January 6, 1992.

35. Geoff Thompson, "Listen up to the voices of indigenous Australia," Sydney Morning Herald, October 17, 1994.

36. The Age, Radio Waves," January 14, 1999.

37. Clay Bailey, "Discrimination Game Deals Kids handful of Insights," Commercial Appeal, February 25, 1999.

38. Germantown News, "Local Holocaust survivor speaks to GMS students," March 4, 1999.

39. Susan Hogan-Albach, "A Hard Lesson," Star Tribune, January 1999.

40. Globe-Gazette, "Riceville puts big bite on mosquitoes," July 3, 1984.

41. Susan Hogan-Albach. "A Hard Lesson." Star Tribune, January 1999.

42. E.M. Messersmith, Riceville Recorder, February 4, 1999.

43. Ibid.

44. James S. Jennison, Riceville Recorder, February 4, 1999.

45. Des Moines Register, "Eye exercise stings, but lesson sticks," March 27, 2008.

46. Elinor J. Brecher, "Here comes trouble," Miami Herald, May 16, 1999.

47. Tallahassee Democrat, "Infamous speaker to be part of race relations conference at Civic Center," January 2, 2000.

48. Ibid.

49. Anjetta McQueen, "Diversity speaker says Bushes are racists," Des Moines Register, March 16, 2000; Corpus Christi Caller-Times, "A speaker speaks out of turn," March 17, 2000.

50. Murial Crabbs, "College reprogramming another thing to worry about," Evening Sun, May 13, 2000.

51. Martin Carcasson and Mitchell F. Rice, "The Promise and Failure of President Clinton's Race initiative of 1997-1998: A Rhetorical Perspective," Rhetoric and Public Affairs, No. 2, summer 1999, 243.

52. Jane Elliott, email message to author, February 17, 2022.

Chapter 21: Angry Eye

1. Kansas City Star, "Bush starts well," January 21, 2001.

2. Journal Gazette, "Brown-eye, blue-eyed lecture at EIU to examine issue of prejudice," February 9, 2001.

3. Sarah Glen, "Landmark study exposed effects of racism," Whitehorse Daily Star, May 29, 2001.

4. Dianne April, "Don't it Make Your Brown Eyes Blue?", June 2, 1996.

5. Ibid.

6. Robin Summerfield, "Former U.S. teacher gives racism lesson," Calgary Herald, August 2, 2001.

7. Desert Sun, "The Angry Eye," August 3, 2001.

8. Jane Elliott, email message to author, March 4, 2022.

9. Jane Elliott, email message to author, March 4, 2022.

10. Angry Eye, directed by Susan A. Golenbock, (2001; Osage, Iowa: Elliott and Elliott Productions, LLC.) DVD.

11. Jane Elliott, email message to author, March 4, 2022. Menifee, CA.

12. "About Admire Productions," Diversity Delivers, 2022, www.diversitydelivers.org/about/.

13. Jane Elliott, interview by author, California, March 7, 2022.

14. The Leader-Post, November 15, 2001; Times Colonist, May 3, 2002.

15. Stolen Eye, directed by Phillip Cullen (2001; location unknown; Angry Eye Productions, LLC.) YouTube, 1:01.13, https://www.youtube.com/watch?v=CCImXKPNN8U

16. Jane Elliott, interview by author, California, March 7, 2022; David Elias, "Bringing it all back home," The Age, May 24, 1997.

17. Jane Elliott, interview by author, California, March 7, 2022.

18. Ibid.

19. Globe-Gazette, "Elliott to receive justice award," July 18, 2001; The Courier, "Area women honored by Iowa's Hall of Fame," July 18, 2001; Iowa Department of Human Rights, "Cristine Wilson Award Recipients," Iowa Department of Human Rights Website, date unknown, https://humanrights.iowa.gov/cristine-wilson-award-recipients; Globe-Gazette, "Elliott to receive justice award," July 18, 2001; The Courier, July 18, 2001.

20. Jane Elliott, interview by author, California, March 8, 2022.

21. Mike Cronin, "Students feel sting of bias in role play," Salt Lake City Tribune, January 22, 2004.

22. Ibid.

23. Marshfield News-Herald, "Hear the kids: Prejudice doesn't make sense," January 21, 2004.

24. Ronnie Blair. "School Cancels Racism Lesson." Pasco Tribune, February 23, 2004.

25. Ibid.

26. Linda Seebach, "This diversity training cruel to kids," Albuquerque Tribune, June 22, 2004.

27. Ibid.

28. Evin Dyer, "Former teacher working to hone our racial conscience," Pittsburgh Post-Gazette, January 30, 2004.

29. Stephen Bloom, "Lesson of a Lifetime," Smithsonian Magazine, September 2005, https://www.smithsonianmag.com/science-nature/lesson-of-a-lifetime-72754306/

30. The McGraw-Hill Foundation, "The McGraw-Hill Foundations of Education Timeline," 2005. Jane Elliott files, Osage, IA.

31. Des Moines Register, "Elliott: A voice against racial discrimination," March 29, 2006.

32. Tom Ashcraft, "Diversity: From simple fact to liberal cudgel," Charlotte Observer, February 3, 2007.

33. Carl F. Horowitz, "Jane Elliott and Her Blue-Eyed Devil Children," Front Page Magazine, December 28, 2006, https://www.amren.com/news/2006/12/jane_elliott_an/.

34. Lisa Rossi, "Eye exercise stings, but lesson sticks," Des Moines Register, March 27, 2008.

35. Globe-Gazette, "Margaret 'Gie' Jennison," June 17, 2008.

36. Corina Knoll, "The woman who opened America's eyes—blue and brown—to the reality of racism," Vancouver Sun, March 28, 2009.

37. Gallup Inc., "Presidential Approval Ratings—Barack Obama, Jan. 21-25, 2009, and Sept. 14-20, 2009," Gallup Inc. https://news.gallup.com/poll/116479/barack-obama-presidential-job-approval.aspx

38. Clarence Page, "Googling racism against Obama," Kitsap Sun, June 14, 2012.

39. In the summer of 2009, a viral news story surfaced when South Carolina Republican activist, Rusty DePass joked that an escaped zoo gorilla was an ancestor of Michelle Obama. In 2010, an email written by a woman in Casco, Maine called the First Lady a monkey. In 2012, Chief U.S. District Judge Richard Cebull was exposed for forwarded a racist email about President Obama.

Chapter 22: Eye on the Prize

1. Robert Epstein, "Lessons in apartheid by eye color," The Independent, November 1, 2009.

2. Diane Abbott, "Dark times for the debate on immigration." The Independent, October 24, 2009.

3. Janes Doussard, "'Eye of Storm' Is Simple, Touching," Courier-Journal, May 11, 1970.

4. Richard Blount IV, Healing America, (Bloomington, IN: WestBow Press, 2021), 104; Channel 4, "The Event: How Racist Are You?" October 29, 2009, YouTube, 47:28, video, https://www.youtube.com/watch?v=6MYHBrJIIFU

5. Robert Epstein, "Lessons in apartheid by eye color," The Independent, November 1, 2009.

6. Drake Bennett, "Who's Still Biased?" Boston Globe, March 7, 2010.

7. Ibid.

8. As of spring 2023, Susan Golenbock's website diversitydelivers.org is expired.

9. Theresa Churchill, "Racism remains cultural concern," Herald and Review, March 31, 2010.

10. Mara Rose Williams, "Future is an opportunity, anti-racism activist says," Kansas City Star, February 18, 2017.

11. Jane Elliott, "As Long as We Have Racism, We'll Have Sexism—and It Starts With Our Word Choice," Ms. Magazine, October 22, 2021, https://msmagazine.com/2021/10/22/racism-sexism-word-choice/

12. Karina Bland, "A Lesson on race endures, 50 years later," Arizona Republic, November 19, 2017.

13. Jane Elliott, email message to author, April 5, 2022. Menifee, CA.

14. UHGCSW, "A Conversation on Race and Privilege with Angela Davis and Jane Elliott," YouTube, September 6, 2018, video, 1:42.39, https://www.youtube.com/watch?v=S0jf8D5WHoo.

15. Jane Elliott, interview by author, California, March 7, 2022.

16. Judy Paulson, "Pupils could relate to discrimination's string," Des Moines Register, February 16, 2011.

17. Jane Elliott, email message to author, March 10, 2022.

18. Jane Elliott, "As Long as We Have Racism, We'll Have Sexism—and It Starts With Our Word Choice," Ms. Magazine, October 22, 2021, https://msmagazine.com/2021/10/22/racism-sexism-word-choice/

19. Deb Nicklay, "Elliott: Racism still prevalent," Globe-Gazette, May 2, 2013.

Conclusion: "If you want to be loved, don't do this."

1. Joyce E.A. Russell, "Inclusive workplace better for your business," Leader-Post, January 17, 2015.

2. Şeydâ Buurman-Kutsal, interview by author, Netherlands. February 25, 2022; Roland Martin, "Anti-racism activist Jane Elliott speakers, dismantles racism on #RolandMartinUnfiltered," Roland Martin Un-filtered, Facebook, July 28, 2020. video, 1:10.27, https://www.facebook.com/rolandsmartinfanpage/videos/anti-racism-activist-jane-elliott-speaks-dismantles-racism-on-rolandmartinunfilt/2743363205886846/

3. Riceville Recorder, "Darald Dean Elliott, 79," October 3, 2013.

4. Steven Thompson, "125th anniversary of Burr Oak Free Baptist Church," Mitchell County Press News, August 2, 2017.

5. Jane Elliott, interview by author, Iowa, June 18, 2021.

6. Elliott, A Collar in My Pocket, viii.

7. Amid a legal dispute between Elliott and Golenbock, diversitydelivers.org has been taken off the Internet. "Store," Diversity Delivers, 2022, www.diversitydelivers.org/about/.

8. Jane Elliott, email message to author, February 13, 2022.

9. Jane Elliott, email message to author, December 21, 2022.

10. Jane Elliott, email message to author, April 22, 2022.

11. Longview News-Journal, "Rapper's comments at Sanders rally spark more controversy," February 18, 2016.

12. Jane Elliott, email message to author, April 22, 2022.

13. T.I. (Clifford Harris), "T.I. - Warzone," YouTube, September 16, 2016, video, 3:50, https://www.youtube.com/watch?v=VKcw35_saLY

14. @troubleman31, "Got a chance to spend the day with my #WCW Jane Elliot yesterday in Chicago," May 21, 2017, Instagram, https://www.instagram.com/p/BUXY7vHjUp_/?utm_source=ig_embed&ig_rid=dd9d61e9-5f3a-4e09-81ad-ea9fe2a96ff1.

15. Arizona Republic, "Elliott's 1968 message endures," November 19, 2017.

16. Chandra Thomas Whitfield, "Educator Jane Elliott Talks Trump, Kaepernick and Fix-ing Racism," NBC News, September 29, 2017, https://www.nbcnews.com/news/nbcblk/educator-jane-elliott-talks-trump-kaepernick-fixing-racism-n747291

17. Jeff Martin, "'You are my slave. School's Civil War Day sparks mom's ire," Rapid City Journal, October 14, 2017; Carolyn Thompson, "Schools struggle with how to teach about slavery," Sheboygan Press, July 8, 2019.

18. Rachel Boon, "Request to Award an Honorary Doctoral Degrees at the University of Northern Iowa," Board of Regents State of Iowa, April 11-12, 2018.

19. Jane Elliott, Interview by author, Iowa, June 18, 2021.

20. Globe-Gazette, "Brian Dean Elliott," July 17, 2018.

21. University of Northern Iowa, Fall Commencement Program, Cedar Falls, Iowa, December 15, 2018.

22. Jane Elliott, email message to author, July 5, 2022.

23. James E. Causey, "Black face is learned racism. It can be unlearned," March 18, 2019.

24. Carolyn Thompson, "Schools struggle with how to teach about slavery," Sheboygan Press, July 8, 2019.

25. Ibid.

26. Michael Judge, "My Grandfather and the 'Blue eyes-Brown Eyes' Lesson," Wall Street Journal Opinion, September 17, 2019, https://www.wsj.com/articles/my-grandfather-and-the-blue-eyes-brown-eyes-lesson-1523052806

27. Bradenton Herald, "What They're Saying," August 25, 2019.

28. Executive Office of the President, "Executive Order 13950. Combating Race and Sex Stereotyping," Federal Register, The Daily Journal of the United States Government, September 28, 2020, https://www.federalregister.gov/documents/2020/09/28/2020-21534/combating-race-and-sex-stereotyping

29. Manhattan Institute, "Woke School: A Toolkit for Concerned Parents," Issue Brief, Manhattan Institute, June 17, 2021, https://manhattan.institute/article/woke-schooling-a-toolkit-for-concerned-parents

30. Executive Office of the President, "Executive Order 13950," https://www.federalregister.gov/documents/2020/09/28/2020-21534/combating-race-and-sex-stereotyping

31. Manhattan Institute, "Woke School," https://manhattan.institute/article/woke-schooling-a-toolkit-for-concerned-parents

32. Jack Panyard, "These are the books and other resources banned by the Central York School Board," York Daily Record, September 14, 2021, https://www.ydr.com/story/news/2021/09/14/books-and-other-resources-banned-central-york-school-board/8333108002/

33. Thomas Dee and Emily K. Penner, "Ethnic studies increases longer-run academic engagement and attainment," Proceedings of the National Academy of Sciences, September 7, 2021, https://www.pnas.org/doi/
10.1073/pnas.2026386118.

34. Jane Elliott, email message to author, May 13, 2022.

35. Jane Elliott, email message to author, February 4, 2022.

36. Elliott, "A Collar in My Pocket Training Manual," 29.

INDEX

ego states, 303

Eissens, Ronald, 274

Election of 2000, 297

Election of 2016, 322–23

Elliott, Bertha Ellen (Elsberry), 67, 332

Elliott, Brian Dean, ix, 80, 97, 106–108, 119, 123, 132, 184–85, 238, 263, 320, 333, 338; death 325–26

Elliott, Darald Dean, ix, 66–74, 79–85, 89–93, 96–101, 125–28, 132, 142, 184–85, 207, 209, 219, 232, 263–66, 282, 288, 325, 332–33; death 320; Elliott Warehouse Mark-It, 219; Red Owl Grocery Store, 185

Elliott, Edwin Vera, 67, 332

Elliott, Jane (Jennison): "1619 Project," 327–29; "A Collar in My Pocket" eye color exercise, 262–63, 269, 276, 286–86; "Anatomy of Prejudice" lecture, 262–63, 267–69, 276, 285; "Children Without Prejudice," 177–84; "Person of the Week," 254, 336; "Project Misery," 2, 168–72, 173; "The Way It Is," 10, 18, 149–52, 158, 173, 279, 334; A Collar In My Pocket (memoir), 146, 158, 299, 320–21; A Collar In My Pocket Training Handbook, 299; academic studies, 175–76, 187–88, 243–45, 284–85, 309, 313; Angry Eye, 10, 298–302, 321, 337; animosity with Riceville 293–94, 309; Australian tour, 18, 287–91, 266, 277, 287–92, 296, 302–303, 313, 337; birth, 21, 29–30; birth control, 81–82; call-and-response, 270; Canada tour, 10, 266, 302, 334, 336; comic books 49–51, 53, 75, 212; copycats, 152–54, 171–73, 198–202, 218, 247–48, 260–62, 264, 292–93, 304–307; corporate training, 229–34; courtship with Darald, 54, 66–70; death of sister Anne 41–43; death threats, 205–207; Department of Defense training, 266–73; Discrimination Day lesson (Blue Eyes/Brown Eyes Exercise), 126–37, 144–45, 189–90, 205–207, 216, 219, 223–25, 230, 232–38, 246–47, 252–53, 257–58, 276–77, 283–86, 293–94, 299–303, 307; elementary teacher, 105–109, 113–18; exercise versus experiment, 191–92, 269; Eye of the Storm, 2, 18, 115, 161–67, 170, 173, 175, 178, 184, 188, 191–95, 199–201, 206–208, 219–25, 259–61, 276, 279, 286, 290, 301, 304, 312, 321, 334; giving

birth to children, 80; Honorary doctorates, 326, 338; Iowa Commission on the Status of Women Christine Wilson Medal for Equality and Justice Award, 304; Iowa State Teachers' College, 56–58, 55–58, 66, 69, 109–110; Jamestown School No. 2, 32-36, 42, 47, 53; keychain souvenir, 232; KIDS! program, 220; legal action, 321-22; see also Golenbock, Susan; Luther College Distinguished Service Award, 185; marketing the exercise, 301–302; McGraw Hill Foundation, 1, 64, 307, 337; melanin vernacular, 16–17, 26, 64, 216, 260, 315–16; middle school teacher, ix, 219–20, 335; National Mental Health Association Award for Excellence in Education, 215; Northwestern Bell Magazine, 195; nursing education, 54–55; Osage home, 185; paranormal activity, 325; Peabody Award, 188–89; plagiarism investigation, 167–71; Presidential Advisory 1776 Commission, 329; rebranding Blue Eyes/Brown Eyes Exercise, 243; retirement from teaching, 230–31; Room 10 Reunion, 220–24; Round Grove, 22–36, 38, 41, 43, 45, 57, 73, 79, 95, 97; sibling rivalry with Mary and Jean, 56–57, 49; student teaching, 58–63; transfer to middle school, 210; Village Green Park, 197–98, 207–209; Vogue, 337; White House Conference on Children and Youth, 177–184

Elliott, Mark Donald, ix, 80–81, 97, 238, 320, 333

Elliott, Mary Jean, ix, 80, 97, 140, 161, 184, 219, 232, 238, 262, 270, 275, 291, 320–21, 323, 333

Elliott, Sarah Jane, 80, 82, 184-85, 232, 263, 325, 347n, 376

Ellsberg, Daniel 212

Elsbury, Barbara Ellen Flockhart, 69

Enovid 10, 81–82

Eugenics, 187

Evers, Charles, 165

Evers, Medgar, 125, 157, 165

Expeditiously, 323

experiential pedagogy, 5–6, 109–18, 171, 197, 199, 213, 215–16, 230, 268, 274, 278, 310, 313, 327

Eye of the Beholder, 10, 18, 243, 253, 279, 336; see also Elliott, Jane

ACKNOWLEDGMENTS

My first encounter with Jane Elliott was in 1994. I was fifteen, and she was sixty. I was in my Harrisburg home, and she was on *The Oprah Winfrey Show*. I couldn't tell if Elliott was authentically callous as I watched her engage with Oprah and the live studio audience. For an hour, she remained stoic, a despotic short-haired woman in glasses. I had never watched more than five minutes of *Oprah* before this episode. There was something about the way she spoke to people. In one instance, she levied hateful words toward blue-eyed audience members. In a sudden change of pace, she condemned others for the bigoted characterization of African Americans and Jews. I figured it was a game because Oprah depended on her to explain the root causes of prejudicial feelings. The episode left an enduring impression.

Almost two decades later, Jane Elliott lectured at a university near my home in central Pennsylvania. I attended the event. Unfortunately, I was not given a chance to meet her. Like everyone in the audience, the only thing I knew about Mrs. Elliott was that she was a teacher from the small town of Riceville, Iowa, and put third-grade children through an eye color simulation on discrimination after Martin Luther King Jr. was murdered. I often watched the PBS *Frontline* documentary "A Class Divided," sometimes discussing it with my students when studying social reactions to King's assassination. My interest in reading and writing biographies made me want to know more about this lightning rod figure. Another decade later, on a whim, I emailed Jane asking if she would be interested in speaking to several elementary teachers for whom I was responsible for designing a professional learning program. She agreed to speak to the group via Zoom pro bono, stating, "Nothing would make me happier than to speak to a group of educators about the problem of racism in our society," adding eagerly, "Send me a time and a date, and I'll be ready."[1] This book results from that first email exchange.

---

1. Jane Elliott, Email message to the author, April 27, 2021.

In writing this book, I owe my greatest debt to the Elliott family, who took my phone calls, answered my emails and text messages, and collected many long-forgotten family documents. I want to single out for special thanks Sarah Elliott, who kept her phone line open and jumped on Zoom calls late into the night after my kids fell asleep and as we managed time zone differences. More than anyone, this book's subject, Jane Elliott, treated me like one of her own. Understandably, it took a few months for her to warm up to this forty-something biographer interrogating every moment of her life. Nonetheless, she allowed me to ask tough questions about her private life, challenge her on many controversial topics, check her accuracy of personal memories, and rummage through boxes of family mementos. The time spent in conversation with Jane will always be amongst my fondest memories. I thank her for welcoming me into her life and allowing for fellowship between our two families despite the questions I asked or what I wrote.

I am deeply indebted to my mother, Maurene, who generously read the entire manuscript of this book and offered corrections and suggestions. My writing has grown because of the insight my father, Tom, provided whenever we could find the time. I also wish to thank Judy Miller and Maria Vita for sharing their thoughts on how Jane Elliott's story intersects with the work of educators and psychologists. Thanks to the hard workers at Sunbury Press, including Lawrence Knorr and my editor, Sarah Illick. Thanks to the Iowa Women's Archives archivists at the University of Iowa Libraries: Margaret Gamm and Anna Holland. I owe a debt of gratitude to Jane's friends, neighbors, colleagues, and former students. I want to single out a few who sacrificed many hours to speak with me: Russ Watson, Ron Stangl, Raymond L. Hansen, Dennis McCabe, Marc Ruckebier, Şeydâ Buurman-Kutsal, and Rex Kozak. Thanks to filmmaker Bertram Verhaag, producer of *Blue Eyed*, civil rights icon Charles Cobb, and journalist Roland Martin for meeting with me on several occasions. A big thank you to filmmaker Muriel "Mikey" Peters, assistant producer of *The Eye of the Storm*, for taking my phone calls and responding to my emails. I would be remiss if I failed to thank my good friend, Todd Allen, for being a curator of civil rights history in his own right.

Most importantly, this book is due to my wife, Melissa, son, Carter, and daughter, Adeline. Together, they are the most important green-eyed, brown-eyed, and blue-eyed people in my life. Not only were they willing to live with Jane Elliott, as it were, for two years, but they selflessly played the role of sounding board, editor, and escape. This book is as much theirs as it is mine.

ABOUT THE AUTHOR

TODD M. MEALY is a historian and biographer of books and articles about the intersection of civil rights and education, including *This Is the Rat Speaking*, which tells the remarkable story of the Black campus movement of the late 1960s; *Glenn Killinger, All-American: Penn State's World War I Era Sports Hero*; and *Displaced: A Holocaust Memoir and the Road to a New Beginning*. A specialist in nineteenth and twentieth century anti-slavery and civil rights history, Mealy is also an adjunct professor in the History Department at Dickinson College with more than two decades of experience  teaching American history and academic writing at urban and rural schools in Pennsylvania. The founder and Executive Director of the National Institute for Customizing Education, Mealy is a sought-after curriculum designer whose work includes the K-12 Nonviolence365 curriculum for The Martin Luther King Jr. Center for Nonviolent Social Change in Atlanta, Georgia.

Mealy attained a Ph.D. in American Studies from Pennsylvania State University-Harrisburg, where he received the institution's Sue Samuelson Award for outstanding academic achievement. He lives with his family in Lancaster, Pennsylvania.

Made in the USA
Columbia, SC
09 November 2024

46073722R00231